RHS

ROYAL HORTICULTURAL SOCIETY
COMPLETE
GARDENER'S
MANUAL

ROYAL HORTICULTURAL SOCIETY

COMPLETE
GARDENER'S
MANUAL

The one-stop guide to plan, sow, plant, and grow your garden

CONTENTS

GROW YOUR OWN

CARE FOR YOUR GARDEN

MAKE A START

If you are fairly new to gardening, start here. This chapter
takes you through the basics that will make gardening
easier and you a better gardener from day one. All the key
topics are covered here: how plants grow and reproduce,
how to improve your soil, how to recognize healthy plants,
and how to choose the most suitable ones for your plot.
Plant names and garden jargon are decoded and there's
a guide to the most useful tools.

WHAT PLANTS NEED

All plants need moisture, nutrients, sunlight, and a suitable temperature for healthy growth and optimum development. However, they will need different levels of each depending on the natural habitats in which they have evolved.

▼ MOISTURE

Water is vital for plants as it is used in photosynthesis (*see facing page*) and to keep leaves and stems firm and upright. Plants have a variety of methods to absorb and store it. Most take up moisture through microscopic root hairs and lose it via the leaves in a process called transpiration. This cycle enables sugars and nutrients to be circulated. Plants from arid regions, such as cacti, often have a reduced leaf area and a waxy coating to control moisture loss.

Water-loving bog plants such as *Gunnera manicata* and some irises need moisture-rich sites at the margins of garden ponds and pools.

▶ TEMPERATURE

Plants are classified according to hardiness: tender specimens tolerate temperatures down to 5°C (41°F), frost-hardy to -5°C (23°F), and fully hardy to -20°C (-4°F). Every plant has specific temperature requirements; young plants are especially vulnerable and usually need protection to survive. Seedlings that have been raised indoors should be gradually introduced to cooler outdoor temperatures, a process known as "hardening off". Frost-sensitive plants should be wrapped up *in situ* or moved to a frost-free location over winter.

Tender, exotic plants such as cacti, aloes, and agaves require a warm, dry site, and need protection against frost in cold winter climates.

◄ SUNLIGHT

Sunlight powers plant growth in the process of photosynthesis. The green parts of plants, which contain the pigment chlorophyll, absorb light and use it to convert carbon dioxide and water to sugar and starches. These compounds make cellulose, the building block of plant tissue. Shoots and leaves will move to trap light as efficiently as possible, but if they receive an insufficient amount or a restricted spectrum they become pale and drawn or "etiolated".

Plants that are adapted to heat and bright light tend to have small or narrow, even needle-like leaves, and may have various "sun screens" such as dark masking pigments or silver-grey felting. Shade-adapted plants often have broad leaves or large leaves made up of smaller leaflets, which allow them to absorb as much light as possible. In full sun, shade plants may scorch as they are unaccustomed to the high light levels.

The large surface area of the leaves of the banana plant enable it to absorb light.

▲ NUTRITION

Plants need three key elements and a range of trace elements for healthy growth. Nitrogen (N) governs the growth of leaves and shoots; potassium (K), or potash, is required for flowering and fruiting; and phosphorus (P) promotes strong root growth. Adverse growing conditions such as incorrect pH or underwatering can inhibit this uptake. When plants run short of these, they show deficiency symptoms including stunted or distorted growth, or discoloured foliage. High-potassium fertilizers suit most plants.

Fast-growing plants such as *Rosa* 'The Fairy' have greater nutritional demands than plants that are adapted to poor or dry soils.

UNDERSTANDING PLANTS

A basic understanding of plants underpins everything you do in the garden. Are you planting annuals for just one season, or a shrub or perennial that will become a fixture? Knowing how plants reproduce also helps you maximize their contribution to your garden.

Seedheads can be an ornamental feature of plants such as poppies (*Papaver*), which will quickly populate a wide area if allowed to broadcast their seeds. For more targeted seedlings, remove the heads and save the seed.

LIFE CYCLES

Annual plants complete their life cycle in a single growing season: growing from seed, flowering, and then dying. Removing fading flowers before they get a chance to set seed tricks them into producing more, and lengthens the floral display.

Hardy annuals, such as pot marigolds, nasturtiums, and candytuft, will germinate outdoors and can be sown in autumn to overwinter as young plants for early summer flowers, but are usually sown in spring as soon as soil conditions allow. Half-hardy annuals require indoor warmth to germinate, and are transferred outdoors after the risk of frost has passed. This group includes most traditional bedding plants, such as petunia, salvia, and French marigold.

Biennials, such as foxgloves and forget-me-nots, usually complete their life cycle in two years. Seedlings appear in summer and then overwinter before producing flowers in spring or early summer, then setting seed and dying.

What is a perennial?

Perennials live on from one year to the next. The term is mainly used to describe non-woody herbaceous plants like delphiniums and geraniums, which die back in winter and re-shoot in spring. Tender perennials, such as pot geraniums, also survive from year to year if kept in temperatures above freezing.

Annual plants, such as nasturtiums (*Tropaeolum*), reproduce by setting seed before they die at the end of their life cycle. You can collect seed from your annuals to sow for new plants the following year (see pp.326–329).

Biennial plants, including foxgloves (*Digitalis*), set seed before the end of their two-year life cycle. They require two growing seasons before blooming – pinch out any buds that form in the first season to ensure a good display.

Perennial plants have a root system that lives for three or more years; "herbaceous" explains the fact that the part above the ground dies down each year, although a few perennials are evergreen and provide winter interest.

REPRODUCTION

Pollination leading to setting seed is by far the most common way by which flowering plants reproduce in nature. Most garden flowers, fruits, and vegetables are pollinated by insects, particularly bees, but grasses, conifers, shrubs and trees with catkins, and crops like sweet corn are wind pollinated.

Pollination is a method of sexual reproduction, and therefore means that a variety of genetic combinations are possible, and the resulting seedlings can vary. Although some flowers are self-fertile, which means they do not need to receive pollen from another flower to reproduce, cross-pollination or cross-fertilization ensures a good genetic mix, giving plants in the wild a greater chance of adapting to their environment.

In horticulture, variation is what enables plant breeders to select and produce cultivars with new combinations of desirable characteristics. Commercial seed production is carefully controlled to minimize this genetic variation and produce predictable results that retain these characteristics. F1 seed (see pp.328–329) is the most uniform and the most expensive, followed by F2, and the cheaper, open-pollinated strains.

Asexual reproduction

As well as pollination and seeding, plants use a number of other ways to reproduce at ground level and beneath the soil. Runners, rhizomes, bulbils, and offsets (see right) are all "vegetative" or "asexual" means of reproduction that are useful for gardeners, as the plants produced are normally identical to the parent and produce garden-ready specimens quickly and easily.

Runners are stems that grow out from the parent plant. They root where they touch the soil surface, and can later be severed and transplanted. Strawberries and spider plants (*Chlorophytum*) reproduce in this way.

Rhizomes are specialized stems that travel through the ground from the parent plant emerging as a cluster of new shoots a distance away. Perennials spreading via rhizomes can be invasive, especially in light soils.

Bulbils are bulb-like growths produced from the stems of some plants, including several ornamental lilies and some members of the onion family. They drop on to the soil and take root, or can be pulled off and planted.

Offsets are miniature versions of a parent plant, usually an alpine or succulent, growing in ground-encrusting colonies. They can be pulled away and potted up separately, and usually root quickly when they make contact with the soil.

Insect pollination relies upon the presence of the right insects. If bees are scarce, perhaps because of cold, wet weather, flowers may not be pollinated and seeding, fruiting, and cropping will be adversely affected.

Wind pollination occurs mainly in grasses and cone- and catkin-bearing plants. These don't rely on coloured or fragrant blooms to attract insects – their pollen grains are small and light, allowing distribution on the breeze.

Plant names may contain useful information about the plant's natural habitat; for instance, *Cryptostegia madagascariensis* (allamanda violet) comes from Madagascar.

GARDEN JARGON

The terminology associated with plants and gardening can seem intimidating if you are new to gardening. However, the Latin name system is used all over the world, and a little knowledge of it goes a long way.

Although many plants have familiar common names such as "rose" or "lavender", not every plant has one. As an added complication, several may share their name with other plants or be named differently in different regions and countries. Botanical names are used universally to avoid this kind of confusion, which makes it useful to know something about them.

Botanical names classify each plant with two Latin words. The first word describes the genus (for example, *Ilex*) and the second, the epithet (for example, *aquifolium*). Together, they make up the name for a particular plant species such as *Ilex aquifolium* (English holly). Other species in the same genus are given different epithets, such as *Ilex crenata* and *Ilex serrata*. The system has been developed so that the entire plant kingdom is divided into a universally recognized "family tree" (see facing page).

A family may contain only one genus (for example, *Eucryphia* is the only genus in the family Eucryphiaceae) or many – the daisy family Compositae has over 1,000 genera. Each genus comprises related plants, such as oaks (genus *Quercus*) or lilies (genus *Lilium*),

BEHIND THE NAME

The two-part Latin name given to each plant can give useful clues to the plant's geographic origins and natural habitat, as well as allowing similar plants to be grouped together.

The second part of the plant's name denotes the species (see facing page), and often reflects the physical characteristic of the plant. For example, *cyanus* describes a blue plant such as *Centaurea cyanus* (right), and *octopetala* (as in *Dryas octopetala*) means "eight petals". The species name can also reflect the person who discovered the plant (as in *Magnolia wilsonii*); its natural habitat (*pratensis* denotes a meadow-growing plant); or the plant's country of origin (species called *sinensis* are from China).

Centaurea cyanus

Magnolia wilsonii

Cardamine pratensis

Hibiscus rosa-sinensis

Many summer annuals originate from South Africa. Here the orange-flowered *Ursinia cakilefolia* and blue-flowered herb, *Heliophila arenaria*, grow wild in the Western Karoo.

with several features in common, and a genus may contain one or many species. For example, a member of the genus *Lilium* could be any lily, but *Lilium candidum* denotes just one type. A species is a group of plants that consistently and naturally reproduce between themselves, generating plant populations that share similar characteristics.

GARDEN SPEAK

Help is at hand
Throughout this book, you will find "Garden Speak" boxes like this one wherever a piece of potentially confusing garden terminology needs to be explained.

Rather than searching through a glossary for these words and phrases, the information is right where you need it, whether you are designing, planting, or maintaining your garden.

VISUAL GUIDE TO PLANT CLASSIFICATION

In horticulture, plants are classified according to a hierarchical system and named primarily on the basis of the binomial approach (genus followed by species epithet). As an example, part of the family Rosaceae has been set out below, showing all levels of this system.

Family A group of several genera that share a set of underlying natural characteristics. Family names usually end in -aceae. Family limits are often controversial.

Rosaceae

Genus (plural: genera) A group of one or more plants that share a range of distinctive characteristics. Several (rarely one) genera are classified into one family. Each genus contains one or more species and its name is printed in italic type with an initial capital letter.

Rosa

Prunus

Species A group of plants that breeds naturally to produce offspring with similar characteristics; these distinguish it from other populations in nature. Each species has a two-part name, conventionally printed in italic type.

Rosa mulliganii

Prunus padus

Subspecies A naturally occurring, distinct variant of a species, differing in one or more characteristics. Subspecies are indicated by "subsp." or "ssp." in Roman type and an epithet in italic type.

Prunus lusitanica subsp. *azorica*

Varietas and forma A *varietas* (var.) is a minor species subdivision, differing slightly in botanical structure. A *forma* (f.) is a minor variant of a species, often differing in flower colour or habit from others in the species.

Prunus incisa f. *yamadae*

Rosa gallica var. *officinalis*

Cultivar Selected or artificially raised, distinct variant of a species, subspecies, *varietas*, *forma*, or hybrid. Cultivars are indicated by a vernacular name printed in Roman type within single quotation marks.

Rosa gallica var. *officinalis* 'Versicolor'

Prunus 'Pandora'

Discovering plants' natural habitats is an important part of planning flower displays, helping you to place them in their optimum position for health and vitality.

RIGHT PLANT, RIGHT PLACE

The choice of garden plants is enormous but the sites you can offer may be more limited. Matching the plants you choose to the varying conditions in your garden, from full sun to damp shade, is key to success.

When plants are in the wrong place, they suffer stress, are more vulnerable to damage during adverse weather conditions, and are more susceptible to pests and diseases. Fortunately, there are plants that will thrive in even the most extreme conditions that you might find in your garden. In the wild, plants occupy almost every possible niche in a range of habitats, and there are varieties that will fill the most troublesome areas in the garden: waterlogged soil, dry, shady places, windswept or sun-baked spots.

Wild plant hunters collect plants from a wide variety of natural environments in countries the world over. The species and varieties growing in our gardens today might have originated from places as varied as high alpine slopes, woodland, meadow, marsh, shoreline, or desert.

Hot spots

Plants adapted to full sun and parched soils are useful if you find yourself with an open garden and very free-draining soil. Where winters are relatively mild,

SITING PLANTS

Plants can be used to perform different functions if chosen carefully. An ugly shed could be camouflaged by a vigorous climber like Clematis montana or a rambler rose, but you would be less likely to use the same plant to decorate a small wooden arch. For this, pick a compact-growing, large-flowered clematis hybrid or a modern, repeat-flowering climbing rose.

For ground cover beneath trees, self-seeding perennials, bulbs, and bamboos with a rhizomatous habit would suit, but these same plants behave like weeds in a flower border. Check plant dimensions when designing borders to avoid ending up with large bulky plants at the front obscuring others (see pp.116–117).

Disguise unsightly structures with climbers.

Naturalize bulbs in a lawn for a woodland effect.

Bamboo screening can hide fences or views.

Train wall shrubs to enhance sheds and fences.

MICROCLIMATES

The area where you live has a general climate but every garden has potential microclimates created by its aspect and surroundings. In cold regions, a sheltered, south-facing plot will experience higher temperatures than the average for the area; cities also generate heat, keeping temperatures high. Even in a north-facing garden, the area around a house may remain frost free in winter. Walls and fences cast shade and may trap cold air, causing frost pockets, while mature tree canopies may provide some frost protection.

succulents, silver- and grey-leaved plants, perennial herbs, and flowering bulbs adapted to Mediterranean climates would do well.

Damp shade

You might find damp, shady spots due to poorly drained clay soils next to buildings. Plants adapted to this environment tend to be those that originated in forests and woodlands. In warmer, sheltered areas, the only limiting factors are nutrients and light, so a range of large-leaved ferns would do well. For more advice on siting plants in difficult corners of your garden refer to the 'plant problem solver' pages in the Plant Chooser chapter (pp.370–435). Here you will find catalogues and lists of plants that fit specific conditions well.

The four main conditions found in various combinations in most gardens are (clockwise from top left): low-lying damp areas where plants such as Gunnera thrive; arid conditions suitable for drought-tolerant plants; deep shade beneath tree canopies; and hot sunny borders for bursts of exotic blooms.

Compare plants before deciding which to buy, and avoid those in full flower unless you are looking for specific colours.

CHOOSING HEALTHY PLANTS

The starting point to a successful garden is to buy strong, healthy plants that establish quickly and give a good display. Shop around for the best plants, and check them over first to find the healthiest specimens.

WHAT TO LOOK FOR

To find the healthiest specimens, compare several examples of the same plant at garden centres and nurseries. Avoid any with obvious problems, such as broken stems, sparse growth, or signs of pests and disease. Also steer clear of plants that don't appear fresh, with old growth, tired-looking compost, and faded or missing labels. Inspect the plants fully, and ease them from their pots to check the condition of the root system (see below right).

The best time to buy and plant most perennials, shrubs, and trees is while they are dormant from autumn to spring. This does make it hard to check their conditions however, so you might prefer to wait until spring when new growth shows. Evergreen perennials should be planted in mid- to late spring so that they can toughen up before the following winter. (Container-grown types can be planted at any time, as long as you keep them well watered.)

For healthy perennials, look for plants with plenty of stems emerging from the compost. You can plant perennials and shrubs in full flower but they will be slower to establish. It is preferable to pick plants in bud or those that have finished flowering. When deciding between new trees and shrubs, look out for balanced, well-branched plants, with plenty of new growth or buds.

CHECK PLANT LABELS

It is easy to be tempted into buying attractive looking plants on impulse at garden centres, but check the label to make sure they are suitable for your soil and site. Check the plant's eventual height and spread too, to be sure it will fit your space.

Any questions? If you're still not sure about a plant after reading the label, ask a member of staff for advice.

CHECKLIST

When buying any new container-grown plants, it's a good idea to give them a quick check before taking them home. It will only take a few minutes for each plant, and is a useful way to avoid potential problems or costly disappointments.

Don't feel awkward doing this in garden centres and nurseries, as they are keen to only sell healthy plants. Most reputable outlets guarantee their plants for at least 12 months, so retain your receipt as proof of purchase, in case of any problems.

Signs of care are a good guide to how well a plant has been looked after. Look for plants that have been well supported, with neat, tied-in growth, and fresh compost. Avoid any plants that are tangled, straggling, or scruffy.

▲ **Bare-root** plants, such as hedging, can be "heeled in" until ready to plant.

◄ **Container-grown** plants will last a short while in their pots if regularly watered.

STORING PLANTS

It is best to plant new plants within a few days of buying them, to help them establish quickly. That might not always be possible however, especially if the weather is wet or you are in the middle of a garden project. Container-grown plants will be fine for a few days if kept well watered. If you need to store them for longer, move them to a sheltered spot so they don't blow over, and keep them out of full sun, or they will dry out too quickly. For longer-term storage, it may be a good idea to repot them into large containers. This will also avoid checking their growth.

Bare-root plants sold in autumn or winter are at a greater risk of drying out and frost damage than container-grown plants, and need protection. As a temporary measure, "heel" plants into the soil, which involves burying the roots in a trench or hole. Choose a sheltered site, in free-draining soil, and keep the plants well watered. Plant them out into their final positions before new growth appears in spring.

If you are unsure when you will be able to plant out bare-root plants, consider potting them up and standing them in a sheltered spot. Keep well watered and fed, and they will survive into summer.

Reject pots with mature weeds, as this suggests plants have not been well maintained; you will also avoid introducing weed species to your garden. Moss-covered pots should be rejected for the same reason.

Look under the pot to see if there are roots growing through the drainage holes. Just a few suggests a healthy root system; lots of roots indicate the plant is pot-bound and should be avoided. Remove the pot to check.

Check the roots to see if they are healthy. Look for pale, plump roots and clear signs of new growth. Avoid plants with dead, black, or hollow roots that fall away from the compost. Also avoid plants with congested roots.

FROM THE GROUND UP

Knowing how to make the best of your garden's conditions by nurturing and improving the soil will help you work wonders on your plot – even with challenging soils like heavy clay or chalk.

Earthworms save work by incorporating organic matter into the depths of the soil, as well as opening up drainage channels.

WORKING WITH YOUR SOIL

Analysing the basic structure and drainage of your soil, its pH (see p.66), organic content, and fertility, is an important first step. If you dig down into soil, you will eventually see a change from the darker, fertile, topsoil layer to the paler, infertile subsoil layer and rock beneath. Some soils have very little depth, adversely affecting cultivation. On the other hand, loams cultivated over many years, with regular additions of manure, can be very deep. The colour difference between topsoil and subsoil is due to the lack of humus or organic matter at depths where earthworms are not active. In clay, the subsoil is orange but in waterlogged conditions, it can be blue-grey due to the lack of oxygen. Never mix subsoil into topsoil; the lower layer can be toxic to plants.

In poor soils, the lack of depth can severely affect the growth of both ornamentals and crops. Raised beds allow more topsoil to be added, contained within a frame.

WHAT IS SOIL?

Soil is a mixture of ground-up rock particles, organic matter or humus, and countless microscopic organisms and tiny invertebrates. In healthy, well-drained soil the particles are clumped together with the spaces in between occupied by water and air. This crumb structure allows earthworms to move through, creating a network of channels that plant roots can make use of. Earthworms are very active "gardeners", pulling leaf litter and other organic debris down into the soil where bacteria and fungi, together with other soil organisms, break it down, releasing and recycling nutrients. Creating conditions that benefit these soil organisms is the best way to maintain fertility.

Sandy soils have coarse grains and lack organic matter, which makes them very free-draining. They are easy to dig, can be cultivated all year round, and warm up quickly in spring for early sowings. Self-seeding plants can become a nuisance as they germinate freely, but weeds and unwanted plants can easily be pulled out.

Loam soils are ideal, having a good balance of clay particles to retain moisture and nutrients, and sand grains to improve drainage. Loam usually has a healthy worm population, and most plants thrive with little extra feeding. A clay loam will be slower to warm up in spring than a sandy one.

Improve your soil's structure by working in plenty of bulky, well-rotted organic matter such as manure (see p.303).

To dig or not to dig?

Soil can be damaged in several ways. Compaction destroys air and rooting channels, impairs drainage, and reduces earthworm activity. Digging is then essential to help loosen up compacted and heavy ground. You will also need to dig over uncultivated soil ready for planting. Some soils are easy to dig and can be cultivated all year round, while others, such as heavy, clay soils, may have a relatively narrow window for sowing and planting.

Generally, there is little need for routine digging in a garden that is already cultivated. Worms will do much of the hard work for you, incorporating organic matter added to the surface. Digging shallow soils can be problematic because there is a risk of bringing infertile subsoil to the surface; digging can also disrupt beneficial soil micro-organisms. Walking on or digging wet clay soil damages its structure. If you need to dig clay, do this in autumn when it is softened but not saturated by rain, or in spring when it is not too wet.

COMPARING COMPOSTS

Soil-based composts, such as John Innes, are the best choice for the long-term health of perennials, climbers, shrubs, and trees grown in containers. Compared with soil-free potting media, they retain their structure better and don't shrink or compact over time.

Multi-purpose composts, ideally peat-free, are good for short-term planting such as summer patio pots, and retain moisture and nutrients well. They weigh far less than soil-based media, allowing pots to be moved more easily.

Ericaceous composts, free of lime, are used for shrubs such as camellias and rhododendrons that require acid soil.

Clay soils are some of the most fertile, because clay particles hold on to nutrients. Poor drainage is a common problem with clay soils, and this can be improved by digging in bulky organic matter such as well-rotted manures and composts.

Chalk soils and other limestone soils have a high pH and are unsuitable for acid-loving plants. Because they are peppered with stony fragments of flint or limestone, they drain freely but are prone to drought. They warm up quickly in spring and are easy to dig, but are often shallow, overlying solid rock.

PROBLEM SOILS

To improve the texture and drainage of heavy clay soils, work in copious amounts of bulky organic matter, about two buckets of organic matter per square metre. This chemically alters the clay and causes the fine particles to cluster, opening up drainage channels. Avoid digging or walking on clay when it is wet; both activities destroy the structure. When it is dry it is very hard to dig, but it may be possible with a fork.

Sandy soils are free-draining, but this can leach nutrients out of the upper layers and away from the roots of plants, leaving the soil impoverished. They can be improved by the addition of well-rotted organic matter to hold nutrients and moisture in the soil; moisture-loving plants can also be mulched.

ENRICHING THE SOIL

To get the best out of your productive crops and ornamental plants, you may need to improve the fertility or moisture-retaining capacity of your garden soil. There are many ways to go about this, following organic or chemical methods.

Organic matter improves soil structure, promotes soil microbes, and adds plant nutrients, all of which encourage plant health.

IMPROVING FERTILITY

Some plants, such as bush and patio roses and many summer bedding varieties (fuchsias and petunias, for example), are particularly "hungry" and need regular feeding to keep them growing and flowering well, especially on naturally poor ground. You can feed border plants by adding well-rotted manures and garden compost to the soil around them, or by applying granular or liquid fertilizers.

Other woodland species like Japanese maples, ferns, and deciduous azaleas can survive with less feed, but the soil needs to be enriched with leafmould or organic matter to create a suitably moisture-retentive rooting environment.

Some plants have evolved to grow on relatively poor soils, and if concentrated granular fertilizers are applied around their shallow root systems, they scorch and suffer shoot die-back. A common example of this

Leafmould makes an excellent soil conditioner. It does not require any special conditions, and can be made by collecting leaves either in a wire cage or in black plastic sacks, wetting them, and composting them for two years.

Farmyard and stable manure should be well rotted before use as fresh manure is liable to scorch roots. Nitrogen can be locked up while soil organisms decompose strawy manure, leading to short-term yellowing of foliage.

Garden compost is ideally made up of 25–50 per cent soft, green garden waste (to feed micro-organisms) to one part woody waste. *(See p.303 for detailed information on recycling garden and kitchen waste for your own compost.)*

is box (*Buxus sempervirens*), which is best fed with well-rotted manure or dilute liquid fertilizer. Hardy annuals and Mediterranean herbs and shrubs also thrive on nutrient-poor soils such as sands, gravels, and chalks.

Fertilizer recipes

Unless you enrich the soil organically, you will need to replenish lost nutrients using an appropriate artificial fertilizer, especially around flowering plants and crops. On the labels of most chemical fertilizers you will often see an "NPK" ratio, which shows the relative proportions of nitrogen (N), phosphorus (P), and potassium (K) in the mix. Other micro-nutrients may also be listed. Feeding with a potassium-rich fertilizer, such as a tomato fertilizer, will suit all plants. High-potassium feeds can particularly help to condition cold-sensitive plants prior to winter and initiate flower bud

Mulching with garden compost will improve the soil structure, as well as adding plant nutrients to the soil. Don't use a commercially produced soil improver without first checking its pH – most are alkaline.

production in shy-flowering shrubs and climbers. For a more specific recommendation, send your soil to a laboratory that carries out soil tests.

Getting the balance right

Follow instructions carefully for the amount and frequency of feeding. Too much fertilizer can be just as damaging as too little, and using the wrong type can also cause problems. Feeding flowering and fruiting plants with a high-nitrogen mix encourages leafy growth at the expense of bloom, and the resulting tall stems are more vulnerable to weather damage. Soft, sappy shoots are also more attractive to pests, such as aphids, and overfeeding lawns makes them prone to frost and fungal infection. (*See pp.302–303 for more information on feeding.*)

MULCHING

Covering soil with a layer of organic matter, such as chipped bark, garden compost, manure, or cocoa shells (if a sustainable source can be found) is known as mulching. To be most effective, a layer of organic mulch needs to be 5–8cm (2–3in) thick. Materials, such as plastic sheeting, pebbles, or cardboard can also be used as a mulch.

Mulches conserve valuable soil moisture and suppress weeds, and organic mulches also release nutrients as they break down, feeding the surrounding plants. Woody mulches, such as chipped bark or shredded wood, last a long time and do not deplete soil nitrogen.

Mulches are applied to the soil surface, rather than dug in, to minimize root damage, keep light from reaching weeds, and enhance soil microbes and earthworms near the surface where they do the most good. (*See p.350 for more information on using mulches to suppress weeds.*)

GREEN MANURES

A green manure is a crop grown and dug in before it sets seed, and is used on vegetable beds to improve the soil. It can also be harvested and soaked in water to produce a liquid feed. Growing green manures improves the soil structure, and can be used to help bind light soils or break up heavy clays. They can also draw nutrients from deep down and add atmospheric nitrogen to the soil.

Clover is grown to add nitrogen into the soil.

Alfalfa adds nitrogen and organic matter

Grazing rye grass helps to bind light soils.

Second-hand tools can be easy to come by and have proven robustness. If buying new, choose the best quality tools you can afford.

BASIC TOOL KIT

To tend a garden you need tools, and a fairly small selection will cover most routine tasks. Tools are versatile and can be used for more than one purpose, and you can build a more comprehensive kit over time.

TENDING THE SOIL

Caring for your soil is a key task in the garden, and plays an important role in keeping plants healthy. Digging prior to planting aerates the soil, mixes in nutrients, and breaks up hard lumps. Either a spade or a fork can be used for digging, but it is worth having one of each. Forks are ideal for working on heavy or stony soils; spades are better for digging holes and for general earth moving. On a smaller scale, hand trowels and forks are indispensable for lighter digging and planting and loosening the soil.

Controlling weeds is another important part of maintaining your plot, and is most easily done using a long-handled hoe that cuts weeds off at the base. This tool is ideal for larger beds, as you can easily weed between plants. You can also make seed drills with a hoe.

You will find a garden rake useful for levelling and tilling the soil surface ready for seed sowing, and for clearing light plant debris.

KEEP TOOLS CLEAN

Cleaning tools after use keeps them in good condition and makes them easier to use. Brush off any soil and debris before putting them away, and clean and sterilize your pruning tools to prevent spreading diseases between plants.

To keep tools sharp, wipe oil onto cutting blades, including spades, to keep them sharp and rust-free.

Spades and forks are used for cultivating the soil, and come in various sizes. Choose one with a long enough handle to suit your height, and light enough to manipulate easily.

Hand tools are useful for light tasks, and allow you to tend the soil in awkward places. They are ideal for planting out seedlings and young plants, and for uprooting small weeds.

Caring for plants

Water is essential to plants, and a watering can is a must. While a hose is useful for watering established borders, a basic can is ideal for new plants, containers and baskets, and greenhouse crops. Fit a fine rose to the spout to water young seedlings, or use the can to apply plant feeds.

Keeping plants to size and shape is important for their health, so you will need pruning tools. Secateurs are useful for pruning light woody stems; it is worth investing in a good-quality pair. If your garden has large trees or shrubs, consider buying long-handled loppers and a pruning saw. Shears are effective when cutting back leafy growth and for trimming lawn edges.

Like other plants, lawns also need care and maintenance; you will need a mower to keep in regular use throughout the summer. There are many types to choose from, and before you opt for the biggest and most powerful, consider the space you have to store it. A manual push-along mower may be all you need on a small area. Another worthwhile lawn tool is a spring rake, which is used to remove moss and to collect fallen leaves. You can also use it to tidy around the garden in general.

Storing tools

Before buying your tools, make sure you have somewhere to store them under cover. Even if you only have space for a covered tool tidy or a garden cupboard, tools last longer and work better if kept clean and dry. A store also helps keep your tools in one place, so you know where to find them. If you have space, install a shed to house costly power tools along with the mass of sundries you will gradually acquire over time, and to prevent children or pets accessing garden chemicals.

Weather-proof storage in a shed or tool tidy is recommended, because tools last longer when kept under cover. Keep expensive tools under lock and key to safeguard against theft.

Watering cans can be used for carrying water wherever needed. It is worth having a few different sizes to use for various tasks, such as watering hanging baskets and general feeding.

Pruning tools are worth having close to hand throughout the year to keep plant growth in check, and to prune out weak or diseased stems whenever you spot them.

Lawn rakes make short work of clearing lawns and borders of debris, and can be used instead of garden brooms to help tidy up in autumn. Garden rakes are used to cultivate soil.

DESIGN YOUR GARDEN

Before you reach for your spade, think about how you would like your garden to look and how you will use it, then create a garden to suit you. Be inspired by the range of styles, layouts, and techniques in this chapter and use them to make your garden beautiful, practical, or productive – or a combination of all three.

ASSESS YOUR GARDEN NEEDS

Try to visualize your dream garden and the features it might include – take inspiration from designs that excite you. How will it fit in with your lifestyle, and how much time will you have to maintain it? How will you use it? Decide whether plants, people, or wildlife will take precedence.

▶ SPACE TO ENTERTAIN

Transform your garden into a useful, comfortable outdoor space and use it as an extension of your house for eating, drinking, relaxing, and socializing. Bring the interior outside by adding homely touches such as colourful cushions, soft lighting, and a fire pit to an al fresco lounge. Combined kitchen and dining spaces make open-air cooking and eating easy and enjoyable, and if you grow your own crops, make the journey from plot to plate even shorter. For a touch of luxury, consider adding a spa with a sauna and day bed.

◀ HOME-GROWN PRODUCE

Whether you have the space to create an allotment sized plot or you simply want to grow a pot of peppers on a sunny windowsill, the rewards will be tasty, wonderfully scented herbs, fruits, and vegetables – an attractive asset to any garden. The best thing about growing your own is that you can select exactly which varieties you want to eat, including unusual types that are not readily available. You will also know exactly what has gone into their cultivation.

▶ FOR ALL THE FAMILY

Maximize outdoor family time by designing the garden so that adults and children can enjoy being outside together. Gardens have more to offer children than just fresh air and exercise – they can create opportunities for wild encounters with nature and encourage imaginative play, so create special areas for these "secret" adventures to occur. Screen these, and larger, unsightly pieces of play equipment, from view if necessary, or leave the garden layout open and construct a relaxing seating area so that you can keep an eye on the activities of younger children.

◀ CALMING RETREAT

Use your garden as a place to escape from everyday stresses and to ground yourself in nature. You can experience feelings of real freedom out in the open air surrounded by birdsong and the rustle of leaves, especially when your private sitting space is shielded from the house and overlooking windows. Consider using water to create a sense of tranquillity. Feed your senses with the sound of a trickling fountain or the sight of reflections in a still pool of water. A single focal point helps to create a perfect space for contemplation.

▲ WILDLIFE HAVEN

Attracting a range of wildlife to your garden is as much about your gardening approach as your plant selection – relaxed and not too tidy works best. Use colourful, highly scented flowers to attract hoverflies, bees, and butterflies. Create a woodland environment for visitors as diverse as beetles, hedgehogs, and wood mice. A pond will be attractive to birds and amphibians, and an eco-pile will provide a welcoming habitat for beneficial insects.

► EASY-CARE GARDEN

Even if you do not have a lot of time to dedicate to your garden, there is no reason why it can't still be beautiful. Making life easier does not necessarily mean resorting to expanses of paving: use easy-care landscaping solutions such as gravel and wooden sleepers and select plants that do not require frequent pruning, feeding, or watering.

◄ A PLACE FOR PLANTS

Some types of plants may interest you more than others, so adapt your garden to suit their needs. With a bit of consideration, fussy plants such as tender types or even exotics can be accommodated if given a warm spot and moved under cover in winter. There is no need to feel limited by your existing garden: consider inserting a pond or bog area; create a shaded woodland zone; or build a rock garden.

FINDING INSPIRATION

Initially, let your imagination run riot. Think about what you like rather than your garden's restrictions. You may already have a favourite gardening style or at least a mental list of must-have features. A mood board with magazine cuttings, fabrics, and colour swatches can help you focus, or you can scan online sources such as Pinterest or Instagram for ideas and direction.

Formal gardens juxtapose topiary colours and textures to striking effect – apply these principles to your plant choices.

Natural habitats allow you to discover plants in the wild. Where possible, mimic these conditions in your garden.

Show gardens are often made to draw attention to exciting, contemporary designs and interesting planting schemes.

Art or mosaics may inspire formal planting schemes or colour themes; re-create your favourite mosaics with paving.

Eye-catching plants inspired by a tropical holiday can brighten your garden; ensure you can provide the conditions needed.

Sculptures make wonderful focal points – collect them on your travels or pick up ideas from any you admire.

A SPACE TO ENTERTAIN

Extend your living space into the garden and create a stylish outdoor kitchen, an intimate dining area for starlit gatherings, or a relaxation space complete with hammock. Mirror your indoor styles for a seamless transition.

Elements for constructing your al fresco room are readily available, from exterior tiles and decking for barefoot garden access to instant "walls" constructed from decorative screen panels or "hedges" of potted bamboo. Make a "ceiling" using a pergola festooned with night-fragrant jasmine or fit a sail-like awning for summer shade. Many stylish sofas and armchairs are designed to stay out whatever the weather. Impromptu seating (from sitting-height raised beds) is perfect to encircle a fire pit.

Finish with paints and stains, matching cushion fabrics and china to interior colour schemes. Dress your outdoor room with topiaries and sculptural foliage in contemporary containers. Add drama at nightfall with low-voltage lighting.

KEY DESIGN ELEMENTS

All-weather surfaces
Many contemporary doors roll back or fold, blurring the barrier between indoors and out. Mirror your flooring – choose feet-friendly tiles, smooth paving, and decking that repels rain and is frost-proof.

Outdoor lighting
Dramatic choices include recessed neon deck lights and coloured floods that turn plain walls into modern art, while candles, oil lamps, and string lights woven through plants create atmosphere.

Dining space
Al fresco summer dinner parties with flickering candelabras, or lunches in the dappled shade of a vine-clad pergola, can be stylish, memorable events. Bring out the best tableware for a dinner party.

Privacy and shelter
Need shade at midday? Try a sail-like awning. Being out of the wind is essential; being beyond the gaze of neighbours is desirable if you want to doze in a hammock or on a sofa.

▼ Colourful, hard-wearing **furniture** creates a versatile outdoor room.

Outdoor furniture

As well as being practical and comfortable, furniture should also add to your garden's design. Whether you favour a traditional feel or modernist fashions, pick furniture and fabrics to mirror interior luxury.

Food preparation area

Cooking and eating outdoors is an epicurean delight. Fit a kitchen with easy-clean surfaces, a stove, and perhaps a log-burning oven. Grow a range of herbs close by to enhance your barbecues.

Fire pit

A fire pit will draw people together at social gatherings and makes a captivating focal point, so position soft seating to make the most of it. Some designs have safety guards and some can be used for cooking.

ALSO TRY

Garden art
Turn your garden into a gallery with pieces that enhance the style of the surroundings.

Pools and fountains
Choose a pool with night-time illumination or a sparkling fountain to add movement.

Soft seating
Convert steps, walls, and raised beds into comfortable perches with outdoor cushions.

SOCIAL STYLE

Extending the house into the garden creates extra living space with a unique backdrop – flowers and foliage, the sights, scents, and sounds of nature, and the open sky – so install a second kitchen, dining room, or lounge.

▼ Fork to fork

You can be sure of the freshness of your herbs and salads when they are growing within arm's reach. Surrounding an outdoor kitchen with crop-filled raised beds and walls of salad leaves is convenient, attractive, and usually highly aromatic. Plant a variety of colours, shapes, and textures for maximum impact.

▶ Café chic

Add a touch of elegance by positioning a small table and colonial-style sunshade in a quiet corner. Create a sense of privacy by surrounding it with tall, dense plants, and introduce glamour by marking the entrance with a stylish pair of corkscrew topiaries.

▲ Summerhouse

Garden buildings can make a wonderfully romantic addition to period and cottage gardens. Here, a curved pathway and deep, well-filled borders help to give a feeling of seclusion. Fit soft furnishings, lighting, and a kettle so that you don't have to go back to the house too often.

▲ **Wilderness sanctuary**
Glimpsed through diaphanous screens of flowers, this sculptural seating arrangement looks remote and wild. In the day it would be a peaceful sanctuary from modern day-living; at night you could sit and stargaze.

▲ **Inside out**
The open-plan design technique employed in contemporary homes can work particularly well in the garden too. A covered veranda or canopied terrace creates a useful transition between the house and open-air cooking and dining areas. Use spotlights or strings of fairy lights to create atmosphere and to highlight favourite plants. If the weather takes a turn for the worse, you can move the party under cover and continue to enjoy the outdoor atmosphere.

◄ **The green room**
In larger gardens it may be possible to position an outdoor seating area well away from the house, creating a peaceful, scenic retreat. An open-sided shelter will protect you from light rain showers, and will provide welcome shade in bright weather. Use pergola posts, climbers, and specimen plants to frame selected scenes. A slightly raised platform gives the area prominence; lead the eye to it with a wide path flanked with colourful flowers and foliage.

ADAPTING THE STYLE

Careful planning will allow you to make the most of your space. Use the plan below for design inspiration and then customize it to suit your needs. Site dining and cooking areas close to the house for easy access. Create extra seating with wide-edged raised beds. Separate the lawn from the patio with a screen of tall potted plants, to give each area an enclosed feel.

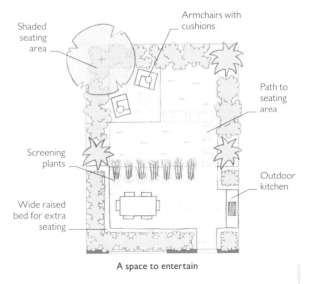

Shaded seating area

Armchairs with cushions

Path to seating area

Screening plants

Outdoor kitchen

Wide raised bed for extra seating

A space to entertain

THE PRODUCTIVE GARDEN

You might start off with just a few potted herbs or an annual crop of greenhouse tomatoes, but "growing your own" soon becomes addictive. Happily, there is a wealth of ingenious options for making even a small plot productive.

Mixing crops into flower borders, cottage-garden style, is useful if you don't have a dedicated vegetable plot, and certain leafy crops are just as good-looking as they are flavourful. Runner beans produce delicate flowers, and the blossom and fruits of apples, cherries, and strawberries are as attractive as any grown for ornament. Redcurrants, followed by the autumn foliage of blueberries, also make eye-catching displays.

Potagers and herb knots are theatrical features and even raised beds with decorative edging can make a statement. Maximize your culinary space by training fruit against walls, and by growing vines and climbing vegetables against trellis. In a courtyard or patio garden, many crops can be grown in pots or hanging baskets.

KEY DESIGN ELEMENTS

Crops in containers
Even in the smallest garden you can grow a variety of crops in pots, growing bags, or windowboxes. Choose compact vegetable types and dwarf fruit trees; tender ones in pots can be moved under cover.

Decorative varieties
There are many delicious and ornamental vegetables to choose from, with colourful foliage, fruits, or flowers. Cabbage, kale, and chard are highly ornamental and look striking grown in a potager.

Chickens
If you have room for a run, chickens make excellent pets. It's best to confine them as they produce a lot of faeces and will scratch up the garden looking for worms. You don't need a cockerel to get eggs.

Wall-trained fruit
Espalier- and fan-trained trees crop better than freestanding types and look beautiful too. Use any vertical space – varieties are even available for north-facing walls. Also try training fruits such as gooseberries.

▼ Break up expanses of green
with a line of purple cabbages and
a colourful border of flowers.

ALSO TRY

Edible flowers
Try petals of sunflower, rose, and
pot marigolds, or whole blooms
of viola and nasturtium.

Herb garden
Create a formal herb garden
edged with clipped hedging,
santolina, or lavender.

Climbing crops
Use trellis, arches, and pergolas
to support climbing squash,
courgettes, and runner beans.

Productive baskets
Mixed displays of herbs, edible
flowers, and trailing strawberries or
tomatoes are full of colour and are
convenient for harvesting if hung
by the back door. Try using novel
containers, such as an old colander.

Raised beds
On heavy or very stony soils, raised
beds can provide you with enough
quality topsoil to grow a wide
range of crops. Add compost and
manure to the surface to develop
a healthy, fertile soil full of worms.

Crop covers
Use polytunnels, cloches, or cold
frames to extend the growing
season and to provide vulnerable
crops with frost protection and
extra warmth. Use barriers such
as fleece or netting to deter pests.

PRODUCE-FILLED PLOTS

There are many attractive ways to incorporate crops into your garden, whether you want to plant a pot of salad on the patio, grow climbing vegetables up a screen of trellis, or dedicate your entire space to drills and rows.

▶ Recycled containers
You can use virtually any container as long as it will hold soil or compost and allow drainage. Ensure that you water smaller pots frequently, as the soil may dry out quickly.

▼ Additional lines
Consider turning the whole garden into a productive plot. Use long straight rows and plant dahlias and sunflowers for colour.

▶ Productive patio
You can nurture a surprising range of fruits, vegetables, and herbs on even a tiny patio. Showcase a variety of heights, colours, and textures for maximum contrast and interest. Mix and match your containers to give the patio a rustic feel.

▲ Squashed up
Some crops will take up a lot of space unless confined. Grow sprawling squash and climbing beans up fencing or trellis and keep them penned within a low raised bed. Many fruits can be wall-trained to save space.

ADAPTING THE STYLE

Before you create a detailed crop plan, position permanent unsightly elements, and those that are likely to smell, such as a compost bin or chicken enclosure, at the far end of the garden. Stock a line of raised beds with an array of colourful crops, and flank them with beds filled with ornamental edibles, to create a lovely view from a garden bench.

▲ Old-world charm
A potager is a highly structured, decorative planting scheme and an ideal way to make vegetable and herb areas more attractive, especially in a period setting. Lay out the design and then edge the segments with gravel boards, dwarf hedging, or an evergreen herb such as cotton lavender. Here, clipped hedges gives the plot definition and old rhubarb forcers are used as ornaments. Bay and rosemary standards could also be used as attractive centrepieces.

◄ Pretty tasty
Save space by mixing edibles and ornamentals together, cottage-garden style. Varieties such as purple-leaved cabbages, kale, sage, or red-stemmed chard provide a lovely foliage contrast when grown with colourful perennials or gold- or silver-leaved herbs. Fruits such as tomatoes, courgettes, and strawberries will add a splash of colour, while many ornamental flowers have edible petals that make a pretty addition to a salad.

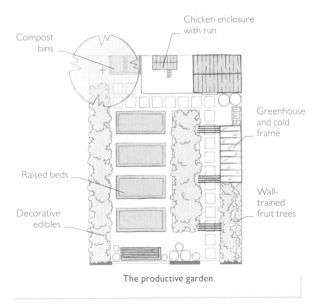

The productive garden

FAMILY GARDEN

A garden can cater to the needs of every member of the family – there's no reason for play areas to dominate. With an integrated design, grown-ups can enjoy more sophisticated pursuits while keeping an eye on youngsters.

First, secure boundaries and deal with potential hazards. Lock away tools and chemicals and remove poisonous, irritant, or spiny plants. Children need the freedom to run around or play ball games, so choose a hard-wearing lawn mix. Make pathways smooth and spacious for pedalling tricycles or scooters, and provide "secret" areas where they can build dens, let their imaginations take flight, or lose themselves in nature. Children love water: pebble fountains are a strong but harmless draw, and a bog garden gives the illusion of water but is also quite safe.

A raised patio or deck creates a vantage point for adults and doubles as a sanctuary for relaxing or family dining, perhaps given extra protection with a pergola and trellis panels.

KEY DESIGN ELEMENTS

Raised beds
Lifting plants above ground level helps to protect them during play, and keeps toy trucks and cycles on the right track. If you have dogs, growing vegetables in a raised bed deters trampling or fouling.

Hard-wearing lawns
Choose durable grass seed or turf mix that contains rye grass. Aerate and resow thin patches and move play equipment to aid recovery. Mixes are available for problem areas such as shade or poor soils.

Play spaces
Consider children's ages before investing in play equipment. Look for adaptability: a sand pit could later be converted to a raised bed or pool. Swings have lasting appeal and can be adjusted over time.

Wide paths
For easy pedalling, keep paths wide, with gentle inclines rather than steps. This helps to protect plants that cascade over the edge of borders, and spreads the wear on grass pathways.

▼ **Separate the lawn** from the seating area using a stylish border of tall, dense plants.

Casual seating

Dot benches around the garden, especially in wilder parts where children can connect with nature. Introduce swing seats, hammocks, or outdoor bean bags. Keep cushions handy for walls and steps.

Built-in storage

Stow toys and equipment away so that they don't clutter the garden. Keep them within easy reach in waterproof cupboards concealed in purpose-built screened storage areas, or fitted under hinged seats.

Private corners

Adults may prefer a summerhouse but for children, any simple shelter will do, whether a tent, a living willow teepee, or an old shed. Raised platforms and treehouses provide an exciting lookout point.

ALSO TRY

Wet-weather play

Include a sheltered area where children can be out of the house whatever the weather.

Nature ramble

Wind narrow paths through wild flowers, or build a zigzag board walk over a bog garden.

Kid's blooms

Grow plants that attract butterflies and bees, and are fragrant, colourful, or oversized.

SPACE FOR EVERYONE

Creating a garden that is suitable yet enjoyable for all
the family can be easier than you might think, and it needn't
compromise on design. An imaginative layout can maximize
the uses of even the smallest garden.

▶ **In the thick of it**
Keep little ones close by integrating toys with
the productive garden. Use vibrant flowers
and decoration to appeal to them.

▼ **Free range**
Secure your boundaries so that children,
pets, and chickens can run around in safety.
Use boundary areas to store a compost bin,
or to create a secret children's hideaway.

▶ **All grown up**
Choose a secluded
corner where you can
sit and recharge your
batteries but which
allows you to observe
children's activities. Fill
surrounding borders
with fragrant plants
in gentle colours, and
use a bird bath or
bubble fountain
as a focal point.

▲ **Explorer garden**
Lay a winding path between borders filled with tall cottage flowers and herbs, and create screened-off, "secret" hideaways so that children can have fun investigating while adults relax and enjoy the scenery.

ADAPTING THE STYLE

Decide which features need to be located furthest from the house, such as the "secret" children's play space. Consider your seating: create an area of raised decking in a position that overlooks the entire garden, and site a bench where you can view a relaxing water feature. Keep useful storage cupboards close to the house for easy access.

▲ **Grow and play**
In a small plot you'll need imaginative design to make the most of the available space. Create privacy with tall fences rather than borders. Integrate features such as built-in seating with raised beds, and plant them with aromatic herbs to create a scented relaxation area. Use a simple layout to create garden "zones", such as a play area and a vegetable patch. Separating them with a different material, such as decking, creates a clear division between them.

◀ **Family room**
If you've got space, a summerhouse can make an outdoor home from home. Install a kettle and a fridge to ensure that hot and cold drinks are always on hand. Choose comfortable but portable armchairs and tables that can be lifted in or out depending on the weather. Use soft furnishings such as a rug, which is ideal for babies and toddlers, or a bean bag or two. Fit built-in storage for toys and wet-weather games, and shelves for books and magazines.

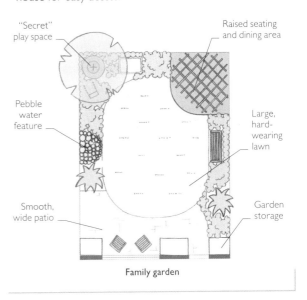

"Secret" play space

Raised seating and dining area

Pebble water feature

Large, hard-wearing lawn

Smooth, wide patio

Garden storage

Family garden

A CALMING RETREAT

Even in the heart of a city, a garden can be an oasis of peace and tranquillity. Cocooned by lush foliage and soft-coloured blooms, and soothed by the sounds of nature, you can escape day-to-day pressures and feel rejuvenated.

Blurring garden boundaries is a first step to establishing your own private sanctuary. Create deep, curving borders and fill them with a number of plants that are head height or taller. Surprisingly, this makes the garden feel larger, while dense planting muffles surrounding noise. Wind chimes, rustling grasses, or a trickling fountain are also pleasingly distracting. Where space is limited, use screening plants like bamboos, strategically placed trees, or a climber-clad pergola to block overlooking windows.

For a contemplative atmosphere, choose muted blues and purples against a green backdrop. Keep lines simple and open spaces uncluttered; try a large, simple container for sculptural contrast or a statue as a point of focus.

KEY DESIGN ELEMENTS

Simple containers
Use large pots with intriguing shapes, colours, or textures as focal points. Weathered terracotta, oxidized metal, and partially glazed finishes all work well. Plant simply, using topiary or grasses.

Spiritual features
Sculptures such as a Buddha or an angel provide a good focus for contemplation, as do plaques and paving carrying quotations or symbols. Site in a reflective space, in dappled shade or beside a pool.

Gentle sounds
Hang wind chimes or set up outdoor speakers to pipe soft music into the garden. For sounds of nature, plant whispering grasses and bamboos, and encourage birds and bees into the garden.

Relaxing water
A natural pond or reflecting pool creates a peaceful ambience. Arrange water features to give a gentle trickling sound rather than loud gushing. Adjust the flow to make the sound more relaxing.

▼ Use a curving low wall as a peaceful seating area in a secluded part of the garden.

ALSO TRY

Grounding experience
Create a treat for tired feet by designing walkways made of turf, stone, and wood.

Soothing shades
Include soft greys, greens, and pinks for their calming and therapeutic effects.

Heaven scents
Introduce heady rose, jasmine, and honeysuckle scents as well as aromatic herbs.

Focal points
Natural elements such as a piece of gnarled olive wood or a stone monolith make ideal focal points. A reflective, weathered mirror or metallic orb can add magic, as can a well-sited bubble fountain.

Informal seating
Avoid hi-tech steel and glass and go for wicker effect and sturdy wooden chairs. A stone or roughly chiselled wooden bench would also work well. Choose sculptural pieces with flowing organic lines.

Subtle screening
The pattern and colour of bamboo stems are a striking feature. Strip the bottom portion of leaves and thin weak stems to reveal their beauty. Use to create partial screens that rustle in the breeze.

PLAN TO RELAX

You can transform a plot of any size into a peaceful oasis using flowing shapes and muted colours, no matter the location. Where space is limited, provide a strong focal point and use screening to shut out distractions.

▼ Natural haven

In a larger garden you may have space to create a secluded, semi-wild area such as a wildflower meadow or a small copse. In this environment you can feel closer to nature, and enjoy the sound of bees, rustling leaves, and birdsong. It's the ideal spot to string a hammock or to position a shady gazebo.

► Zen approach

There's a Japanese saying that a garden is only finished when you can take nothing else away. This rock and gravel garden, or karesansui, is both simple and stylized. The shapes and textures can create drama in even a tiny space.

▲ Simple landscape

It is worth considering a minimalist approach to planting if you are creating a contemplation garden. Here a three-fold colour palette is used: white-stemmed birches are underplanted with soft green ferns and feathery, vibrant pink astilbe.

▲ Tranquil water
If you have enough space, a naturalistic pool makes a beautiful, calming garden feature and will attract a range of wildlife. Use lush marginal plants in a variety of colours and textures to create an attractive reflection.

ADAPTING THE STYLE

Think about the way the eye will be drawn around your garden: choose flowing, circular shapes that lead towards a focal point in the distance. Create deep, curving borders and plant them up with tall trees and shrubs, and soft colour-themed flowers. Use striking features on a compact scale, such as potted bamboos or a small circular water feature.

▲ Cool seclusion
The use of deep, generously planted borders filled with tall plants can make a garden feel bigger than it really is and seclude it from the rest of the world. Create partially screened-off areas to increase the illusion of space. Choose an organic layout, natural materials such as stone, gravel, and wood, and a limited palette of greens, browns, and grey-blues to give the garden a soothing feel.

◄ Spirit garden
The colour white is associated with purity and the sacred, and can be used in a variety of places, most strikingly here, as paving. Create a strong focal point and direct the garden towards it. Here, the ribbons of green act as markers on the journey. Play with shapes: provide symmetry with the rounded hummocks of greenery and the shapes of the pebble sculptures, and use angular tree branches and sword-like phormium foliage as a contrast. Choose greens, blues, and purples for a soft, gentle colour palette.

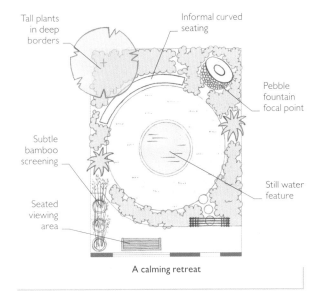

Tall plants in deep borders

Informal curved seating

Pebble fountain focal point

Subtle bamboo screening

Still water feature

Seated viewing area

A calming retreat

WILDLIFE HAVEN

Gardens are a prime resource for insects, birds, and amphibians. Whether yours is a city patio or a sprawling rural plot, there are simple ways to create a refuge for wild creatures without compromising on aesthetics or practicality.

Many cottage garden perennials attract bees with their pollen- and nectar-rich flowers. Encouraging butterfly breeding is more difficult, but if you include native plants, butterflies are more likely to visit and lay their eggs, as they may find suitable food plants for their caterpillars. Birds will feast enthusiastically on the berries of ornamental shrubs and, in winter, perennial seedheads are appreciated by gardeners and foraging finches alike. Large shrubs and evergreen climbers create safe nesting sites, and small trees offer vantage points for birds checking for predators.

Ponds attract a host of creatures from dragonflies to frogs, but if you don't have room, just provide water for drinking and bathing. Long grass, compost heaps, and log piles can harbour invertebrates – a crucial food for birds.

KEY DESIGN ELEMENTS

Winter food plants
Plant a range of fruiting shrubs, trees, and climbers to cater for visiting migrants as well as local residents. Plants such as holly, rowan, honeysuckle, and crab apples are also highly ornamental.

Bird feeders
Pick a location that has shelter from airborne predators but that won't encourage cats to lie in ambush. Remove stale or mouldy food, which can cause fatal poisoning, and keep feeders clean.

Nooks and crannies
Dry-stone walls and bundles of pruned twigs and branches known as eco-piles provide habitats for a range of creatures. Don't disturb over winter, when hedgehogs and queen bumble bees hibernate.

Green roofs
Turn a flat roof into prime insect real estate. Ensure that the surface is waterproof and well supported before laying pre-planted sedum matting or buying plug plants and creating your own ground cover.

▼ Plant a rainbow meadow of highly decorative, insect-friendly flowers.

Ponds and water

Even tiny pools can accommodate a frog or two and provide drinking and bathing water for birds; larger pools can support many species. Sloping sides allow safe access, and marginals and aquatics offer cover.

Insect nests

Provide a nest site for mason bees or a hibernation station for ladybirds and lacewings by filling pots with hollow bamboo stems, or fit a purpose-built box. Position in a warm, sheltered spot.

Nest boxes

Wild birds often lack nest sites, so position a range of boxes around the garden. Attach to trees or climber-clad walls, or fix beneath the eaves of a shed or other garden building in cool shade.

ALSO TRY

Long grass

Allow areas of long grass for the benefit of butterflies, mammals, and amphibians.

Mini woodland

Create a fast-growing, shady woodland habitat with close-planted silver birch.

Bog garden

Attract insects and provide a home for amphibians with moisture-loving bog plants.

NATURAL BY DESIGN

You don't need a large garden, or even one in the countryside,
to foster nature. It's all around you, but the design of your
garden and the plants you choose will have an impact on
how much wildlife you attract to your plot.

▶ Suburban bliss
Hedges, lawns, ornamental shrubs, and trees
offer birds food, sites for nesting, and vantage
points from which to watch for predators.

▼ Meadow haven
Long grass can support many beneficial
insects, including butterflies. At night, listen
for foraging mice and voles – if you're lucky
you may see bats and owls too.

▶ Wall habitat
Rock gardens and raised
beds made from loosely
arranged stones create
nooks and crannies that
make perfect homes
for beneficial insects
such as ground beetles,
queen bumble bees,
and centipedes. They
may also encourage
toads, which kill slugs.

▲ Designer wilderness
Create a stylized meadow or scrubland – birch trees provide sites for nesting and roosting, while the long grass can be sown with insect-friendly daisies and wild-looking perennials like the bee-magnet *Knautia*.

ADAPTING THE STYLE

Your layout will affect the amount of wildlife you will attract. Features such as a wildlife pond or bird and bat boxes are best at a distance from the house. Allow your plot to develop its own style: let the lawn merge into meadow at the far end of the garden. Place pots of scented flowers around a seating area to attract butterflies near the house.

▲ Aquatic life
A naturalistic pool is a huge draw for insects that attract dragonflies, birds, and even bats; birds will also use the pool to drink and bathe. Provide at least one shallow spot for safe access to the water. Use marginals and submerged aquatics to filter the water, and a few floating leaves to reduce the amount of light and heat that reaches the surface. These will also provide shelter and camouflage for amphibians and beneficial insect larvae.

◄ Winter garden glory
Providing an abundance of colourful fruits, berries, and seeds not only enriches views of the garden in winter, it also means there's a supply of food for birds and mammals, which will feast in autumn to build up fat reserves. There is a range of striking berries in colours as diverse as yellow and violet-purple. Ornamental grasses and other seedheads are also a valuable food source; tree ivy provides late nectar and fruits. Bees will appreciate early heathers.

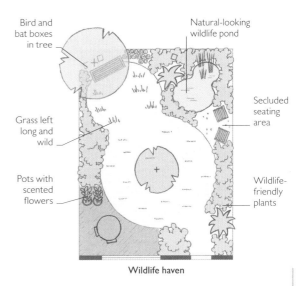

Bird and bat boxes in tree

Natural-looking wildlife pond

Grass left long and wild

Secluded seating area

Pots with scented flowers

Wildlife-friendly plants

Wildlife haven

ENTHUSIAST'S GARDEN

Most gardeners love plants, but for some they are a real passion. Providing conditions for unusual specimens is part of the challenge, as is creating year-round beauty. With research and planning, you can adapt your space to suit almost any plant.

Familiarize yourself with microclimates and soil conditions (*see pp.66–67*) so that you can develop diverse planting situations. Deep borders can offer scope for attractive plant arrangements, and even walls and fences can be utilized by attaching supports, pots, and baskets. Favoured specimens and collections will look even more striking if mixed with a variety of foliage and flowers.

Squeeze in a seating area, growing fragrant plants over a pergola, and conceal propagation or maintenance areas behind screening plants or vine-covered trellis panels. Create narrow, foliage-fringed paths leading to open spaces to provide contrast and variety in the garden, and to give additional planting opportunities.

KEY DESIGN ELEMENTS

Vertical planting
Use wires or trellis to create a climbing frame on any vertical surface; grow climbers and wall shrubs over archways or pergolas. In the right conditions, specimens can be combined to great effect.

Unusual varieties
Creating the right environment for a prize plant can be a challenge. It could entail creating a particular microclimate or soil type or, for large, frost-sensitive plants, wrapping them *in situ* over winter.

Special collections
Once you have the collecting bug, you may focus on acquiring specific genera or groups, such as succulents. Show these off with an auricula theatre or tiered displays on greenhouse or patio staging.

Generous planting
If you have trouble squeezing in new plants, curb over-vigorous types and give away those that no longer interest you. Use potted plants to fill gaps in borders and to invigorate your planting designs.

▼ **Line the banks of a shallow pool** with a mix of plants for colour and foliage.

Niche habitats
Some plant groups can't be accommodated in conventional borders so you'll need to create conditions to suit them, such as a water garden, boggy area, or shady woodland.

Plant protection
Exotic and tender plants require a frost-free shelter, ideally a heated greenhouse or conservatory. Some alpines need protection with a cold frame, while ferns and some orchids will thrive in a humid shade house.

Tender specimens
In warmer months, cacti, palms, tender succulents, and citrus may be moved outside to add a Mediterranean feel to patios and terraces. Others may be plunged into borders for an exotic touch.

ALSO TRY

Behind the scenes
Invest in a greenhouse or cold frame to store any plants that are temporarily off display.

Naturalistic plantings
Create wild-looking groupings of plants from a particular geographic region.

Trained shapes
Show off your skills with clipped topiary shapes, trained fruits, and flowering standards.

PLANT HAVENS

Creating a variety of conditions, such as a bog garden, woodland, or alpine scree, allows you to incorporate diverse, even exotic plants into your collection. Plan your design carefully to make a feature of your favourites.

▶ Tropical paradise
If you can shelter tender plants over winter it's possible to create a summer garden with jungle appeal. Use sculptural bananas, tree ferns, and cannas for an exotic flavour.

▼ Topiary theatrics
Even simple clipped shapes, spheres, or pyramids, can look striking, especially when arranged as part of an abstract design.

▶ Show-time
Put your favourite plants on show using simple displays of pots. Stepped stands or walls are ideal for maximizing the visibility of foliage and flowers. Plants can be changed around throughout the year to make the most of their seasons of interest.

▲ Water world
Creating a pond or bog garden is perhaps the most extreme way to cater for a specific group, but most aquatics and marginals are easy to please, and often have sculptural blooms and large, architectural foliage.

ADAPTING THE STYLE

Erect trellis or screening to disguise any areas of the garden that you don't want on view, such as potting sheds, a greenhouse, or a maintenance area. Use a winding path to separate the different planting zones, such as a bog garden and gravel garden. Site your favourite plants as focal features and position a seating area so that you can fully appreciate them.

▲ Building borders
Most gardens aren't naturally equipped with the conditions you'll need to support every type of plant. It's easier to control conditions, such as drainage and pH, if you grow plants in raised beds, or build up soil behind retaining walls. Mix and match to include as many species as possible, using bulbs like alliums to grow through perennials and alpines. You could also sit pots of lilies, dahlias, or other "fillers" on the soil to fill temporary gaps, or make the most of your prize specimens by showing them *in situ*.

◄ Drifting with nature
You can mimic the way plants grow in the wild by creating drifts and large blocks of the same species, such as *Kniphofia* or grasses. This naturalistic approach works particularly well in larger, rural gardens. Rather than straight-lined, formal beds or borders, allow the garden's borders to form in organic, flowing shapes. The mixing of perennials with grasses in this way is often referred to as prairie planting.

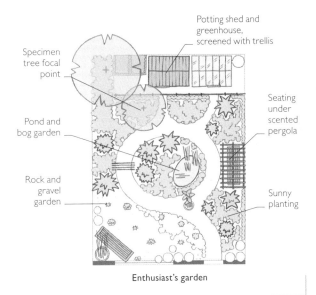

Specimen
tree focal
point

Potting shed and
greenhouse,
screened with trellis

Pond and
bog garden

Seating
under
scented
pergola

Rock and
gravel
garden

Sunny
planting

Enthusiast's garden

EASY-CARE GARDEN

You can enjoy a beautiful garden even if you can't devote a lot of time and effort to it. There is a wealth of low-maintenance plants to choose from, and you can still create dramatic effects without resorting to expensive landscaping.

By adopting a few simple techniques you can keep your garden looking vibrant and attractive. Choose pest- and disease-resistant plants and cut down on weeding by using mulches (see p.23). Select drought-tolerant plants where possible, and maintain more demanding types with automatic irrigation. Instead of annual displays of tender bedding, grow permanent, colourful evergreens and long-flowering perennials; select those that do not need support or deadheading. Some shrubs do not require pruning, while others may only need one simple cut per year.

Consider replacing a lawn with a gravel garden or meadow. Adding easy-care design features, such as a pebble fountain, helps to keep the garden interesting during winter months.

KEY DESIGN ELEMENTS

Colourful evergreens
Though planting emphasis is often on flowering annuals and perennials, evergreen shrubs, herbs, and grasses have longer-lasting displays and many are equally colourful and attractive.

Drought-proof containers
A row of architectural specimens can make as much impact as a multitude of high-maintenance bedding plants. Use automatic irrigation or plant drought-tolerant herbs, alpines, and succulents.

Raised beds
Easy-care raised beds can be filled with alpines, herbs, compact perennials, or even a pool. You can garden at a comfortable height, with no digging, and they can also be used as impromptu seating.

Living carpets
Species adapted to long periods without rain, such as alpines and succulents, are often tough in other ways. Many can withstand harmful insects, and don't require regular feeding or pruning.

▼ Line your floors and walkways with gravel for an attractive surface that needs minimal upkeep.

Decorative ground cover
Laying colourful pebbles or aggregate on top of a weed-suppressing membrane is an attractive solution to weeds, and is striking combined with creative planting.

Hard landscaping
Create clean lines and surfaces with natural stone or manufactured paving. Bricks can be laid in patterns or as edging. Mix materials: try cobbles with decking, or brick with sandstone.

Ornamental features
Display sculptures or use large, empty containers for architectural effects or as part of a colour theme. Use furniture as a focal point, or consider a paving feature such as a mosaic or circular patio insert.

ALSO TRY

Handy storage
Store soft furnishings, tools, and toys in built-in units so they're within easy reach.

Wild ways
Leave areas wild or convert lawns to meadows (see p.340) to free up your spare time.

Simple lighting
Use solar lights – there is a wide range of easy-to-install products available (see pp.76–77).

DESIGNED TO BE EASY

Make your garden easier to maintain by reducing the need for ornamental plants with creative landscaping. The textures and colours can create a striking foil for features such as fountains, vases, and sculptural plants.

▼ Water features

Self-contained water features with a reservoir and small submersible pump look and sound good, and need very little maintenance compared with pools and ponds; as the water is moving, they don't become clogged with algae and weeds. Surround with foliage that will contrast with the shape of the structure.

▲ Sculptural plants

To cut down on work, use easy-care, evergreen plants, shrubs, grasses, and compact bamboos, and limit the number of flowering varieties. To compensate, position eye-catching specimens in key spots such as the corner of a bed next to paving or decking.

► Lawn conversion

Large lawns can feel overwhelming if time is limited. You could adopt a more relaxed approach. It's easy to establish drifts of spring bulbs and snowdrops in grass. Just mow paths until September, when you can do an overall mow to prevent tussocks forming.

▲ Clean sweep
This elegant courtyard with built-in bench seating and slate paving is a useful, stylish outdoor room. With automatic irrigation the bold planting could almost look after itself – it will only need an occasional sweep up.

ADAPTING THE STYLE
Construct a simple design by lining the edges of the garden with easy-care, raised beds and borders, and then divide the rest of the space into a gravel garden and paved patio area. Place sculptural, decorative features or a pond at the far end of the garden to lead the eye across it, and site dining areas close to the house. Use evergreen hedging as a screen.

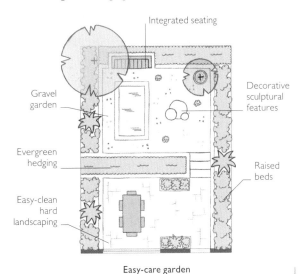

Integrated seating

Gravel garden

Decorative sculptural features

Evergreen hedging

Raised beds

Easy-clean hard landscaping

Easy-care garden

▲ Ornamental focus
In an easy-care garden, a wide range of decorative elements can be used to make an interesting focal point. The simple sculptural shapes of individual pieces such as an avant-garde recliner, a large simple container, or a boulder demand attention. Here a large amphora is the garden's central focus and is given extra prominence with a setting of pebbles and terracotta tiles.

◄ Gravel garden
Covering the soil with landscape fabric virtually eliminates the need to weed. After planting through the membrane, disguise the fabric with a range of decorative aggregates from gravels and pebbles to slate chippings. Over larger areas, it's important to introduce other shapes and textures. Here a line of wooden sleepers directs the eye to the container, which is set on a mosaic of slate shards ringed with stones. Select plants of differing heights, colours, and textures to complement the gravel surface.

WHAT IS ACHIEVABLE?

Keep an open mind. It's easy to be seduced by an attractive garden design but it's important to be practical about what you can realistically achieve, and how well the design will suit you and your lifestyle.

▼ SET YOUR PRIORITIES

When deciding on a design for your garden, think about how you live and the resources you have available. In addition to how much the garden will cost to build, also take into account how much maintenance it will take, and what skills and time that will require. For example, a border of varied shrubs planted through a weed-suppressing membrane with an attractive mulch will need much less care over time than a bed of annuals. It's also vital to choose a design that suits your site. Soil type and pH largely determine the plants you can grow, and aspect and exposure will influence where you position features such as seating areas. Slopes, drainage, and access for machinery and materials are important factors too.

To look their best, these extensive plantings of clipped hedes and pleached lime trees require time-consuming care.

POINTS TO CONSIDER

Time available
Estimate the time needed to build the design, as well as that needed to maintain the scheme. Looking after this topiary bed, for example, would be a time-consuming labour of love.

The budget
Shop around to get the best prices for materials, and compare quotes for labour and tool hire. Building a raised bed like this from timber is cheaper than using bricks.

DIY or get someone in?
Do you have the skills to complete the design yourself or will you need professional help? Laying a brick path like this yourself is fairly easy; pouring a concrete one is less so.

SITE CONSTRAINTS

The success of any design is greatly improved by understanding the plot, particularly soil type, growing conditions, and microclimate. In unfamiliar locations, look at what is thriving in nearby gardens and seek local advice on seasonal variations. Making even small improvements, like creating shelter, can increase the range of plants you can grow, but get to know the plot before making major changes.

▲ Soil and aspect

Many plants require specific soil conditions, such as acid, alkaline, moist, or well-drained, which will influence what you can grow. Aspect also affects plants, which often have a preference for sun or shade, but is equally important when siting features; seating areas, for instance, are best in warm, sunny spots. Watch the garden during the day to see where sun and shade fall, and adjust your plans and planting accordingly.

Planting large shrubs will create areas of shade in your garden for those plants that will benefit from it.

▲ Exposure and shelter

Unlike sheltered spots, exposed gardens can be prone to gusting winds, which may damage plants and will test the durability of garden buildings. Even urban gardens can be exposed, suffering damage caused by wind racing between neighbouring buildings. Sheltered sites are often warmer and allow a wider range of plants to be grown. Garden structures can be more lightweight, and more open designs are possible.

A sheltered spot provides the ideal site for large-leaved plants that would be damaged by wind.

◄ Access and obstacles

Whatever you're planning for your garden, don't forget that you need to be able to bring materials in and take debris out. In a ground-floor flat, that could even mean carrying everything across the living room carpet. Find the best location for skips and decide where to store bulky deliveries. Seek access from neighbours, perhaps.

Don't assume you can change everything in your garden to suit your design. Existing trees and features may be protected, so check with your planning office.

A wheelbarrow, is ideal for moving large or heavy materials on or off site, providing you have access for one.

WHERE TO START

For most people, moving house involves taking on a garden shaped by at least one previous owner. If you are a new gardener, adopting a richly planted garden can be exciting as well as daunting. To avoid mistakes, learn as much as you can before taking action.

▲ Assess the site

An established garden may contain mature trees and shrubs, some hard landscaping, and a variety of structures and buildings. Carrying out a thorough site review will highlight problem areas as well as plants and features to retain or enhance. Do a soil analysis to find any deficiencies. Look for shrubs and trees in need of pruning, regeneration, or removal, or that are mismatched.

Take photographs throughout the year to document the seasonal changes of plants and flowers.

▼ WAIT AND SEE

If possible, leave the major reconstruction of a mature, well-stocked garden for up to a year. There may be plants that aren't visible at the time you move in and it's easy to dismiss a dull shrub in autumn only to find it completely transformed with blossom and taking centre stage in early spring. Delaying not only allows you to experience the seasons, but also to view colour schemes, to see where the light falls, and to assess the amount of privacy the planting creates. It also allows you to review the productivity and health of mature plants and decide whether any need restoration or removal. Mark the position of bulbs or herbaceous plants that you want to keep before they die back. It is a good idea to make a planting plan of existing material in advance of digging and restructuring borders. Local horticultural colleges, social media, garden centres, and nurseries can help to identify mystery specimens as well as problems with pests and diseases.

Spring is the season when plants begin to emerge.

Check for unsightly gaps in your summer borders.

Leave plants to develop their autumn features.

Structural plants and seedheads create winter interest.

QUICK FIXES

While you're working out the details of a major overhaul, consider giving your garden an interim mini-makeover; this will refresh tired-looking hard landscaping and rejuvenate beds and borders. There are plenty of improvements that can be made with immediate benefits, which won't cost a great deal. Tackle eyesores such as dilapidated sheds or badly pruned trees first and if summer is approaching, make upgrading terraces and patios a priority.

▲ Reshape beds and lawns

You can turn a lawn into a feature simply by giving it a crisp, well-defined shape. For a modern touch, go for geometric forms such as intersecting rectangles, squares, or circles. Replace meandering border edges with strong, sweeping curves that lead the eye to a focal point. Adding a brick or paving mowing edge makes upkeep easier and gives the lawn some designer flair.

Reshaping this established lawn and adding edging has given the whole garden a new, fresh look, improving the appearance of flower borders too.

▶ Make good

Apply a fresh coat of paint or stain to existing features. On rendered walls, clean off loose flakes and scrub away any algae before repainting. Wobbly fences can sometimes be rescued rather than replaced; hide mismatched or missing panels with willow screens or trellis. Replace torn roofing felt on sheds and garden buildings, restore broken panes, and replace any cracked paving slabs.

Revitalize old fences with fresh paint.

▶ Clean up

Stripping out unwanted plants, removing rubbish, and generally decluttering provides an instant uplift. Weed paths and patios and hire a pressure washer to restore grimy paving and slabs. Remove unused plant supports, cut back dead stems, and weed beds. Mow and edge lawns and repair worn patches. Finish by sweeping and washing down surfaces.

Power-wash patios to remove stains.

▶ Cut back

Left untouched for a few years, some shrubs can outgrow their allotted space. Fast-growing types can also become clogged with unproductive wood, spoiling their shape and flowering ability. Cutting back sprawling plants can restore balance in a border and will free up space for new plantings. Neglected climbers might also need some attention.

Prune unruly shrubs back to size.

OLD GARDEN, NEW GARDEN

Starting with a bare site is the easiest way to design and build the garden you want. New-build sites are often a blank canvas but if you have taken over an existing plot you may need to clear it first. Keep the best plants and features, and don't be afraid to remove the rest.

► CLEAR AWAY RUBBISH

When clearing a site you are likely to come across a wide range of materials for disposal. Some plant waste can be composted, sent as green waste to local composting, or you can hire a shredder to chip larger, woody branches, which make excellent mulch. As a last resort, you can burn dry organic waste and untreated wood on still, dry days.

For bulky materials that can't be composted, shredded, or burned, such as rubble or rubbish, hire a skip or check what materials your local refuse site accepts; they may collect.

Wear gloves when clearing a site in case of sharp or hidden rubbish.

Removing trees may require planning permission.

◄ REMOVE PLANTS

Established gardens may contain plants that you don't want to keep. Perennials, bulbs, and small shrubs can be dug up and given away or possibly replanted

In some cases, weedkiller may be the best solution.

elsewhere. Most trees and shrubs can't realistically be moved, so are best cut down and dug out. To remove large specimens, contact a tree surgeon for advice, and where necessary remove stumps too large to dig out using a "stump grinder", which can be hired. Before pruning or felling any trees, however, check with your local planning authority that there are no preservation orders in force; this can also apply to hedges. When clearing plants, remove all obvious weeds, then lay down a weed-suppressing fabric, securely pegged down, to help to keep the area weed-free in future. As a last resort, if the plot is overrun with tough perennial weeds, use a chemical weedkiller.

▶ NEW BUILDS

If you buy a house on a new development, you may start out with just a stretch of bare ground in place of a garden. Although unsightly, this fresh start gives you the ideal opportunity to design your dream garden from scratch. Other than the barest bones, such as a path, new-build gardens are devoid of existing features that might otherwise restrict your choices. Such a blank canvas also allows you to start designing and building as soon as the weather permits, and access for machinery and deliveries is often easier.

The downside of new-build sites is that with a lack of established trees and shrubs, it can take several years before the garden develops a sense of maturity or privacy. Depending on how the site was used before it was developed, there may be issues with soil quality (see below). You may also discover there are planning restrictions and bylaws, often specific to that development, limiting what you can plant and build, especially in front gardens.

New-build gardens often lack plants and features but offer a wealth of design opportunities.

▼ Assess the soil

New build soils are often very poor. In a new garden, don't assume that rubble was removed from the site – it may have been buried under a thin layer of topsoil. Dig test holes across the site to check, and also look out for other soil problems, such as compaction (see right). Mark out any problem areas so you can resolve them later or plan around them. Also check how deep the topsoil goes, measure its pH, send soil to be tested at a laboratory, and assess whether it is mostly clay, sand, or loam (see pp.20–21).

▼ Soil compaction

It's not unusual to find a cosmetic topsoil dressing used to disguise an impenetrable base of compacted soil, caused by heavy machinery. Compacted soil contains little air and drains poorly, which restricts plant growth. Scrape back the topsoil to look for patches of soil that are hard to dig and fork through the soil as much as possible, incorporating bulky organic matter such as composted bark. Compaction is most common on heavy clay soils and can take several years to alleviate.

▼ Other considerations

Look at deeds and covenants to find out whether planting added when the house was being built (specified by local planners) has to remain. Check for preservation orders (TPOs) on established trees. In communal front gardens, dividing fences and hedges are outlawed, and some areas may have to remain lawned. Check the routing of gas and water pipes, drains, and electricity cables before work begins to prevent them being disturbed or damaged.

Dig test holes to assess the quality of your soil.

Puddles may indicate areas of compacted ground.

Check your site plan when designing your garden.

SURVEYING THE SITE

Analyzing the key characteristics of your plot will help you to create a garden that works. If you know your challenges, such as a border that floods in winter or an area that's always in shade, you can find planting or landscaping solutions.

▶ CONSIDER THE SOIL

Understanding the type and structure of your soil is paramount. Plants require differing conditions, and knowing which you can provide allows you to make better planting choices. Although certain soil types can be improved, it's best not to try too drastic a change: a thin, lime-rich soil formed over limestone bedrock will have a high pH – ideal for lavender, but lethal for pieris, rhododendrons, and other ericaceous plants that need deep, acidic, humus-rich soil. Using soil additives to increase the soil's acidity may solve the issue in the short term, but water rising from the bedrock will return the ground to its original state, and it's usually better to work with the existing pH. The consistency and drainage of soil can also adversely affect construction projects such as ponds or building foundations, so plan carefully to avoid disappointment.

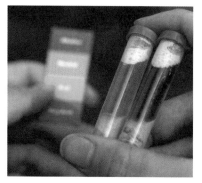

Soil pH
Use a pH test to analyse your soil. Most plants prefer conditions around pH 6.5. But some, such as pieris, prefer acidic conditions, around pH5.5. Alkaline soils suppress clubroot disease of cabbage family plants.

Heavy soil
Clay-rich or "heavy" soils can be tough to dig. If they dry out they can become solid and cracked and, as they drain poorly, they can become very sticky when wet. Dig in organic matter to improve the soil structure.

Sandy soil
Sandy, stony, or gravelly soils drain quickly, and therefore tend to lack water-soluble nutrients, which are easily washed away. Rake in fertilizer and apply a 5–8cm (2–3in) mulch of well-rotted manure or compost.

▼ ASPECT AND SHELTER

Factors such as the direction in which your garden faces, how much sun it receives, where the prevailing wind blows from, and how sheltered the plot is should strongly influence your garden design and planting decisions. By observing the sun as it moves across the garden you can identify which areas will make the best locations for eating and relaxing – you could have one patio for breakfast or morning coffee and another for evening dining. These observations will also help you to site a herb or vegetable plot or a gravel garden, which all need as much sunshine as possible. As the sun moves from east to west, the house, neighbouring buildings, trees, and hedges can cast shadows over different areas. The amount of shade will also vary according to the time of year: in summer, the sun is higher, which results in more of the garden receiving warmth and light.

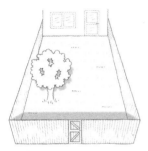
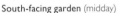

South-facing garden (midday)

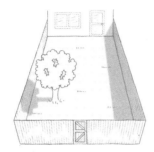

West-facing garden (midday)

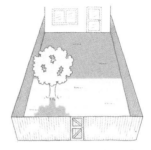

North-facing garden (midday)

East-facing garden (midday)

▲ Frost pockets

Hot air rises, and in sloping gardens the cold air will sink to the bottom of the gradient. If prevented from escaping by a dense hedge or wall, it accumulates, forming a frost pocket. Select plants carefully as tender and newly planted specimens, especially evergreens, may not be able to survive the cold in winter months.

Observe your garden to identify frost pockets. They can be very localized: the plants surrounding the *Sambucus*, *Acanthus*, and grasses above are unaffected.

▼ Exposed seaside sites

Strong winds can strip moisture from foliage and damage weak stems, so the more sheltered your garden, the better your plants will cope. Use tall wind-, salt-, and cold-tolerant plants to create a "shelter belt", to shield the plot from prevailing winds. This barrier of plants will allow you to grow more delicate types in sheltered spots.

Use tough plants such as large, spiky phormiums and tall, feathery pampas grass on exposed, sea-facing aspects. Their height and foliage make them an asset, but even plants such as these benefit from a shelterbelt to reduce exposure.

DEALING WITH SLOPES

Gradients add interest to a garden, allowing you to create different levels, but they can pose a challenge. Achieving level surfaces and easy access may require substantial digging, soil retention, and drainage.

▼ CREATING LEVELS

Gently sloping sites provide a wealth of opportunities to create interesting paths, steps, and spaces. Individual areas can be easily levelled, either by cutting in and building retaining walls, or by building upwards to form decks and terraces. On larger plots, or on those that slope in more than one direction, different levels can be interconnected to create a multi-level space. Where gradients are gentle, this is something you can probably achieve yourself, or at least with minimal help and advice.

Major earth-moving is very expensive and difficult, however, and on steeply sloping sites it may be better to design with the gradient rather than try to level it. Instead, work with the natural contours. Seek expert advice to see what is achievable, and what it may cost.

A multi-level terrace like this provides a variety of linked spaces.

▼ RETAINING THE SOIL

When cutting into a slope to make a level area, you may need to retain surrounding soil to hold it in place. On gentle slopes, a low wall or a row of railway sleepers may be adequate, which you could build yourself. Steeper sites, with more soil to hold back, require substantial retaining structures, capable of supporting the weight of soil, as well as the water it contains. Speak to a professional landscaper, or for walls over 1m (3ft) high, contact a structural engineer.

Use wooden sleepers to level shallow slopes.

Substantial walls are needed to retain steeper sites.

▶ CHANGING LEVELS

An essential aspect of any sloping site is being able to move between levels safely and easily. Ramps and steps are the obvious solution, and whichever you choose, plan them carefully. They should be wide and deep enough to climb safely, but shallow enough so you don't struggle to reach the top. The materials used should not become slippery in wet weather, and you may need to plan in surface drainage and handrails. You may be able to achieve this yourself on simple slopes but seek advice on steep, challenging sites.

Simple steps are easy to build with basic DIY skills, and provide space for decorative pots.

Shallow ramps are the safest way to ascend a slope. One like this could be made using decking planks.

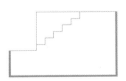

Retaining wall

Steep steps are useful where space is limited but can be dangerous or difficult to climb without a secure handrail.

Shallow steps are safer and easier to climb but take up more space. Ideal for larger plots, wider steps can be decorated with planters.

Continuous ramps are ideal for wheelchairs and bikes but must be long enough to be sufficiently shallow. This takes up lots of space.

Stepped ramps take less space than full ramps, and are easier than steps for wheelbarrows and wheelchairs. The surface must not be slippery.

▶ PROVIDING DRAINAGE

Drainage is vital on sloping sites to control the direction in which ground- and rainwater travels. Unchecked, water flows downhill, below or over the surface, and can collect anywhere, even indoors. Drainage is critical in areas with heavy soils and in urban sites, where there is run-off from roofs, paths, and roads. Angle your hard surfaces to direct water away from buildings, and dig gravel-filled sumps, or interceptor drains, to control water movement. Building raised beds can lift plants out of wet conditions. Again, seek professional advice if unsure.

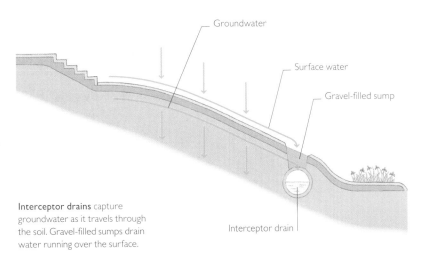

Groundwater

Surface water

Gravel-filled sump

Interceptor drain

Interceptor drains capture groundwater as it travels through the soil. Gravel-filled sumps drain water running over the surface.

CREATING BOUNDARIES

The role of a boundary is to define a space, whether that's the whole plot or an area within it. Boundaries have many functions, from providing privacy and intimacy to forming the backbone of the entire garden design.

▼ SETTING LIMITS

Garden boundaries have the fundamental task of containing the site and providing a physical barrier to intruders, prying eyes, and the weather. In most gardens, they are highly visible and form the backdrop to everything else. When designing with boundaries, there are two approaches: either try to blend them in, or make a feature of them. Once in place, the materials and style you choose are hard to change, so design your boundaries carefully.

Ample planting softens this wall, blurring its lines.

▲ DEFINING SPACES

Dividing spaces often makes them seem larger, especially when the different areas are then given a specific use, such as for formal dining or as a play area for children. You don't need tall barriers to create the divisions – you can achieve the same effect with low walls, woven screens, and see-through planting. The idea is merely to suggest a space and purpose. Using screens also means that the divisions are temporary and can change as your need for different spaces evolves.

Bright paint and a low wall mark out this seating area.

Stark modern fencing sets the tone here.

◄ BEYOND THE BOUNDARIES

Garden boundaries don't have to block views or be continuous and unbroken, and can be used to lead the eye to specific features. Niches clipped into hedges provide a prime spot for statuary, while trellis panels inserted into fences can reveal a neighbouring focal point. Alter the height along the length of your boundaries to give a varying sense of enclosure and openness. Gates don't just provide access, they can also be used to frame views in or out of the garden, and can be made features in their own right.

Within the garden, leave gaps in divides and screens to give a taste of what lies beyond. This will also allow you to take full advantage of garden features by enabling them to be enjoyed from different angles. Be creative with the design of your garden and consider how and from where you will view its features.

A moon gate like this defines the entrance and frames the view.

► MATERIALS TO CONSIDER

When deciding on what materials to use for garden boundaries, it is important to consider the overall scheme first. Aesthetically, natural materials suit traditional designs better but can look out of place in contemporary schemes, and vice versa. On a practical level, think about durability and what the boundary is for. If it's intended to keep people out or to act as a windbreak, you'll need something sturdy. Likewise, if your garden is exposed to the elements, even temporary internal dividers will need to be fairly robust. Maintenance is also a factor. Hedges need trimming regularly in summer, and fences last longer if they are treated every year. Even walls need looking after.

Brick walls offer a traditional look.

Fences and screens are quick to erect.

Traditional hedges take several years to establish.

Trellis fencing is useful for internal garden divides.

SURFACES

Surfaces are one of the main elements of a garden, literally underpinning almost everything else. They can be expensive and time-consuming to install, but get it right and they will last a lifetime.

▼ CHOOSING MATERIALS

There are many factors to consider when deciding on surface materials. Cost and appearance are obvious, but don't overlook practicality: think about the site and how it will be used. For example, choose tough, hard-wearing materials for heavily used areas such as paths. Consider porous materials, like gravel, at the foot of sloping sites where drainage is an issue. If access is difficult, think about using lightweight materials that can be easily carried to the site. Another important consideration is that, although the surface is the most visible element, it is often the easiest to complete; it is the foundation that can be challenging. Decking, for example, needs minimal footings, which you can do yourself, but stone tiles require a solid base, best left to professionals. The payback, however, is that while a deck lasts 10–15 years, tiled surfaces can last indefinitely.

Hard surfaces are best for seating areas; lawn is ideal for play spaces.

DRAINAGE

Hard surfaces must drain in a controlled way to prevent puddles forming and to stop rainwater entering buildings. Slope surfaces and incorporate drainage channels to direct flow. Ensuring good drainage also helps prevent smooth surfaces such as slabs and tiles becoming slippery in wet weather.

Plants between paving slabs can help to absorb excess water from the non-porous surface. Trim as needed if they spread.

► HARD SURFACES

Hard surface materials include bricks, blocks, slabs, and tiles, whether natural or man-made. Their advantage is that they provide a firm, level surface that is very hard-wearing. They are also available in a wide range of materials, suitable for most designs. Smaller units, like bricks, are best for sloping or angular sites, where corners are required, or where materials must be carried on site. Slabs are ideal for paving areas quickly and are simple to lay. The drawbacks, depending on the material, are the need for foundations and drainage, and often the price.

◄ GRAVEL

Gravel is very versatile and comes in a range of colours and textures. It can be laid almost anywhere, regardless of slopes and corners, and requires only a weed-proof membrane for a foundation. It can be carried in bags to site, and if bought in bulk can be very economical. It can be used as a temporary solution. Laying it requires no special tools or skills, so is easy to do yourself. The downsides are that it does not form a solid surface, and can make walking, and pushing wheelbarrows and prams, more arduous. Weeds may eventually grow through it.

► DECKING

Decking is usually made of weather-resistant, pressure-treated wood, which must be treated regularly to protect against rot. Decks are adaptable, ideal for sunny areas, and can be built to suit most sites, whether on different levels or awkwardly shaped. Their advantage is that they are easy to build, using basic tools and DIY skills, and the materials are cheap. You can also adapt or expand them over time. The drawbacks are that decks can be slimy when wet, and that wood decays and needs replacing. Composite decking is made from recycled plastic and wood and lasts longer.

◄ LAWNS

Lawns are the most traditional garden surface. Like gravel, they are ideal for sloping and awkwardly shaped sites, and the materials can be easily brought to site, assuming the soil beneath is suitable. They are also ideal for families, providing a safe surface for children and one that will grow back if damaged. A big drawback is maintenance, as they require regular mowing in summer and treatment and care in autumn and spring. They are not suitable for shady sites and can turn to straw in hot summers, although they usually recover.

GARDEN BUILDINGS

Even the humble tool shed can become an attractive feature when positioned and finished with care, so it's worth integrating your garden buildings into your design. With sheds, greenhouses, and other working buildings, pay particular attention to access and location.

▶ SITING SHEDS AND STORES

Sheds offer convenient storage for items such as tools, compost, toys, and bicycles. In a small plot, consider a garden store or locker. Fit sheds with a sturdy padlock and check home contents insurance to see whether they are covered. Consider location carefully. It might be better to put a shed out of sight – down a side passage or behind shrubs and trees – rather than in full view.

When selecting a shed, examine the quality of the joints, frames, and fittings of doors and windows and reject any where you see chinks of light through the framework. The base should feel solid and the roof should have a decent overhang and a good covering of thick roofing felt.

Wooden sheds look attractive but need paint, stain, or preservative treatments to prevent rot. Rust-proof metal or fibreglass types may be easier to maintain.

◀ Access

If you will be manoeuvring large equipment such as a lawn mower or wheelbarrow in and out of your shed, select a model with large entrances and doors that open fully. Wide access paths are ideal and you may want to replace steps with a ramp, or gravel paths with paving, for easy access. For leisure buildings, garden offices, and studios – where you will not regularly need to move bulky items – use steps and stairways to enhance the architectural impact of the structure; surround it with plants to integrate it into the garden. For any garden building, ensure that the base is level and that surrounding surfaces and paths slope away slightly to divert rainwater.

Make a grand entrance by using a striking spiral staircase for access to an exterior office or studio.

► GREENHOUSES

Commonly constructed from metal, such as lightweight aluminium, or from naturally rot-resistant woods like cedar, greenhouses are available to suit any garden design. A sheltered position is best, avoiding nearby walls, hedges, and trees that cast unwanted shade. Site away from boundaries to lessen the risk of vandalism.

Consider what you are likely to grow: a lean-to on the north side of a wall would be perfect for a cool, shady fernery but much more light will be needed for ripening grapes. An east–west orientation for a freestanding greenhouse is ideal for raising spring seedlings, and for overwintering plants. Choose a model with roof vents and exterior shading blinds to keep plants cool in summer. If you need extra heat and light, lay cabling to supply electricity.

A large, traditional greenhouse makes an attractive feature in a rural garden. Surround it with plants to soften its appearance.

Check planning rules when siting a garden room.

Customize a shed with a stained-glass window.

Install a play house and walkway.

Fit a garden office with an insulating sedum roof.

◄ TYPES OF BUILDINGS

There is a wide range of garden buildings available, but if you can't find the design you want, some companies will create bespoke pieces or can convert an existing building. You might need planning permission depending on the size, height, and proximity to boundaries, so check before positioning.

Customize a wooden building using paints, stains, or even a stained-glass window, or leave structures a natural shade to blend in with their surroundings. For a green roof try pre-planted sedum matting; you may need to strengthen the structure to take the extra weight. Fit insulation in sheds, garden offices, and workshops, especially if you plan to heat them. Consult an electrician when installing heating and lighting.

LIGHTING

Outdoor lighting can serve a variety of purposes, from providing safety and security to creating a relaxing atmosphere. It can transform the look of your garden by night, so decide which plants or focal points you want to illuminate and then choose lights to fit your design.

▼ SECURITY

Lighting up entrances to the house can be decorative and welcoming but can also help to deter burglars; if possible, keep a clear line of sight to the road. LED wall lights can be set to switch on at dusk and off in the morning, but this can result in light pollution that disturbs wildlife. A more eco-friendly option is to install security lights fitted with infra-red movement sensors that illuminate your home as people approach it. Adjust the sensitivity so that lights aren't triggered by passing cats and foxes. Also keep nearby plants well pruned to prevent them activating the lights on a windy night. Be sensitive in the placement and power of lights to avoid upsetting your neighbours.

A clear line of sight along well-lit paths leaves no hiding places for unwelcome visitors.

▲ SAFETY

If you plan to use the garden at night you'll need to light paths and steps for safety. Concentrate on potential hazards such as ponds, or where ground levels change or land falls away sharply from a pathway. Use post lights or low-level mini spotlights angled to cast light over the edges of paving or decking, or install recessed paving lights; choose a style that complements the design of your house and garden. Recessed deck lights are relatively easy to install and will highlight the edge of the deck as well as changes in level. Safety lights don't have to be on continuously: sensors are available which will switch lights on as you approach and off again after a set time. You can also control garden lights using a remote or mobile phone.

Outdoor LED post lights are plugged into a transformer. Solar-powered lights are also available.

◄ DECORATION AND MOOD

With strategic lighting it's possible to transform the look of a garden at night. Individual mini spotlights, uplighters, and downlighters can be used to illuminate sculptures, decorative wall panels, garden buildings, and structures such as pergolas. Used sparingly, coloured lights will add drama to plain walls, and recessed lights can make a feature of steps and retaining walls. Fountain lights make water features sparkle at night, while submersible lights add drama to contemporary pools.

Uplighting a tree picks out the texture of the bark and leafy canopy. With diaphanous subjects like grasses, shining low-level lighting through the stems and flowers works well. Tiny string lights woven through overhead climbers and wall shrubs creates a romantic atmosphere.

Use recessed lighting to illuminate a seating area and to highlight focal plants and screening.

► LIGHTING OPTIONS

There is a range of lighting types, so pick those that fit your design. Any lights powered by a mains circuit must be installed by an electrician.

LED lights make striking features. They can be plugged into a transformer in a waterproof unit in the garden or attached to the house. Submersible LEDs can be used to illuminate ponds and water features.

You can also buy wireless, battery-powered lights that are recharged by plugging them into a USB socket. Solar-powered lights are eco-friendly and many will work even in winter; position them so that they can absorb enough sunlight to recharge.

Candles and lanterns are inexpensive and create a wonderful atmosphere. Make sure to position them well away from flammable materials and plants.

Lantern-style lights provide an atmospheric touch to a garden.

Solar-powered lights are safe and easy to install.

Ensure that candles are safely positioned.

LED lighting should be installed by a professional.

DESIGN PRINCIPLES

Decide on a look for your garden – sleek contemporary, relaxed informal, or strongly structured traditional – and base your layout on this. Consider different ways of navigating the garden, where to place various features, and in what direction main sight lines will run.

◄ SHAPES AND SPACES

Designs work best if there is a good balance between flat, open spaces, such as lawns, decking, and patios, and upright elements, such as trees, borders, and buildings. The vertical features provide contrast with the horizontal, and help to divide up the plot. Overlap bold geometric shapes for a simple but unusual design.

Mark out the key zones on a rough plan, designating approximate areas of use, such as seating or planting. Decide whether you've given sufficient space to different areas, and try different ideas. If the lawn or terrace is too big relative to the borders, the garden could feel stark and uncomfortably open. On the other hand, lack of open space could feel claustrophobic.

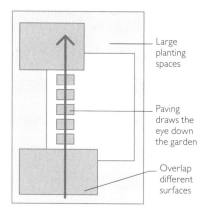

Large planting spaces

Paving draws the eye down the garden

Overlap different surfaces

Right angles Use straight-sided shapes to make the garden seem bigger – position down the centre for length, or side to side for width.

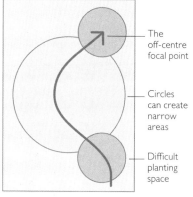

The off-centre focal point

Circles can create narrow areas

Difficult planting space

Circles Use the circular areas to create an organic, natural-looking design. Here the eye is led through the centre to the rear right corner.

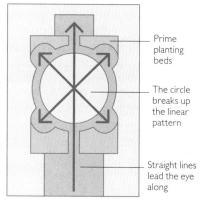

Prime planting beds

The circle breaks up the linear pattern

Straight lines lead the eye along

Mixed shapes When blending straight and rounded shapes, keep the design simple as it can create odd-shaped planting areas.

▼ ROUTES AND NAVIGATION

Deciding the garden's access points, and figuring out how to move around it, results in a pattern of pathways that will influence the overall design. A straight path forming the primary route down the centre creates a formal look. Strengthen the axis further by placing a focal point at the far end. A route that meanders creates a more relaxed ambience, with the promise of partly hidden spaces to explore. A circular route can provide access to all parts of the garden, linking to different areas such as a dining terrace or utility area.

Use sharp topiary to accentuate formal symmetry.

Create a winding, river-like walkway lined with slate.

A circular path makes the whole plot accessible.

▼ FOCAL POINTS

In a small plot, use one strong focal feature, such as this large slate vase, to draw the eye; for a traditional feel, place it at the end of a straight walkway. Positioned in a corner, it can pull focus along a diagonal axis to make a short plot feel longer. Choose features in interesting shapes, textures, and colours, to contrast with their surroundings.

▼ EXPERIMENT WITH PLANS

The plans below illustrate just how different the same-sized plot could look simply by rearranging the position and shape of various key garden features. Each design contains lawns, borders, a pool, and a patio, but the left-hand plan is formal and highly ordered while the plan on the right-hand side is fluid, relaxed, and dynamic. Place a grid over your plan – by keeping the lines adjacent to the paper's edges you will find it easier to plot the straight-lined grid formation of the first design. Alternatively, rotate this grid by 45 degrees to plot your features on the diagonal, as in the second design. Link features together by plotting them on a curved, swooping line.

Choose plants that act as a foil for your feature.

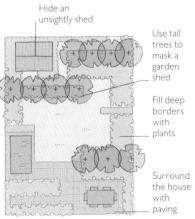

Hide an unsightly shed

Use tall trees to mask a garden shed

Fill deep borders with plants

Surround the house with paving

Use a grid-like layout and parallel screens of trees and hedging to encourage the development of secluded, intimate areas.

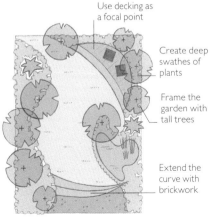

Use decking as a focal point

Create deep swathes of plants

Frame the garden with tall trees

Extend the curve with brickwork

Use organic shapes and a small number of materials to create a space that is relaxing and will be easy to maintain as plants develop.

DRAWING SIMPLE PLANS

Once you've examined your garden's soil and aspect, and chosen which features you want to include, you can begin designing. You'll need an accurate site plan, so ensure that you measure carefully.

▶ REGULAR SHAPES

On a piece of A4 or A3 paper, sketch out a rough outline of the garden, drawing it approximately to scale. If the site is attached to, or flows around a building, make this your main point of reference.

Using a long tape measure, note the exact shape and dimensions of the building, including the position of doors and windows, and also the distances between the building and the site boundaries. This will show the full extent of the garden area. Next, measure the length and angles of the garden boundaries, and also the distances from corner to corner to help you work out the true shape of the plot, relative to the house.

Finally, note down any remaining elements, including any existing features or buildings that you intend to keep, and mark on their positions in relation to the boundaries and house.

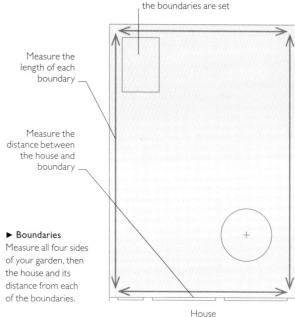

Add in features once the boundaries are set

Measure the length of each boundary

Measure the distance between the house and boundary

▶ Boundaries
Measure all four sides of your garden, then the house and its distance from each of the boundaries.

House

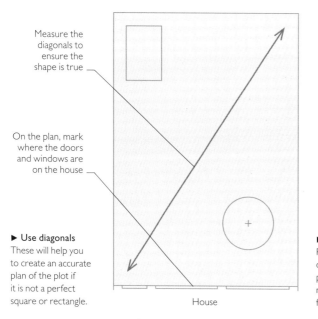

Measure the diagonals to ensure the shape is true

On the plan, mark where the doors and windows are on the house

▶ Use diagonals
These will help you to create an accurate plan of the plot if it is not a perfect square or rectangle.

House

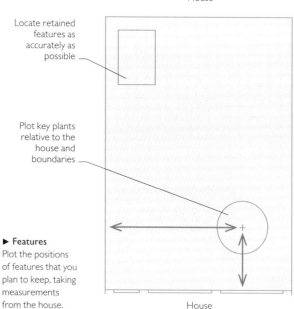

Locate retained features as accurately as possible

Plot key plants relative to the house and boundaries

▶ Features
Plot the positions of features that you plan to keep, taking measurements from the house.

House

▼ MEASURING OUT

Once you've gathered your measurements, transfer them to a scale drawing on graph paper. Choose a scale that relates to the size of your plot and the amount of detail you require. For a small garden, a scale of 1:25 (1cm/½in on paper measures 25cm/10in on the ground) or 1:50 is ideal. When transferring measurements to the plan, a scale rule and a pair of compasses will be useful for plotting features. Draw it out using a fine-nibbed pen, and take photocopies so you can experiment with ideas.

▼ IRREGULAR SHAPES

To measure out an irregularly shaped garden accurately, you will need to use offsets. These are worked out by first laying a tape measure along the length of the garden at a 90-degree angle to the house. Holding a second tape measure at 90 degrees to the first, measure the distance to the boundary on each side at regular intervals, also recording the measurement to any feature you plan to keep. Scale down the measurements and draw out the plot, linking the boundary offsets to draw the perimeter.

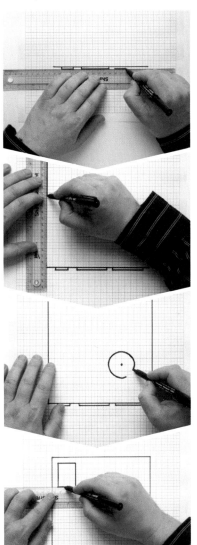

1 Begin by drawing the façade of the house along one edge. Use a pen and a ruler to mark the size and position of windows and doors.

2 Draw in the boundaries and then the diagonal measurements. If the lines don't match up, adjust the boundary lines accordingly.

3 Draw in the position of trees and their canopies using measurements taken in relation to the house and boundaries.

4 Finish by plotting the position of sheds, ponds, patios, and other hard elements. Don't waste time filling the plan with features you don't intend to retain.

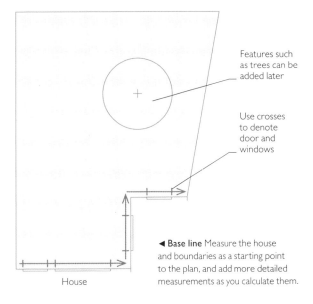

Features such as trees can be added later

Use crosses to denote door and windows

House

◄ **Base line** Measure the house and boundaries as a starting point to the plan, and add more detailed measurements as you calculate them.

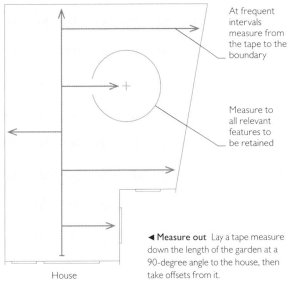

At frequent intervals measure from the tape to the boundary

Measure to all relevant features to be retained

House

◄ **Measure out** Lay a tape measure down the length of the garden at a 90-degree angle to the house, then take offsets from it.

CREATING A DESIGN

There are a number of useful ways to firm up your ideas and help you visualize the various stages of development in your garden plans. Start off with a basic sketch or photo and roughly superimpose your design. It's also handy to have photocopies of a scale plan to experiment with.

1 BUBBLE PLANS

This is one of the easiest ways to visually display your ideas and will help you to establish the best positions for functional areas and decorative features. Bubble plans help to show the relationship between, and relative scale of, component elements, such as lawns, borders, seating areas, and play equipment. Link and overlap the bubbles and change their size and orientation as you experiment. You may find it useful to colour code the bubbles according to their different uses.

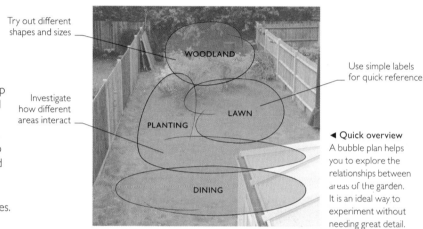

Try out different shapes and sizes

Investigate how different areas interact

Use simple labels for quick reference

◄ Quick overview
A bubble plan helps you to explore the relationships between areas of the garden. It is an ideal way to experiment without needing great detail.

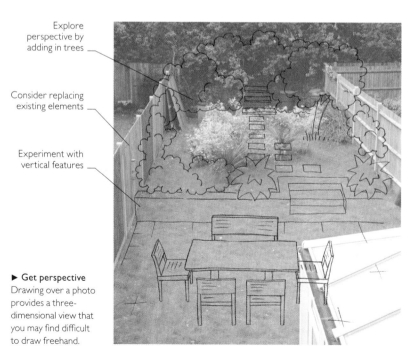

Explore perspective by adding in trees

Consider replacing existing elements

Experiment with vertical features

► Get perspective
Drawing over a photo provides a three-dimensional view that you may find difficult to draw freehand.

2 SKETCH OVER PHOTO

Take photographs of your garden from as many different angles as possible. These will act as a handy reminder for drawing plans, especially for checking the position of trees and buildings outside the perimeter. Try to get a view from above to help you better visualize the garden. When experimenting, place sheets of tracing paper over one of your photographs, and sketch out a range of three-dimensional ideas. The photograph's boundaries and trees will help to keep the drawn elements to scale, but try not to let existing features, such as patios or borders, influence your design. Sketches like these are invaluable for showing others what you have in mind, as many people find bird's-eye plans difficult to visualize.

3 OVERHEAD PLAN

Create a scale plan showing the exact size and location of all the garden's features – you may want to employ a qualified garden designer to do this for you. Draw in vertical elements such as fences, hedges, and trees. Map out horizontal surfaces and if possible, draw in individual paving units or decking planks. Going into detail will help you to predict the costs accurately. If your garden slopes and there are dramatic changes in level, annotate these clearly, or produce a cross-sectional plan. More complex drawings for steeply sloping gardens may need to be produced by a surveyor for ease of planning.

4 PLANTING PLAN

If your planting plan is for a landscaper or nursery, be precise so that they know how many plants to supply, and what spacing to use. Indicate lines, drifts, or blocks of the same plant using symbols, a numbered key, or a colour code (see pp.116–117). Show where shrubs, trees, or topiary will overlap ground-level planting.

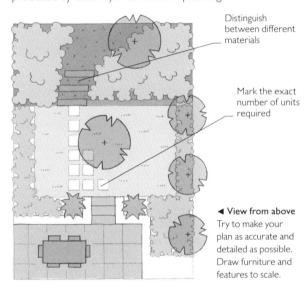

Distinguish between different materials

Mark the exact number of units required

◄ **View from above** Try to make your plan as accurate and detailed as possible. Draw furniture and features to scale.

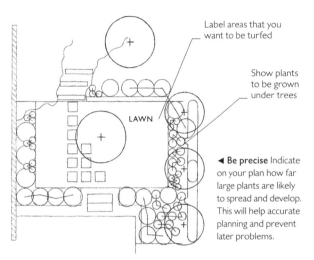

Label areas that you want to be turfed

Show plants to be grown under trees

LAWN

◄ **Be precise** Indicate on your plan how far large plants are likely to spread and develop. This will help accurate planning and prevent later problems.

5 THE FINAL STAGES

When a design is drawn to scale and shows accurate locations and dimensions of all its elements and features, as well as the layout of electric cables, lighting, and drainage, it is ready for use. Whether you do all the work yourself or pass it over to a contractor, the plan will be invaluable when measuring up and laying out. Laminate it, or make several copies, as it will probably end up muddy and torn.

6 THE FINISHED GARDEN

By following a detailed plan you maximize the chances of a smooth, organized project. Once construction and planting are completed, add finishing touches that will enhance your design. Here the furniture (*right*) echoes the clean lines and square shapes of the stonework.

PUTTING UP FENCE POSTS

The strength of a fence lies in its supporting posts. Choose 75×75mm (3×3in) pressure-treated wooden posts, and set them in quick-drying concrete or alternatively support in concrete spurs. Your chosen fencing panels can then be nailed in place.

▶ **A new fence** makes an attractive backdrop to planting, and will last for years if put up correctly.

FENCING BASICS

Installing a new fence post involves digging a deep hole and partially filling it with hardcore to provide a firm foundation. The post is then set vertically using "post-mix" concrete that dries in under an hour. Ask your neighbours' permission if you need access, and hang the fair side of the panel facing their side.

YOU WILL NEED

Claw hammer or screwdriver
Tape measure, spirit level, rope
Bricks, timber, hardcore
Spade
Fence posts and finials
Metal spike or pole
Timber battening
"Post-mix" concrete

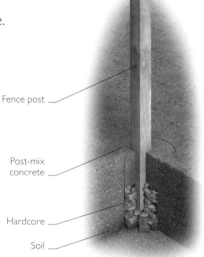

Fence post

Post-mix concrete

Hardcore

Soil

1 If replacing an existing fence, dig out any weak or damaged posts first. If these are set in concrete, use improvised levers to prise them out of the ground.

2 Mark out where the new post holes need to be. Dig them 30cm (12in) square, and roughly a third as deep as the fence will be tall – deeper in exposed sites.

3 Place pieces of hardcore in the bottom of the hole and stand the post on top. Holding the post vertical, pack more hardcore around the sides until the hole is half filled.

4 Use a heavy metal pole or a length of timber to ram the hardcore in place and help settle the material. Top up as required, so the hole remains about half full.

5 To test that the post is vertical, hold a spirit level against each of its four sides. Make adjustments as necessary. Check the post is at the right height for the panel.

6 To keep the post upright, tack on a temporary wood brace, fixed to a peg driven into the soil. Fix it to the side that won't have fencing panels attached.

7 Fill the hole with water and let it drain to settle the hardcore. This will also improve the adhesion of the concrete. Check that the post is completely vertical.

8 Add quick-drying "post-mix" concrete to the hole and leave to set fully before hanging the panels. To protect the tops, nail on wooden finials to deflect rain.

FENCING OPTIONS

The style of fencing you choose has a major impact on the overall effect of your garden; the right choice can act as a foil for planting or make a bold design statement. Select the highest-quality elements that you can afford for the most attractive and durable results. A concrete or wooden gravel board at the fence base prolongs the life of the panels.

Natural screen
A framed and oiled willow screen provides a neat yet natural backdrop for planting.

Hurdle
These surprisingly robust, hand-woven panels are perfect for cottage-style gardens.

Trellis panel
With an inset of trellis down the centre, these panels are ideal for training climbers.

Shiplap
One of the cheapest and most popular fencing options, but not the most durable.

METAL SPIKE SUPPORTS

If you have firm, stone-free soil, metal spike supports are an option. Position the spike in place and insert a "dolly", a post-driver, into the square cup. Hit the dolly with a mallet to drive the spike into the ground. Check the angle to ensure that it is straight; they are difficult to remove once inserted. When the spike is in the ground, remove the dolly and insert the post, tapping it into place.

Featheredge
These sturdy panels of vertical softwood timbers are a good choice for boundaries.

Picket fence
This simple wood fence has rustic charm, yet also works well with a modern property.

LAYING A PATH

Paths can be laid using a wide range of materials. Bricks, blocks, and other small units are hard-wearing and adaptable for slopes and angles. Creating a simple block path requires only basic tools, and is easy to do yourself.

▶ **Taller edging** blocks can be used to hold back soil from paths that run alongside raised garden borders. They prevent soil washing onto the path every time it rains, keeping it neater.

PAVING BASICS

Block paths are laid onto a very simple foundation, consisting of a compacted layer of soil, hardcore, and sand, set into the ground. The blocks are then laid on top and held in place with sand and gravel.

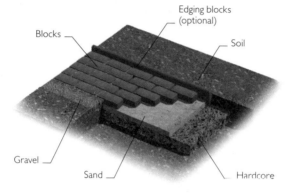

Blocks

Edging blocks (optional)

Soil

Gravel

Sand

Hardcore

YOU WILL NEED

Tape measure, spirit level

Pegs and string

Hammer and nails

Spade, trowel

Shuttering boards

Hardcore

Sharp sand, gravel

Hand rammer or plate compactor

Paving blocks or bricks

Rubber mallet

Garden brush

1 Measure the path and mark with string and long wood pegs, spaced every 1.5m (5ft). Allow enough room for shuttering boards and decorative edging.

2 Dig out enough soil between the string to accommodate layers of hardcore and sand, as well as the blocks. Check levels along the path using a spirit level.

3 To prevent puddles, the path must slope gently to one side to drain. Angle it away from house or garden walls to avoid damp problems. Check levels again.

4 Nail the shuttering boards to the pegs to enclose the area of the path. Check levels once more; any adjustments can be made by easing the pegs up and down.

5 Spread a 8–10cm (3–4in) layer of hardcore along the length of the path. Use a hand rammer or hired plate compactor to tamp it down thoroughly.

6 Spread a layer of sharp sand over the hardcore. Level the surface by pulling a length of timber across the path towards you. Fill in any hollows with extra sand.

7 Here, shallow carpet blocks that sit on the sand's surface are used. Full-sized paving bricks should be tamped into the sand and left proud by 2cm (¾in).

8 Paving bricks are butted up close together, but other types of paving need more space. When you have finished laying and tamping, brush kiln-dried sand into the gaps.

9 Once the path is laid, consider removing one or two small pavers to provide planting holes. Plant with low alpines; these will soften the appearance of the path.

10 Finish off block paths by brushing decorative gravel into the gaps between them. This isn't necessary for brick paths, as the blocks are butted up together.

MATERIALS

There is a broad range of materials available for block paving laid using this method, with both natural and man-made products in a wide variety of sizes and finishes. Price and appearance are obvious factors when choosing, but also consider how durable the material will be, whether you can get it on site easily, and how simple it is to lay.

Granite setts
Tough, natural, and non-slip, setts are ideal for uneven surfaces and areas in heavy use.

Paving bricks
These are cheap to buy, easy to lay, and come in a wide variety of colours and styles.

Mixed materials
In informal schemes, use a mixture of tiles, slabs and stones for an eclectic look.

Concrete blocks
These are a cheaper alternative to granite setts but give a similar effect when laid.

Other materials
Paths don't have to be stone. Consider other materials, such as wooden sleepers.

Crazy paving
Bed stone or broken slab pieces into gravel and sand, or mortar for a more solid finish.

LAYING A PATIO

Slabs and pavers are available in a wide range of shapes, sizes, and materials, and make a neat, practical surface. Laying large, regular pavers is relatively easy; preparing the foundation is the hardest part of the job.

▶ **The patio surface** forms the backbone of the design, with subtle colours and smooth surfaces that blend into the background. Finely mortared joints complete the look.

PATIO BASICS

Patio slabs and pavers are laid onto a simple foundation consisting of compacted soil, hardcore, and sand, set at a slight gradient for drainage. Each slab or paver is then sat onto five "dabs" of mortar and tapped level. To finish, wet or dry mortar is worked into the joints to create a solid, weatherproof surface.

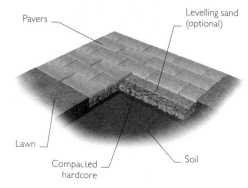

Pavers

Levelling sand (optional)

Lawn

Compacted hardcore

Soil

YOU WILL NEED

Pegs and string
Builder's square
Spade or turf cutter
Rake
Builder's trowel and brick jointer
Hand rammer or plate compactor
Spirit level
Pavers or slabs
Hardcore, sharp sand
Ready-mix mortar
Rubber mallet or club hammer
Spacers
Stiff brush

1 Mark out the paved area with pegs set at the height of the finished surface, and join with string. Use a builder's square to check corner angles are 90 degrees.

2 Remove any turf with a spade, or hire a turf cutter for large areas. (Reuse turf or compost it.) Dig out the soil to 15cm (6in) deep, plus the thickness of the paving.

3 Use a hand rammer or powered compactor to tamp down the foundation area. Adjust the marker pegs to ensure the finished surface has a slight gradient for drainage.

4 Spread a 10cm- (4in-) deep layer of hardcore over the area, rake level (ensuring you retain the slope), then tamp firm with a hand rammer or plate compactor (*above*).

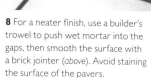

5 Level out the hardcore, where required, with sand. Lay the first pavers along the perimeter string, bedding each on five trowelfuls of wet mortar.

6 Tamp down the pavers using a rubber mallet or the handle of a club hammer. Insert spacers to ensure evenly sized joints, and cement around the outer slabs.

7 Remove spacers after two days, once the pavers are firm, and brush dry ready-mix mortar into the joints between them. The mortar will harden over a few days.

8 For a neater finish, use a builder's trowel to push wet mortar into the gaps, then smooth the surface with a brick jointer (*above*). Avoid staining the surface of the pavers.

MATERIALS

The range of materials to use for patios is vast, with choices to suit all designs and budgets. Laying a patio is time-consuming and costly, so consider your choice of materials carefully. Some materials are more hard-wearing than others, while others, including some natural stones, need routine care. Also remember, fashions change.

Concrete slabs
There is a huge variety to pick, some very naturalistic or modern, others very basic.

Natural stone
Attractive but costly; some types need annual treatment to make them weatherproof.

Tiles
Tiles can't be laid with the "dab" method (left) but must be laid on a solid concrete bed.

Moulded slabs
These add texture and interest to a finished patio. Use sparingly to create a feature.

MAKING CUTS

To finish the patio you may need to cut some pavers to size or shape, using an angle grinder (see right). First measure and mark out the cut you need to make, and lay the paver on a deep layer of sand. Holding the angle grinder firmly, draw the cutting disc along the desired cut until complete. For your own safety, wear goggles, gloves, ear defenders, and a dust mask when cutting.

Patio kits
Centrepiece designs, such as this stylized sun, come as a kit and fit together like a jigsaw.

Reclaimed stone
Using reclaimed stone will give your patio a "period" look but can be very expensive.

LAYING DECKING

Decking is very adaptable and can be built to fit most sites, blending with modern and traditional garden styles. It is usually built from hardwood or pressure-treated softwood, and often comes in kit form.

▶ **Decks can offer** the ideal solution to awkward plots that feature slopes or poor access. They can be raised to level a site and the materials are fairly lightweight.

DECKING BASICS

Decks consist of a wooden frame supported by evenly spaced posts. The posts are set upright into holes filled with hardcore and concrete, then trimmed to provide a level base. The deck is constructed on top to create an even, raised platform.

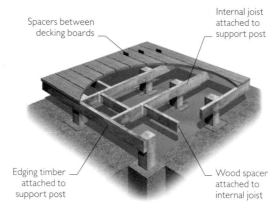

Spacers between decking boards

Internal joist attached to support post

Edging timber attached to support post

Wood spacer attached to internal joist

YOU WILL NEED

Pegs and string, tape measure

Builder's square, spirit level

Weed-proof membrane

Spade

Hardcore

75 x 75mm (3 x 3in) support posts

Post-mix concrete

100 x 50mm (4 x 2in) timber joists

Drill

Galvanized nuts, bolts, washers, screws, nails, brackets

Saw and hammer

Decking boards

Spacers

1 Mark out a rectangular or square deck with pegs and string. Check the corners are at a 90-degree angle using a builder's square. Mow any grass very short.

2 Lay a weed-proof membrane over the area, overlapping joints by 45cm (18in). Roll it back when setting the outer posts but cut through it for internal supports.

3 You will need a post in each corner and the rest spaced in a grid pattern, one every 1.2m (4ft). Dig holes 38cm (15in) deep, and fill the bottom 8cm (3in) with hardcore.

4 Fill the hole with water to dampen the hardcore and allow to drain. Insert the post and pour in post-mix concrete (see p.84), using a spirit level to check it is vertical. Leave it to set.

5 Cut edging timbers to length and drill bolt holes through them and also the posts. Attach one end of the first edging timber to a post using nuts and bolts.

6 Level the first timber and fix in place with nuts and bolts. Trim the post ends flush. Repeat these steps until all three sides are fixed, then tighten the bolts firmly.

7 Pre-drill holes and use nails to fix internal joists between the edging timbers, across the shortest span, spacing them 40cm (16in) apart. Make sure they are all level.

8 To hold the joists rigid, cut short lengths of timber and insert them between the joists at 1.2m (4ft) intervals. Secure them using long nails or metal brackets.

MATERIALS

Decks are predominantly made of timber, and often come in kit form. Being made of wood, they are easy to adapt and personalize with your own ideas, although ready-made deck accessories are available. The advantage of decks is that they are easier to change than traditional patios, allowing you to be more creative with materials.

Wooden decking
The most common material for decking is wood that has been treated against rot.

Plastic decking
Impervious to rot and bad weather, plastic surfaces are ideal for a low-care garden.

Decking tiles
Made from light soft-wood, these tiles are easy to replace when they start to wear.

Wood stain
Pretreated timber can either be left natural, or transformed with a coloured stain.

Railings
Some decks must have safety railings, which may be a feature in their own right.

Finials
Personalize your deck posts with attractive finials, which come in many designs.

9 Cut a decking board to length. Pre-drill holes in the board, then attach it to each joist using two corrosion-resistant decking nails or countersunk screws.

10 Cut remaining boards to size and attach them to the deck, making any joints above the joists. Space the boards 5mm (¼in) apart, using spacers, to allow for expansion.

LAYING A LAWN

The quickest way to achieve a beautiful lawn is to lay turf in early autumn or spring to give the grass plenty of time to establish. Watering is critical to prevent drying out. To cover a large area, sowing seed is a cheaper option.

▶ **A well-maintained lawn** creates a sense of space in the garden, as well as providing the perfect foil for border flowers.

LAWN BASICS

Buy your turf from a reputable supplier, and if possible, inspect it before purchasing to ensure that it is weed- and disease-free. Prepare the site carefully before laying the turf, and ensure that you lay the pieces very closely together to create tight seams. Once the strips are in place, you can cut a curved edge using a hosepipe or rope as a guide.

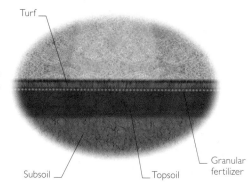

Turf

Subsoil

Topsoil

Granular fertilizer

YOU WILL NEED

Spade or fork

Rake

Hoe

All-purpose granular fertilizer

Sieved topsoil mixed with horticultural sand

Wooden plank

Broom

Hosepipe

Edging iron

1 Two months before the turf arrives, weed the site thoroughly and dig a little organic matter into the soil.

2 Level the area with a rake and apply an all-purpose fertilizer. Keeping your weight on your heels, tread over your plot, and repeat at right angles across the width.

3 Rake the ground level to remove any depressions. Leave for five weeks for the soil to settle, then hoe to remove weeds.

4 Carefully unroll the turf, laying whole pieces and working out from an edge. Stand on a plank to distribute your weight, and tamp down turves with a rake.

5 Continue to lay the turves in rows, and stagger the joints like a wall of bricks; this produces a much stronger structure. Use an old knife for cutting if necessary.

6 Create a tight seam between turves by butting them together so they almost overlap and then pressing the crease down firmly with your thumbs.

7 Don't use small pieces of turf at the edge of the lawn as they will dry out and shrink – instead lay them in the middle of the site. Firm in well with a rake.

8 To shape lawn edges, use a hosepipe or rope to mark out the curves, and then cut around your template with an edging iron or sharp spade.

SEEDING A LAWN

For large areas of lawn, seeding is the cheapest option and, although it will be about a year before the grass can take heavy use, it should start to green up and look good in under a month. The best time to sow is in late spring or early autumn when the soil is warm and moist.

1 Prepare the site as for turfing. Before sowing, remove weeds and add a top dressing of fertilizer. Weigh out seed for a square metre (yard) and pour into a paper cup; mark where seed reaches.

2 Rake soil level. Remove any stones and other debris. Mark out a square metre (yard) using canes or string, then measure out the right amount of grass seed using the marked paper cup.

3 Scatter half the seed in the cup over the marked area in one direction, and then the other half at right angles. Set out the next square, and repeat the sowing process.

4 Rake the seed into the soil to just cover it. Water with a can fitted with a rose, or spray lightly with a hose. Cover the area with bird-proof fleece. The seedlings should appear within 14 days. Water regularly.

9 To help adjacent pieces of turf to grow together and root firmly, brush in a blend of sieved topsoil and horticultural sand using a stiff broom.

10 Keep the lawn well-watered during dry spells (particularly in summer) to avoid shrinkage. Take care not to overwater in winter, as this may kill the grass. If cracks do appear, brush in some soil.

MAKING A PERGOLA

A pergola is a series of cross-beams linked together to form a covered walkway, providing the perfect support for climbing plants. A wood frame kit, demonstrated here, makes it easy to put the structure together.

▶ **Create a shady retreat** by training climbing plants up and over your pergola using wires attached to the upright posts.

PERGOLA BASICS

Each pergola arch consists of a cross-piece supported by two upright posts. Most have extra cross-pieces along the length of the roof timbers to strengthen the roof and support the areas between the upright posts. These additional cross-pieces do not sit on uprights, so are unsupported.

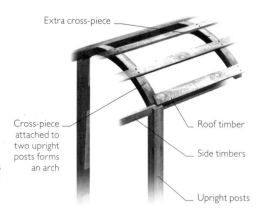

Extra cross-piece

Cross-piece attached to two upright posts forms an arch

Roof timber

Side timbers

Upright posts

YOU WILL NEED

Pergola kit
Pegs and string, tape measure
Builder's square, spirit level
Vice
Drill and screwdriver
Galvanized screws or bolts
Hammer
Temporary wooden battens (optional)
Spray paint
Spade
Hardcore
Metal spike
Ready-mix fast-set concrete

1 Unpack and identify all the pieces. Mark out the layout of the pergola on the ground with pegs and string, using a builder's square to check right angles.

2 To make an arch, attach each end of a cross-piece to the top of an upright post. Nail wooden battening between the upright posts to prevent them splaying.

3 Mark the two post positions for the first arch using spray paint. Dig out holes about 60cm (2ft) deep and 30cm (12in) across. Fill with 10cm (4in) of hardcore.

4 Ram the hardcore firmly in place with a metal spike. Place the posts in the holes and check that each one is vertical by holding a spirit level against each of its sides.

5 Holding the posts steady and upright (or using wooden battens if necessary), concrete the first arch into place (see p.84).

6 Position the second arch, allowing for a slight overlap. Dig post holes and check their position by placing side timbers on their respective uprights.

7 Using a spirit level, check that the side timbers are horizontal and the uprights are vertical before concreting the posts in position. Repeat steps 3–7 for all the arches.

8 Once the concrete has set, screw or bolt all the side timbers in place, butting the joints together. It's best to pre-drill the holes to prevent splitting.

9 Screw or bolt the extra cross-pieces in place midway between the uprights. Check that all the fixtures on the frame are tight.

10 Pre-drill holes and screw the roof timbers on top of the cross-pieces. Leave the wooden battens in place until the concrete has completely set.

OBELISKS

Timber obelisks suit almost any garden design, be it formal or a relaxed country-cottage style. Use them draped with clematis or other flowering climbers to add height to a border, as a feature to flank an entrance, or to create a focal point at the end of a walkway.

Although you can make an obelisk from scratch (if you have good DIY skills) or from a kit, ready-made structures are available in a range of materials and sizes and can be inexpensive. Choose a contemporary metal structure for a mixture of climbing roses and clematis, or a more short-lived woven wicker frame to support a profusion of colourful sweet peas (*Lathyrus*).

Woven
For a rustic look, choose a woven obelisk for beans in a productive garden.

Metal
Delicate climbing flowers provide a contrast to a modern metal obelisk.

MAKING A POND

Designing a pond with a flexible butyl rubber or PVC liner allows you to create a feature of any size and shape. Mask the edges of the liner with overhanging stones on a bed of waterproof mortar.

▶ **Plant up your pond** with water lilies and marginal plants once the waterproof mortar is completely dry.

POND BASICS

A pond usually has a deeper central section; the depth must be at least 45cm (18in) to prevent the pond freezing solid in winter. The pit is covered with underlay to cushion the liner. To work out how much liner you need, add twice the depth of the pond to its maximum length plus width.

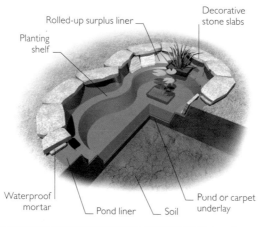

Rolled-up surplus liner

Decorative stone slabs

Planting shelf

Waterproof mortar

Pond liner

Soil

Pond or carpet underlay

YOU WILL NEED

Hosepipe

Spade

Pickaxe

Spirit level/plank

Sand

Pond or carpet underlay

Flexible pond liner

Waterproof mortar, bucket, trowel

Sharp knife

Decorative stone

1 Use a hose to mark out the outline of the pond; the relative inflexibility of the hose will create a smooth, curving shape.

2 Before you start digging, skim off turf for reuse elsewhere. Keep the fertile topsoil separate from the subsoil, and loosen compacted subsoil with a pickaxe.

3 Dig out the pond to a depth of 45cm (18in). Leave a shelf 30–45cm (12–18in) wide around the edge, then dig out the centre to a further depth of 45cm (18in).

4 Use a spirit level placed on a straight piece of wood to check that the ground around the top of the pond is level. Remove loose soil and large or sharp stones.

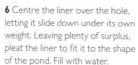

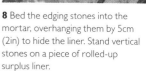

5 Line the sides and base of the pond with pond or carpet underlay. On stony soils, spread a 5cm (2in) layer of sand over the base first.

6 Centre the liner over the hole, letting it slide down under its own weight. Leaving plenty of surplus, pleat the liner to fit it to the shape of the pond. Fill with water.

7 When the pond is full, trim the liner leaving 45cm (18in). Pleat the excess so it lies flat, and bury the edges in the soil. Lay a bed of mortar; don't let it fall into the water.

8 Bed the edging stones into the mortar, overhanging them by 5cm (2in) to hide the liner. Stand vertical stones on a piece of rolled-up surplus liner.

BUILD A BUBBLE POOL

Suitable for even the smallest of gardens, a bubble pool makes an interesting water feature. Adjust the flow so that the water bubbles up over the top of the pot and down the sides. Seek advice from a qualified electrician to install an outdoor electricity supply, and ensure that all electrical connections are fitted with an RCD circuit-breaker.

1 Dig a hole bigger than the size of the water reservoir that will be positioned below the bubble pool. Install a waterproof electricity supply with assistance.

2 Edge the hole with damp sand and position the reservoir, packing the area around it with sand. When in place and level, place the pump inside and add the lid.

3 Place the pot over the reservoir with the pump pipe protruding through the hole in the base. Seal the pipe in place with silicone sealant and leave to dry.

4 Attach the delivery pipe to the water flow adjuster, then attach them to the pump tube inside the pot. The delivery pipe should sit just under the rim of the pot. Fill the reservoir and pot with a hose.

9 Wait a week for the mortar to set, then add aquatic plants and marginals. Top baskets with a layer of well-washed pea gravel.

10 If adding fish, float their bag on the water and open the top to allow more air inside. Release the fish into the pond after 20 minutes.

BUILDING A RAISED BED

Creating a timber-framed raised bed is easy, especially if the pieces are pre-cut to length. Untreated wood is best for growing edibles, to avoid any risk of chemicals leeching into the soil. If the bed is to sit next to a lawn, make a brick mowing edge.

▶ **A neat mowing edge** makes the perfect finish for your raised bed, and creates a clean edge as well as a decorative feature.

RAISED BED BASICS

To create a raised bed, build up the timbers, overlapping the joints at the corners. Part-fill with a layer of rubble, including stones and broken crocks for drainage and to fill up deep beds, before adding at least 15cm (6in) of topsoil or compost, and topping with a layer of mulch.

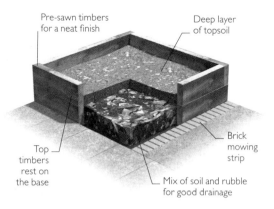

Pre-sawn timbers for a neat finish

Deep layer of topsoil

Top timbers rest on the base

Brick mowing strip

Mix of soil and rubble for good drainage

YOU WILL NEED

Spade
Pre-cut wooden timbers
Spirit level
Tape measure
Rubber mallet
Drill
Screwdriver
Heavy-duty coach screws
Rubble and topsoil (ideally mixed with well-rotted garden compost or manure)
Bark

1 Dig out strips of turf wide enough to accommodate the timbers. Pressure-treated wood or reclaimed hardwood are economical options.

2 Lay out the timbers *in situ* and check that they are level with a builder's spirit level; use a plank of wood to support a shorter spirit level. Check levels diagonally too.

3 Make sure that the base is square by checking that the diagonals are equal in length. For a perfect square or rectangular bed, it's a good idea to use pre-cut timbers.

4 Using a rubber mallet, gently tap the wood so that it butts up against the adjacent piece, remaining level and upright. Remove soil as needed.

5 Drill holes through the end timbers into the adjacent pieces at the top and bottom. Secure with long, heavy-duty coach- or timberlock screws.

6 Attach the next layer on top of the base, joining them together and making sure the joints overlap those below. Check levels before screwing together.

7 For extra drainage, partially fill the base with rubble – this may not be necessary in shallower beds. Add at least 15cm (6in) of quality topsoil, free from perennial weeds.

8 Fill up to about 8cm (3in) from the top, then mulch with a layer of bark or gravel. Plant up your bed with ornamentals or productive plants, and water in well.

MATERIALS

Consider size carefully when selecting a material for a raised bed: railway sleepers will allow you to create a large bed, but unless you are very tall you should build your beds no more than 1.2m (4ft) across, so you can reach to the centre. Beds can be narrower if you choose, and taller beds are ideal if you need your plants within easy reach.

Sleepers
Unused railway sleepers can be built up layer by layer to suit your needs.

Stone
Perfect for a country-style border of rambling ornamentals. Doesn't require mortar.

Wicker
Choose a lined, woven wicker bed for a short-term, rustic, cottage-garden appearance.

Brick
Create beds of any size using bricks, making sure that you include drainage channels.

Ready-made kits
The simplest option, ready-made raised bed kits are available in various sizes.

Slate
Use reclaimed slate tiles upright to edge and retain temporary raised beds.

MAKING A MOWING EDGE

Dig out a strip of soil deep enough to accommodate the bricks plus 2.5cm (1in) of mortar. Lay a level mortar mix in the bottom of the trench as a foundation, and set the bricks on top with a small gap between each one. Check that the bricks are level and tap them into position with a rubber mallet. When fully set, brush dry mortar between the bricks, working it in with a trowel.

PLANT YOUR GARDEN

From scrambling climbers to majestic bamboos, the gorgeous plants offered in this chapter suit every garden, regardless of soil conditions, aspect, or garden size. Follow the planting recipes to create year-round interest – from naturalized spring bulbs and wildflower summer meadows to autumn berries and colourful winter stems.

PLANT FAMILIES

Plants in each of the major groups have different habits and behave in different ways, so it is useful to have a basic understanding of how they look and perform before creating a planting scheme for your garden.

TREES

These large woody evergreen or deciduous plants usually produce a canopy of leafy stems above a single clear trunk, although many conifers bear branches from top to bottom. Trees lend height to designs and provide shade in sunny sites, but position them carefully as they are difficult to move once established.

SHRUBS

Together with trees, shrubs form the backbone of a garden design. They can be evergreen or deciduous and come in many different shapes and sizes, but all are characterized by a permanent framework of woody stems. Grown for their attractive foliage, flowers, and stems, shrubs provide colour and interest all year.

PERENNIALS

Living for three years or more, a few perennials are evergreen but the majority are deciduous, their top growth dying down in winter and reappearing in spring. Their stems are generally non-woody and many multiply to form large clumps. They are mainly grown for their flowers; some also provide foliage interest.

GRASSES AND BAMBOOS

Grasses grow from the stem and leaf bases, and produce strap-like foliage. They encompass annuals and both evergreen and deciduous perennials, and their flowers are wind-pollinated. Sedges are very similar to grasses, but tend to be evergreen, while bamboos are simply grasses with woody stems.

BULBS

A bulb is a plant with a food-storage organ that sustains its growth when the optimum conditions prevail. The group includes true bulbs, such as daffodils; corms, such as crocuses; tubers, including dahlias; and rhizomes like irises (see p.160). They are valued for their colourful flowers; some also have decorative foliage.

ANNUALS AND BIENNIALS

Plants that grow, flower, and die within one year are known as annuals; those that produce stems and leaves in their first year, then bloom and die in the second year are biennials. The flowers of hardy types are often used to brighten up borders, while tender plants that flower all summer are ideal for pots.

CLIMBERS

These climb host plants or structures to search out sufficient light. The group includes evergreen and deciduous forms; some have lax stems while others are woody. Most need a framework of trellis or wires, or a host tree or shrub to climb, and cling via a number of different methods (see p.144).

WATER PLANTS

Plants that live in and around water comprise four main categories: oxygenators help to keep the water clear by starving out weeds; aquatics such as water lilies root at the bottom of a pond; marginals live at the water's edge; and bog plants grow in the moist soil that typically surrounds a natural pond.

PLANTING FOR A LIFESTYLE

The plants you choose and the way that they are used have an impact on the time you will need to spend caring for them. If you want an easy-care garden, opt for robust, hardy plants that perform year after year and require little maintenance.

High maintenance

If you enjoy being outside and tending your garden, you can choose from a wide range of planting schemes and garden styles. Include a lawn if you don't mind mowing, and try tender plants that require cosseting in a warm greenhouse or room indoors over winter. Keen gardeners can also sow annuals each year in beds and containers, and plant tender summer bulbs, such as dahlias and gladioli, which need lifting and bringing indoors in autumn. Trees with flowers that require frost protection, such as magnolias, are also options if you are happy to cover them with fleece when temperatures dip.

Moderate care

Those who enjoy gardening but only have limited time can still maintain a lawn and perhaps a few large container displays, as well as trees, shrubs, and perennials in beds and borders. Any plant in a pot needs more nurturing than one in the ground, where it has access to greater reserves of nutrients and water, but large containers require watering less frequently because they hold greater volumes of soil. You could also plant climbers like clematis that only need to be pruned annually, and some hardy bulbs, which are left *in situ* over winter.

Low maintenance

Small trees and hardy shrubs make life easy for gardeners. Most require very little maintenance if planted in the right conditions. Shrubs may need trimming back every couple of years, while trees shouldn't require much pruning, except to remove dead or diseased stems. Hardy perennials are also easy; just cut back the dead growth in autumn or early spring.

High-maintenance gardens filled with annuals, tender summer bulbs, and lawns require constant care in the growing season.

Low-maintenance gardens include easy-care perennials, such as grasses, shrubs, and *Hylotelephium* (sedum). Gravel is a low-maintenance surface option.

DESIGNING WITH PLANTS

To produce an exciting design, combine a range of plants with contrasting structures, textures, and forms. You can also create a specific look, such as a modernist or cottage style, simply by using specific plants or grouping them in a particular way.

PLANT FUNCTIONS

Before planning a planting scheme, take time to compile a list of your favourite plants. Visit gardens and jot down the names of any that inspire you, and look through books, magazines, and plant catalogues for additional ideas. Make sure that the plants on your list will thrive in your garden, and then map out a simple plan (see pp.116–117).

Start by planning in trees and shrubs to add height and structure to your scheme. Then fill in around these forms with perennials and ground-cover plants, and include plenty of seasonal interest with a range that perform at different times of the year. Finally, inject drama with focal plants set in key positions within your design.

Beautifully blended shapes, colours, and textures create a dynamic visual feast in this garden.

Structural plants
Woody plants, like trees and shrubs, can be used to create a structure, such as a hedge or flowering screen, a tree-lined walkway, or a mixed group to form a backdrop to a flower bed.

Mid-range plants
Most perennials fall into this group, together with small shrubs. Use them between structural plants, or combine them with grasses to produce rippling seas of colour and texture.

Focal plants
Plants with bold colours and shapes catch the eye, directing the line of vision to a planting scheme, punctuating the end of a pathway, or sharpening the focus on a patio.

Ground cover
Ground-hugging plants can be shrubs, grasses, or perennials. Smothering weeds with their leafy stems, they help fill difficult areas beneath trees and next to sun-baked patios.

Seasonal plants
All the main plant groups include seasonal interest. Both trees and shrubs offer flowers and autumn leaf colour, while bulbs, annuals, and perennials provide seasonal blooms.

GROUPING PLANTS

Your choice of plants and their grouping and arrangement should reflect the garden style you are trying to create. A traditional approach for a border design is to line plants up in order of size, with the largest at the back and smallest at the front; beds work in a similar way with plants of ever-decreasing sizes fanning out from the tallest in the middle. Modernists have adopted a different approach, and use blocks of a single species to mirror Cubist paintings. Cottage-garden schemes interlink lozenge-shaped swathes of perennials to create a naturalistic effect, while modern perennial schemes are also inspired by nature, weaving together wide ribbons of tough hardy perennials and grasses to create an undulating landscape of flowers and foliage.

Traditional schemes

To create a traditional border, either plant a hedge or use shrubs and tall grasses to form a backdrop, and then add perennials with contrasting leaf shapes and flowers in front. Pompon-headed alliums work well with floating grasses, while flat-headed achilleas make a good match for flower spikes. Edge the front of your scheme with ground-cover plants, compact grasses, and annuals to form a line of flowers.

Contemporary blocks

Inspired by the modernist art movement, planting in blocks produces a clean, minimalist design. You can use a single type of grass, such as a *Miscanthus* species, which will have a dynamic effect when the leaves rustle in the wind; clumps of bulbs or perennials, such as irises; or heavier blocks of closely clipped box or yew. Set them out on an asymmetrical grid, and use lawns and pools to break up the planting.

Woodland planting

Even small gardens can play host to a woodland scheme. Underplant a small collection of trees with shade-tolerant shrubs, grasses, ferns, and other perennials that would naturally occur in similar sites in the wild, but don't be tempted to cram in lots of different species, as this will look too styled. Add some meadow flowers in open areas around the trees and in brighter areas within your woodland to mimic a glade.

Naturalistic schemes

Contemporary designs combine a limited palette of hardy perennials and grasses in bold swathes to resemble a prairie or steppe landscape. These schemes work best on medium-sized to large sites, but you can shrink them to fit smaller spaces by reducing the number and diversity of plants. Perennials such as *Rudbeckia*, *Eupatorium*, and *Hylotelephium* are ideal, combined with grasses like *Stipa*, *Miscanthus*, and *Calamagrostis*.

WHAT PLANT WHERE

When selecting plants for your garden, it's important to test your soil and assess your site carefully before you start (see *pp.66–67*). Failure to do so may end in disappointment, with sun-loving plants in shady sites growing tall and gangly as they strain to find the light, or shade-loving plants scorching in full sun.

Test your soil's acidity too, as mistakes can be expensive if plants are given the wrong conditions. For example, azaleas, rhododendrons, camellias, and pieris only thrive in acid soil and will suffer in chalky, alkaline conditions. Remember, too, that the soil close to a house wall or permanent structure will be significantly drier than other areas of the garden – these areas are called "rain shadows".

Roses will not flower well, if at all, in a shady site and their stems may grow tall and leggy. Plant them in open, sunny areas in nutrient-rich, moist but well-drained soil.

All ferns thrive in shade as their fronds will scorch in full sun. Most also require moist soil, although a few, including *Dryopteris filix-mas*, cope with drier conditions.

CREATE A PLANTING STYLE

Plants enhance and define a garden style or theme. Geometric beds set out in a symmetrical pattern instil a sense of formality; modern schemes are defined by minimalist planting, while sinuous borders filled with billowing grasses and native flowers convey a wilder look.

▶ FORMAL STYLE

Chic and orderly, formal styles are all about control. To achieve the look, lay out your beds in a symmetrical pattern, and use clipped hedges to define them. Take your lead from the formal gardens of Versailles in France and plant low hedges of box filled with colourful gravel, roses, or lavender to create a theatrical effect. Lollipop-shaped trees or topiary will lend height and structure. Enclose flowering perennials or annuals with looser forms in square or rectangular beds. Formal styles are quite easy to care for; simply clip the hedges and topiary twice a year.

Formality is created using a balanced design, mini-fountains, and a mirror.

◀ COTTAGE STYLE

Evoking an English country idyll, the cottage style has long captured the imagination of gardeners with a passion for plants. It is essentially a romanticized version of 19th-century cottage gardens, where most of the planting was productive, with a few flowers thrown in to create a colourful mix.

Today, flowers tend to dominate these designs; perennials and annuals are woven together in swathes, and beds are punctuated by structural shrubs, such as bay. Rose- and clematis-covered arches and arbours are also typical of these gardens, adding height and structure to designs, while scented roses and lavender are included for their fragrance. This is a high-maintenance style, ideal for keen plant lovers.

Classic combinations of delphiniums, lupins, and scabious are edged with frothy *Alchemilla mollis* and *Persicaria*, spilling over onto gravel or brick pathways.

▶ URBAN STYLE

City gardens tend to be small and need to look good all year round as the whole space is permanently on view. They may also be overlooked by neighbouring properties and require tall planting to increase privacy. Inject colour with painted walls, which make great foils for evergreen foliage specimens, such as bamboos and phormiums, or use plants including heucheras, day lilies (*Hemerocallis*), and sedums to add colour. Also use plants that perform well without taking up valuable ground space. Ideas include pleached trees (*see pp.118–119*) along the boundaries to enhance privacy, and climbers that provide walls of flowers and foliage. In a roof garden, lightweight pots of wind-proof hardy grasses, geraniums, and lavender are ideal.

Colours and shapes of bamboos and grasses, box topiary, and purple heucheras stand out against painted surfaces.

◀ MEDITERRANEAN STYLE

Use the sun-baked landscapes of the Mediterranean region to inspire you, with plants that evoke a rural setting or a café-style courtyard. In a medium-sized or large garden, try mass plantings of lavender with the odd scarlet poppy dotted here and there to mirror the fields of southern France. Alternatively, use large terracotta pots filled with this quintessential Mediterranean herb on a patio. Established olive trees offer much-needed shade in both country and city gardens, and are hardy enough to survive winters outside in a sheltered spot and free-draining soil. Patios edged with rock roses (*Cistus*) and self-seeded annuals create a sense of relaxed informality.

A gravel scree, laid on a weed-proof membrane, makes an easy-care foil for sun-loving lavenders and poppies.

▲ WILDLIFE GARDENS

Ever popular, wildlife gardens offer an attractive natural setting for people, plants, insects, birds, and animals.

A pond or pool is a vital ingredient, unless you have small children where open water can pose a danger, and can be planted with a whole range of beautiful aquatic and moisture-loving plants (*see pp.176–177*). Include an area of long grass and nectar-rich flowers to lure bees and insects. Star attractions for beneficial insects include the butterfly bush (*Buddleja*), *Mahonia*, thyme, lavender, asters, and foxgloves. A mixed hedge and a fruit tree will provide nesting sites and winter food for birds.

Wooden walkways, fringed with naturalistic planting of iris and *Circium rivulare*, allow easy access for close study of water life.

▶ MODERNIST STYLES

Sharp and sophisticated, modernist designs are based on the principle "less is more". Map out your garden on an asymmetrical grid, with planting limited to key areas, and a restricted palette of different species. Architectural plants will help to define the style. Set out topiary box balls in rows or blocks, or try spiky bearded irises in a regimental line. Many modernist designers also employ tightly trimmed hedges to carve up the space and divide different areas of the garden. In a courtyard, a tree with a graphic shape, such as an *Acer palmatum*, would make an effective focal point set against a brightly painted screen.

Glossy bamboo stems are underplanted with white peonies in chunky marble chippings in this green and white minimalist garden.

◄ FAMILY GARDENS

Gardens for grown-ups and children have to be multi-functional, offering both a relaxing and stimulating environment. If your garden is large enough, break it up into "rooms", with areas for entertaining and spaces to play. Throughout the garden, the planting has to be resilient and bounce back if trodden on or hit by flying balls. Decorative grasses are ideal, as are many perennials – snapped flowerheads will, in most cases, simply stimulate the plant to produce more blooms.

Use tough plants, such as *Aucuba*, *Elaeagnus*, and *Euonymus*, around swings and sandpits. They are practically indestructible.

DESIGNING CONTAINER DISPLAYS

As well as using plants in beds and borders, add a selection of containers to embellish your garden style. Choose pots that suit your theme, and fill them with foliage and flowers to decorate patios or provide focal points in the garden.

Pots made from metals like zinc and man-made materials tend to suit contemporary designs, especially when moulded into smooth, geometric shapes. Use a set of three large identical containers planted with leafy phormiums, astelias, or topiary for a modern look, or try squat pots filled with houseleeks (*Sempervivum*) or aeoniums.

Classic and period garden styles can be enhanced with pots made from terracotta or natural stone, or composites that resemble these. Patio roses make superb feature plants for large urns in a traditional setting, or try an old trough filled with herbs, perennials, or alpines in a cottage scheme. If you have a naturalistic style garden, complete the look with a rustic container made from recycled wood.

Rustic
Use recycled fruit boxes, old kitchen pans or wooden planters for a cottage or naturalistic style.

Tropical
Colourful glazed containers suit tropical foliage and leafy shrubs or topiary specimens.

Contemporary
Metallic containers lend a modern note to a patio or garden. Team them with architectural foliage.

Traditional
Terracotta containers are ideal for traditional gardens, and their earthy tones suit cottage plants.

INTRODUCING COLOUR AND TEXTURE

Awakening our senses, colour can excite and energize us, or create a calm, tranquil atmosphere. Combine hot pinks, reds, and oranges in areas where you want borders to sparkle, and cool blues, greens, purples, and white close to relaxing seating and dining areas.

THE COLOUR WHEEL

Many artists and designers use a device called a "colour wheel" to help them create pleasing colour combinations. The wheel is made up of the primary colours (blue, red, and yellow) and secondary colours (green, orange, and purple). The secondary colours are directly derived from the adjacent primaries, for example when blue and red paints are mixed they make purple, and red and yellow combine to produce orange. The same principle applies to the tertiary colours, which result when adjacent secondary and primary colours are mixed.

You can use the wheel to create a colour palette in the garden. Combine colours directly opposite each other, such as yellow and purple, to create dramatic contrasts that will help to enliven a planting scheme, or try adjacent colours to produce more subtle blends.

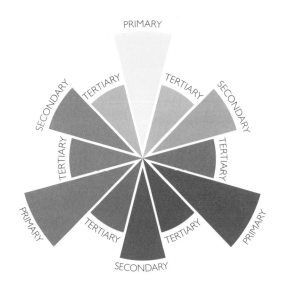

Shades and tones of purples and greens make an elegant planting combination.

CHOOSING COLOURS

As well as using the wheel for ideas, also consider the effects that colours have on the senses. Hot hues, including red, yellow, and orange, are bright, arresting colours that catch the eye: use them as focal points in borders or in pots on a patio. These sizzling shades will also foreshorten a space, and can make a garden look smaller if set at the back.

Cool colours, such as blue, green, and mauve, have the opposite effect and help to lengthen a view, just as colours pale towards the horizon. Blues and mauves are easy on the eye, but a scheme with only these colours may look recessive, so inject warmer colours to liven it up.

USING COLOURS

Use the colour wheel as a guide when mixing and matching colours in your garden, and try the following ideas to create successful schemes. You can also incorporate shades and tints of the main hues: shades are colours with additional black, making darker hues, while tints are colours mixed with white and are paler.

Single-colour and duotone schemes allow you to create a sophisticated look. The famous white garden at Sissinghurst in the UK has inspired many to adopt a monochrome palette, using a combination of white flowers and silver and variegated foliage. Or try planting a border with just two colours, such as purple and yellow, or pink and mauve.

Opposite colours on the colour wheel will produce a successful planting scheme when used in combination with each other. These contrasting colours are known as complementary shades and used by many top garden designers. Try pairing purple salvias with yellow *Doronicum* (*left*), or opt for maroon alliums with lime green euphorbias.

Triadic colours are those that are evenly spaced around the colour wheel. Like opposite colours, they often create a sense of excitement when used in combination, as they are contrasting hues. Triadic colour combinations are useful if you have cool hues, such as purple and blue, which need a matching hot shade to enhance the design.

Adjoining colours create harmonious combinations – when you select soft purples and blues, a soothing effect is produced. Paler tints that reflect light will help to inject highlights into your scheme. If you are more adventurous, try a fiery mix of the hot shades, such as red and orange, with a foil of darker shades, and watch your borders blaze under the sun.

USING PLANT TEXTURES

Successful planting schemes combine leaf, stem, and flower textures as well as colours. Select shiny leaves, berries, and fruits to reflect light into gloomy areas, and use soft, downy foliage close to the front of a bed or border where its tactile texture can be fully appreciated. Also, plant trees with rough or peeling bark to create focal points in winter gardens.

When creating your planting designs, pair up plants with contrasting textures. Try matching grasses with plants that produce felted or ferny leaves. Think, too, about the texture of flowers, combining the satin petals of roses, for example, with the spiky bracts and rough, prickly flowerheads of sea holly (*Eryngium*), or the brush-like blooms of red-hot pokers (*Kniphofia*).

Prickly
The prickly stems of roses and spiky sea holly flowers (*above*) contrast well with silky petals.

Silky
The petals of large flowers, such as tea roses (*above*), camellias, and hibiscus have a satin-like texture.

Shiny
The leaves of *Fatsia*, camellias, and other plants add a shiny texture, as do berries and fruits.

Matt
Plants with matt leaves include *Gunnera*, *Cercis*, hydrangeas (*above*), and many others.

Soft
Stachys byzantina (*above*) and *Verbascum bombyciferum* are prized for their downy foliage.

Hard
The rigid trunks of trees, like *Acer pensylvanicum* (*above*), contrast well with their soft canopies.

SEASONAL EFFECTS

Creating a spectacular design with year-round appeal requires careful planning. Find inspiration and ideas by visiting open gardens at different times of the year, note the plants that are looking their best, and add these to your displays.

▶ WINTER

Many herbaceous perennials are beneath the soil at this time of year, but those with sturdy stems and enduring seedheads make decorative displays when married with grasses and evergreens. Colourful dogwoods (*Cornus*) also come into their own in winter with their scarlet or bright yellow stems, while white birches (*Betula*), golden bamboos, and the red trunks of *Prunus serrula* are picked out by the sloping rays of the winter sun. A few shrubs dare to bloom, including *Mahonia japonica*, witch hazels (*Hamamelis*) and scented winter box (*Sarcococca*). Conifers add evergreen interest, with blue- and gold-leaved forms injecting extra colour.

Frost transforms the garden, adding sparkle to conifers, plumed grasses, and the leaves of shrubs such as purple *Cotinus*.

◀ SPRING

Heralding the start of the growing season, spring arrives with a burst of colour as the sun warms the soil and buds unfurl. Delicate blossoms adorn tree branches like bolts of lace, while a few shrubs beneath their canopies also put on an early show. Magnolias are the queens of the spring garden, their beautiful flowers striking a pose against the graceful stems. Perennials are also starting to show their faces in spring, with a range of beautiful hellebores and also dainty bleeding hearts (*Lamprocapnos*) leading the way.

Cherry blossom is the star of the show in this spring garden, complemented by mass planting of tulips in harmonizing colours.

▶ SUMMER

Long sun-drenched days epitomize early summer when the garden is in full swing, with plants vying for attention at every turn. The choice is legion, but remember that too many contrasting plants can look messy. Include a few attractive foliage subjects to offset perennials and flowering shrubs. Trees perform a similar function, and also help to regulate temperature fluctuations in the garden. As summer draws on, beds and borders may look past their prime, so include Michaelmas daisies (*Symphyotrichum*), rudbeckias, crocosmias, and decorative grasses that flower as the season comes to a close.

Summer colour continues with dahlias, salvias, *Lavatera*, and begonias and French marigolds.

◀ AUTUMN

It's easy to forget about autumn when you're planting up a border in spring, but this can be a dramatic season, with flaming red and orange foliage firing up the proceedings, and branches laden with shimmering fruits. Trees and shrubs valued for their autumn tints and berries include maples, cherries, crab apples, *Sorbus, Cotoneaster, Cotinus,* and *Viburnum opulus.* The violet bead-like berries of *Callicarpa bodinieri* are also well worth including. Some flowers, such as *Verbena bonariensis*, Michaelmas daisies, and *Abelia*, continue to bloom as temperatures plunge, while hydrangeas, *Hylotelephium* (sedums), and the grasses that bloomed earlier have ornamental seedheads, many of which will persist into winter. Include some autumn-flowering bulbs, such as nerines and crocuses, at the front of a sheltered sunny border.

The fiery leaves of *Acer palmatum* and dense red berries of a towering *Cotoneaster* set the garden on fire in autumn.

MAXIMIZE PLANT POWER

Think of your garden as an outdoor room, with leafy walls and a protective canopy of trees and structures. You can either fill the room with plants to confer a sense of enclosure or restrict the planting to key areas to create an airy open space.

▶ CREATING A ROOM

To create an intimate area for dining or relaxing, use trellis covered with climbers or a hedge or bamboo screen to enclose the space. In a small garden you could surround a seating area with tall, airy perennials and annuals, but this will only give shelter during the summer months.

Low plants allow more light to penetrate and can extend the views through a garden, but they may also expose the boundaries, which will make the area look smaller. To create the illusion of a larger space, plant tall shrubs and trees to disguise fences and walls, and site a low hedge towards the end of the garden with a doorway cut into it or a path weaving round it, so that the plot appears to continue beyond it.

A backdrop of dense yew provides privacy for a decked seating area, and clipped low hedging adds to the sense of discovery as you approach.

◀ WALLS OF FLOWERS AND FOLIAGE

The walls around a garden may provide useful vertical spaces for flowers and foliage and help to create a three-dimensional design. Think of the surfaces as you would those in the house, and paper them with climbers, including ivy, roses, clematis, and jasmine. Introduce screens within the garden to create different areas, such as a kitchen and lounge. The screens can be adorned, and will create microclimates, providing conditions for a greater range of plants. Use a mixed hedge to make a wall of decorative flowers, foliage, and berries.

Integrate a seating area into a garden wall, and clothe it with attractive climbers or wall shrubs.

▼ MAKING AN ENTRANCE

Make dramatic entrances to your garden rooms with decorative doorways. Train a pair of trees, such as hornbeams – which have flexible stems and tolerate clipping – to form an archway over a gate. Period and formal gardens suit a simple doorway, such as an arch cut into a closely clipped yew hedge.

Contemporary designs require something a little different. One idea is to flank the entrance with lines of grass-like *Libertia* set against rusty steel panels, or try a metal arch with an evergreen *Trachelospermum*, with its scented white summer flowers, trained over it.

A rustic arch or pergola at the entrance to a cottage garden is adorned with scented roses and honeysuckle to set the scene as visitors pass through.

PLANTING IN RESTRICTED SPACES

Pack your courtyard, balcony, or roof terrace with plants in pots fixed to walls or suspended in baskets. Green roofs will also increase your planting space and make great wildlife habitats, as will a few well-chosen climbers used to clothe bare walls, or even a full living "green wall" vertical planting system, now widely available.

Space savers

Planting in tiny spaces requires a little ingenuity. As well as using climbers to clad the walls, dress them up with pots and windowboxes filled with seasonal flowers and foliage, or train an espaliered tree to a wall or fence and use the space in front for some well-behaved flowering perennials or small shrubs. Pencil-thin conifers and fan-trained trees also take up very little ground space, and make excellent accent plants in pots or borders.

Light ideas

The weight of plants and pots can pose problems on balconies and roof terraces, so select light metal containers or polycarbonate and recycled plastic types. Faux terracotta, lead, and stone pots are very realistic and, once planted, it is difficult to distinguish them from the real thing. Trees grown on dwarf rootstocks will add height to a tiny garden, while grasses, bulbs, and perennials offer year-round interest. You can even plant a dwarf shrubby evergreen, such as *Lonicera nitida*, in a long, deep container to create a slim green screen.

Green roofs

There is a variety of green roof systems to choose from, but check the load-bearing capacity of your roof before investing in one. You can choose between easy-care succulents or more sophisticated grass and flower schemes if your roof will take the weight of the deeper soil required. As well as looking fantastic, green roofs also provide excellent habitats for birds and insects, help to insulate your property, reduce flash flooding by absorbing rainwater, and minimize noise pollution in homes near airports and motorways.

CREATING A SIMPLE PLANTING PLAN

Planting plans are quite easy to draw up and they will help you to organize your ideas and plot the position of the plants. You can also use a plan to visualize how much space you have and the number of plants needed for your scheme.

MEASURING AND VISUALIZING YOUR BORDER

Before making a plan, first carry out a survey of the site, checking how much sun it receives and the soil type (see pp.66–67). Then measure your planting area accurately, and draw the outline to scale on graph paper (see pp.80–81). Look through your chosen list of plants and double check that each will suit the specific conditions of the bed or border, and note their heights and spreads to calculate the space they require.

Many people find it difficult to look at a two-dimensional plan and visualize how their three-dimensional planting scheme will look, so try using props to create an impression. Set out tripods, buckets, and pots that are approximately the same heights and spreads as your plants in the area you have allocated for them. Even top designers use this trick to check that their planting ideas will work on the ground.

◄ **Visualization technique**
Mocking up your planting plan using garden equipment is a good way to find out what works.

MAKING A PLAN

You can either plot your plants to scale within your outline plan using professional symbols (see below) or simply use a bubble diagram to show roughly where you are proposing to site different species (see p.82). The benefit of a scale drawing is that you can estimate the number of plants you will need more accurately. Large plants, such as trees and shrubs, are relatively easy to plot using a compass to draw circles to scale. Remember that young trees and shrubs will be smaller than your plan suggests, so fill in the spaces with annuals or perennials that can be lifted and moved easily as your woody plants grow. Plot smaller plants, such as perennials and bulbs, in groups, rather than as individual plants.

CALCULATING PLANT QUANTITIES

The quantity of trees and large shrubs you require will be obvious from your plan, but numbers of perennials may be more difficult to calculate. To make an accurate estimate, mark out a square metre (yard) on the ground, then buy one or two mature plants and place them in the square. Allowing some space for spread, you can then calculate the number that would fill the square and therefore the quantities needed for your border. Bulbs can be packed quite closely together and if you are planning on large-scale plantings, check out specialist suppliers that offer discounts for bulk purchases.

Plant symbols
These are the most widely understood and commonly used planting plan symbols, which form part of a visual design language.

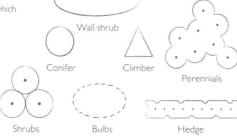

Wall shrub

Conifer

Climber

Perennials

Existing tree

New tree

Shrubs

Bulbs

Hedge

THE FINAL PLAN

This garden design, by top British designer Chris Parsons of Hallam Garden Design, is for a small woodland area, featuring three silver birches (*Betula utilis* var. *jacquemontii*). To produce a similar plan, first mark out the trees using circles, and calculate the areas beneath the canopies that will sustain shade-loving plants, such as the epimediums used here. Tall grasses are accent plants that need sun, so should be set where the trees cast little or no shade. Note that the more dramatic plants, such as *Helleborus foetidus* and the purple *Actaea simplex*, have been used as single specimens, while a mass of the yellow-flowered *Alchemilla mollis* fills the areas in between and spills on to the gravel patio.

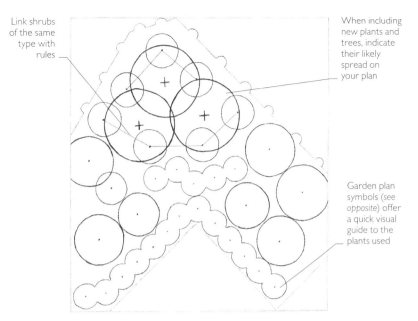

Link shrubs of the same type with rules

When including new plants and trees, indicate their likely spread on your plan

Garden plan symbols (*see opposite*) offer a quick visual guide to the plants used

YOU WILL NEED

1 *Betula utilis* var. *jacquemontii*
2 *Actaea simplex* 'Brunette'
3 *Alchemilla mollis*
4 *Helleborus foetidus* Wester Flisk Group
5 *Epimedium* x *versicolor* 'Sulphureum'
6 *Calamagrostis* x *acutiflora* 'Karl Foerster'

INTRODUCING TREES

Offering colour and structure throughout the year, trees are an essential ingredient for any garden scheme. As well as lending height and beauty, they cast cooling shade, absorb greenhouse gases, and provide homes and food for wildlife.

► CREATING A WOODLAND SETTING

You can create a woodland effect with just a few well-chosen specimen trees in a small garden, or with a more varied selection on a larger plot. Look for varieties with unusual stems for a striking effect, even after the leaves have fallen in winter. The dappled shade cast by your chosen trees will offer sufficient light for an understorey of shade-loving plants. When choosing underplanting for your scheme, look for a selection of plants that will provide year-round interest.

A mix of textured trunks, underplanted with rhododendrons, hostas, ferns, and ivies frame the steps to a woodland pond. The corky bark of *Cordyline australis* contrasts with the papery surfaces of silver birches, and a lantern tree brings a splash of colour to the canopy.

▲ ADDING HEIGHT AND PRIVACY

Any tree will add height to a garden, but to give a more contoured effect, underplant it with shade-tolerant shrubs. Trees' imposing stature can be deployed to great effect in a city garden overlooked by many windows. Use species with airy canopies to shield a seating area; plant them close to the space that needs extra privacy, rather than on the boundary where taller trees will be needed to mask upstairs windows. Alternatively, plant a wall of pleached trees, which form a line of clear stilt-like stems topped by a screen of leafy branches just above head height.

A row of pleached hornbeams creates a suspended boundary – perfect for adding privacy without resorting to dense hedgerow planting.

▼ USING TREES AS FOCAL POINTS

When selecting a tree for a focal point, opt for a year-round star performer. Choose a cherry or crab apple that will be covered with delicate blossom in spring, provide a leafy canopy in summer, and put on a finale of blazing colours and shining fruits in autumn. Alternatively, in a modern or formal garden, you could opt for a shapely evergreen, or a smart topiary specimen. Site your tree in the centre of a lawn, at the end of a pathway, or in a border to punctuate a corner or curve in the design, and use small trees in pots to make an impact on a patio or in a courtyard garden.

The glow of this Japanese maple's beautiful summer foliage stands out in an otherwise verdant scheme.

◄ FRAMING FEATURES

A long, tree-lined avenue makes an impressive entrance, and a similar effect is possible in a small garden with fewer trees and a little pruning and training. Plant six to ten trees on either side of a pathway and train their stems on to frames to form arches of foliage. Use the same technique with a pair of matching trees to create a decorative arbour over a seat.

Highlight a focal point, such as this sculpture, by positioning it centre-stage at the end of a leafy walkway.

◄ PROVIDING COLOUR AND TEXTURE

Before buying trees for colour effects, look for those that offer more than one decorative feature. Spring blossom has instant appeal but lasts just a few weeks, while the deep red bark of a *Prunus serrula* or stunning white birch trunks provide colour all year. If flowers are your passion, include a few different species, such as a cherry and the early summer blooms of *Cornus kousa*, to extend the display.

Plenty of good tree choices are available for autumn colour, prolonging the season of interest into early winter when the fallen leaves carpet the ground. Textures also add an extra dimension to planting designs; consider the pleated foliage of hornbeams, or the spiky needles of pines and other conifers.

Match an ornamental cherry (see pp.124–125) with contrasting deep-red foliage specimens and evergreen conifers for theatrical impact in the garden.

SELECTING AND PLANTING ORNAMENTAL TREES

Every garden has room for a tree, whether it's a majestic oak in a large plot or a compact conifer on a patio. Choose a healthy specimen, plant it with care, and water well for a beautiful feature that will last for many years to come.

When buying trees, you will find that most are sold as container-grown plants. Look for those in white or black woven fabric bags (known as Air-Pots), which are designed to promote healthy roots and encourage trees to establish well once planted. Trees are a long-term investment so buy from specialist nurseries, where stock will be grown in ideal conditions and a quality guarantee or replacement is offered if plants fail.

Hedging and fruit trees are also available in bare-root form from late autumn to late winter. These are young, dormant plants lifted from nursery fields and supplied without a pot. They are cheaper than container-grown trees but must be planted as soon as you receive them.

A greater choice of trees is usually available if you buy them container grown; most large, mature specimens are only available in this form.

SELECTING SIZES AND SHAPE

Check the plant label carefully and seek advice before buying a tree to ensure that its size and habit suit the style of your garden, and that it will fit your space when it matures. Also site your tree carefully when you get it home; if planted in the wrong place, it will be very difficult to move once established.

Spreading These may be small or large but all spreading trees produce horizontal branches and are often wider than they are tall. They are ideal as focal points in a lawn or gravel garden, but may take up too much space in a small plot.

Weeping Trees with this graceful habit include the weeping willow as well as many smaller trees, such as flowering ornamental cherries (*Prunus* spp.) Use the elegant silhouette of a weeping tree as a focal point in the garden for maximum impact, or add trees with light canopies to a mixed border.

Fastigiate With erect branches, held close together, fastigiate trees have a slim shape that makes them perfect for small gardens or tight spaces. Conical trees produce horizontal branches from the top to the bottom of the trunk; the shape is similar but broadens out more.

Round-headed Many trees, such as this hornbeam (*Carpinus betulus* 'Variegata') produce a rounded canopy on a single clear stem; those with this form usually allow light beneath them for underplanting. You can prune the stems to accentuate the lollipop shape and use the tree as a focal point.

WHEN AND WHERE TO PLANT

The best time to plant trees is in late autumn, although container-grown types can be planted at any time, as long as the ground is not frozen, waterlogged, or bone dry. Bare-root trees must be planted in winter, at the same depth as they were grown in the nursery field – indicated by a brown soil mark on the stems. Check your soil and aspect (see pp.66–67) and match your tree choices with your garden conditions, since planting a tree in the wrong place may cause it to grow lopsided or fail to thrive. Remember that trees cast shade and draw large quantities of moisture and nutrients from the soil, affecting other plants growing nearby. They can also undermine foundations with their roots, so be careful to site your tree at a distance from buildings. Where there is space, consider a tree with a strong structure to act as a stand-alone focal point.

A row of slender silver birches planted directly into a lawn can act as an informal division between areas of your garden, as well as adding height and shade in summer.

Create a focal point with a flowering tree such as this decorative dogwood (*Cornus kousa* var. *chinensis*) in the centre of a lawn, or use one at the end of a vista to draw the eye.

GARDEN WISDOM

Don't plant too deeply

Trees that are planted too deeply may fail to establish well, or even die because their trunks become too wet and rot. Ensure your tree is planted so that the point where the roots start to flare out from the trunk is at soil level – you may need to scrape away some soil from container-grown trees to see this point.

Use a cane as a guide.

PLANTING A CONTAINER-GROWN TREE

Get your new tree off to a flying start by preparing the ground well before planting. Loosen the soil with a fork to improve drainage, remove weeds, and incorporate some organic matter and all-purpose fertilizer at the specified rate over 2–3m (6–10ft) of ground surrounding the planting area to ensure that your tree is well nourished. Stake large trees after planting (see p.122) to prevent damage from wind-rock.

1 Soak the tree roots thoroughly. Dig a planting hole the same depth as the root ball and up to three times as wide. Break up any compacted soil around the sides with a garden fork.

2 Place the tree in the hole and check the planting depth by laying a stick or bamboo cane across the top (see *Garden Wisdom box, below*). This may be easier if you remove the container first.

3 When the container has been removed, scrape away excess soil from the base of the trunk and tease out any roots that have grown around the edge of the root ball.

4 Put the tree back in the hole and spread the roots out evenly. Water in well, thoroughly soaking the roots. Ask someone to help you hold the tree upright while you replace the excavated soil.

5 Replace the excavated soil in and around the roots and firm in well with your foot to eliminate any air pockets, but take care not to compact the soil. Water the tree well. Apply a mulch, leaving a gap around the trunk.

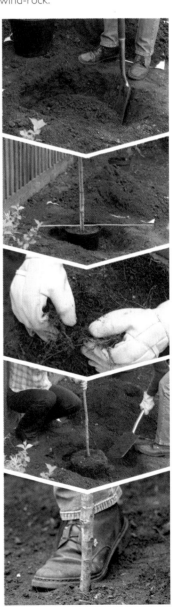

AFTERCARE AND MAINTENANCE

Most newly planted trees will need extra irrigation for up to two years until they are fully established. Drought stress can cause permanent damage, so it is vital that you water frequently and sufficiently, so that moisture reaches the roots.

After planting, winter-planted deciduous trees will not need further watering until early spring when they come into bud; evergreens may require extra irrigation during a dry winter. Water deeply once or twice a week from spring to autumn. Use a hose, but turn the tap only halfway on to restrict the water flow, and soak a wide area up to 2m (6ft) around the trunk to encourage the roots to follow the moisture. Keep the same area around the tree free of weeds to give it the best chance of thriving.

Apply a thick mulch, such as composted bark chippings, after planting and watering in to suppress competing weeds and seal in moisture; keep the mulch clear of the tree's stem to prevent rot.

Staking trees

Large trees will require staking to guard against wind rocking the plant and tearing new roots. After three years, they will have sufficient anchoring roots to hold them steady and the stake can be removed.

An angled stake is commonly used, although an upright one can be used for bare-root trees. Drive in a wooden stake at a 45-degree angle, leaning it into the prevailing wind. Use a flexible tree tie to secure it about a third of the way up the trunk. On windy sites, use two upright stakes either side of the root ball, attached to the trunk with long ties. Check ties every few months, loosening if necessary to prevent damage to the tree as it grows. '

Watering bags slowly release moisture, wetting the roots more efficiently than surface watering.

When staking, use adjustable tree ties that can be loosened as the tree grows.

TREES FOR WILDLIFE

One of the major benefits of owning a tree is the huge variety of wildlife it attracts to the garden. Birds nest among the branches and feed on the flower buds and berries; insects are also drawn to all parts of a tree.

Berries are an attractive feature in a garden, as well as providing a valuable source of food for birds and other animals in the winter months when food is scarce. If you have space, plant several fruiting trees that ripen at different times to ensure a long-lasting supply. Good choices for an abundance of berries are hawthorn (*Crataegus*), *Cotoneaster* x *watereri* 'John Waterer', rowan (*Sorbus*), mulberry (*Morus nigra*), elderberry (*Sambucus*), and cherry (*Prunus*). Most windfalls are readily eaten by birds, small mammals, and insects.

Other excellent trees for wildlife include thorny types that provide cover from predators, such as hawthorn and holly (*Ilex*), and those with nectar-rich flowers for bees and other insects, including crab apples (*Malus*). Hazels (*Corylus*) are also useful, producing an abundance of nuts for overwintering creatures.

Sambucus nigra

Corylus avellana

Crataegus persimilis

Ilex aquifolium 'Madame Briot'

TREE RECIPES

PARADISE ISLAND

Tree ferns (*Dicksonia*) lend a tropical flavour to any planting scheme and marry well with the purple foliage of a Japanese maple (*Acer*) and lush ferns (*Dryopteris*). Add a dash of colour with some moisture-loving bright red astilbes set around a pool. Although reasonably hardy, tree ferns will need some winter protection (*see p.130*).

1 In autumn, dig over the planting area and add some well-rotted manure a few weeks before planting. Plant the *Acer* using the technique outlined on page 121, and water in well.

2 You can also plant the astilbes and ferns at the same time, using the method for planting perennials on page 137. Plant the ferns between the trees, and the astilbes in sun.

3 In mid-spring, plant the tree ferns at the back of the scheme, in the same way as you planted the *Acer*. Water the crowns, not the roots of the ferns, and cover the bed with an organic mulch.

YOU WILL NEED

1 *Dicksonia antarctica*

2 *Acer palmatum* var. *dissectum* Dissectum Atropurpureum Group

3 *Astilbe* 'Köln'

4 *Dryopteris affinis*

VIBRANT WINTER BORDER

Willows (*Salix*) have a graceful habit and some are also valued for their colourful winter stems. Young stems produce the best effects, so pollard them in late winter by removing all stems above a clear trunk every couple of years. Dogwoods (*Cornus*) also have bright winter stems; cut them back to the ground every year in late winter.

YOU WILL NEED

1 *Salix alba* var. *vitellina* 'Britzensis'

2 *Cornus sericea* 'Flaviramea'

3 *Cornus alba* 'Sibirica'

4 Dwarf conifers

5 *Erica carnea*

6 Variegated ivies

1 Plant your trees and shrubs in autumn after digging over your border and incorporating plenty of well-rotted organic matter. Set out your plants in their pots.

2 Plant the *Salix* at the back with a frill of ivies in front, but not too close to the tree. The *Cornus* are about hip-height; site them in the middle of the border.

3 Plant the conifers in the gaps and the low-growing *Erica* at the front. Apply an organic mulch. Water the plants for two growing seasons.

ORNAMENTAL CHERRIES

Celebrated for their dazzling spring flowers, many ornamental cherries have a range of other eye-catching features, including decorative bark, autumn leaf colour, beautiful structure, and glistening fruits that provide food for birds and other wildlife. They are also available in a range of sizes to suit gardens large and small.

Prunus padus 'Colorata'

Choose from a huge range of flowering cherries for a spectacular display of delicate blossom in your garden each spring. Some types also have coppery-red young foliage and many display excellent autumn colour, so when making your selection look for a cherry that offers more than one season of interest. There is a wide variety of species and forms available (*see below*); be sure to ask suppliers for a compact or dwarf type if you need a tree for a small garden.

▶ **Create a sensational spring border** with an abundance of floral underplanting such as viola, tulips, and tiarella paired with the beautiful blossom of *Prunus* 'Kanzan' and *P. triloba*.

CHERRIES TO CHOOSE FROM

Prunus avium The wild cherry is a tall tree best suited to large gardens. As well as masses of white flowers in spring, it has good autumn colour along with red fruits.

Prunus padus The bird cherry is ideal for urban gardens. Its long flower panicles are accompanied by green leaves that turn yellow and bronze in autumn.

Prunus rufa The Himalayan cherry is grown for its wonderful reddish-brown and amber bark. This small tree also bears small clusters of pale pink flowers.

Prunus serrula The Tibetan cherry has willow-like leaves and small flowers. It is prized for its mahogany-red bark that peels as it ages, adding colour and texture.

Prunus sargentii This Sargent's cherry has single pink spring flowers and chestnut-brown bark, while autumn tints are often fiery. It casts a light shade.

Whatever type of garden you have, an ornamental cherry is guaranteed to boost its spring appeal. Choose from single or double flowers in shades of white or pink. Check the final height and spread of your chosen tree before buying to make sure that it will fit the space you have. Some have a weeping habit, such as *Prunus* 'Cheal's Weeping', which forms arching branches laden with double

pink flowers, while others, including *Prunus* 'Spire', are more upright, providing a vertical accent. There are many compact forms suitable for small gardens, such as the pink-flowered *Prunus* 'Accolade', 'Kanzan', and 'Pandora', or the dainty *Prunus* 'Shimidsu-zakura' with white blossom.

Ideal as focal points in the centre of a lawn or paved patio garden, cherries also make eye-catching features in mixed borders. Alternatively, plant a cluster of trees to mirror Japanese gardens during the cherry blossom festivals. Try underplanting with spring bulbs that flower at the same time, such as grape hyacinths and snake's head fritillaries, and include some late flowers like Japanese anemones to complement the autumn leaf colour.

Plant your tree in a sunny site, although some tolerate part shade, and free-draining soil. To plant a tree in the ground, see page 121, or plant in a large pot (*see right*). Many cherries have a beautiful natural habit and need little pruning, but if you do cut back your tree, do so in summer to reduce the risk of silver leaf disease (see p.267).

POTTING UP A CHERRY

If you're short of space, you can still enjoy an ornamental cherry's gorgeous spring blossom by planting a tree in a container, which will restrict its size and keep it from outgrowing its container. Make sure that you choose a large, weatherproof pot with drainage holes in the base.

1 Place broken crocks in the bottom of the pot. Wearing gloves, add a layer of soil- or loam-based compost and mix in controlled-release fertilizer, following the product guidelines.

2 Soak the tree roots in a bucket before planting. Tease out any roots that are circling around the root ball, and stand the tree on the compost, ensuring it is upright.

3 Plant the tree at the same level it was growing at in its original pot. Fill in with compost and firm down, leaving a 5cm (2in) gap between the rim of the pot and the compost for watering.

4 Give the planted tree a good soak. Water regularly – every couple of days in summer – and feed annually in spring with a slow-release fertilizer. Underplanting will add floral interest through the summer.

Prunus x *subhirtella* 'Autumnalis' This popular cherry produces delicate, blossom sporadically through autumn and winter, and is ideal for small gardens.

Prunus 'Taihaku' The great white cherry is a popular and celebrated Japanese form. Its winning features include large white flowers, coppery young foliage, and autumn tints.

Prunus x *yedoensis* 'Somei Yoshino' The Japanese Yoshino cherry bears almond-scented white blossom on arching branches in mid-spring, followed in autumn by dark red fruits.

STYLES WITH SHRUBS

Spanning a vast range of woody plants from sprawling ground-huggers to statuesque specimens, shrubs are a diverse group that also includes stylish evergreens, colourful foliage plants, and spectacular flowering forms.

▶ FILLING DIFFICULT SITES

When looking for a plant to fill a difficult site, you will always find a shrub to suit. There are those that thrive in deep shade, such as skimmias and daphnes, while sun-loving bottlebrush will sail through dry periods. On poor soils, buddlejas are almost guaranteed to succeed, and sprawling specimens like *Cotoneaster horizontalis* will cover a slope or bank. There are even shrubs that are happiest in the salt-laden air near the coast, such as sea buckthorn (*Hippophae*) and *Tamarix*.

Squeezing into a gap, the bright red flower spikes of this crimson bottlebrush add colour and texture.

▲ INJECTING FOLIAGE INTEREST

Shrubs are indispensable foliage plants, with the evergreens providing permanent colour and deciduous types offering bright new spring leaves and autumn fire. Those with colourful foliage inject highlights into dull green displays, while variegated evergreens perform a similar function, illuminating gloomy areas with splashes of light. Choose shrubs with dramatic leaf shapes to provide points of interest: the bold, glossy, finger-like forms of *Fatsia japonica* and the pointed spikes of a yucca are sure to catch the eye.

Mix the spiky, dark red foliage of a *Berberis* with vivid grasses in a border for contrast and long-lasting interest.

◄ CREATING CONTAINER FEATURES

Many shrubs make excellent container specimens and, when planted in large pots, most are easy to care for. Compact evergreens offer sculptural year-round displays, either planted on their own or with seasonal companions. Alternatively, choose a small conifer with textural foliage and architectural shapes, such as a pencil-thin juniper or the round *Pinus mugo* 'Mops'. To create a flowering container display, look no further than the vast range of patio roses, available in almost every colour except blue. Shrubs that flower for many months, such as the new hydrangea hybrids, also make elegant container plants and will make a superb focal point on a patio.

The long-lasting blue flowers of this *Hydrangea serrata* 'Blue Deckle' make a beautiful and enduring shrubby container feature.

▲ PROVIDING STRUCTURE AND SCREENING

Use a selection of shrubs to create walls and structures in your garden; box and others with dense foliage make excellent hedges for edging, boundaries, and low screens. Shrubs with elegant forms, like hebes and *Nandina*, offer sculptural interest in borders and gravel gardens, and try plants with arching stems, like *Buddleja alternifolia*, in an open site. Large foliage shrubs are also useful, providing beautiful backdrops to planting designs.

Perfectly trimmed evergreen hedges provide sturdy, structural contrast with the soft, romantic planting in this early summer garden.

◄ ADDING SEASONAL FLOWERS

The choice of flowering shrubs is vast and varied, ranging from inconspicuous winter flowers to big, blowsy blooms. Most shrubs flower for only a brief spell, but as there are options for every month, you can enjoy colour all year round. The fragrant flowers of witch hazels get the ball rolling in winter, followed by a huge selection of spring blooms and early summer gems, including the scented *Philadelphus*. The colourful flowers of summer, such as fuchsias, roses, and hydrangeas, are followed by autumn blooms like heathers (*Erica*), which maintain interest as the seasons turn.

***Rhododendron mucronulatum*'s vibrant pink blooms** bring a splash of much-needed colour into the winter garden, especially when paired with a witch hazel's yellow flowers.

SELECTING AND PLANTING SHRUBS

Most hardy shrubs need very little care once established, making them ideal for those with little time to spare. Tender types require more attention, but when grown in pots they can be easily moved indoors over winter.

Their sheer diversity makes shrubs a highly appealing group of plants, but before you buy, check the labels carefully for final heights and spreads, as different species can have widely differing habits. Azaleas are a case in point, with the deciduous *Rhododendron luteum*, for example, growing to a lofty 4m (12ft) in height, while the compact evergreen

Rhododendron 'Rosebud' reaches no more than 90cm (3ft).

Look for healthy plants that show no signs of disease on the leaves and stems, and slip them out of their pots to check that the roots are not congested, as this will hinder their development once planted. Also reject any that have poor or underdeveloped root systems.

Always check your chosen shrubs are healthy and undamaged before purchasing.

SHRUBS FOR DIFFERENT CONDITIONS

To guarantee the best performance, choose shrubs that suit your site and soil; in the wrong conditions, their foliage and flowers are likely to suffer.

As well as checking plant labels, also consider shrubs' native habitats. Those from warm climates such as the Mediterranean need a sunny position in free-draining soil, and often have small leaves that deflect the heat and light. Forest or woodland natives are shade-lovers, and can be identified by their larger, dark green foliage, which is perfectly adapted to absorb the low light beneath tree canopies.

Check that shrubs do not require specifically acid or alkaline soils before buying, to prevent an expensive mistake. Most shrubs will tolerate both, but there are some exceptions.

Sun Shrubs with small, silver or grey-green leaves, such as rock roses (*Cistus, above*), lavender, and *Perovskia*, need a sunny site. Plants with colourful leaves, such as *Berberis thunbergii* and the purple forms of *Cotinus*, also thrive in sun.

Shade Many large-leaved and some pretty flowering shrubs, such as hydrangeas (*above*), prefer a shady site. A few variegated shrubs, such as *Elaeagnus*, also cope with shade but need a little sun to bring out their colours.

Acid soils Some shrubs, such as camellias (*above*), rhododendrons, and *Pieris*, are only happy if grown in acid soil. Others that prefer acidic conditions include witch hazel, heathers, *Enkianthus*, *Leucothoe*, and *Arctostaphylos*.

Alkaline soils A greater number of plants will tolerate alkaline conditions, including sun-lovers such as *Ceanothus* (*above*), *Cytisus*, and *Hebe*, and plants for shade, such as *Deutzia*, *Sarcococca*, and *Viburnum tinus*.

PLANNING A SHRUB BORDER

Many shrubs produce a dense thicket of branches and form a block of solid colour, so arrange them in height order, with the smallest at the front. Also select plants with different heights and structures, and think of them as living sculptures to create a visually exciting display. For example, you could use a *Cornus controversa* 'Variegata', with its horizontal flowering stems, behind compact shrubs with contrasting strap-like or rounded foliage (*see below*).

You can also enhance the interest of some small-leaved shrubs, such as box or shrubby honeysuckle (*Lonicera nitida*), by clipping them into topiary shapes. Try planting a prized specimen in a large pot and set it at the front of, or within, your border. Also consider shrubs with decorative or unusual foliage to inject textural and colour contrasts, and add grasses, sedges, and perennials, such as rudbeckias or asters, to bring flowers and colour to your border in late summer and autumn when few shrubs are in bloom.

Pair the delicate white flowers of a *Cornus controversa* 'Variegata' with a silvery *Pittosporum* and red annual *Atriplex hortensis* var. *rubra*.

GARDEN WISDOM

Heavy loads

Architectural shrubs, such as clipped bay, palms, and fatsias, make excellent container plants. However, large shrubs, or those in weighty containers, can be very heavy, so it is wise to plant them *in situ*, or set them on plant trolleys, which can be wheeled around your plot with ease. You can buy decorative cast iron trolleys that make attractive additions to a patio display.

Plant heavy pots *in situ*.

PLANTING A SHRUB

If your soil is very heavy, or light and sandy, improve it before planting and select suitable shrubs (*see p.66*). A few weeks before planting, dig over the area to reduce soil compaction and incorporate some organic matter. Plan your layout carefully and site shrubs with sufficient space for them to grow to their full size. While they are maturing, fill in any gaps with annuals and perennials, which can be then lifted and moved when necessary.

1 Measure the distance from neighbouring plants to ensure your shrub has space to mature. Dig a hole about twice the width of the container and the same depth as the root ball.

2 Place the shrub, in its container, into the hole, and use a cane as a guide to ensure that when planted the shrub will be at the same level as it is in its pot. Water it thoroughly.

3 Enrich the excavated soil with controlled-release fertilizer. Remove the shrub from its pot, and place it in the hole. Fill in around the roots with the enriched soil.

4 Firm the soil down around the roots with your fingertips to expel any air pockets. Water in well and apply a mulch of well-rotted organic matter, leaving a gap around the stems.

CARING FOR SHRUBS

Many shrubs require very little aftercare, but they will need regular watering until their roots are fully established. Water during the growing season from spring to autumn; evergreens may also need watering during prolonged dry spells in winter.

Supplement poor soil with all-purpose fertilizer.

Once established, most shrubs will only require extra water during a severe drought. Mature shrubs should not need feeding, either – just lay a mulch of well-rotted organic matter, such as manure or compost, around them each spring. If your plants are looking unhealthy, or if your soil is poor, apply an all-purpose granular fertilizer before mulching.

Overwintering tender shrubs

Many tender shrubs, such as *Cordyline australis*, will not survive a harsh winter unprotected, but this should not deter you from growing them. The easiest solution is to grow compact types in small pots and bring them under cover during winter. If your plants are too large or your pots too heavy to move, cover them with a double layer of horticultural fleece. Make sure you also wrap up the container to insulate the roots, especially if your plants are in terracotta pots, which may crack in frosty conditions. Alternatively, make

Frost-proof delicate roots by insulating pots with sacking, fleece, or bubble wrap.

a cage around shrubs planted in the ground, using chicken wire attached to canes. Pack the cage with dry straw for insulation, and cover it with plastic to keep out the rain. This method should keep the plant warm and dry. Remember to remove the plastic on warm days to prevent the plant "sweating" and rot setting in.

SMALL SHRUBS FOR EDGING

Diminutive shrubs make excellent edging plants, either clipped to form a low hedge, or planted in a line at the front of a bed or border.

Thymes are useful edging for sunny, formal or wildlife gardens, where their flowers will attract many beneficial insects. They are available in a variety of colours and look attractive when used to cover slopes and banks, especially when planted in colourful blocks (*top left*). Consider combining them with other herbs, such as lavender.

Excellent choices for low, formal hedges, or as edging for a potager, include box, *Ilex crenata* (*top right*), and forms of *Euonymus fortunei*; their linear forms lend themselves to traditional garden designs.

On acid soils, include heathers and heaths to form a dense carpet of evergreen, needle-like foliage. They naturally form domed shapes (*bottom left*), and can be clipped to accentuate this trait. Line up plants or use them in clusters, or plant in swathes for a naturalized effect (*bottom right*). Different forms flower in autumn, winter, spring, and summer, and by mixing and matching a range you can create an edge with flowers all year round.

Scented strips of thyme

Crisp corners on hedging

Compact spheres of heather

Soft swathes of heather

SHRUB RECIPES

COOL CONTEMPORARY ROSE BED

Disease-resistant roses, such as Winchester Cathedral, make beautiful focal features in a bed of perennials. The monochrome scheme is perfect for a contemporary or formal garden, where the elegant flowers create an air of cool sophistication. The rose is best in full sun, but the surrounding plants will cope with some shade.

YOU WILL NEED

1 *Actaea simplex* 'Brunette'
2 *Veronica spicata* 'Alba'
3 White violas
4 *Rosa* Winchester Cathedral
5 Hardy white geraniums
6 *Alchemilla mollis*

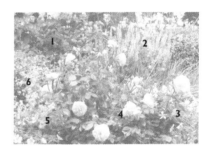

1 To plant the rose, follow the steps on page 133, setting it in pride of place in the middle of the border. Water the other plants.

2 Plant the low-growing violas, *Alchemilla*, and geraniums in the front, and the taller *Actaea* and *Veronica* behind or to one side.

3 Water well and add an organic mulch, leaving gaps around the stems. Keep the border watered while the plants are establishing.

RICH MIX

The sumptuous dark purple foliage and structural habit of the *Cotinus* dominate this scheme, and are set off by layers of foliage colour and form, with a golden hop (*Humulus*) growing over a rail in front of a *Cotoneaster* hedge. The box (*Buxus*) balls provide a formal note, while the perennials pick up the colour of the *Cotinus*. The plants will thrive in full sun or partial shade and moist but free-draining soil.

YOU WILL NEED

1 *Cotinus* 'Grace'
2 *Cotoneaster* hedge
3 *Humulus lupulus* 'Aureus'
4 *Lysimachia ciliata* 'Firecracker'
5 *Buxus* topiary

1 This scheme will get off to a good start if planted in autumn. Prepare the bed by digging and incorporating well-rotted organic matter.

2 Plant the shrubs as described on page 129. The hop is a twining climber and will need a support to scramble over (see p.145).

3 Either clip the box balls *in situ* or buy ready-made topiary specimens. Apply an organic mulch, keeping it clear of the stems. Water well.

Rosa 'Sunblest'

CLASSIC ROSES

Reigning supreme as queen of the flower garden for hundreds of years, the rose's exquisite beauty, elegance, and fragrance remains unrivalled. Today, modern disease-resistant hybrids that combine the best of the species' charms have caught the eye of contemporary designers and made roses more fashionable than ever.

With around 150 species roses and thousands of hybrids and cultivars to choose from, you cannot fail to find a rose that appeals to your sense of style and taste. Choose from elegant hybrid teas – the classic flowers of traditional rose gardens; thorny species with their large, beautiful blooms and glossy rosehips; or compact patio roses to dress up summer containers. In confined areas, use the vertical space and train a climber to decorate your walls and fences with foliage and sumptuous blooms.

TYPES OF ROSE

Shrubs This diverse group includes species roses that usually bear single flowers over a relatively short period, as well as modern shrub roses that flower for longer and include a wider range of flower forms.

Hybrid tea Sometimes called large-flowered roses, these have blooms of a classic shape, with long, pointed buds opening to petals that surround a central cone. The flowers are borne singly; many are fragrant.

Floribunda Also known as cluster-flowered roses, floribundas are similar to hybrid teas but with a more informal style, bearing flowers in great quantities from summer to autumn. Many are scented.

Old Bearing one flush of flowers in summer, often followed by large hips, old roses include groups such as Alba, Bourbon, Damask, China, and Moss roses. Most are very thorny, and many have a rich scent.

Patio and dwarf polyantha Patio roses are dwarf floribundas, growing to just 45–60cm (18–24in) in height. Polyanthas are rarely scented, but are tough bushes of a similar size with lots of small flowers.

Miniature These repeat-flowering, dwarf shrubs have very compact growth, and rarely spread. Flowers are tiny and rarely scented, and appear in flushes of 3–11 from summer to autumn. Ideal for containers.

Ramblers With long, flexible stems, rambling roses produce one flush of small to medium-sized flowers in early summer. They grow vigorously, and are ideal for training over fences and pergolas and into trees.

Climbers With a more rigid framework than rambling roses, climbing roses are a diverse group including some types of hybrid tea and floribundas; most flower from summer to autumn.

PLANTING ROSES

Roses thrive in a sunny position in fertile, moisture-retentive soil. If your soil is free-draining, dig in plenty of well-rotted farmyard manure a few weeks before planting to increase water retention. Whatever your soil type, apply a 5cm (2in) mulch of manure after planting, leaving a space around the stems.

1 Dig a bucketful of organic matter into your proposed planting area. Then dig a hole a little deeper and twice the diameter of the container in which your rose is growing.

2 Place the rose, in its pot, into the hole. Using a cane, check the graft union (swelling at base of the stems) will be below the surface, or slightly above in heavy soil. Add fertilizer to the excavated soil.

3 Water the rose and leave to drain before removing from its pot.

4 Wearing gloves, place the rose in the hole. Backfill around the root ball with the excavated soil, and firm in gently around the stems with your hands. Water in well.

With such variation in flower form and structure, roses are among the most versatile of all garden plants. Traditionalists may like them confined to their own beds, but if you choose this style, opt for disease-resistant roses that will not succumb to blackspot and lose their leaves. Alternatively, mix and match roses with other shrubs and perennials, which not only extends the season of interest but also helps to disguise leggy or leafless plants.

Standard roses make striking features in parterres and formal gardens, and look stunning when underplanted with lavender. Or use one as the centrepiece in a large container display on a patio surrounded by summer bedding.

Species shrubs, such as *Rosa alba* and *R. rugosa*, and modern hybrids are excellent choices for hedges, their thorny stems providing cover for wildlife and acting as a deterrent against human intruders. Climbers and

▲ **Make the most** of the vertical space in your garden by training vigorous rambling roses up bare walls and boundary fences.

ramblers are also effective in wildlife gardens, but really come into their own in cottage-style schemes. The tried-and-tested pairing of roses and clematis epitomizes a romantic idyll when plants are left to scramble over an arch or around a doorway.

Plant container-grown roses at any time of year and bare-root roses in winter, after soaking their roots in water just before planting. Many roses fall prey to the fungal disease blackspot, which, although not fatal, produces ugly black spots on the leaves and stems and causes foliage to fall. Reduce the risk by selecting disease-resistant hybrids. Aphids (see p.360) do not kill established plants, but may damage new flower buds and new stems.

PLANTING WITH PERENNIALS

Celebrated for their infinite variety, perennials (see p.12) never lose their charm and remain as popular as ever. With flowers of every colour, texture, shape, and form, this group includes plants for both sun and shade, and varieties suitable for all types of soil.

▶ FILLING THE GAPS

Perennials are ideal for filling gaps and adding ground-cover interest between shrubs and beneath trees in mixed borders and woodland gardens. Shade-lovers, such as hellebores, suit situations where their planting partners block the sun, putting on an early show of flowers beneath a deciduous tree, or use ferns to carpet the ground with a leafy design. In sunnier spots, your options are wider, but choose tough perennials like achilleas that can cope with competition for moisture from their neighbours.

In this neutral-coloured scheme, *Alchemilla mollis* and a purple *Actaea simplex* add colour and texture.

▲ INJECTING TROPICAL FLAVOUR

In warm, sunny, sheltered areas, re-create the gardens of tropical climes close to home with a combination of tender perennials and hardy types with eye-catching looks. Set the scene with large-leaved plants, and add to the effect with colourful leaves and vibrant flowers. Tender plants are best grown in pots and brought inside before the frosts to avoid damage. Match these with hardy perennials that can remain outside all year.

Team the hardy banana (*Musa basjoo*) with fiery cannas and annual purple *Ricinus* to inject an exotic flavour to a border.

◄ PROVIDING SUMMER ABUNDANCE

No plant group can compete with perennials for sheer flower power. The queens of the summer border, they include traditional favourites such as delphiniums and peonies. These prima donnas dazzle and glow, but others, like pastel-hued *Astrantia major*, are more delicate and reserved, forming a chorus to the bright stars and tempering the flower display.

From early to midsummer, perennial borders heave with flowers but the choice diminishes as autumn approaches. To keep your garden in full bloom at this time, seek out late starters like red-hot pokers (*Kniphofia*) to carry you through the late season.

Create a cottage garden brimming with summer blooms, such as tall spikes of *Delphinium*, purple salvias, and classic roses.

▲ DECORATING DRY LANDSCAPES

Drought-tolerant perennials are perfect for gravel gardens and desert-like landscapes. These styles are ideal if you garden on dry, sandy soil, and if you choose your plants carefully, you should not have to water them once they're established. Small succulents, together with *Rhodanthemum* and *Stachys*, will form a dense carpet of colour on a gravel or scree surface; mix them with taller plants like salvias and valerian (*Centranthus*) to add height.

To create this look, mix grasses with flowering perennials such as yarrow (*Achillea*) in a range of yellows and oranges.

◄ CREATING NATURALISTIC EFFECTS

Prairie schemes are best suited to larger gardens where plants can be amassed in bold swathes. Choose a limited selection of perennials that enjoy the conditions you can provide and plant them in large groups. A number of perennials also suit meadow plantings. To create this style, imagine the plants have self-seeded between the grasses: create small groups here and there, dotting a few of the same species close to these clusters.

Combine swathes of catnip (*Nepeta racemosa* 'Walker's Low') with *Betonica officinalis* 'Hummelo' and *Salvia nemorosa* 'Amethyst'.

SELECTING AND PLANTING PERENNIALS

Perennials provide spectacular flowering displays for many months of the year. Although some tall types require staking, most will look after themselves, reappearing year after year following their winter rest.

STAGGERING VARIETY

From the towering *Eupatorium purpureum* to the low, sprawling *Campanula poscharskyana*, there is a perennial for any area or planting scheme. They are available in a huge range of colours and shades, making it difficult to decide which to plant. Begin by assessing your site and soil and selecting those that do best in these conditions (see p.66). Next, map out your border or planting area, and assign plants according to their size and stature. Generally, lofty plants provide a backdrop to medium-sized and ground-hugging perennials, but remember that a few, such as the ever-popular *Verbena bonariensis* and

elegant *Dierama pulcherrimum*, can be planted towards the front of a scheme as they have slender stems and an airy, see-through structure. Finally, take your pick from the wide range of flower colours and foliage forms to complete your design.

Spectacular blooms

For borders bursting with colour, include a few flamboyant blooms. Try peonies, which boast large flowers prized for their ruffles of delicate petals in pink, red, or white. Lupins join the peonies in early summer, and produce eye-catching cones of small flowers in many hues, while in midsummer, the towering spires

Plant perennials in groups of three or more. Buy mature plants or young "plugs" which are more cost effective for bulk purchases.

of delphiniums are hard to beat, with their spikes of open flowers in shades of blue, purple, pink, and white. Also add a selection of oriental poppies. Although their sumptuous blooms are relatively short-lived, the decorative seedheads that follow extend their interest.

► **A pink rhododendron bush**, surrounded by foxgloves, red valerian, and *Centaurea montana* (perennial cornflower), brings a splash of colour to a border in spring and early summer.

PLANNING A LONG SEASON OF INTEREST

There are perennials for all seasons, starting with hellebores (*top left*), which flower between late winter and mid-spring. Next are the dainty forget-me-not-like blooms of *Brunnera,* and dancing flowers of *Epimedium* and *Lamprocapnos spectabilis*, all of which prefer some shade, followed later in spring by aquilegias in a variety of shapes and colours. A host of geraniums and vibrant geums (*top right*) then appear in early summer.

For dramatic colour from late summer to autumn, opt for blue or cerise asters (*bottom left*) and golden rudbeckias, toned down with the white daisies of *Leucanthemum*. In autumn try the knee-high, sun-loving *Ajania pacifica* (*bottom right*), which bears yellow button-like flowers surrounded by beautiful silver-edged lobed foliage. The evergreens then come into their own in winter, with round-leaved bergenias, grassy *Libertia*, and colourful heucheras leading the show.

Helleborus × *hybridus* 'Pluto'

Geum coccineum

Aster amellus 'Rosa Erfüllung'

Ajania pacifica

GARDEN WISDOM

Planting depths explained
Most perennials should be planted at the same depth as they were when in their original pots, but exceptions include those that dislike damp soil around their stems, such as *Verbascum*, *Sisyrinchium*, and *Hylotelephium*. Plant these 2–3cm (1–1½in) above the surface, and pull up the soil around the root ball to encourage water to drain off. Moisture-loving plants, including hostas, prefer to be planted more deeply, so that their roots are never exposed to the dry conditions nearer the surface.

PLANTING A PERENNIAL

To prepare the ground for planting, dig over the soil to aerate it, reduce compaction, and remove any weeds. Then dig in some organic matter, such as well-rotted manure or compost. Most perennials are planted in early autumn or spring; more tender types or those that dislike cold, wet conditions, such as *Verbena bonariensis*, are best planted in spring, allowing them a full growing season to establish before the winter rains.

1 Dig a hole twice as wide as the plant pot and a little deeper. Set the plant in the hole and check that it will be at about the same depth when planted as it was in its original pot.

2 Fork the bottom of the hole to loosen any compacted soil, and rake in a little general fertilizer to the hole. Water the plant well, then carefully slip it out of its pot.

3 Gently tease out any circling roots from the rootball. Place the plant back into the hole. Fill in around the root ball with it, firming it down with your fingers.

4 Water the plant well and apply an organic mulch of compost or well-rotted manure. Lay gravel around plants that like their stems kept dry, such as achilleas, stachys, and sedums.

AFTERCARE

If you plant perennials in their optimum conditions, they should only need watering for one season after planting. Some may require extra irrigation during extended periods of drought, but don't be tempted to water plants whose leaves droop at midday, as this is simply their mechanism for conserving moisture – they should bounce back again in the evening.

Once they are established, greedy perennials, such as *Symphyotrichum novae-angliae*, will need an application of all-purpose granular fertilizer once a year in spring. Also mulch around perennials with organic matter such as well-rotted manure, compost, or bark chips at the same time.

Tall plants, such as delphiniums and some asters, will need staking, especially in exposed sites. Insert stakes in spring when new growth appears, and tie in the stems as they grow. Stake single stems with bamboo canes; insert twiggy hazel or pea sticks, or use link or ring support

Stake clump-forming plants such as peony early in the season, raising as the plant grows.

frames, around clump-forming plants. These may not look very attractive at first, but the plants will soon grow large enough to disguise them.

Cutting back perennials

Perennials require very little other maintenance and most will be happy doing their own thing for the rest of the growing season. Some plants, such as hardy geraniums, will form fresh foliage if you cut them back after they have bloomed. Others, including

Dianthus, will produce a fresh flush of blooms if deadheaded. In late autumn, cut old plant stems down to ground level, unless their foliage or seedheads are attractive over winter, in which case leave this task until spring. Remove the old foliage of evergreens, including bergenias, in spring to allow space for new leaves to form.

GARDEN SPEAK

The Chelsea chop
In late spring, at the same time as the end of the famous RHS Chelsea Flower Show, you may want to try what is known as "the Chelsea chop". Simply cut or pinch back plants by half, and this will help to spread out the overall flowering season. The plants will also produce more flowering stems, so although they will bloom a little later than usual, the display will be more spectacular. Plants that respond to this include *Rudbeckia*, *Hylotelephium*, *Echinacea*, and *Helenium*.

PERENNIALS FOR DIFFICULT SITES

Versatile and beautiful, perennials can be relied upon to fill even the most challenging sites. Plan carefully and you will be able to create year-round interest in any garden.

Alpines are perfect for squeezing between paving or the gaps in a dry stone wall. *Aubrieta* (top left), *Alyssum*, and *Arabis* will fill these areas with exhilarating spring colour, while *Frankenia* and *Cerastium* offer later seasonal interest.

The glaucous blue-leaved evergreen *Euphorbia rigida* (top right) is ideal for sunny slopes and produces frothy yellow flowers in spring, or choose the fern-like, silver-leaved *Artemisia* 'Powis Castle' for sun-baked gravel gardens.

In dry shade, use the pretty *Vinca minor* (bottom left) with its lax stems of evergreen foliage and beautiful blue spring flowers or *Lamium*, with variegated foliage.

Most ferns are at home in deep shade, while other good choices for shady borders include low-growing *Pachysandra*, *Alchemilla mollis*, and *Brunnera*, or *Bergenia* and some *Lysimachia* where taller plants are required. For damp shade, try hostas (bottom right), which produce attractive foliage (but most need protection against slug and snail attacks).

Crimson *Aubretia*

Euphorbia rigida

Vinca minor

Hosta 'Francee'

PERENNIAL RECIPES

HIGH-SUMMER COLOUR

Nothing compares to a midsummer border brimming with colourful perennials. This mix of contrasting yellows, blues, and purples, with red highlights, also combines interesting shapes and forms, which lead the eye around the scheme. Plant this group in a sunny area and apply an organic mulch over the border each spring.

YOU WILL NEED

1 *Lupinus* 'The Governor'
2 *Pittosporum tenuifolium* 'Silver Queen'
3 *Anchusa azurea* 'Loddon Royalist'
4 *Achillea* 'Moonshine'
5 *Rosa* Rose of Picardy
6 *Verbascum* 'Gainsborough'

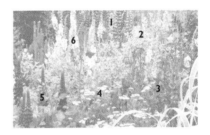

1 In spring, dig over the border, add some organic matter, and set out your plants. Plant flower spikes next to flat-headed achilleas.

2 Plant the tall lupins and verbascums in groups of three or more towards the back of the border, but ensure they are still in sun.

3 Water the border well after planting and regularly for the first year. In late winter, cut back the old perennial stems.

PRAIRIE DRIFTS

This beautiful border comprises large drifts of stout perennials that, together with groups of grasses, provide stunning late summer colour. The plants also offer interest in autumn when the blooms fade and seedheads form, followed in winter by straw-coloured stems that look fabulous when iced with frost. Plant in a sunny site.

YOU WILL NEED

1 *Deschampsia cespitosa*
2 *Hylotelephium spectabile*
3 *Echinacea purpurea* 'Rubinstern'
4 *Lythrum virgatum*
5 *Eupatorium*

1 Before planting in early autumn or spring, dig plenty of organic matter into the border to enrich the soil.

2 Buy ten or more plants of each type and plant them in teardrop-shaped, interlinking swathes. Vary heights and textures to create the effect.

3 Keep plants well watered for the first growing season until they are established. Leave the dried stems over winter and then cut them down in spring.

PERENNIALS FOR FOLIAGE

Swathes of flowers look wonderful in beds and borders, but many perennials bloom for a relatively short period. For a longer-lasting scheme, select plants for foliage effects as well as for blooms, and combine different shapes and colours for a long season of interest.

Perennials follow the general pattern of most plants, with larger-leaved species tending to prefer shade, and those with small, silver, or downy foliage enjoying sunny sites. Most colourful foliage perennials need some sun to bring out their hues, but a range of variegated plants, such as arums and pulmonarias, do well in shade. Contrast plants with different features (*see right*) and use each type in bold groups or swathes for the greatest impact.

FOLIAGE OPTIONS

Large leaves One of the best perennials for large leaves is *Bergenia* (*above*), with its oval, leathery leaves and clusters of pink flowers in early spring.

Colourful foliage For the widest variety, opt for heucheras (*above*), which thrive in most soil types. Hostas include a good choice for shady sites.

Dryopteris affinis

Sword-like leaves Sun-loving phormiums (*above*) are hardy and make exceptional focal plants. Shade-tolerant astelias produce a similar effect.

Patterns *Brunnera* cultivars (*above*), and *Pulmonaria* species, many of which are variegated, will brighten up shady areas with their patterned foliage.

Grassy leaves *Ophiopogon* species (*above*) form compact plants with variegated leaves or black grass-like foliage. *Libertia* is a taller option for beds and borders.

Finger-like foliage Not all euphorbias are perennials, but the striking red-purple foliage of *Euphorbia amygdaloides* 'Purpurea' makes it one of the best.

Ferny leaves Choose an *Achillea* (*above*) for a mix of fern-like foliage and flowers. Ferns themselves make beautiful specimens for shade.

Soft, downy foliage For tactile effects, try downy-leaved lambs' ears, *Stachys byzantina* (*above*), and the velvety foliage of *Verbascum bombyciferum*.

◀ **Nestle shade-loving perennials**, such as *Hosta* and *Dicentra* 'King of Hearts', under a bench to add an extra layer of planting to a secluded corner of the garden.

PLANTING FERNS IN A POT

Even if you don't have much space, you can create a verdant display by planting a mix of contrasting ferns in a container on a patio. These are ideal in a shady spot.

1 Choose a pot with holes in the base to allow for adequate drainage. Apply a layer of soil-based compost. Add some slow-release fertilizer granules.

2 Soak the ferns in a bucket of water for 15 minutes. Place them, still in their original containers, in the pot to ensure that you are happy with the arrangement.

3 Tip the ferns out of their containers, and place on the layer of compost. Fill in around the root balls, firming the compost gently with your fingers.

4 Plant the ferns at the same depth as in their original containers, leaving a gap of 5cm (2in) between the pot rim and top of the compost to allow space for watering. Water in well.

Leafy perennials are versatile plants, suitable for gardens of all sizes, with diminutive types squeezing comfortably into tiny spaces and dramatic crowd-pleasers, like phormiums, providing excellent container plants for patios. Add to these the mid-sized perennials, which create bold, textured effects when used *en masse* in larger spaces. There are even tough little plants, including the prettily patterned deadnettle, *Lamium maculatum*, that will survive the dry shade beneath trees.

Make the most of perennials

in a small urban garden by tucking shade-lovers such as hostas, pulmonarias, and ferns beneath a bench, or use them to produce a frill of foliage alongside a pathway. In boggy areas close to a pond or pool, inject drama into a larger garden with the massive leaves of a *Gunnera manicata*, or use the shapely foliage of *Ligularia* and *Rodgersia* species where space is more restricted. Areas that bask in full sun will provide the perfect home for an edging of furry lambs' ears (*Stachys*), swathes of colourful succulents, including purple forms of *Hylotelephium telephium*, and focal plants such as *Melianthus major*.

Plants grown for foliage effects

come from a wide range of habitats, so check the labels for specific site and soil requirements before you buy. Many, like ferns (*see right*), make superb container specimens, but remember to keep perennials in pots well watered and feed them annually in spring with an all-purpose granular fertilizer to keep the foliage looking lush.

INTRODUCING CLIMBERS AND WALL SHRUBS

Climbers and wall shrubs are versatile plants, perfect for decorating small gardens where space is tight or for clothing large structures and screens. Prized for their lush foliage, they also offer a variety of decorative fruits and flowers.

▶ PROVIDING WALLS OF SCENT

The beauty of a scented climber is that the blooms are perfectly placed at nose height. The choice is legion, with climbing and rambling roses producing a range of heady scents. Deciduous honeysuckles (*Lonicera periclymenum*) and jasmines (*Jasminum*) are also hard to beat for fragrance, while scented evergreens include the star jasmine (*Trachelospermum jasminoides*). Wisteria's purple or white lanterns of flowers reign supreme in spring, blessing gardens with a rich scent. Best grown on a sturdy pergola or frame, this towering beauty needs plenty of support.

Star jasmine (*Trachelospermum jasminoides*) is a highly scented evergreen, which is easily trained onto wires or trellis. Although the summer flowers are small, they emit a delicious fragrance.

▲ CREATING LEAFY SCREENS

When grown up a wooden or chain link fence or a trellis, climbers offer a fast-growing alternative to a hedge. These hybrid fence cum hedges are known as "fedges", and ideal plants include ivy (*Hedera helix*) and the deciduous Virgina creeper (*Parthenocissus*). For a shady wall or fence, try the climbing hydrangea, which produces a leafy screen with flat-headed white flowers. The stunning pink, white, and green *Actinidia kolomikta* is a great choice for a sunny site.

The dramatic foliage of *Parthenocissus tricuspidata* creates a dense, leafy wall with beautiful autumn tints.

▲ DECORATING STRUCTURES

Soften the hard lines of a pergola, arch, fence, or shed with a veil of plaited stems, textured foliage, and flowers and fruits for all seasons. Wire up vertical supports for twiners, and ensure your structure will take the weight of heavy-limbed specimens. Try combining two varieties, but check plant labels for vigour to ensure one half of a climbing pair will not swamp the other. Also consider wall shrubs such as *Pyracantha,* which makes screens of spiny stems, evergreen foliage, and masses of autumn and winter berries.

The classic combination of roses and clematis makes a romantic, cottage-garden style feature of these iron railings.

◄ ADDING HEIGHT TO CONTAINER DISPLAYS

Climbers are not just for beds and borders. In a courtyard or on a patio, create focal points with large pots of annuals. Traditional flowering climbers such as sweet peas are ideal for a cottage-garden scheme, supported by a tripod of rustic canes. For a contemporary effect, choose an unusual flower shape, such as *Rhodochiton*. Patio clematis are also worth considering, their compact growth festooned with summer flowers.

An eye-catching container wigwam of scrambling sweet peas (*Lathyrus odoratus*) provides a floral focal point in a border.

◄ CLIMBING THROUGH TREES AND SHRUBS

Deciduous trees provide the perfect hosts for large scrambling climbers like roses and early-flowering clematis. These vigorous plants will need a little support from bamboo canes at first, but once latched onto the tree branches, they will soon find their way up through the canopy. Choose pairings of trees and climbers carefully to give a long season of interest with flowering seasons in quick succession. For summer and autumn colour, add a late-flowering species, such as the flame creeper (*Tropaeolum speciosum*). Adorn shrubs with more compact climbers; try a scrambling annual like the cup and saucer vine (*Cobaea scandens*), or in a tropical-style garden, choose sizzling orange *Eccremocarpus* flowers.

Pair a pale pink climbing rose with a deciduous tree to support an abundance of beautiful flowers, creating an atmospheric and fragrant seating area in a secluded corner of the garden.

SELECTING AND PLANTING CLIMBERS AND WALL SHRUBS

There are many beautiful climbers and wall shrubs on offer, and plants for both sun and shade, but whatever you choose, make sure you know how yours climb and provide them with appropriate supports.

Climbers have developed a range of methods by which they scramble up vertical surfaces, and understanding the one your chosen plant uses will help you to provide the right support for it. Twining climbers, such as clematis and honeysuckle, need trellis, wires, or a large shrub or tree to cling to, while some vigorous climbers, including wisteria, become very heavy over time, so make sure the supporting structure will hold their eventual weight.

A self-clinging plant, such as ivy or Virginia creeper (*Parthenocissus*), will climb over a house wall without your help, but once established, these plants need to be cut back regularly and may damage old pointing and block guttering.

Look for plants with lots of healthy stems, and remember to remove plastic or metal ties fixing them to their canes before planting.

CLIMBING TYPES

Climbers have evolved a variety of methods to cling to their hosts, from sticky pads to twining stems and tendrils. Read the labels on plants when you buy, or examine stems and shoots to decide what support they need. Even the self-clinging types will require some canes at first to guide the stems to their supports.

Aerial roots Self-clinging climbers such as ivy and climbing hydrangea use aerial roots to fix on to surfaces unaided. Ivies will scramble over anything in their path, from trees and shrubs, to walls, fences, and posts.

Hooks and thorns Plants such as roses use hooks and thorns to latch on to taller plants. They will happily grow through a host plant but will need to be tied to trellis or wires against a wall or on a structure like a pergola.

Adhesive pads Some self-clinging climbers, including Virginia creeper and Boston ivy, produce adhesive pads that stick the plants to their supports. They will need no other help from you after they have attached themselves.

Twining stems or tendrils Popular climbers such as passion flowers and honeysuckle thread their way through a host plant using twining stems or tendrils. Cover a structure, such as a fence or arch, with mesh or wires for them to cling to.

COVERING WALLS AND SCREENS

To clothe walls and fences, roses and twining climbers such as clematis will usually need additional wire or trellis supports. If using trellis, attach two wooden battens to the vertical surface and screw the trellis onto them. This creates an air space behind the trellis, which allows climbers to get a better grip.

When attaching horizontal wires, drill parallel sets of holes at 45cm (18in) intervals up the wall or fence posts, and insert rawl plugs into the holes (these are not required in timber posts). Screw in vine eyes, and attach durable garden wire. Tighten the vine eyes to pull the wires taut. To encourage your climber to cover the surface evenly, spread the stems out and attach them to the wires or trellis with soft twine. Rose stems flower more profusely when trained horizontally, so train as many as you can along the wires.

Decorate a rustic wall with clematis, supported by wires and vine eyes that will be hidden from view.

GARDEN WISDOM

Wiring up posts

The posts of a pergola or arch are easy to wire up. Simply twist in four screw eyes on each side of the post at the top, and repeat at the bottom. Fix plastic-covered wires between them, and twist the eyes until the wires are taut. Alternatively, give climbers more support by wrapping wire or plastic netting around the posts and securing it with metal pins.

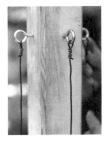

Quick and easy supports.

PLANTING A CLIMBER

Fix wire supports or trellis panels in place before you plant your climber against a wall or fence. Then dig over and enrich the soil with organic matter, such as well-rotted compost or manure. Avoid planting your climber too close to the wall or fence because the soil there is likely to be quite dry. Most hardy climbers are best planted in the autumn; plant more tender types, such as potato vines (*Solanum*), in spring.

1 Dig a planting hole about 45cm (18in) from a fence (or a little closer to a post), making it twice as wide and slightly deeper than the plant pot. Place the pot in the hole to check the planting depth.

2 Place bamboo canes in the hole and arrange them in a fan shape. Attach the canes to the horizontal wires on the fence to provide a temporary support for the climber until it reaches the wires.

3 Water the plant, then remove it from its pot. Place it in the hole and lean it towards the fence; ensure the root ball is not above the soil surface. Add fertilizer to the excavated soil.

4 Fill in around the roots with soil, firming it down with your fingers. Make a saucer-shaped depression with the surrounding soil around the base of the climber to create a water reservoir.

5 Tie the stems loosely to the canes with twine. Water the plant – the reservoir will guide moisture to the roots. Apply a mulch of organic matter or bark chips, leaving a space around the stems.

AFTERCARE

Climbers take a couple of seasons to fully establish and may need extra water during this time. Water every week during dry spells from early spring to autumn; evergreens may need watering during the winter too. Turn the tap halfway on and aim your hose at the base of the plant to thoroughly soak the root area. Alternatively, attach a rose to a watering can and empty the whole can around the plant.

Each spring, apply a mulch of organic matter, such as well-rotted manure or garden compost, leaving a gap around the climber's stems. If your soil is reasonably fertile, most plants will not require additional feeding once established. If growth is slow or your climber is lacking vigour, apply an all-purpose granular fertilizer in spring. Tie in young stems throughout the growing season to ensure supports are covered evenly. For pruning advice, see pages 316–317.

BEAUTIFUL BERRIES

The flowers of climbing plants are eye-catching, but those with berries should not be under-estimated for late-season ornamental value and a long season of interest. Good choices include the glossy violet, red, pink, or white berries of *Billardiera longiflora*, which make an unusual garden feature, or the red, bead-like rose hips that stud the stems of rambling roses such as *Rosa* 'Seagull' and *R.* 'Albertine', adding to their appeal after the flowers have faded.

Alternatively, choose *Ampelopsis brevipedunculata*, whose white berries shine like pearls before maturing to a rich purple-blue, or the bright orange, red, or golden berries of wall shrubs such as *Pyracantha*, which will bring a splash of colour to a gloomy corner.

Billardiera longiflora Dainty greenish-yellow flowers are followed by the colourful fruits that adorn this pretty evergreen in autumn. It needs a sheltered, sunny position to survive the winter; cover it with fleece during cold spells.

Rose hips Many roses produce pretty hips, but if you deadhead the flowers you'll remove the fruits too. Leave a few stems of ramblers unpruned after flowering, and don't deadhead repeat-flowering climbers after midsummer.

WALL SHRUBS FOR YEAR-ROUND INTEREST

Woody plants that can be trained on a wall or fence but have no facility to climb are known as wall shrubs. There are beauties for all seasons, with the blue-flowered *Ceanothus*, such as *C.* 'Concha' (*top left*), which bears abundant clusters of blooms, and the flowering quinces, *Chaenomeles*, leading the way in spring.

In summer, the golden-yellow blooms of *Fremontodendron* 'California Glory' (flannel bush, *top right*) will brighten up a sunny wall. Alternatively, try the dainty bell-like, pendent flowers of the evergreen *Abutilon megapotamicum* (*bottom left*), or tender *Carpenteria californica* (tree anemone), with its fragrant, cup-shaped flowers.

Autumn colour comes in spades from the profuse berries of pyracanthas and cotoneasters, while winter is the time when the silky tassels of *Garrya elliptica* (*bottom right*) appear. The variegated evergreen foliage of *Euonymus fortunei* cultivars, such as *E. f.* 'Emerald 'n' Gold' and 'Silver Queen' are also useful in winter, adding interest to a shady wall.

Ceanothus 'Concha'

Fremontodendron 'California Glory'

Abutilon megapotamicum

Garrya elliptica

CLIMBER RECIPES

QUICK-COVER SCREEN

Annual climbers, such as morning glory (*Ipomoea*) and black-eyed Susan (*Thunbergia*), quickly scramble over a wire trellis to create a temporary screen or backdrop to a raised bed or container. Both need free-draining soil and a sunny site to coax the flowers to bloom.

1 Plant *Ipomoea* and *Thunbergia* seeds in pots indoors in early spring. When the frosts have passed, fill a raised bed or large container with soil-based compost, such as John Innes No 2. Fix a trellis to the back of the display.

2 After the frosts, plant two seedlings of each plant at the base of the trellis, and day lilies that match the colours of the climbers on either side. Firm in the soil with your fingers.

3 Water in the plants, and keep the bed or container well watered throughout the summer. The climbers will not need to be tied to the trellis, but ensure the stems cover it by spreading them out evenly.

YOU WILL NEED

1 *Ipomoea* 'Heavenly Blue'
2 *Thunbergia alata*
3 *Hemerocallis* (day lily)

CLASSIC COMBINATION

The dainty small-flowered rambling rose hybrid *R.* 'Minnehaha' makes an ideal partner for *Clematis* 'Comtesse de Bouchaud'. Just as the scented rose begins to fade, the clematis bursts into bloom and keeps the show going until early autumn with its pastel pink flowers. Both the rose and clematis will need a sturdy trellis, wired wall or fence, or tree for support. Underplant them with contrasting blue perennials, such as the hip-high *Campanula lactiflora*; its bell-like blooms persist throughout summer and will cover any leggy stems at the base of the climbers. All plants will be happy in full sun or partial shade, and moist but well-drained soil.

1 These climbers like fertile soil, so dig plenty of organic matter into the bed before you start planting and add some fertilizer.

2 Plant the clematis and rose as shown on page 145, about 60cm (24in) apart. Firm in the soil well around the stems, and water in the plants.

3 Plant the campanulas about 45cm (18in) in front of the climbers. Keep the bed well watered for the first two growing seasons.

YOU WILL NEED

1 *Clematis* 'Comtesse de Bouchaud'
2 *Campanula lactiflora*
3 *Rosa* 'Minnehaha'

Clematis x durandii

CLIMBING CLEMATIS

The flexible, flowering stems of clematis provide many ways to create exciting effects in the garden, and with a vast range of colours, shapes, and forms to choose from, it's no wonder they're so popular. From tree-huggers to container varieties, there's a clematis for every garden size and flowers for almost every month of the year.

Clematis comprise a large group of climbers, and include a range of different flower types and growth habits. The larger species, such as *Clematis montana* and *C. tangutica*, need little support when allowed to scramble through host trees and shrubs. The large- and late-flowering hybrids are not as vigorous and, like all clematis, need wires or trellis to climb vertical structures. Late-flowering viticella types are similar in habit to the large species and ideal for weaving through host plants.

Clematis offer a rich source of exciting features for year-round displays, with patio hybrids, large-flowered early summer performers, the subtle, bell-like blooms of late-flowering species, and the sweet aroma of winter- and early

TYPES OF CLEMATIS

Early-flowered species These include the tall, often scented, open-flowered montanas, ideal for growing through trees, and the smaller, early-flowering alpina and macropetala species.

Large-flowered hybrids The large, showy blooms of the early summer-flowering hybrids make up a large and varied group, with a broad colour palette. Many also sport stripes and colour blends.

Late-flowering hybrids These include *C. jackmanii* and its many relatives, and the flowers tend to be smaller than the earlier-flowering hybrids. The colour ranges mirror those of the large-flowered types.

Double-flowered hybrids Much sought after, double-flowered clematis are prized for the ruffles of petals that surround the central anthers, giving the flowers a fuller, more rounded appearance.

spring-flowering forms. And for the brief moment in midwinter when clematis are not in bloom, *C. tangutica* brightens gloomy days with its lantern-shaped seedheads.

Some clematis types, such as *C. montana* and its cultivars, can reach up to 10m (30ft) and when planted with a host tree that flowers just before its late spring blooms appear, the pair provide many weeks of colour. The late-flowering viticella types also make good partners for trees and shrubs, or allow them to scramble through herbaceous plants in a border.

To cover a wall, fence, or screen, train a large clematis along wires. A good choice for late-season colour is *C.* 'Bill McKenzie', which forms a tangle of leafy stems and bright yellow nodding flowers followed by decorative seedheads. The myriad clematis hybrids afford eye-catching displays for pergolas, arches, and posts, and all combine well with climbing roses, jasmine, and annual morning glory (*Ipomoea*).

Plant clematis in moist but well-drained, fertile soil; they thrive in full sun or partial shade. Keep the roots cool by shading them with other plants or placing a layer of pebbles or flat stones at the base. To prevent the fungal disease clematis wilt, plant in deep, fertile soil and ensure the plant's roots don't dry out.

◄ **Send a clematis** such as *C.* 'Perle d'Azur', scrambling over a wall for an informal mass of colourful blooms in late summer.

PRUNING CLEMATIS

There are three methods of pruning clematis: most plant labels will tell you which group your plant belongs to, and when it is best to prune.

Group 1
Shear over vigorous winter- and spring-flowering clematis after flowering to keep them tidy. Renovate old, congested plants by cutting them back almost to ground level after flowering.

Group 2
Early summer-flowering clematis, including the large-flowered hybrids, require light pruning. Remove dead and diseased growth and cut back remaining stems to a pair of healthy buds.

Group 3
Clematis that flower after midsummer should be cut back hard in winter or early spring. Prune the stems to a pair of strong buds 15–30cm (6–12in) above the ground. New stems will soon appear.

Patio clematis As well as some compact hybrids such as *C.* 'Bees' Jubilee' (*above*), the clematis in Raymond Evison's Boulevard collection have been bred specifically for containers.

Evergreen species *C. armandii* (*above*) and *C. cirrhosa* are popular for their evergreen foliage and their profusion of late winter and early spring flowers. Those of *C. armandii* are sweetly scented.

Small-flowered species This group includes the late-flowering viticella clematis, the yellow-red *C. koreana* (*above*), yellow *C. tangutica*, and *C. flammula*, with its clouds of tiny star-shaped blooms.

BAMBOO AND GRASS EFFECTS

From wispy fountains of rustling leaves to stands of colourful poles topped with feathery foliage, grasses and bamboos lend stature and drama to any planting scheme.

▶ INJECTING COLOUR AND FORM

Planting flowers isn't the only way to ensure a broad spectrum of colour in your garden: bamboo varieties are available with beautiful purple, ice-blue, gold, or black stems. Some, like the blue-stemmed *Borinda papyrifera* and *Phyllostachys*, measure up to 5m (15ft) in height, and provide a fantastic way to add colour and drama to your outdoor space if you have the room to make the most of them.

Grasses can also add a splash of colour, and unusual cultivars make great focal plants. Look for varieties with striking yellow stripes or spectacular scarlet tips, such as *Miscanthus sinensis* 'Zebrinus' or the scarlet-tipped *Imperata cylindrica* 'Rubra'.

In this gravel garden, clumps of black and yellow-stemmed bamboos (*Phyllostachys nigra* and *P. aureosulcata* f. *aureocaulis*) lend height and colour to a foliage scheme.

▲ PROVIDING TEXTURAL CONTAINER DISPLAYS

Grasses make exceptional container specimens, either planted on their own or together with annuals and perennials in mixed displays. Add structure and interest to patio schemes with a mix of tall leafy fountains, golden flowing forms, and those with long, soft flowerheads, and bronze or bluey-grey foliage. Bamboos also look great in containers, but are quite demanding, requiring plenty of water all year round.

Combine evergreen *Stipa tenuissima* and *Carex comans* with deciduous *Eragrostis* for a multi-coloured display.

▼ CREATING SCREENS AND HEDGES

Densely planted bamboos make unusual hedges and are superb windbreaks. Use non-invasive types, such as *Fargesia* and *Phyllostachys*, planted in the ground or grown in containers. Seek expert advice, as invasive types can be very difficult to eradicate.

Some deciduous grasses, including *Miscanthus sinensis*, can also be used for screening. Their dried stems and flowers will still provide cover in winter, but need to be cut down in spring, when the plants offer no shelter for a few weeks before the new growth takes over.

Plant tall bamboos in large terracotta containers to create a flexible screen for a sheltered seating area.

◄ MAKING MEADOWS

Soft grass species provide the perfect foil for bright annual meadow flowers. Alternatively, use them on their own to produce a summer hay meadow with feathery flowers and decorative seedheads. As well as looking beautiful and requiring just one or two mows a year, depending on the type you choose, meadow grasses also provide the perfect habitat for insects and invertebrates. The grasses are usually available in seed form, and should be planted as for a meadow (*see p.340*).

Sow meadow grasses beneath deciduous trees to soften their silhouettes with a sea of airy foliage.

◄ ADDING INTEREST TO MIXED DISPLAYS

Both deciduous and evergreen grasses provide a textural contrast to perennials and offer an airy foil to blocks of shrubs. Tall grasses make excellent backdrops to herbaceous plantings in sunny sites, while well-behaved bamboos that do not spread too rapidly perform a similar function – but do keep a check on their growth. There are many beautiful grasses and sedges for the middle of beds, including those with see-through stems; low-growing *Carex* and fescues are perfect for the front of a display.

A wonderful choice for height, *Stipa gigantea* does not dominate thanks to its see-through flowerheads. Add contrast at the front with the golden sedge, *Carex elata* 'Aurea'.

SELECTING AND PLANTING BAMBOOS AND GRASSES

Tough and versatile, there are grasses and bamboos for sunny or shady positions, and dry or damp soils. Select them carefully to produce a year-round display of foliage, flowers, stems, and seedheads.

Grasses are a varied group and can be found on every continent on the planet; those selected for garden use have graceful habits and decorative flowers and seedheads. They range from tiny types, such as the squat fescues, to towering giants like *Arundo donax*, which reaches up to 4m (12ft) in height. Most grasses prefer full sun and free-draining soil, although *Holcus*, *Milium*, and the prairie cord grass, *Spartina*, thrive in moist conditions and some shade. Most bamboos, and the evergreen *Carex* family and other sedges, which closely resemble grasses, are also perfect for shady sites and damp soils.

Planting an invasive species can be a costly, irreversible mistake. A good nursery can offer invaluable advice on invasiveness before buying.

SELECTING WELL-BEHAVED BAMBOOS

Bamboos are simply grasses that form woody stems, and they tend to be more tolerant of shady conditions than their close relatives; a few, including forms of *Pleioblastus*, are even happy in deep shade. They thrive in moist but well-drained soil.

Despite their elegant appearance, some bamboos have a dark side – their invasive, spreading roots can take over a garden, transforming beautiful planting schemes into dense jungles. Bamboos that fall into this group include *Indocalamus*, *Pleioblastus*, *Pseudosasa*, *Sasa*, and *Sasaella*. If you want to grow these, restrain their roots by planting them surrounded by bamboo control sheets.

Clump-forming species, such as *Fargesia*, *Chusquea*, *Thamnocalamus*, *Himalayacalamus*, *Phyllostachys*, and *Semiarundinaria* are better behaved, but will still benefit from a root barrier to keep them in check.

Phyllostachys One of the most popular tall, clump-forming bamboos. Choose from golden-, black-, or green-stemmed forms; all are ideal for use as screening or as focal points.

Thamnocalamus A tall, graceful bamboo that makes a beautiful garden specimen. It produces small leaves and either blue, fading to deep red, or pinkish-brown stems.

Fargesia All members of the *Fargesia* family are well behaved, hardy, and tolerate dry soils. They make excellent hedges and look stunning when grown in large patio containers.

Borinda This non-invasive bamboo is closely related to *Fargesia* and *Thamnocalamus*. Its vivid blue stems and strong upright growth make a colourful focal point or screen.

WHEN AND WHERE TO PLANT

Most grasses, sedges, and bamboos are available in pots, and can be planted like perennials (see p.137) at any time of the year, unless the soil is frozen, waterlogged, or very dry. However, it is best to plant them in spring, allowing a full growing season for them to establish before winter. Some bamboos, especially those used for hedging, are also available as bare-root plants in winter; plant them as soon as you receive them.

Grasses suit most sunny mixed borders and gravel gardens, and they also make effective container plants. Bamboos will be happy in both sunny and partially shaded areas, and are best used as focal points or backdrops to mixed planting schemes, or to create a screen or hedge. Most grasses and bamboos dislike waterlogged soils, so add horticultural grit to heavy clays to improve drainage, and incorporate plenty of well-rotted manure or garden compost into all types of soil a few weeks before planting.

Grasses can be planted alongside herbaceous perennials to create contrast and variety in beds.

PLANTING A BARE-ROOT BAMBOO

Available from specialist nurseries, bare-root bamboos tend to be cheaper than those grown in containers, and most are available via mail order. The drawback is that you will need to plant them as soon as possible to prevent them from drying out and failing to thrive once planted. When you receive them, stand the plants in a bucket or large pot filled with soil or moss, keeping them damp until you are ready to plant. Then prepare your bed by digging it over to loosen any compacted soil, and apply some well-rotted manure or compost.

1 Dig a hole deep enough to fit the whole root ball, and use a fork to loosen the soil at the bottom. Add a layer of well-rotted manure or compost to the base.

2 Unwrap the bamboo, and place it in the hole. Check that the soil marks on the stems (culms) will be at ground level when the bamboo is planted.

3 Keep the plant upright with one hand, and carefully work the excavated soil in between the roots. Fill in the hole gradually and water to remove any air pockets around the roots.

4 Firm the soil with your fingers, pushing it between each of the stems. Water in well, and apply a mulch of rotted manure or composted bark, keeping it clear of the stems.

AFTERCARE AND MAINTENANCE

Grasses rarely need extra irrigation once established as they have adapted to survive periods of drought. Bamboos may need watering for longer, and will need a constant supply of water if grown in containers, so you may wish to invest in an automatic system, such as a seep hose or drip nozzles attached to a hosepipe. An automatic timer will also allow you to regulate watering times.

Apart from watering, bamboos and grasses require very little extra maintenance. In spring, comb out the dead growth from evergreen grasses and sedges with a spring-tined rake or kitchen fork. The dead stems of deciduous grasses have decorative value in winter, but should be cut back in spring.

Cut out dead bamboo stems when you see them and mulch plants every year in spring with rotted manure or composted bark. Leave a carpet of dead foliage beneath the plants, as this contains silica, which bamboos need in order to form wood.

Automate watering to ensure that plants receive enough water to establish successfully.

Use a root barrier to prevent vigorous bamboo plants colonizing the garden.

Controlling bamboos

Bamboos spread via underground root systems or rhizomes that travel horizontally just beneath the soil surface, throwing up new stems as they do so; some can be invasive. To prevent them taking over, dig a narrow trench around your clump and insert a proprietary root barrier of non-perishable material, such as strong plastic, or a wall of slate slabs. Alternatively, use a sharp spade to slice through the roots around your bamboo and dig out and remove the severed roots.

BEAUTIFUL SEEDHEADS

Among the most alluring features of decorative grasses are their seedheads, which can grace a garden from midsummer to winter if you mix and match varieties, and are especially valuable during the winter months when there is little else on offer. Choose a variety of different forms, such as feathery plumes and caterpillar-like brushes.

The best choices for grasses with attractive and interesting seedheads include forms of *Stipa*, *Pennisetum*, and the reed grasses, *Calamagrostis*, as well the larger grasses, such as pampas grass (*Cortaderia*) and the many forms of *Miscanthus*.

Stipa calamagrostis
The feather grass is so named because in late summer it forms beautiful plumes of greenish-white flowers, shaped like giant feathers. These then dry to produce tawny seedheads that persist over winter.

Pennisetum alopecuroides
In late summer, the fountain or foxtail grass bears long stems of pinkish-brown, foxtail-like flowers that dry to form decorative seedheads. It needs a sunny, sheltered site to survive the winter.

Briza Both the annual *Briza minor* and perennial quaking grass, *B. maxima*, produce spear-shaped seedheads that dance in the breeze during summer and autumn. Plant in full sun and any soil – even in wet conditions.

BAMBOO AND GRASS RECIPES

POOL OF COLOUR

Add depth and drama to a garden with differing textures and colours of grasses. The eye lingers on the bands of 'Pink Feather' pampas grass, *Calamagrostis*, *Miscanthus*, and *Pennisetum* in this display. Taller, structural background plants such as *Arundo donax* (a giant reed) and *Stipa gigantea* bring depth to the arrangement.

YOU WILL NEED

1 *Stipa gigantea*
2 *Miscanthus* 'Adagio'
3 *Miscanthus* 'Ferner Osten'
4 *Cortaderia* 'Pink Feather'
5 *Calamagrostis* 'Karl Foerster'
6 *Pennisetum villosum*
7 *Calamagrostis brachytricha*
8 *Pennisetum macrourum*
9 *Pennisetum* 'Fairy Tails'

1 In autumn, dig over the site, removing weeds and compaction. For each sq m (3sq ft), work in a bucketful of rotted organic matter.

2 Buy the plants in spring and set them out, with ripples of grasses leading the eye across to the taller background plants.

3 Add a mulch of gravel around the grasses to reflect light and suppress weeds. Water during dry spells for the first two summers.

JAPANESE-STYLE DISPLAY

Graceful bamboos planted in glazed containers lend an oriental note to a patio scheme. Most require large pots, but you can use smaller ones if you're prepared to repot regularly. In this context, you can also use more invasive types like *Pleioblastus*, as the pots contain the roots' spread. The bamboos will be happy in a partially shaded area.

1 Choose a selection of pots with drainage holes, then add a layer of soil-based compost, such as John Innes No 3, to each pot. Add some slow-release fertilizer granules.

2 Water the plants and then tip them out of their containers. Plant the bamboos in the pots at the same level they were at in their original containers. Firm in the compost around the stems.

3 Water the pots regularly during the growing season. Each spring, remove the top layer of compost and add fresh, mixed with some slow-release fertilizer granules. Repot the plants as necessary.

YOU WILL NEED

1 *Phyllostachys bambusoides* 'Holochrysa'
2 *Pleioblastus variegatus*
3 *Indocalamus tessellatus*
4 *Pleioblastus variegatus* 'Tsuboii'
5 *Fargesia murielae*

FOCUS ON GRASSES

Knit together a range of different grasses to form a spectacular textured border, or mix and match with complementary perennials for a colourful display of flower and foliage forms. The graceful leaves and delicate flowers shimmer and glow when backlit by morning or evening sun, so try to site your border to capture this effect.

Grasses range from lofty giants that stretch up over 2m (6ft) or more to tiny tufts that barely reach ankle height, with a whole variety of sizes in between. Weave a selection of tall types in swathes through a large border using prairie-style planting or use them to form a backdrop in a smaller space. Also integrate evergreen and deciduous grasses for year-round appeal. In summer, the wisps of delicate flowers will appear in a range of colours and contrast with the bold shapes of the leaves. In winter, many deciduous types lose their summer colours but retain their stature, creating interest at a time of year when there is little else on display.

▶ **Mix blue-green** *Helictotrichon sempervirens* with plants of contrasting shapes and colours, such as *Euphorbia* and *Leucanthemum*.

Chasmanthium latifolium 'River Mist'

CHOICE OF GRASSES

Miscanthus Eulalia grasses are deciduous, upright, and drought tolerant; most are fairly large. The flower plumes are borne in late summer.

Pennisetum Deciduous fountain or foxtail grasses have arching foliage and long, soft flowers. Most do not exceed 1m (3ft).

Deschampsia 'Goldtau' is a popular border cultivar, with deciduous dark green leaves and cloud-like sprays of tiny golden summer flowers.

Most grasses need a sunny site to thrive, so choose the brightest spot in your garden for the best display. Most species also like free-draining conditions, and will withstand periods of drought once established. Ideally, plant them in spring to allow the root systems a full season to develop before winter. Although most grasses prefer a sunny site, *Deschampsia* will tolerate some shade and thrives in a range of soil types.

In large borders, weave together a selection of medium-sized and large grasses, such as *Calamagrostis*, *Deschampsia*, *Miscanthus*, and

◄ **In winter**, displays of *Phlomis russeliana*, *Hakonechloa macra* 'Aureola', and *Pennisetum* look beautiful when dusted with frost.

Panicum species, with contrasting perennials such as *Eupatorium*, Michaelmas daisies (*Symphyotrichum*), and *Verbena bonariensis*.

In smaller gardens or at the front of large borders, try a mix of *Calamagrostis brachytricha*, with its beautiful late summer, feather-like plumes, the wispy *Stipa tenuissima*, and silvery-blue *Helictotrichon*. Match these with rusty-orange achilleas, cream *Astrantia major*, and dark red *Hylotelephium* 'Herbstfreude'. Also use the flowing form of *Anemanthele lessoniana* at the edge of a border, to add a sense of movement as it spills over a path or patio.

All the border grasses suit gravel gardens, which also make good seedbeds for annuals. Sprinkle the seeds of *Briza minor*, with its dainty, dangling, summer flowers, through a gravel border for a naturalistic effect; it will self-seed thereafter, repeating the effect year after year. Other annuals to try include *Lagurus ovatus*, or bunny tails, which features furry little pompon blooms, and *Setaria macrostachya*, with its caterpillar-like flowerheads.

PLANTING GRASSES

1 Dig a hole as deep as and a little wider than the container. Place the plant in the hole to check that the top of the root ball will be level with the soil when you plant it out.

2 Water the plant well. Remove it from its container and gently tease out the outermost roots. This encourages them to spread and develop well after planting.

3 Place the plant in the hole and fill in around the root ball with the excavated soil, firming it with your fingers. Water it well using a can with a fine rose. Water regularly until it is established.

4 The dead growth of deciduous grasses can be left over winter; use a spring-tined rake or kitchen fork to remove dead growth from evergreens in early spring.

Anemanthele This knee-high evergreen bears gauzy flowers and arching clumps of foliage with yellow and red tints from autumn to spring.

Stipa Choose popular, wispy-leaved *Stipa tenuissima*, or *S. gigantea*, with evergreen leaves and tall stems of golden, oat-like flowers.

Calamagrostis Most feather reed grasses are good in borders. They bear deciduous upright foliage and feather-like flowerheads.

Helictotrichon Evergreen blue oat grass is steely-blue and a good foil for flowering plants. Its flowers appear from late spring to summer.

Panicum Prairie-type switch grass bears clusters of tiny flowers that float above clumps of wide leaves. Some forms have blue-grey foliage.

USING BULBS EFFECTIVELY

From diminutive winter-flowering snowdrops to the soaring stems of vibrant dahlias in autumn, bulbs, tubers, corms, and rhizomes offer a huge choice of flowers for all seasons, while their diversity of colour and form will enrich any garden.

▶ INFUSING GARDENS WITH SCENT

Many bulbs boast colourful blooms, but a number are also celebrated for their delicious fragrance. Position them at the front of borders or grow them in pots near the house. To create a perfumed paradise, seek out beautiful scents for all seasons, starting in spring with forms of *Narcissus jonquilla*, *N. tazetta*, and *N. poeticus*, as well as hyacinths and bluebells. In summer, select the powerfully scented oriental and longiflorum lilies, or try the turkscap *Lilium martagon* in shady sites. End the year with the autumn-flowering *Crinum* x *powellii*.

Vibrant in scent and colour, the blooms of *Lilium* Golden Splendor Group make beautiful edging for a walkway.

▲ DECORATING LAWNS

Create carpets of colour and texture by planting spring bulbs beneath the turf in autumn. Plant bulbs, such as snake's head fritillaries, in a random pattern to mimic a wildflower meadow, or in a more formal garden, try planting in narrow lines to create stripes of delicate flowers. Experiment with colour combinations: choose a limited range of pastel shades, or plan for an explosion of colour. Leave the bulbs to die down naturally before mowing in late spring and the plants will then multiply to give even greater displays in future years.

Soften a formal, structured scheme by planting lines of delicate *Anemone blanda* 'White Splendour' and 'Blue Mist'.

◄ MAKING SEASONAL DISPLAYS

Inject colour into your patio displays throughout the year with a range of bulbs for different seasons. Some, such as snowdrops, will flower year after year if planted in a cool spot; team them with other woodlanders, such as small ferns and hellebores. Other diminutive early-flowering bulbs, such as irises and species tulips, are perfect for a sink or trough as part of an alpine collection. Grow dwarf narcissi and *Muscari* in windowboxes and wall pots and combine these with heucheras, violas, and evergreen grasses for colour from winter to late spring. In summer, surround a central planting of tall dahlias or cannas, and edge with trailing plants.

For a late summer display, plant striking dahlias with the feathery fronds of *Pennisetum orientale* and arching stems of *Gaura lindheimeri*.

▲ CREATING TROPICAL EFFECTS

Tender bulbs grown for their sparkling blooms, such as dahlias, cannas, and gladioli, fit perfectly into planting schemes that mirror the landscapes of the Far East or Caribbean. Plant them in late spring in free-draining soil or in containers and combine their vibrant flowers with a foil of lush foliage. Some hardy bulbs work particularly well as part of this kind of themed display.

Create a tropical paradise using cannas with their flame-like flowers and colourful leaves. Intersperse with heleniums and rudbeckias.

◄ WELCOMING IN SPRING

Gracing beds and borders with sunny yellows, hot pinks, sizzling reds, and cool blues, spring bulbs are a great way to kick off the growing season. Some, such as snowdrops, will appear once winter comes to a close, and will be followed in quick succession throughout the season by dwarf irises, crocuses, and daffodils. By the middle of spring, the garden will be ablaze with hyacinths, fritillaries, and the queens of the show, tulips. Underplant taller types with spring bedding in complementary shades.

For an eye-catching display of colour, plant up pots of bright pink, red, and yellow tulips and mix and match them with violas, saxifrage, and grasses.

SELECTING AND PLANTING BULBS

Bulbs are very easy to grow; simply plant them a few months before they are due to bloom. Most prefer full sun and free-draining soil but some will thrive in shady sites beneath deciduous trees.

This diverse group of plants offers interest almost all year round, from snowdrops at the end of winter to colchicums and nerines in autumn, with a vast array of bulbs in bloom in between. For a year-round display, start with colourful spring bulbs, such as tulips and daffodils, and mix in some alliums, which will flower on the cusp of the new season, their pompon blooms providing dramatic accents in beds and borders. Lilies are the stars of summer, with their large, fragrant blooms in shades from cool white to dark maroon stealing the show. From midsummer, spice up your garden with tender dahlias, gladioli, cannas, and long-flowering Peruvian lilies (*Alstroemeria*), and end the year with a display of delicate nerines, if you have a sunny, sheltered garden to suit them, or cyclamen and colchicums in colder spots.

Label bulbs planted in pots so that you can identify them before they burst into flower.

WHAT IS A BULB?

It can be confusing when you discover that the word "bulb" is often used as a blanket term for any plant that has an underground food-storage organ. As well as true bulbs, there are three other forms: corms, rhizomes, and tubers.

Each type of bulb has evolved to cope with a variety of growing conditions and allows the plants to survive when dormant and during adverse conditions, such as prolonged periods of drought.

◄ True bulbs

Daffodils, tulips, and *Eucomis* (*see left*) are all true bulbs. The bulbs are made of leaves layered like an onion, covered with a protective papery skin or tunic. Lily bulbs are looser in form and lack a skin – plant them on their sides to prevent water seeping in and rotting them.

◄ Rhizomes

The most common rhizomatous plants are bearded irises (*see left*), although Dutch and reticulata irises are bulbs. Rhizomes have a swollen root that grows horizontally near the soil surface and produces several buds along it which then develop into leaves and flower stems.

◄ Corms

Gladiolus and crocus (*see left*) are typical corms. These are formed by the swollen bases of the plants' stems and are more rounded in shape than true bulbs. They produce one or two buds at the top, and tiny cormlets grow around the base.

◄ Tubers

Tubers fall into two categories: root tubers, such as dahlias, which are basically enlarged roots, and stem tubers, like begonias, which are swollen underground stems similar to rhizomes (*see left*). Tubers produce buds or eyes along their length, and each can form a new plant.

WHEN TO PLANT

Spring flowers
Plant spring-flowering bulbs, such as daffodils, tulips, grape hyacinths (*Muscari*), crocuses, and other hardy types in autumn to overwinter and then flower the following year. Most can be planted early on in the season, but leave tulips until late autumn to minimize the risk of plants developing the disease tulip fire.

Summer flowers
Alliums, which flower in early summer, are best planted in autumn, but the majority of other summer bulbs should be started off in spring. Plant tender types, such as dahlia tubers and gladioli corms, in pots indoors to be moved out later or plant outside when the soil has warmed up and the worst frosts have passed.

Autumn and winter flowers
Plant nerine bulbs in a warm, sheltered, free-draining site or in a container in autumn to flower the following year. Cyclamen and colchicums are also planted in autumn. Snowdrops are an exception: plant them after they have flowered when still in leaf, known as "in the green".

PLANTING IN A BORDER

Choose healthy, disease-free, firm bulbs and select a site with free-draining soil. If you have heavy clay either dig in plenty of grit and well-rotted manure a month or so before you start, or plant your bulbs in pots. Bulbs can be planted *en masse* in a large trench or hole or naturalized in grass (see p.162). Mark the area where you have planted your bulbs to prevent digging them up later by mistake.

1 Dig a hole to a depth of about 3–4 times the height of your bulbs and large enough to accommodate them at the correct planting distances. Lightly fork over the bottom.

2 Apply some granular fertilizer to soil in the hole. Then set out the bulbs with the pointed growing tips facing upwards. Discard any that are soft or show signs of disease.

3 Fill in the hole with soil, taking care not to damage the growing tips. Firm it down with your hands to push out any air pockets around the bulbs.

4 Cover the area with chicken wire held down with pins or stones to prevent animals digging the bulbs up. Remove the wire when the first shoots appear in early spring.

PLANTING DEPTHS AND LAYERING

For bulbs to flower successfully, you need to plant them at the optimum depth. Most, including daffodils, grape hyacinths, and alliums, should be planted at about three times their own depth (*see below*).

However, there are exceptions. Tulips prefer deeper planting, at four times their own depth, while cyclamen species should be planted with the top of the tuber at, or just below, the soil surface.

Bulbs make beautiful container plants and by layering two or three different types in one large pot you can either produce a sequential display or, with careful planning, one that will flower simultaneously for a big burst of colour.

To create a long-lasting display, place a layer of compost or bulb fibre at the bottom of a pot. Lay some tulip bulbs on it, then add more compost on top and set small crocus bulbs on this. Finish off by adding the final layer of compost. Store the pot in a sheltered spot and move into the sun in spring.

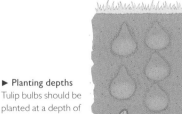

Daffodil   Tulip

▶ **Planting depths**
Tulip bulbs should be planted at a depth of about four times their height; daffodils should be planted at three times theirs.

▶ **Layering early**
and late bulbs together, such as crocus and tulips, will create a longer display.

AFTER FLOWERING

After spring bulbs have bloomed, remove the flowerheads to prevent them setting seed, and apply a tomato fertilizer. Allow the foliage to die down naturally before cutting it off. Many bulbs will bulk up year after year to produce large clumps, but tulips may stop flowering if they are not lifted every year after the leaves have died down. Dig them up carefully with a fork and remove any diseased bulbs. Clean the compost from the healthy bulbs and store in paper bags or boxes in a cool dry place. Replant them in late autumn. If large swathes of snowdrops have developed, you can lift and divide them in spring after they have flowered. For further dividing advice see pages 332–333. Lift tender bulbs, such as dahlias, begonias, and gladioli before the frosts (see p.165).

NATURALIZING BULBS

Decorate your lawn with a sprinkling of colourful bulbs. Arrange them in random groups or swathes, or opt for ordered stripes across the lawn (see p.158). You could also plant them in rings around the base of large trees or shrubs. Choose robust types, such as snowdrops, daffodils, or crocuses, which can compete successfully with the grass and spread over time, creating a colourful carpet of blooms.

Before planting in autumn, remove perennial weeds, such as dandelions, and mow the grass. If you are planting bulbs over a wide area, scatter them across the lawn and plant each individually – a bulb planter will make this job easier.

Plant smaller areas by lifting a section of turf. Use a sharp spade to cut an "H" shape into the grass. Holding the

Gently push bulbs into the soil, ensuring that you plant them at the correct depth and provide them with enough space to spread.

spade horizontally, slice under the turf and carefully roll it back to reveal the soil. Add a small amount of fertilizer and space the bulbs out on the soil; you may need to dig deeper to accommodate larger bulbs such as daffodils. Gently replace the flaps of turf, firm down gently, and water well.

UNUSUAL VARIETIES

Create a talking point by growing a range of unusual bulbs in borders or containers for a striking mix of foliage and flower forms. Seek out specialist suppliers for the widest choice, and ensure that your site and soil are suitable; growing bulbs in containers will allow you to control the growing conditions more easily.

In spring, try the elegant maroon or cream bells of the stately bulb *Fritillaria persica* (*bottom left*). Unlike its diminutive cousin the snake's head fritillary (*F. meleagris*), this large plant grows up to 1.5m (5ft) in height, creating a dramatic statement in a border. *Triteleia hyacinthina* (*top left*) is smaller but equally impressive, producing umbels of starry white flowers on slim stems.

For summer colour, try *Dichelostemma* (*top right*) with its tubular bell-like blooms in reds, pinks, and purples, and the elegant corn lily, or *Ixia viridiflora* (*bottom right*), which produces dainty star-shaped blooms. Also add a few brightly coloured *Sparaxis* hybrids, which come in an assortment of fiery shades and in pots, beds, or borders are guaranteed to turn heads throughout the summer months.

Triteleia hyacinthina

Dichelostemma ida-maia

Fritillaria persica

Ixia viridiflora

BULB RECIPES

SPRING HOT SPOT

Fire up your late spring garden with a range of hot-hued tulips, including orange-red 'Ballerina' and pinky-red 'Jimmy', mixed with sizzling euphorbias. Add a cooling note with the dainty white bell-shaped flowers of a Solomon's seal (*Polygonatum*), held on graceful arched stems. Plant in an area that receives some sun.

YOU WILL NEED

1 *Tulipa* 'Ballerina'

2 *Polygonatum* x *hybridum*

3 *Tulipa* 'Jimmy'

4 *Euphorbia griffithii* 'Fireglow'

1 Prepare the border in early autumn by digging in well-rotted organic matter. Then plant the *Polygonatum* at the back of the border.

2 Plant the *Euphorbia* about 45–60cm (18–24in) in front, leaving a space for the tulips. Wait until late autumn to plant the tulips.

3 Plant groups of *Tulipa* 'Ballerina' between the perennials, and *T.* 'Jimmy' in front. The bulbs will then appear in mid-spring.

CONTRASTING COLOURS

Mixing and matching spring bulbs in a riot of bright colours makes a dazzling display beneath a blossoming cherry or crab apple tree. Use flowering perennials, such as primulas and saxifrages, to complement your designs, and interplant with perennials that bloom later, so that their foliage disguises the dying leaves of the bulbs. Lift the tulips after flowering and store the bulbs in a dry area.

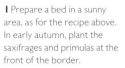

YOU WILL NEED

1 *Tulipa* 'Ballade'

2 *Tulipa* 'Golden Apeldoorn'

3 *Hyacinthus*

4 *Muscari*

5 *Saxifraga*

6 Purple primulas

1 Prepare a bed in a sunny area, as for the recipe above. In early autumn, plant the saxifrages and primulas at the front of the border.

2 Plant the *Muscari* and hyacinth bulbs at the same time as the perennials, but leave gaps for the tulips and mark the planting areas.

3 In late autumn plant the tulips between the markers for the hyacinths and *Muscari*. The border will be in full bloom from mid-spring.

DAZZLING DAHLIAS

Prized for their bright, bold, and extraordinarily diverse blooms, dahlias are impossible to ignore. Choose from fiery oranges and reds, cool whites, and pretty pinks to boost your beds, borders, and container displays from midsummer to late autumn.

Dahlia 'Hillcrest Royal'

Comprising so many different forms, dahlias offer something for everyone. Those with a penchant for large, dramatic focal plants will be drawn to the giant-flowered types that exceed 25cm (10in) in diameter. For more relaxed or informal designs, opt for the small or medium-sized blooms, and if you are planting up pots, try the miniatures, which measure just 10cm (4in). In addition, dahlias are divided into ten main groups that reflect the size, shape, and structure of their flowerheads (*see below*).

Most dahlias bloom from midsummer to the first frosts, providing a long season of colour and texture. There are tall types in each of the flower categories that make excellent back-of-the-border plants, with some reaching up to 1.5m (5ft) in height. By

TYPES OF DAHLIA

Single Flowers are usually open with a single set of petals surrounding a central disc. They are usually less than 10cm (4in) across.

Anemone The fully double anemone flowers have two sets of petals surrounding a dense group of shorter tubular petals in the centre.

Ball These fully double flowers are ball-shaped or slightly flattened at the top and produce densely packed, almost tubular petals.

Water lily With broad, overlapping petals that resemble those of a water lily, these fully double flowers have no central disc.

Decorative Flowers are fully double with no central disc, and have a domed appearance. The petals are often tear-shaped or oval.

positioning them among other late-flowering grasses and perennials you can also disguise the stakes needed to support their stems.

For pots or the front of a border, choose the compact forms. Look for the label 'dwarf bedder', which describes plants that do not exceed 60cm (2ft) in height. The gallery dahlias, with flowers named after

◀ **Let your prima-donnas** take centre stage by setting them against a foil of cool green foliage. Dahlias' vivid blooms perform their star turn just when most summer flowers are fading.

famous artists and art movements, such as *D.* 'Art Deco' and *D.* 'Gallery Cézanne', fall into this group. Remember, too, that many small or miniature flowers are held on tall plants, so check labels carefully before buying.

Choose a range of flower types to add interest to your planting scheme – try pairing tiny pompons with large cactus blooms for an exciting contrast. As well as their compelling flowers, many dahlias offer colourful foliage into the bargain. The dark bronze leaves of the 'Bishop' range, for example, are well worth including in borders and container displays.

Plant dahlias in a sunny site with sufficient space to allow them to grow to their full potential. Plant the tubers in the ground a few weeks before the final frosts in late spring, or grow plants in pots indoors, harden them off by placing them outside during the day for a couple of weeks, and plant out when the frosts have passed.

OVERWINTERING TUBERS

By lifting your dahlia tubers, storing them carefully indoors over winter, and planting them out again in spring, you can enjoy their beautiful flowers in your garden year after year. Check the stored tubers regularly during the winter; if any mildew or rot has developed, cut it out with a clean, sharp knife.

1 After the first autumn frosts have blackened the foliage, trim stems back to 15cm (6in) with secateurs. Use a fork to lift the tubers, label them, and store upside down for two weeks.

2 Once the tubers have dried out, place them the right way up in boxes of dry vermiculite or coir and keep them in a cool, dry, frost-free place over winter.

3 In spring, plant the tubers in pots of fresh compost and grow on inside. Plant outside when the frosts have passed. For tall dahlias, add a stake when planting.

Pompon A smaller version of the ball dahlias but with a more spherical shape, pompons are never more than 5cm (2in) in diameter.

Collerette Similar to single dahlias with broad outer petals, but distinguishable by the inner "collar" of smaller petals around a central disc.

Cactus The narrow, pointed petals of the fully double flowers are straight or curled inwards, giving a spiky, spherical appearance.

Semi-cactus The spiky, pointed petals of the semi-cactus dahlia have broader bases than cactus types and curve at the tips.

Miscellaneous This broad category includes dahlias that do not fit into any of the other groups, including peony, lilliput, and orchid types.

EASY-GOING ANNUALS AND BIENNIALS

They may be short-lived, but annuals and biennials make up for their brief spell in the limelight with a wealth of dazzling flowers. Some also sport colourful foliage, and most are easy to grow from seed, sown direct or indoors.

► CREATING FLEETING COMBINATIONS

Shrubs and perennials can leave gardens looking under-planted until they become more established, but with a sprinkling of annuals and biennials you can fill your borders with blooms without cramping the permanent plants. Hardy annuals can be sown where required for almost instant effect – although they may not grow if sown too close to shrubs – while biennials have a two-year life cycle and give colour early the following year. Many annuals and biennials, including love-in-a-mist (*Nigella*) and forget-me-nots (*Myosotis*), self-seed freely; you may only need to sow once to enjoy them in your garden for many years to come.

Summer annuals, such as these chrysanthemums (*Chrysanthemum carinatum*) and pot marigolds (*Calendula officinalis*) grow fast and bulk out beautifully to fill bare ground.

▲ MAKING FOILS OF FOLIAGE

Although the flowering annuals draw the eye, foliage plants provide equally compelling displays. Multi-coloured coleus, with patterned leaves in rich purples, reds, yellows, and greens, are a match for any bloom, while tall *Perilla frutescens* provides the perfect backdrop to colourful flowers. Silver-leaved and trailing annuals are useful foils for container displays, or for something a little more dramatic, consider *Euphorbia marginata*, with its tall stems of green and white leaves, and the exotic hand-shaped foliage of *Ricinus communis*.

The leaves of coleus (Solenostemon) come in a huge variety of shades and patterns – try planting several together to create a riot of colour in a border.

▲ GOING WILD

Meadow planting is increasingly popular, not just because it has a natural beauty, but because it is low-maintenance once established – simply cut back once or twice a year (see p.341). The brightest and most beautiful annual flowers thrive on very poor soils, so some may require you to strip off the topsoil before sowing your seed mixes. You can also sow annual mixes to add sparkle to perennial meadow flower displays, creating a backdrop of subtle colour topped up with bright poppies and corn marigolds.

This small orchard is underplanted with meadow-style annuals including poppies (*Papaver* species) and love-in-a-mist (*Nigella damascena*).

◄ PLANTING CLASSIC CONTAINERS

The long flowering season and colourful blooms of annuals make them the perfect plants for pots and baskets. In spring, garden centres are brimming with the traditional favourites, including petunias, impatiens, and pelargoniums in every shade under the sun. However, most of these are tender, so keep your displays under cover until early summer to avoid losses. Although it's tempting to cram your containers with lots of different flowers, their effect will be lost if they're all competing for attention. To prevent this, select one feature plant, such as a white-flowered marguerite, and team it with matching flowers and foliage plants.

Cascading lobelia with its mass of tiny blue flowers and cool white impatiens create a beautiful pastel container scheme with a pink fuchsia.

◄ BRIGHTENING THE GLOOM

Most annuals and biennials will not burst into bloom unless flooded with sunlight, but a select few thrive in some shade. Natural woodlanders such as foxgloves grow best in the dappled light beneath deciduous trees, while annuals that flourish in part-shade include sweetly scented tobacco plants (*Nicotiana*), colourful busy lizzies (*Impatiens*), and violas with autumn-, winter-, spring-, and summer-flowering forms, so you're sure to find one that will suit your conditions.

Nestling beneath a cluster of silver birches, foxgloves (*Digitalis* species) inject a splash of eye-catching colour into this small woodland garden.

SELECTING AND PLANTING ANNUALS AND BIENNIALS

Most annuals and biennials are easy to grow from seed, providing an inexpensive way to fill your garden with a sea of colour. If you don't have the space or time to sow seeds, choose from the wide selection of young plants.

Buying young annual plants is the quickest way to fill containers and borders with colour.

You will find a huge choice of annual and biennial seeds online or via mail order from specialist suppliers. Hardy annuals, such as love-in-a-mist (*Nigella*) and pot marigolds (*Calendula*) can be sown directly outside in mid-spring; sow them where you want them to flower. Sow tender and half-hardy types in early spring in a heated greenhouse or on a windowsill indoors. For these

you will need seed trays or pots, seed compost, and some patience, as they must be nurtured until they are ready to go outside after the frosts (see *pp.328–329*). If you sow with care, you can be rewarded with 20–50 plants or more per packet.

Plug plants offer another economical way of purchasing annuals and biennials. These are seedlings that need potting

on into larger containers or trays when you receive them, but they cost much less than mature plants. Specialist suppliers offer a good range, although not as extensive as the choice of seeds. Finally, you can buy mature plants, which provide instant effects and are ideal if you want just a few plants to fill a summer container, or to add colour to a border.

Shade Plant up a partially shady site with the blue flowers of *Myosotis sylvatica* 'Music'.

Sun A colourful mix of *Papaver rhoeas* will brighten up a sunny border or meadow.

PROVIDING IDEAL CONDITIONS

There is a range of annuals and biennials for almost any location, so select those that suit your site.

To encourage the best performance from your plants you will need to provide them with sufficient light; browse through a seed catalogue and you will find that the majority of annuals listed prefer to grow in a sunny position. Colourful types, including marigolds, lobelia, petunias, and asters, will light up a sunny spot with their striking blooms. However, there are a few annuals, including busy lizzie (*Impatiens*), nasturtiums, and fibrous-rooting begonias, that are happy in partial shade, while foxgloves (*Digitalis*) and forget-me-nots (*Myosotis, see left*) are among the biennials that will thrive in partially shaded sites.

The majority of sun-lovers prefer average to free-draining soil, and can

tolerate periods of drought. For example, cornflowers and annual poppies (*see left*) are ideal for a meadow on a large expanse of dry, sandy soil. True annual wild flowers perform best on infertile soil. If you want to grow wild flowers and your soil is too rich, you will find that grasses and weeds dominate, and the flowers will not be able to compete. To remedy this, strip off the top layer of soil before sowing, as this usually contains the highest levels of nutrients.

Plants from tropical areas that are grown as annuals for bedding, such as coleus (*Solenostemon*) and heliotrope, as well as woodlanders such as foxgloves, prefer moist soil conditions. Also, annual bedding plants that are used for summer container displays, such as petunias, asters, and marigolds, will perform best when they are grown in moist potting compost.

EASY SEEDS

Growing annuals and biennials from seed is not difficult as long as you can provide the right conditions at crucial stages of their growth – check individual seed packets for site and soil advice. However, if you are new to sowing seeds and want to guarantee success, put the following at the top of your list: hardy nasturtiums, pot marigolds, love-in-a-mist, Californian poppies, English marigolds, *Iberis*, and *Cerinthe major*. These are among the most dependable hardy plants. Sow outdoors where they are to flower in free-draining soil and a sunny site to promote a good display of blooms.

Sow the following easy tender seeds indoors in early spring for a sparkling collection of summer flowers: annual dahlias, cosmos, petunias (select the upright plants as the trailing forms are less reliable), *Bidens*, *Tagetes*, and zinnias.

SELF-SEEDING PLANTS

Annuals and biennials that self-seed either true to type or with minor variations:

Agrostemma (Corn cockle)
Calendula officinalis (Marigold)
Centaurea cyanus (Cornflower)
Clarkia amoena (Satin flower)
Collinsia bicolor (Chinese houses)
Digitalis purpurea (Foxglove)
Eschscholzia californica (Californian poppy)
Hesperis matronalis (Dame's violet, sweet rocket)
Lunaria annua (Honesty)
Malcolmia
Myosotis (Forget-me-not)
Oenothera biennis (Evening primrose)
Papaver (Poppy)
Silene armeria (Campion)
Tropaeolum majus (Nasturtium)
Verbascum (Mullein)

SOWING BIENNIALS

Spring-flowering hardy biennials, such as wallflowers (*Erysimum cheiri*), should be sown between spring and early summer in the year before they bloom. They grow best in a sunny site and free-draining soil, so dig plenty of organic matter, such as well-rotted manure or compost, into heavy clay soils in the autumn before sowing.

1 Remove any weeds and stones from the soil before sowing, and rake it over to ensure an even surface. Sow seed thinly and evenly and then water using a watering can with a fine rose.

2 When seedlings reach 5cm (2in) tall and have a few leaves, lift them carefully with a fork. Retain plenty of soil around the roots. Water the soil around the plants thoroughly an hour before lifting.

3 Replant 15–20cm (6–8in) apart, firming them in with your fingers. Keep them well watered in summer. If they are not in their final position, you can lift and replant them again in autumn.

4 Plant them out in sunny borders with tulips and other spring bulbs, or in a container. Many biennials do not like excessive winter rain, so protect them with a cloche during wet periods.

Sow meadow mixes on poor soils and in full sun for a dazzling flower display.

PLANT CARE

Watering young seedlings is vital if you want them to grow into mature, healthy plants, but once they are established, many require little extra irrigation except during long periods of drought. The exceptions are those grown in containers, which will need watering daily during hot spells, and every few days at other times.

Feed container-grown annuals with slow-release fertilizer granules when you plant them. This one application should provide them with sufficient nutrients for most of the season, but if displays start to flag at the end of summer, top them up with a dose of liquid feed.

Remove faded blooms regularly as this encourages the plants to form flowers rather than putting their energies into making seeds. Don't deadhead the flowers if you want to collect seeds to sow next year.

Zinnia 'Carousel' is attractive to beneficial insects.

FLOWERS FOR BEES AND BUTTERFLIES

Many annuals and biennials are rich in nectar and attract pollinating insects such as bees, butterflies, hoverflies, and moths. These beneficial insects are especially useful in productive gardens, where pollinators are needed to set fruits, such as tomatoes and strawberries, and seeds like broad and runner beans.

Another good reason to stock your garden with insect-friendly plants is to maximize bee food supplies, as worldwide populations of these vital insects are in serious decline as a result of the loss of their preferred flower-rich habitat, and any extra help you can give them will benefit your garden too. The best nectar-rich plants to include in your displays are spring-flowering *Iberis*, sweet alyssum (*Lobularia maritima*) and sweet williams (*Dianthus barbatus*). Cornflowers (*Centaurea cyanus*), corn cockles (*Agrostemma githago*), and other meadow flowers, the yellow and white poached-egg plant (*Limnathes douglasii*), pot and French marigolds (*Calendula* and *Tagetes*), Californian poppies (*Eschscholzia*), *Cerinthe major*, and *Phacelia tanacetifolia* produce blooms for insects throughout summer.

CUT FLOWERS

Some annuals make stunning cut flowers for the home. Combine *Moluccella laevis*, with its tall spikes of unusual green flowers, with larkspur (*Consolida ajacis*), and try the annual aster *Callistephus chinensis* in late summer and autumn arrangements, or *Bracteantha*, which can be used fresh or dried.

Moluccella laevis (*top left*) The bells of Ireland make the perfect foil for colourful flowers. Grow in full sun in moist, free-draining soil. Chill the seed for five days in the fridge and soak before sowing.
Consolida ajacis (larkspur, *top right*) This pretty annual looks like a dwarf delphinium with spikes of blue, pink, or white flowers. Sow seed in spring and enjoy vases of blooms all summer.
Callistephus chinensis (*bottom left*) Sow seeds of the annual or China aster indoors in early spring. Plant out after the frosts in a sunny site with moist, free-draining soil. Buy long-stemmed varieties for indoor displays.
Xerochrysum bracteatum (*bottom right*) The everlasting flower is so called because it will literally last for years when dried. Sow the seed indoors in early spring and plant out after the frosts in a sunny site and free-draining soil.

Moluccella laevis

Consolida ajacis

Callistephus chinensis

Xerochrysum bracteatum

ANNUALS RECIPES

CREATIVE MIX

Annuals can be used as excellent fillers for the gaps in borders between groups of perennials that have yet to become established. Here, orange French marigolds (*Tagetes*), leafy lime-green *Ipomoea batatas*, and white cosmos brighten up a sunny border of Shasta daisies (*Leucanthemum*), penstemons, and dahlias.

YOU WILL NEED

1 White *Cosmos bipinnatus*

2 *Penstemon*

3 *Tagetes*

4 *Leucanthemum*

5 *Ipomoea batatas* 'Sweet Caroline Light Green'

6 Yellow dahlias

1 In early spring sow cosmos, *Ipomoea*, and marigold seeds indoors in pots or trays. Keep the seedlings in a warm place, and water them frequently.

2 When all danger of frost has passed, plant out the seedlings in a sunny border, and protect them against slug and snail attacks.

3 Water well while plants are establishing; they will cope with some drought later in summer. Apply a liquid fertilizer if the annuals start to flag.

SUMMER BRIGHTS

Sun-loving annuals and tender perennials that are grown as annuals, such as *Pelargonium* and *Osteospermum*, will thrive in the shelter of a south-facing brick wall. The wall will also absorb heat from the sun during the day and radiate it back out during the evening, emitting even more of the heat these plants enjoy. Combine bright reds with yellows for a fiery display, together with blue nemesias and the leafy *Helichrysum* to provide a contrasting foil to the hot shades.

YOU WILL NEED

1 *Begonia* 'Waterfall Encanto Orange'

2 *Nemesia* Golden Eye

3 *Pelargonium* 'Horizon Deep Scarlet'

4 *Helichrysum petiolare*

5 *Osteospermum* 'Banana Symphony'

1 In late spring, buy young plants or "plugs" and grow them on indoors. After the frosts have passed, fill large pots with multi-purpose compost.

2 Leave a gap of about 10cm (4in) between the compost and pot rim, and add some slow-release fertilizer granules.

3 Plant up, setting the smallest plants and cascading foliage at the front of the pots. Water the plants every other day in summer.

STRIKING SUNFLOWERS

For many, a love affair with sunflowers begins at an early age when, as children, we watch them grow from tiny seeds into towering giants. Many artists have been inspired by their graphic blooms, while the sturdy stems and cheerful, open flowers are great for cutting. In addition, the seeds offer a rich source of food for birds.

Helianthus annuus

Sunflowers have been bred to be tall plants, measuring 2.4–4.6m (8–15ft) in height, with heavy heads held on sturdy stems punctuated with rough, heart-shaped leaves. However, smaller cultivars are also available, with many dwarf varieties growing to just 30cm (12in). The classic golden petals and chocolate-brown centres are not the only colours on offer. For a more sophisticated palette, choose from pale cream, dusky pink, or dark, smouldering maroon blooms.

To form a picture of the conditions sunflowers enjoy, just think of sun-drenched fields of golden flowers in the south of France. Use this image

TYPES OF SUNFLOWER

Multi-stemmed varieties Ranging in size from towering giants to more compact types, these have a branching habit and produce an abundance of slightly smaller blooms than the single-stemmed plants.

Double-flowered The cushion-like flowers are more rounded in appearance than those with single blooms. Good choices include yellow 'Teddy Bear', orange 'Golden Cheer', and red 'Double Dandy'.

Dwarf varieties Ideal for the front of a sunny border or in pots, the dwarf ranges come in an assortment of colours, including shades of yellow, cream, orange, and red. They measure up to 60cm (24in) in height.

Tall single stem Grow incredibly tall varieties, such as 'Giant Russian' and 'Titan', which rise up to 3m (10ft) and 3.6m (12ft) respectively. These types produce a single large flower at the top of each pole-like stem.

Bi-coloured Among the most popular are those that resemble Catherine wheels, with rings of colour radiating from the centre. 'Pastiche' is a pale-coloured form, while 'Florenza' sports dark red and cream blooms.

Cream-flowered For an elegant border, select a pale cream form. 'Vanilla Ice' and 'Italian White' are both tall varieties, while 'Buttercream' has yellow-tinted flowers and will only reach about 1m (3ft) in height.

Dark-flowered Strikingly different, these are popular for their rich red, maroon, or brown flowers. Choose 'Earthwalker' for its terracotta and brown blooms, claret-coloured 'Ruby Sunset', or dark maroon 'Black Magic'.

as inspiration and plant bold swathes of blooms. Group them with other late-flowering sun-lovers, such as *Echinops*, *Kniphofia*, *Veronicastrum virginicum*, hardy salvias, and ornamental grasses, including species of *Stipa*, *Miscanthus*, and *Panicum*.

In smaller gardens, opt for the dwarf or medium-sized varieties. Sunflowers with small blooms look best in borders, where giant-flowered types can look overbearing. Use 1m (3ft) high sunflowers in colours to match your designs at the back of a sunny informal or wildlife scheme, or line up compact types to edge formal beds or fill a parterre. Sunflowers make good

container specimens too. Dwarf types are the obvious choice, but taller plants can be equally effective in large pots. Try them with an edging of annual millet (*Pennisetum glaucum* 'Purple Baron') and ferny *Lotus maculatus* for a contrast in form and texture.

Sunflowers are best sown from seed in pots in early spring (see *right*), but they can also be sown directly in the ground in mid-spring in a sunny, sheltered spot. Guard against slugs, and bird-proof your seedbed with netting until plants are about 10cm (4in) tall. Stake sunflowers in windy sites, tying them in regularly as they grow.

PLANTING SUNFLOWERS

1 Fill small pots with seed compost and make a hole in the centre with your finger. Place one seed in each hole and then cover over. Ensure pots have drainage holes or use biodegradable types.

2 Water with a can fitted with a fine rose to protect the delicate seedlings from damage. Keep the seed pots in a warm, frost-free place during germination.

3 Plant out seedlings once they reach about 15cm (6in) tall, when the danger of frost has passed. Support taller varieties with canes, especially in exposed sites.

4 Dwarf sunflowers are ideal for patio containers; taller varieties are best planted direct in sunny borders. Keep plants well watered until they are fully established. Mature plants will cope with some drought.

◄ **Brighten up your border** with a bold-coloured mix of medium-sized sunflowers, *Salvia*, lilies, and *Tropaeolum*. Use whites and complementary blues as a foil to the bright flowers.

WATER GARDENING

Water enhances a garden with graphic reflections, sparkles of light, and a whole range of diverse plants that thrive in and around ponds and pools. Combine colourful deciduous plants with a few evergreens for year-round interest.

▶ DRESSING UP FORMAL FEATURES

Formal water features require restraint. Choose just one or two plants to add interest to a raised pool, rather than cramming in a whole range of different types. Match the flat pads and elegant flowers of water lilies with the dramatic vertical leaves of horsetails or miniature reeds to create a sophisticated scheme. Alternatively, use a basket of beautiful spear-shaped foliage, such as *Pontederia cordata* to create a focal point in an otherwise clear pool.

To keep the water in your formal feature clean and free of algae, try adding a black dye, which will inhibit the growth of weeds and accentuate plant reflections; some shade from the leaves of water lilies will help too (see *pp.180–181*).

The sleek, geometric lines of this raised pond provide the perfect backdrop for the architectural reed foliage. Lily pads decorate the water's surface with elegant patterns.

▲ MAKING A HOME FOR FISH

Fish help to bring a pond to life, but many feed on aquatic plants so choose tough greenery that will regenerate after being nibbled. Good choices include grassy, clump-forming *Acorus calamus*, marsh marigolds (*Caltha*), and pickerel weed (*Pontederia*), which will also provide cover from herons and other predators. Site plants carefully in aquatic baskets topped with well-washed pea gravel.

The floating foliage of water lilies (*Nymphaea*) provides fish with much-needed shade and protection.

▲ PLANTING BEAUTIFUL BOGS

Bog and moisture-loving plants include a compelling range with brightly coloured flowers and dramatic foliage. A natural pond will be edged with the damp soil these plants require, but if your conditions are too dry, make a bog garden by digging out an area and lining it with perforated plastic to help retain moisture. In spring, edge your pond with a range of flowering plants, such as primulas, teamed with a carpet of low-growing bugle (*Ajuga reptans* 'Multicolor'). If space allows, spectacular displays can be created by combining the massive leaves of a *Gunnera* with vivid red or pink *Astilbe* and purple-leaved *Filipendula rubra*.

Create a kaleidoscope of colour around a pond with the bright red flower spikes of *Astilbe*, variegated hostas, and spiky irises.

◀ INTRODUCING SMALL SCHEMES

You don't have to deny yourself a water feature if you have just a small patio or balcony garden. A watertight glazed container filled with a dwarf water lily or an arum lily (*Zantedeschia aethiopica*) will add a touch of class to a modern garden design, or opt for a more informal barrel pool, easily constructed from an old barrel lined with butyl. Plant it with a selection of compact aquatics, such as ragged robin (*Lychnis flos-cuculi*) and marsh marigolds (*Caltha palustris*), opting for a good mix of foliage and flowers and taking care not to overwhelm the feature.

Add a new dimension to a small garden with a pool planted with iris (*Iris laevigata*) and water forget-me-nots (*Myosotis scorpioides*).

◀ CREATING A WILDLIFE HAVEN

Any amount of water will attract wildlife, including insects, frogs and toads, birds, and small mammals. To create the most attractive and safe environment, ensure that one side of your pool slopes down into the water so that creatures can get in and out easily, or use containers in and around a raised feature to act as stepping stones. Protect aquatic creatures from predators with marginals for cover, and create a refuge for land animals by edging at least half the pond with bog plants. Although native aquatics will give your pond a naturalistic look, some, like *Iris pseudacorus* and the bulrush *Typha latifolia*, are very invasive. Instead, look out for better-behaved compact varieties, and add oxygenating plants to keep the water clear.

Plant a wide variety of marginals and bog plants, such as these irises, to provide shelter and nesting places for creatures living in and around your pond.

SELECTING AND PLANTING WATER PLANTS

Caring for aquatic plants is not difficult and after planting many take care of themselves, although in small ponds, vigorous types may need dividing occasionally, and you will have to remove pond weeds.

Before planting a pond, check that your favourite plants suit its size and location. Site ponds and water features away from overhanging trees as these may cast too much shade for your plants to thrive. The fallen leaves in autumn also produce harmful toxins as they decompose in the water. Ideal plants for small ponds include marsh marigolds (*Caltha palustris*), *Sagittaria*, *Butomus*, the corkscrew rush *Juncus effusus* f. *spiralis*, and dwarf water lilies, as well as the oxygenating plant hornwort. Larger, deeper ponds provide the conditions needed to support a greater range of plants, including many water lilies.

Choose plants for boggy, marginal areas as well as aquatics, to create a smooth transition from pond to land.

WHAT PLANT WHERE

There are four main types of water-dwelling plants. To enjoy the benefits of all of them, make shallow ledges in the pond for marginals, which live at the water's edge, and create an area of moist ground around the sides to accommodate bog plants. Ensure a depth of about 50cm (20in) or more for aquatic plants, whose leaves float on the water's surface, and include oxygenating plants, which either behave like aquatics or float in the water.

Bog plants These thrive in a moist or wet soil. There is a wide range available, which includes some of the most colourful waterside plants, such as several irises, primulas, *Lythrum*, and *Lysimachia*.

Marginal plants Growing in a few centimetres of water, these plants soften the line between water and land. Some have colourful flowers (*Mimulus*) and many have dramatic foliage (*Sagittaria*).

Aquatic plants These deep-water plants root on the bottom of ponds. There are relatively few plants in this group, but it includes water lilies, which require a minimum water depth of 50cm (20in).

Oxygenators Essential plants in a pond, oxygenators provide oxygen and absorb nutrients otherwise used by algae. Some, like *Ranunculus aquatilis*, flower above the water surface.

marginal plant depth

aquatic plant depth

KEEPING WATER CLEAR

Weeds can ruin the appearance of a pond and compete with valuable ornamentals for light and nutrients. Help keep them in check by including oxygenating plants in your scheme; these starve weeds of the nutrients they need to thrive. Check before buying to avoid introducing invasive oxygenators, as these can cause environmental problems by clogging up natural waterways if they escape from domestic ponds (*see list, right*). In naturalistic features, you can also add bags of barley straw; straw releases hydrogen peroxide, which kills algae.

If you have a contemporary pool with just a few plants and an expanse of clear water, you may want to use a proprietary black dye designed for water features. The dye blocks the light, minimizing the growth of submerged pond weeds and algae.

OXYGENATORS

Plants to include

Ceratophyllum demersum (Hornwort)
Potamogeton crispus (Curled pondweed)
Orontium aquaticum
Nuphar japonica
Ranunculus aquatilis
Aponogeton distachyos

Plants to avoid

Azolla filiculoides (Fairy fern)
Crassula helmsii (New Zealand pygmy weed)
Eichhornia crassipes (Water hyacinth)
Elodea nuttallii (Nuttall's waterweed)
Hydrocotyle ranunculoides (Floating pennywort)
Lagarosiphon major (Curly waterweed)
Ludwigia spp. (Water primrose)
Myriophyllum aquaticum (Parrot's feather)

PLANTING UP A CONTAINER

Large containers and half barrels can make attractive diminutive pools for patios and small gardens. Plant them up with aquatics and marginals in fine-meshed plastic pond baskets, which are available in an assortment of shapes and sizes. Alternatively, if your container has an uneven base or curved sides, buy a flexible aquatic bag, which will fit snugly into it.

1 Choose aquatic baskets or bags that will fit the size of your plants when they are mature. Place a layer of aquatic compost in the bottom of each bag or basket.

2 Insert plants and fill around the root balls with compost, gently firming it down. If you are planting oxygenators, use a pencil to create holes in the compost, insert the stems, and firm down.

3 To prevent soil floating out of the bag or basket and muddying the water, cover the surface with a layer of pea gravel.

4 Place your plants in the container and stand them on bricks if they are not at the correct level when sitting on the bottom. Slowly fill the container with water.

Water lilies limit algal growth by reducing light availability, making it difficult for algae to survive.

AFTERCARE AND MAINTENANCE

Remove any dead or diseased foliage as soon as you see it, to prevent it polluting the water. In small ponds, you can deadhead water lilies and marginals to keep your displays looking neat, but this is not strictly necessary. Although you can minimize weeds, some will inevitably find their way into your pond. Remove excess duckweed with a fishing net, and wind algae around a stick to pull it out. Leave the weeds on the edge of the pond for a day or two to allow trapped creatures to return to the water. Dispose of aquatic weeds on a compost heap; never down a drain or in a ditch.

Top up the water levels of ponds and small water features regularly during hot summers. Check that any submerged planting baskets have not fallen off their supporting bricks – you may also need to remove bricks from beneath baskets of water lilies as the plants mature and the stems grow up to the surface.

If pests, such as aphids, slugs, and snails, become a problem, lure natural predators, including frogs, toads, and newts, to your pond by creating damp habitats for them under stones or logs close by, and avoid pesticides. If plants become unruly or outgrow their planting baskets, lift and divide them in the spring. See pages 344–345 for further information.

Cut away any diseased or yellowing foliage, to maintain the appearance of your pond and to prevent the spread of disease.

Remove algae from the water as it can hamper the growth of other plants. Vigilant removal will eliminate the problem over time.

EYE-CATCHING BLOOMS

Some pond plants are demure and unassuming, offering a simple foliage backdrop, but specimens such as these are the beauty queens, prized for their eye-catching flowers. Water irises offer a fleeting splash of colour in early summer, elegant arums add a sophisticated note to midsummer displays, while the dramatic scarlet flares of *Lobelia cardinalis* and fiery *Mimulus* appear later in the year.

Iris laevigata (*top left*) Japanese water irises come in shades of blue, purple, and white, and dress up ponds and water features with their elegant blooms, bulking out quickly to form large clumps, which you can divide easily to make more plants.
Mimulus (*top right*) The monkey flower bears an abundance of small, red flowers (*M. cardinalis*) or yellow blooms with red throats (*M. guttatus*) among a mass of light green foliage.
Zantedeschia aethiopica (*bottom left*) Arum lilies are among the most beautiful of all aquatic plants. The white forms are the hardiest, while many rich pinks and purples are tender and need a frost-free home in winter.
Lobelia cardinalis (*bottom right*) This showy marginal is not hardy and needs to be overwintered indoors. The rewards for your trouble are 1m (3ft) spikes of brilliant red flowers from late summer to autumn.

Iris laevigata

Mimulus

Zantedeschia aethiopica

Lobelia cardinalis

WATER PLANT RECIPES

LILY POND

An elegant formal pool makes the perfect stage set for a water lily (*Nymphaea*) or two. Ensure your pool is deep enough for your chosen lilies, and if you want to include marginals such as irises, raise them up to their optimum level on ledges around the sides or on bricks.

1 Plant the water lilies as shown on page 181 in fine-meshed aquatic baskets and place them on the bottom of the pool. Then plant up the irises and arum lilies.

2 Use the planting method outlined on page 177. Set the irises at a depth of 10–15cm (4–6in) and the root balls of arum lilies 15cm (6in) below the water surface.

3 Include a few oxygenating plants to keep the water clear. Plant the edges with bergenias, *Lysimachia*, and other perennials, using the method on page 137.

YOU WILL NEED

1 *Zantedeschia aethiopica*
2 *Bergenia*
3 *Nymphaea* 'Pygmaea Rubra'
4 *Nymphaea alba*
5 *Iris laevigata* 'Variegata'
6 *Iris laevigata* var. *alba*
7 *Lysimachia nummularia* 'Aurea'

STREAM-SIDE PLANTING

Take advantage of the permanently moist soil beside a stream to grow some beautiful bog and moisture-loving plants, such as primulas, *Persicaria*, and ferns.

Horsetails (*Equisetum*), which can be invasive in the soil, are best restricted to planting baskets and set in the water. Disguise the baskets with rocks and pebbles.

1 If your stream is artificial and the edges are dry, create boggy conditions by digging out a trench on either side of the water.

2 Line the trench with pond liner and use a fork to puncture it at regular intervals. Replace the soil on top, incorporating some well-rotted manure, too.

3 Plant the primulas, ferns (*Dryopteris*), and *Persicaria* into the moist soil. Plant the horsetails in fine-meshed baskets (see p.177).

YOU WILL NEED

1 *Canna indica*
2 *Carex comans*
3 *Primula pulverulenta* Bartley hybrids
4 *Equisetum hyemale*
5 *Persicaria microcephala* 'Red Dragon'
6 *Dryopteris filix-mas*

PERFECT WATER LILIES

Few can resist the magical quality of these starry summer flowers floating on a pool of sparkling water. Whether your chosen design requires formal elegance or has a wild, naturalistic look, or you have a large lake or small barrel pool to plant up, you can be sure to find a water lily to suit your purpose.

Create stunning containers with beautiful white water lily blooms as a focal point.

When selecting a water lily (*Nymphaea* species), first assess the size and depth of your pond or water feature. Large species lilies, such as *N. alba*, spread up to 1.8m (6ft) across the surface and require a minimum water depth of 1m (3ft), while tiny types, including *N. tetragona*, are happy in tubs or small pools.

As well as producing exquisite flowers, the majority of water lilies are tough, functional plants. Their exotic-looking blooms belie their hardy nature – most will survive the harshest winter unscathed – while the plate-like leaves inhibit the growth of algae. The exceptions are the exotic blue- and purple-flowered water lilies, which are tender and must be given winter protection.

For the best effects in large or medium-sized pools, ensure your water lilies are not crowded by too many other plants or they will lose their impact. Plant a single lily in a raised pool for a sophisticated look in a formal garden. In an informal or wildlife garden design, make a pond with a pebble beach effect and plant your water lilies in the deeper water at the other end.

Water lilies combine well with other aquatics including irises, *Pontederia cordata*, and the arrow-shaped foliage of *Sagittaria sagittifolia*. For a patio display, plant a dwarf water lily in a glazed container or watertight tub, and pair it with one or two well-behaved marginal plants,

Nymphaea 'Conqueror'

TYPES OF WATER LILY

Vigorous types Only suitable for large, deep, naturalistic pools, these impressive water lilies include the wild, white-flowered *N. alba*, the popular red hybrid *N. 'Escarboucle'* (*above*), and the white *N. 'Gladstoniana'* with its dinner-plate-sized blooms.

Small and dwarf These diminutive water lilies, including *N. 'Pygmaea Helvola'* (*above*), are the perfect choice for small pools and large containers. They need 45cm (18in) of water (less for the dwarfs), and spread up to 30–90cm (1–3ft).

Medium-sized This large group includes hybrids in white, yellow, pink, and red. They need a pond depth of 30–60cm (1–2ft), and spread about 1.2m (4ft) over the surface. Popular cultivars include the fragrant *N. 'Marliacea Albida'* (*above*).

◀ **Floating on the surface**, the water lily's leaves shade the water, restricting the growth of algae.

PLANTING A WATER LILY

When choosing water lilies, look for healthy plants free from algae and other weeds. Make sure you position them in a sunny site, and don't overfeed the plants.

1 Choose an aquatic plant basket with fine-meshed sides. Add a layer of aquatic compost. Carefully remove the water lily from its original container, and position it in the centre of the basket.

2 Fill the basket with aquatic compost; gently firm in. Wipe the leaves gently with a cloth to remove any duckweed or algae, and spray with water to prevent drying out.

3 You can stabilize the surface of the soil in the basket by covering it with a layer of pea gravel. Wash the gravel well in several changes of water beforehand to remove dust and impurities.

4 Place the basket in the pond, raising it up on bricks if the water lily's leaves do not reach the surface of your pond or container. The bricks can be removed as the stems grow.

such as the miniature reed, *Typha minima*, and the magenta blooms of *Iris versicolor* 'Kermesina'.

Water lilies object to fast-moving water, so are not suitable for streams or areas close to waterfalls or fountains. They also prefer a sunny position in order to flower well, and may not bloom in shade. Plant them in aquatic baskets (*see right*); when they outgrow their allotted space, simply lift and divide them and repot the smaller plants individually. In frost-prone areas, grow tender varieties in a conservatory.

Scented Fragrant water lily blooms are available in all plant sizes, including the medium-sized rose-pink *N.* 'Rosennymphe' (*above*), the vigorous vanilla-scented *N.* 'Marliacea Carnea', and the dwarf *N. odorata* var. *minor*.

Colourful foliage Many water lilies have variegated foliage, providing interest and a decorative feature when the flowers are not in bloom. The maroon-flecked, purplish-green leaves of *N.* 'James Brydon' (*above*) are a good choice.

Tender types These include exotic blue and purple varieties, as well as flowers in the usual water lily colour range. Some will survive outside in summer, but for the rest of the year they will need a minimum temperature of 10°C (50°F).

GROW
YOUR OWN

Whether you have an allotment or just a small patch of
growing space in your garden, this chapter will equip you
with all you need to produce delicious home-grown fruit
and vegetables. You can also use vegetables like silvery
globe artichokes and ruby chard as ornamental plants
in your flower beds and borders.

WHAT TO GROW

Pick up a seed catalogue and the choice is inspiring. There are practical considerations, such as the space and time available, but beyond that, select for taste and variety, and take pleasure in growing the fruit and veg you love to eat.

▶ QUALITY AND TASTE

Home-grown vegetables always seem to taste better than shop-bought, especially crops such as sweet corn, lettuce, and peas, which deteriorate within hours of picking. Consider heritage varieties not sold in shops, which offer more interesting tastes and qualities. Grow vegetables you enjoy, organically if you prefer, and focus on those that are expensive to buy, such as baby varieties, asparagus, new potatoes, and shallots. Also consider varieties resistant to pests and diseases, which improves yield and makes them easier to grow.

▶ ORGANIC CROPS

If you are concerned about using synthetic pesticides, you may wish to grow your crops organically. Some can simply be planted early or late to avoid the worst problems, while others are available in varieties that have natural pest and disease resistance. Sowing or planting the crops in different beds each season also helps to prevent the build-up of soil diseases. In addition, you can help to keep your beds healthy by growing plants that encourage predators (see p.356). Some have the bonus of being ornamental, too.

◄ TIME AVAILABLE

The amount of time you have to dedicate to your plot is a crucial factor in deciding what to grow. If you only have a few hours a week and your allotment is a distance away from home, choose crops that are largely self-sufficient once established and do not need constant feeding, watering, staking, and tying in. Equally, if you can't get there to harvest regularly, don't grow vegetables that need constant picking. If your plot is closer to home, and you have some time every day to give to tending your fruit and vegetables, you can grow more demanding crops.

▲ CONTINUOUS HARVEST

For a continuous supply all year, choose crops and varieties that mature at different rates, and sow them every three weeks or so. You can also choose varieties for storing, such as late-season apples. Maximize your space by intercropping slow-growing vegetables, such as swedes, with quick-maturing lettuces, for example.

▲ ROOM TO GROW

The size of your plot will determine the amount and type of crops you can grow. If space is short, don't grow something that will only produce enough for one meal. Make the most of your space with fast-growing or high-yielding varieties, choose dwarf forms for containers, and plant trailing crops, trained vertically.

WHERE TO GROW

How and where you grow your vegetables depends on your soil, site, and aspect. Large gardens and allotments usually offer ideal conditions, especially if you add a greenhouse, but there are raised-bed options for smaller gardens, and crops that can be grown in sunny beds and borders.

TRADITIONAL BEDS

If you have enough space and good, well-drained soil, consider growing vegetables in traditional narrow beds, sited to take best advantage of aspect. The best width is 1.2m (4ft), which allows you to work without trampling and compacting the soil. For this reason, it is a good idea to build a path between the beds to walk along, ideally wide enough for a wheelbarrow. In plots without beds, lay boards to work. To make the beds more attractive, which may be important on smaller plots, add elements such as brick paving, or surround beds with herbs or stepover fruit trees.

▶ RAISED BEDS

If your soil is poor, growing crops in raised beds may be the simplest solution. They are easy to build, (see pp.98–99), and if filled with high-quality topsoil, they can provide ideal growing conditions for a wide variety of crops and herbs. The good drainage in a raised bed helps the soil to warm up more quickly in spring, giving your crops a head start, although you will need to water and feed more often. Raised beds also add interest to your garden and bring your crops up to a more comfortable working height.

◀ UNDER COVER

In cooler areas, crops such as tomatoes and aubergines grow best under cover in a greenhouse or polytunnel. If you can fit one of these in, you will find it invaluable. The warmth and protection provided gives a growing season from early spring, until temperatures and light levels fall in late autumn. You can sow early crops under cover, give seedlings a head start, and protect tender plants.

Greenhouses and tunnels should be sited in full sun, away from trees and overhanging branches, but also in a position that is not too exposed. Installing power will allow you to run heaters, lights, and propagators, and having a water butt or water supply nearby is also useful.

CONTAINERS

Containers are suitable for growing a wide range of fruit and vegetables, and are a useful solution in smaller plots where border space is limited, or if the soil is poor or unsuitable. They also allow you to grow crops in ideal positions, or close to the house for easy picking. You can use any container, provided it has drainage holes in its base; from traditional terracotta and glazed earthenware, to all sorts of recycled materials, such as tin baths.

Plants grown in containers require feeding and regular watering, particularly in hot, dry weather. Where space allows, use larger pots, as these retain moisture better and provide more growing space. Smaller containers are portable, allowing you to move plants if required (to avoid full sun or shade, for instance). Most vegetables can be grown in containers, but also consider dwarf fruit trees, fruit bushes, and strawberries.

Repurposed containers make excellent plant pots, as long as they have holes in the bottom to allow excess water to drain out.

Windowboxes

For those with minimal growing space, window-boxes are a useful option, and bring produce within easy reach. Dwarf or cascading varieties are the best to grow, including lettuce and tomatoes. Herbs are particularly good, especially for your kitchen windowsills. Always ensure boxes are firmly secured to prevent them falling, especially from upper windows.

Windowboxes suit colourful crops.

Growing bags

These provide a flexible way to grow vegetables, and are sold prefilled with compost and ready to plant, or empty to fill yourself. They can be used inside or out, and for a wide range of annual crops, such as tomatoes and courgettes. Deep bags can also be used for root crops, such as potatoes. Discard or refill with fresh soil or compost each year.

Growing bags make patio crops easy.

Hanging baskets

Hanging baskets offer similar benefits to small containers, and allow you to use walls or fences as growing spaces. Cascading and low-growing crops are the most suitable, but for the best crop, don't over-plant. Position the baskets in sunny, sheltered spots, away from wind, fixing the brackets securely. In summer, water daily and feed every week.

Hanging baskets crop at eye level.

◄ WALLS AND FENCES

To help maximize your yield, make use of walls, fences, and other upright structures in the garden, including pergolas, to grow climbing vegetables and to train fruit, such as redcurrants. As long as they are sited in a sheltered spot, these provide useful places to grow plants vertically, without taking up valuable ground space. Walls are especially good for tender plants, like peaches.

Before planting, attach trellis or wires to walls and fences to provide support, and to make it easier to train stems. Improve the soil at the base of the structure with well-rotted organic matter, especially near walls. Regularly water any plants growing in rain shadows.

▲ CONVENIENT COVER

If you don't have space for a greenhouse, a cold frame or mini-greenhouse is the next best thing. These are ideal for raising seedlings and protecting plants in cold snaps. By opening them up on warm days, you can harden off plants ready for planting. Mini-greenhouses are perfect for growing tomatoes and peppers, and can be folded away at the end of the season when crops are finished, or used to protect tender fruit.

▲ MIXED PLANTING

Exclusive vegetable-only beds are not essential, as you can grow many crops in flower beds and borders. Some plants, such as globe artichokes, winter kale, and Swiss chard, are ornamental in their own right. Mixed planting is an excellent way to make a small garden productive, and provides interest when flowers have faded. The mix of plants also helps "hide" crops from pests, and attracts beneficial and pollinating insects.

TOOLS AND EQUIPMENT

Having the right tools and equipment to hand makes growing your own produce much easier. Most are things you will use elsewhere in the garden, so are a worthwhile investment. Start with the essentials, and build up your tool kit over time.

Choosing tools

The tools you need to grow fruit and vegetables are fairly basic; even if you're new to gardening, you probably own several of them already. When buying tools, choose the best quality you can afford and keep them in good shape so they will last for years to come. Gather them together after use, wipe them clean and store them in a dry place.

Spades and forks These are vital for preparing the soil, digging holes, and earthing up. Spades are more use on light soils. Forks are best for heavier soils and for lifting plants.

Hand fork and trowel Both are useful for planting out, harvesting, and for tending small areas of soil or containers. Use a small fork for weeding. Long-handled types are available.

Rake Use a rake to create a fine tilth when sowing and covering seed. Rakes are also handy for clearing plant debris when crops are over. They have many general uses in the garden.

Secateurs These are used to prune fruit trees and bushes, and should be kept sharp. They are also used to harvest larger fruit and vegetables, such as cucumber, without damaging stems.

Hoes These tools are invaluable for weeding between plants, tending the soil before planting, and making seed drills. Of the various types, Dutch hoes are the most versatile.

Pruning saw If you have fruit trees or shrubs, a sharp pruning saw is the best tool for pruning larger branches without causing damage. It can also be used for ornamental trees and shrubs.

Garden fleece This lightweight fabric is ideal for protecting young plants against frost or for draping over spring-flowering fruit trees. Keep it handy for when late frosts are predicted.

Netting Protect fruit and vegetable crops from insects and birds using fine- and medium-grade netting. Very fine, insect-proof mesh protects crops such as carrots and cabbages.

Cloches Use these to warm the soil in spring before planting, to protect newly planted crops, and to encourage an early harvest. There are types to suit large or small plots.

Canes and pea sticks These are essential in the fruit and vegetable garden to provide support for tall or weaker plants. Keep a range of sizes to suit different crops.

Seed and module trays These are useful when raising your own vegetable plants from seed. They tend to be fragile and short-lived, but are cheap to replace.

String and raffia Use raffia to tie tender stems to supports, and string for more robust jobs. Choose jute or other natural fibres as, unlike plastic twine, these will rot down in the compost heap.

Garden trugs Modern trugs are made of rubber or plastic and are useful for carrying small items, such as crops, seedlings, or tools, as well as compost and garden debris.

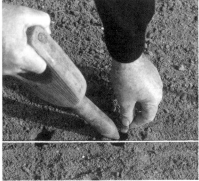

Dibber These are useful for sowing large seeds individually, such as beans, or for transplanting young seedlings. They can also be used to plant bulbs.

Hand sprayers Keep these handy for spraying pesticides or to spray water on tomato flowers to improve pollination, or to increase humidity around indoor crops.

PREPARE A SITE

Before sowing or planting vegetables, you first need to prepare the site. When starting from scratch, this involves creating new beds or preparing new containers. Existing plots may just need a good clear up: weeding, feeding, and preparing the soil in time for spring.

STARTING FROM SCRATCH

To create a new fruit and vegetable plot, choose a sunny, sheltered spot, away from frost pockets, ideally where the soil is fertile and well-drained. Mark out the shape of the beds, making them no wider than 1.2m (4ft) so you can reach plants in the middle, and leaving room between them for a wheelbarrow. If building raised beds, break up the soil surface before building the sides, then fill with improved topsoil. Conventional beds also need digging over and preparing before being planted up.

Make raised beds no wider than 1.2m (4ft) so that the crops can be easily tended.

PREPARING THE SOIL

Digging the soil is essential to keep it healthy. It's best done in autumn or winter to give it time to settle before planting in spring, but don't dig the soil when it is wet or frozen. Working in rows, dig to a spade's depth, lifting and flipping the soil back on itself; at the same time, dig in well-rotted organic matter. On new beds, weed the area first, remove any large stones and rubbish, and fork it over to break up large clods.

Dig the soil to at least one spade's depth. Work across the bed and from one end to the other to avoid standing where you have already dug.

Improve the soil with well-rotted organic matter, such as manure or garden compost. On heavy clay soils, dig in composted bark.

Apply balanced fertilizer before planting, or use organic pelleted chicken manure. Water well if it doesn't rain within a day or so.

GETTING A HEAD START

In colder areas, the soil can be slow to warm up in spring, which delays seed germination, slows plant growth, and can reduce harvests. To make up time or even get ahead, use covers in late winter and early spring to warm the soil and to dry the surface a little, making it easier to work. Do not cover clay soils; they don't drain and so need to dry by surface evaporation.

First dig the soil (*see below left*) and rake the surface fine and flat. Cover the bed with plastic sheeting to keep out the rain and trap heat; secure the edges by digging them into the soil. Black plastic is best for new beds as it will help kill weeds, although clear plastic traps more heat. You can use garden fleece, but since it is permeable, it is less effective than plastic.

Remove the covers after a few weeks, just prior to sowing or planting out, or make cuts and plant through, leaving the cover in place to suppress summer weeds.

▶ **Cloches** warm and dry soils (even clay soils), protect young plants, and provide invaluable extra warmth for tender crops such as melons and cucumbers.

RAISED BEDS, POTS, AND GROWING BAGS

In autumn remove any weeds and plant debris, fork over the soil surface of existing raised beds, and incorporate well-rotted manure or compost. Unless your soil is clay, cover the bed with plastic sheeting during winter to keep down weeds, and to warm the soil before planting.

In spring, remove the covers and any lurking weeds, and lightly fork over the soil. Apply a balanced fertilizer before planting to give new crops a boost. Newly built raised beds are ready to plant as soon they are filled with soil. If you are growing crops in existing containers, use fresh compost, which also helps discourage the build up of pests and diseases. When planting up new containers, plant up smaller ones under cover, harden off, and move them outside later, when the risk of frost has passed. Site large containers in sunny, sheltered spots, ensure they have plenty of drainage holes, and fill with compost.

To prepare growing bags, fluff up the compost by shaking it before opening the bag, then put them in their final position, make drainage holes, and cut holes in the top for planting. Water well and allow to drain before planting.

Growing bags make ready-to-go planting places for crops such as tomatoes, salads, and peppers.

SOW YOUR OWN

Raising crops from seed is usually the only way to grow sufficient plants for a worthwhile harvest. Always check the seed packet for specific instructions, but otherwise a few golden rules apply: provide the correct temperature and soil conditions; prepare seeds, if necessary (see p.329); and sow indoors or outside at the recommended time of year.

SOWING INDOORS

Although some seed can be sown directly in the ground, some crops, such as tomatoes, aubergines, and peppers, need to be sown under cover in early spring and then planted out later. Sow seed in trays, modules, or biodegradable pots, which can be planted straight into the ground once the seedling has developed. Use heated propagators or cover pots with clear plastic bags to provide extra warmth to encourage germination.

1 Prepare the seed trays or modules by filling them with multi-purpose or seed compost, leaving a gap below the rim. Break up any large lumps, and firm it down gently to remove any air pockets.

2 Water the compost lightly before sowing. If seeds are very fine or are mixed with sand, pour a small amount into the palm of your hand so that you can easily control them as you sow. Larger seeds can be sown individually.

3 Sow seed thinly on the surface of the compost or, if sowing in module trays, place one or two seeds in each module. Lightly cover the seeds with a thin layer of compost, depending on their size, and water lightly.

4 Put the tray in a warm place and check daily to make sure the soil is moist, and to see if any seeds have germinated. Prick out the growing seedlings into new trays when the second pair of leaves appear.

5 As they grow, seedlings will develop a stronger root system and will be easier to handle. Push them out of their seed trays or pots from below, and replant them into larger pots filled with potting compost.

6 Keep seedlings well watered. Transfer them to a greenhouse or cold frame when they are ready to harden off (see right): they should have 4–6 true leaves. Water them well before planting out, and try to retain as much potting compost as possible.

PLUG PLANTS

If you don't have the time or space to grow plants from seed, or you only want a few, buying plug plants is the solution, although it is more expensive than raising plants from seed. Plugs are available by mail order or from garden centres, but the choice of varieties can be limited. In mid-spring, select plugs with undamaged leaves and healthy root systems. If you buy via mail order, they will be sent to you at the optimum planting time. Water well, and pot on or plant out immediately.

HARDENING OFF

Plants grown indoors or overwintered in heated greenhouses should be gradually acclimatized to lower temperatures before they are planted outside. This process is known as "hardening off" and starts after the last frosts. Move plants into a cool greenhouse or cold frame for a month, or cover with cloches, removing the lid during the day, and increasing their exposure to outdoor temperatures.

SOWING OUTDOORS

In spring many vegetables, such as beetroot, carrots, spinach, and turnips, can be sown directly into the ground. To prepare a seedbed, dig over the bed at least two weeks before sowing, removing any weeds, and incorporate well-rotted manure or garden compost. If time permits, allow weeds to germinate, then remove them by hoeing.

1 In spring, warm the soil if necessary using cloches or plastic sheeting (see p.193). Rake the soil to a fine tilth and use string to mark lines. If possible, water the day before sowing. Make a drill by pulling the edge of a draw hoe along the length of the string.

2 Sow seeds along the drill as thinly as possible, or for larger seeds, singly, spacing them according to the instructions on the packet. For some crops this will be their final position, but sow generously as they can be thinned out later.

3 Gently cover the seeds with soil and firm the seedbed with the back of the rake to ensure the seeds are in good contact with the soil, then very lightly and carefully rake over the surface. Mark the position of the row with a label.

A YEAR IN THE VEGETABLE GARDEN

The vegetable garden is a busy place for many months of the year, starting with ground preparation and sowing seeds in spring, followed by crop care and harvesting through summer and into autumn. Use the winter months for clearing up, digging over, and planning for the year ahead.

SPRING

Preparation

• **In early spring**, give your greenhouse a really good clean. Remove any bubble plastic if the frosts are over, and clean all the window panes – inside and out. Replace any cracked panes and check that automatic vents are working. Paint any timber panels and wash down the greenhouse floor and shelves with water and disinfectant.
• **Dig over the soil** to ensure that it has not become compacted – try to avoid stepping on it if possible.
• **Put supports in place** for climbing plants; construct wigwams from bamboo canes to support climbing beans.
• **In late spring**, prepare beds for early summer sowings.

Sowing seeds

• **Sow vegetable seed** in a greenhouse to give both hardy and tender varieties a head start. Begin with aubergines, beetroot, cucumber, peppers, and tomatoes.
• **Sow hardy vegetable seed** such as broad beans, Brussels sprouts, cabbages, carrots, kale, leeks, lettuce, peas, and parsnips under cloches outdoors in early spring.
• **In mid-spring**, sow seeds such as French and runner beans, sweet corn, beetroot, broccoli, cabbage, carrots, cauliflowers, spinach, and Swiss chard directly in the ground and cover with cloches if frost threatens.
• **In late spring**, sow courgette, marrow, and squash seeds under cover in a greenhouse.

Planting out

• **In early spring**, plant out early seed potatoes, garlic, and onion and shallot sets.
• **In mid-spring**, plant out second early and maincrop potatoes and globe and Jerusalem artichokes.
• **Prick out and pot on seedlings** of leeks, aubergines, and early summer cabbages, and harden off those that will be planted outside. Use cloches or cold frames to protect vulnerable seedlings from frosts or pests.
• **In late spring**, harden off and plant out seedlings such as peppers, tomatoes, celery, and Brussels sprouts.
• **Begin to transplant well-developed seedlings** of cauliflowers, courgettes, and Florence fennel, and provide them with protection from cloches as necessary.
• **Plant out** shop-bought pre-grown herbs in late spring.

Routine care

• **Remove and dispose of weeds** as they appear.
• **Earth up potatoes** to protect them from frost.
• **Put fleece on young plants** on chilly nights.
• **Water plants regularly**, especially those in containers.
• **Top-dress plants** in containers if necessary.

Harvesting

• **Harvest cabbages**, cauliflowers, kale, herbs, salads, purple sprouting broccoli, Swiss chard, asparagus, and spring onions.

Other tasks

• **Prune perennial herbs** such as rosemary, thyme, and sage. Divide clump-forming herbs and replant if necessary.
• **Shade the greenhouse** by applying whitewash to the glass.

Sow seed under cover for a head start.

SUMMER

Sowing seeds

• **In early summer**, sow beetroot, carrots, courgettes, outdoor cucumbers, beans, herbs, peas, radishes, squashes, swedes, Swiss chard, and turnips. Continue to sow successively over the summer months and make late-summer sowings for autumn and winter harvests.

Planting out

• **Transplant all indoor-sown seedlings** to their final outside positions in early summer.

Routine care

• **Feed and water plants regularly**, particularly as the weather warms up and the plants begin to bear a crop.
• **Keep plants well weeded** and clear beds of debris.
• **Tie in climbing plants** and nip out their topmost shoots to encourage bushy growth.
• **Remove sideshoots** from cordon tomatoes.
• **Earth up potatoes and leeks**.

Harvesting

• **Harvest crops** such as beetroot, broad beans, cabbages, cauliflower, courgettes, cucumbers, artichokes, lettuce, peas, garlic, onions, tomatoes, aubergines, sweet corn, peppers, potatoes, carrots, and Swiss chard. Harvest fruits as they appear, as this will encourage crops such as courgettes and peppers to produce a greater yield.

Other tasks

• **Feed, weed, and water greenhouse plants** regularly and ventilate on hot days to prevent temperatures rising too high. As summer goes on, shade the greenhouse by applying whitewash to the glass and on very hot days damp down the floor by splashing water on it. Remove pests and diseases on sight or buy biological controls.

AUTUMN AND WINTER

Sowing seeds

• **In early autumn**, sow spinach and Swiss chard under cover, and transplant spring cabbages outside. Sow hardy lettuce varieties for winter and early spring picking.
• **Plant out autumn garlic,** shallots, and hardy onion sets and sow broad beans, carrots, and peas to overwinter.
• **From midwinter onwards**, sow hardy crops under cover ready for planting out in early spring, such as broad beans, early carrots and cauliflowers, leeks, lettuce, onions, shallots, spring cabbages, and peas.

Harvesting

• **Harvest the last crops** of many vegetables, including beetroot, carrots, chillies, cucumbers, cabbages, French and runner beans, peppers, potatoes, sweet corn, tomatoes, squashes, and turnips. Kale, leeks, and parsnips should also be ready for harvesting as required, but can be left to stand in the ground for longer.
• **Over winter**, continue to harvest Brussels sprouts, cabbages, kale, parsnips, and leeks.

Other tasks

• **In autumn**, remove any spent plants and give the greenhouse a good clean after the busy summer months, before bringing in the plants that will overwinter there.
• **Tidy the garden**, removing all dead plants – if the debris is disease-free, transfer it to the compost heap.
• **Gather up any fallen leaves** to use to make leaf mould.
• **Dig well-rotted manure** into beds and borders.
• **Plan your crop rotation** and order seeds, seed potatoes, onion sets, and bare-root plants. Chit your seed potatoes.
• **If the greenhouse is not heated**, line the windows with bubble plastic to slow heat loss and take the edge off short frosts. Check plants for pests and diseases, and ensure their compost is slightly moist but not wet.

Hand weed vegetable beds to avoid damaging crops.

Collect fallen leaves for leaf mould.

Harvest sprouts ready for Christmas.

HEALTHY CROPS

No crops are immune to pests and diseases, and you will inevitably come across a few problems in the course of growing your own fruit and vegetables. Prevention is better than cure, and many setbacks can be avoided by good plot management and giving your plants the best care and attention.

Although almost any crop you grow will be under threat from some form of pest or disease, certain groups of crops, such as brassicas, are especially prone to specific diseases such as clubroot. Fortunately, there are alternatives to simply reaching for a bottle of pesticide: basic plant care is the place to start. Regular feeding and watering will encourage plants to become as strong and naturally robust as possible. You can also start them off under cover to give them an advantage or grow resistant varieties. Weeds can provide breeding grounds for pests and diseases, as well as competition for crops, so remove them on sight. In some cases, appropriate chemical controls may be the best option; ensure that you use them safely (see p.359).

CROP ROTATION

This technique provides optimum growing conditions for your plants. The basic premise is to avoid planting the same groups of vegetables in the same place more than once every four years. This discourages the build-up of diseases that affect specific plant groups and also allows plants to benefit from the nutrients left behind in the soil by its previous occupants. Think of your crops as belonging to three distinct groups for rotation:
• potatoes and tomatoes
• brassicas, such as cabbages and broccoli
• legumes, such as peas and beans, with onions and roots, such as carrots and parsnips.

Bed one
Year one: Potato family and tomatoes

Year two: Legumes – peas, broad beans, French beans, runner beans – and also onions, carrots, beetroot, parsnip, and celeriac

Year three: Brassicas – Brussels sprouts, cabbage, cauliflower, kale – radish, and turnips

Bed two
Year one: Legumes – peas, broad beans, French beans, runner beans – and also onions, carrots, beetroot, parsnip, and celeriac

Year two: Brassicas – Brussels sprouts, cabbage, cauliflower, kale – radish, and turnips

Year three: Potato family and tomatoes

Bed three
Year one: Brassicas – Brussels sprouts, cabbage, cauliflower, kale – radish, and turnips

Year two: Potato family and tomatoes

Year three: Legumes – peas, broad beans, French beans, runner beans – and also onions, carrots, beetroot, parsnip, and celeriac

▶ GENERAL HYGIENE

Good gardening practice is key to producing healthy plants and a high yield of good-quality produce. Plant out healthy seedlings, plants, or trees into well-prepared, disease-free soil, and tend them using clean tools. It is important to keep the growing area clear of dead or decaying plants – remove any diseased plant material as soon as you see it and destroy it; do not place it on the compost heap as you will risk further infection. Keep plants well fed and watered so that they are better able to fight diseases.

◀ BARRIERS, TRAPS, AND CONTROLS

Attacks from some pests can be prevented if you protect fruit and vegetables. Covering plants in tents of fine, insect-proof netting or horticultural fleece provides a barrier against pests such as carrot fly, cabbage root fly, flea beetle, aphids, butterflies, and birds. Grease bands wrapped around tree trunks stop winter moths climbing up to lay their eggs. Traps, such as sticky wasp traps, can catch and kill specific pests. Organic slug pellets help to control slugs, and nematodes applied regularly in the growing season are a biological control for slugs.

▶ RESISTANT VARIETIES

Your chance of success with certain crops is greatly increased if you grow resistant varieties, bred to withstand specific problematic pests, for example, carrots bred to resist carrot fly. Another option is to choose varieties that have been awarded the RHS Award of Garden Merit. AGM crops have good general resistance to pests and diseases, are reliable, not prone to reversion, do not require specialist care, and are widely available. The list is regularly reviewed and updated as new varieties become available.

◀ ORGANIC GROWING

Choosing to grow fruit and vegetables organically is a personal decision, but some gardeners find that it improves the health and vigour of their plants. They also feel happier eating unsprayed crops and knowing exactly what has gone into producing them. Your plant health need not suffer if you refuse to use chemicals: allow nature to assist by reducing pests and diseases with the help of natural predators and biological controls (see pp.356–358). Using natural fertilizers such as compost and manure is also a part of this philosophy.

CONTINUOUS HARVEST

The key to achieving a succession of fruit and vegetables is careful planning. The aim is to produce enough food to consistently supply you throughout the seasons, without being overwhelmed by gluts or growing nothing at all.

INTERCROPPING

This technique maximizes your space and yield by allowing you to grow more than one crop simultaneously, using small crops in the gaps between larger crops. Plants such as sweet corn are ideal: with tall stems that cast little shade, they can be underplanted with lettuces, radishes, or onions, or grown with squashes beneath and beans climbing the stems – a planting trio dubbed the "Three Sisters" by indigenous groups across the Americas. You can also intercrop with ornamentals that attract pollinators, like the poached egg plant, or those that divert pests, such as nasturtiums.

CATCH CROPPING

The catch cropping technique is similar to intercropping, but specifically involves sowing fast-maturing crops – usually those that take about 30 days or so to mature from seed, such as salad leaves or radishes – before or after slower-growing ones, such as parsnips or swede. This allows the quick-growing crops to take advantage of ground that will not be required until the long-term plants are further developed. Faster-growing seed can also be sown successionally in small batches every few weeks. This will provide a manageable supply so that you do not end up with a glut.

SUCCESSIONAL SOWING

Prevent gluts by sowing seed in batches, every few weeks, rather than all at once so that cropping is spread over a long period. These crops do not store well so are best used fresh.

Fast-growing crops:
Baby beets • baby carrots • baby spinach • calabrese • cauliflower • French beans • kohl rabi • lettuce • pak choi • peas • radishes • salad leaves • spring onions • summer cabbages

Fast-growing crops such as lettuce can either be grown successionally or as catch crops that precede the emergence of slower plants.

STORING VEGETABLES

If you find yourself with a larger yield than you can cope with, or poor weather threatens and you need to harvest large amounts at once, there are plenty of ways to minimize wastage.

Use air-tight jars to store chutneys and pickled vegetables.

Surplus vegetables can be reliably stored in various different ways to keep for the leaner winter months. Many can be cooked and used to make chutneys, pickles, and preserves, which will allow you to enjoy them long after harvesting. Store some vegetables chopped or whole, either pickled in vinegar or brine, or blanched and frozen. If you have the equipment, many crops can be used to make delicious homemade wines in a matter of months, such as parsnip and rhubarb.

Alternatively, use vegetables, such as broccoli, peppers, and tomatoes to make soups, freezing them if you don't want to eat them straight away. If you lack inside storage space, large harvests of root vegetables can be usefully stored outside in frost-proof clamps.

FREEZING

This is an excellent way to store a variety of crops for up to six months, and one of the best ways to preserve their fresh flavours, if you freeze them promptly. Blanch all vegetables in boiling water before freezing to preserve colour, texture, and flavour.

Herbs are particularly good for freezing – chop them finely and freeze in an ice cube tray.

Freeze gluts of French beans, broad beans, runner beans, and sprouting broccoli.

Sweet corn should be frozen quickly as it rapidly loses sweetness after harvesting.

PRESERVING

A traditional technique for storing vegetables is to pickle them raw in cold vinegar, or to cook them and use in chutneys or preserves. These techniques conserve the flavour of the vegetables, which will often improve over a couple of months.

Pickle vegetables such as cucumbers, peppers, beetroot, cabbage, garlic, and shallots cold in vinegar, leaving for a month to mature.

Use a range of crops such as beetroot, courgettes, and beans to make chutneys or preserves, or mixed vegetables to make piccalilli.

CLAMPING

Choose a sheltered patch of well-drained soil which won't be needed over winter, and cover it with a 20cm (8in) layer of sand. Lift the vegetables, trim away any top growth and make a pyramid with them on the sand. Cover with a 20cm (8in) layer of straw, then a 15cm (6in) layer of soil, leaving one section of straw exposed.

Root vegetables such as carrots, celeriac, parsnips, swedes, and turnips, as well as potatoes, can be stored throughout autumn and winter.

French beans are best trimmed before freezing.

Beetroot chutney will keep well until needed.

Potatoes can be stored in clamps for months.

VEGETABLE CROP PLANNER

Use this table to check when to sow, plant, and harvest your vegetable crops.
The timings will vary for different climates, so adjust them according to your
site and weather conditions.

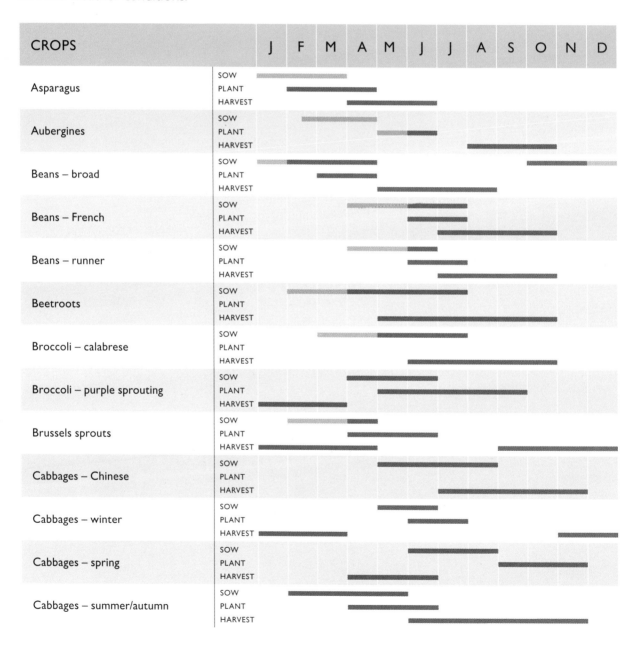

CROPS		J	F	M	A	M	J	J	A	S	O	N	D
Asparagus	SOW	▬	▬	▬									
	PLANT		▬	▬	▬								
	HARVEST				▬	▬	▬						
Aubergines	SOW		▬	▬	▬								
	PLANT					▬	▬						
	HARVEST								▬	▬	▬		
Beans – broad	SOW	▬	▬	▬								▬	▬
	PLANT			▬	▬								
	HARVEST					▬	▬	▬	▬	▬			
Beans – French	SOW				▬	▬	▬						
	PLANT					▬	▬						
	HARVEST							▬	▬	▬	▬		
Beans – runner	SOW				▬	▬	▬						
	PLANT					▬	▬						
	HARVEST							▬	▬	▬	▬		
Beetroots	SOW	▬	▬	▬	▬	▬	▬	▬					
	PLANT												
	HARVEST				▬	▬	▬	▬	▬	▬	▬	▬	
Broccoli – calabrese	SOW			▬	▬	▬	▬						
	PLANT												
	HARVEST							▬	▬	▬	▬		
Broccoli – purple sprouting	SOW				▬	▬	▬						
	PLANT					▬	▬	▬	▬	▬			
	HARVEST	▬	▬	▬									
Brussels sprouts	SOW		▬	▬									
	PLANT					▬	▬						
	HARVEST	▬	▬	▬								▬	▬
Cabbages – Chinese	SOW					▬	▬	▬	▬	▬			
	PLANT												
	HARVEST								▬	▬	▬		
Cabbages – winter	SOW					▬	▬						
	PLANT						▬	▬					
	HARVEST	▬	▬	▬								▬	▬
Cabbages – spring	SOW							▬	▬	▬			
	PLANT									▬	▬	▬	
	HARVEST				▬	▬	▬						
Cabbages – summer/autumn	SOW		▬	▬	▬								
	PLANT				▬	▬	▬						
	HARVEST							▬	▬	▬	▬		

Key

▬▬▬	SOWN, PLANTED, HARVESTED UNDER COVER
▬▬▬	SOWN, PLANTED, HARVESTED OUTDOORS

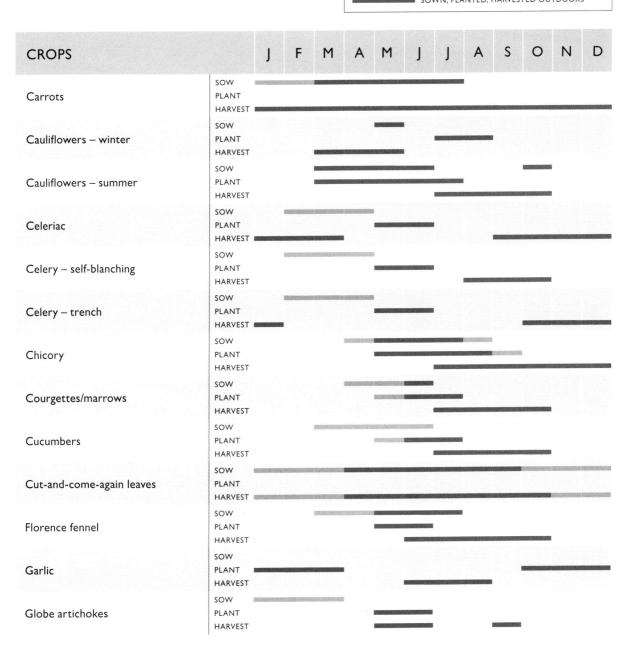

CROPS		J F M A M J J A S O N D
Carrots	SOW	
	PLANT	
	HARVEST	
Cauliflowers – winter	SOW	
	PLANT	
	HARVEST	
Cauliflowers – summer	SOW	
	PLANT	
	HARVEST	
Celeriac	SOW	
	PLANT	
	HARVEST	
Celery – self-blanching	SOW	
	PLANT	
	HARVEST	
Celery – trench	SOW	
	PLANT	
	HARVEST	
Chicory	SOW	
	PLANT	
	HARVEST	
Courgettes/marrows	SOW	
	PLANT	
	HARVEST	
Cucumbers	SOW	
	PLANT	
	HARVEST	
Cut-and-come-again leaves	SOW	
	PLANT	
	HARVEST	
Florence fennel	SOW	
	PLANT	
	HARVEST	
Garlic	SOW	
	PLANT	
	HARVEST	
Globe artichokes	SOW	
	PLANT	
	HARVEST	

CROPS		J	F	M	A	M	J	J	A	S	O	N	D
Jerusalem artichokes	SOW												
	PLANT	■	■	■									■
	HARVEST	■	■	■							■	■	■
Kale	SOW				■	■	■	■					
	PLANT						■	■					
	HARVEST	■	■	■							■	■	■
Kohl rabi	SOW		■	■	■	■	■	■	■				
	PLANT					■	■	■	■				
	HARVEST							■	■	■	■	■	
Leeks	SOW	■	■	■	■	■							
	PLANT						■	■					
	HARVEST	■	■	■						■	■	■	■
Lettuces	SOW	■	■	■	■	■	■						
	PLANT												
	HARVEST				■	■	■	■	■	■	■	■	■
Onions – overwintering	SOW								■				
	PLANT									■	■	■	
	HARVEST							■					
Onions – summer	SOW	■	■	■					■				
	PLANT		■	■	■	■	■						
	HARVEST							■	■	■	■	■	
Parsnips	SOW		■	■	■	■							
	PLANT												
	HARVEST	■	■	■							■	■	■
Peas	SOW	■	■	■	■	■	■	■	■	■	■		
	PLANT		■	■	■								
	HARVEST					■	■	■	■	■	■		
Peppers – chilli	SOW	■	■	■									
	PLANT				■	■	■						
	HARVEST							■	■	■	■	■	
Peppers – sweet	SOW		■	■									
	PLANT	■	■	■	■	■	■						
	HARVEST							■	■	■	■	■	
Potatoes – earlies	SOW												
	PLANT		■	■	■								
	HARVEST					■	■	■	■	■			
Potatoes – maincrop	SOW												
	PLANT			■	■								
	HARVEST							■	■	■	■	■	
Potatoes – late maincrop	SOW												
	PLANT			■	■								
	HARVEST									■	■	■	■

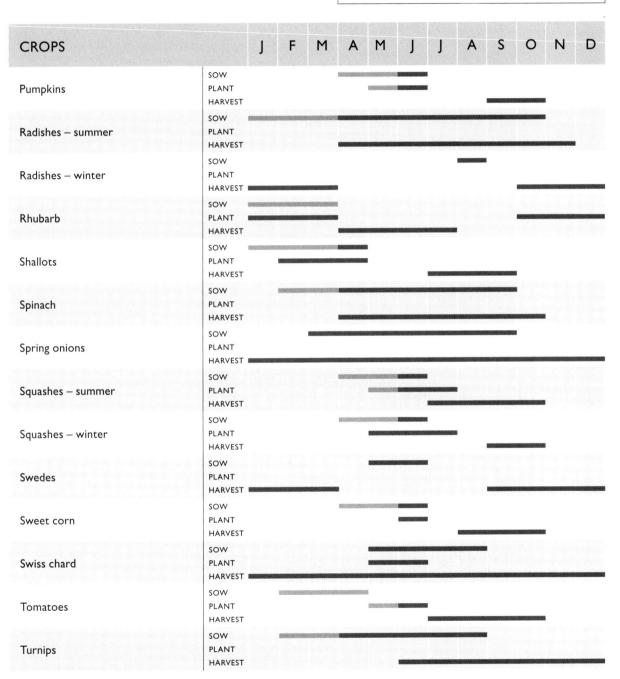

Key

▬▬▬ SOWN, PLANTED, HARVESTED UNDER COVER
▬▬▬ SOWN, PLANTED, HARVESTED OUTDOORS

CROPS		J	F	M	A	M	J	J	A	S	O	N	D
Pumpkins	SOW												
	PLANT												
	HARVEST												
Radishes – summer	SOW												
	PLANT												
	HARVEST												
Radishes – winter	SOW												
	PLANT												
	HARVEST												
Rhubarb	SOW												
	PLANT												
	HARVEST												
Shallots	SOW												
	PLANT												
	HARVEST												
Spinach	SOW												
	PLANT												
	HARVEST												
Spring onions	SOW												
	PLANT												
	HARVEST												
Squashes – summer	SOW												
	PLANT												
	HARVEST												
Squashes – winter	SOW												
	PLANT												
	HARVEST												
Swedes	SOW												
	PLANT												
	HARVEST												
Sweet corn	SOW												
	PLANT												
	HARVEST												
Swiss chard	SOW												
	PLANT												
	HARVEST												
Tomatoes	SOW												
	PLANT												
	HARVEST												
Turnips	SOW												
	PLANT												
	HARVEST												

LETTUCE

Probably the easiest and most rewarding of crops, fast-growing lettuce can be grown in the smallest of spaces, including containers, and will provide you with fresh salads all summer and even into the winter months.

Crisp, fresh lettuce is a summer staple.

		SPRING	SUMMER	AUTUMN	WINTER
SOW/PLANT					
HARVEST					

HOW TO GROW

Lettuce need a bright spot, shaded from midday sun, and grow best at temperatures of 10–20°C (50–68°F). They also prefer moist, free-draining soil, improved with well-rotted organic matter. For an early-summer harvest, sow hardy types outdoors from late winter. Tender varieties can also be sown under cover in winter and early spring, 1cm (½in) deep in modules, to be planted out when the frosts have passed. For summer crops, sow outdoors once temperatures rise to above 5°C (41°F). Lettuce should be thinned or planted 15–30cm (6–12in) apart, but this depends on the variety so always check the packet.

Keep plants well watered, especially during dry spells to help prevent bolting, and weed them often to reduce competition. Loose-leaf varieties can be harvested leaf by leaf, as soon as they are large enough; harvest traditional hearting varieties as soon as a small heart develops, cutting them cleanly through their stems with a sharp knife. To prevent disease, clear away all plant debris after picking.

TYPES AVAILABLE

Loose-leaf lettuces don't form a heart, and can give a continuous supply of leaves if grown as a cut-and-come-again crop (see facing page).

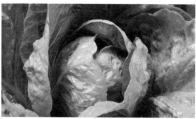

Butterhead lettuces are some of the most popular varieties, and have soft, round heads with either flat or frilly leaves.

Cos and semi-cos lettuces (sometimes called romaine lettuces) are upright and more oval in shape, with longer, crisper leaves.

Crisphead lettuces have round, dense heads and very crunchy leaves – this group includes iceberg lettuces.

VARIETIES TO TRY

Loose-leaf
'Catalogna' • 'Cocarde' • 'Green Salad Bowl' • 'Laurenzio' • 'Lollo Bionda' • 'Lollo Rossa' • 'New Red Fire' • 'Red Salad Bowl' • 'Rossa a Foglia Riccia da Tavolo' • 'Verde a Foglia Riccia'

Butterhead
'All The Year Round' • 'Buttercrunch' • 'Cassandra' • 'Clarion' • 'Marvel of Four Seasons' • 'Mottistone' • 'Tom Thumb'

Cos
'Chartwell' • 'Dazzle' • 'Freckles' • 'Frisco' 'Little Gem' • 'Little Gem Pearl' • 'Lobjoits Green Cos' • 'Nymans' • 'Pandero' • 'Parris Island' • 'Pinokkio' • 'Tintin' • 'Winter Gem'

Crisphead
'Challenge' • 'Great Lakes' • 'Iceberg' • 'Red Iceberg' • 'Saladin' • 'Sioux' • 'Webbs Wonderful' • 'Winter Density'

CUT-AND-COME-AGAIN

Quick-maturing leaf crops are perfect for growing as a cut-and-come-again salad. Just one sowing will provide you with tasty leaves for several weeks. It's the ideal way to grow salad if you have limited space.

	SPRING	SUMMER	AUTUMN	WINTER
SOW/PLANT				
HARVEST				

Grow fresh, handy salad in patio containers.

HOW TO GROW

As the name suggests, cut-and-come-again crops are sown, harvested young, left to grow back, then cropped again. Leafy crops are best suited to this approach, and you can buy seed mixes for different tastes and uses. Sow seeds as you would lettuces (see *facing page*); indoors in early spring in pots, or outside in pots or into well-drained, fertile soil, once the temperature has risen above 5°C (41°F). After 2–3 weeks leaves should be ready to pick. To harvest, either pick the larger leaves individually, leaving the smaller ones to grow on, or crop the whole plant with scissors. The latter approach is quicker, although the plants are slower to recover. Once they have regrown, however, plants can be harvested again in the same way. Plants will regrow a number of times but for the strongest crop, resow a fresh batch every three weeks for a succession.

Keep the plants well watered at all times, and feed crops in containers every two weeks. Clear plant debris after picking to avoid diseases, and keep plants well weeded.

TYPES AVAILABLE

Corn salad, also known as lamb's lettuce, produces a steady supply of small leaves when picked individually and continues into winter.

Mibuna is similar to mizuna (*below*), and is grown for its slender summer leaves. It can be harvested whole or as single leaves.

Land cress has a peppery taste, and can be used instead of water cress. Harvest as seedlings or leave to grow on for about six weeks.

White mustard has a mild mustard flavour, and can be harvested at seedling stage (*above*) or when more mature as young plants.

Pak choi is commonly grown as a mature crop (*see p.209*), but the seedlings are just as tasty and provide instant salad. It has a mild flavour.

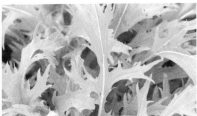

Mizuna has a mild mustard flavour and a crisp texture. It can be harvested as seedlings or allowed to grow on for a few weeks.

LOOSE-LEAF CROPS

There's a surprising range of leafy crops that take little space, and are easy and attractive plants to grow. They give a delicious crop of crisp, tasty leaves and stems, and most are ideal for smaller gardens and containers.

		SPRING	SUMMER	AUTUMN	WINTER
SOW/PLANT					
HARVEST					

Swiss chard 'Lucullus'

HOW TO GROW

Leaf crops are generally quick growing, and prefer a sunny spot with well-drained, fertile soil that has been improved with plenty of well-rotted organic matter, such as garden compost or manure. Where space is limited, small crops can be grown in containers (see below).

For an early start, sow under cover into modules in spring and plant them out when the risk of frost has passed. Sow main-season crops directly outside in the soil into drills, thinning them to their final spacing, according to the crop and variety. Cover young plants with fleece if cold weather is predicted. Keep the plants well-watered throughout the growing season and weed often to reduce competition and encourage quick growth. Some leaf crops can be harvested as whole, mature plants, but most are picked as individual leaves (see right).

▶ **Pick leaf crops** when young or fully grown, depending on space available.

WATCH OUT FOR...

Downy mildew causes yellow patches with fluffy mould beneath them on leaves, which may die, weakening plants. Remove infected leaves and improve airflow.

Fungal leaf spot causes dead patches on the leaves, which may join up, killing larger areas. Remove infected leaves and autumn debris.

Slugs and snails are major pests, spoiling leaves or eating whole plants. Apply slug pellets, use beer traps, or lay gritty trap barriers.
(For more pests and diseases advice, see pp.356–369.)

GROWING IN CONTAINERS

1 Ensure the container has drainage holes before filling with compost, leaving a gap below the rim to allow for easy watering. Make shallow drills, sow seeds, and cover. For an early start, sow indoors.

2 Seeds germinate after about two weeks, depending on the crop. Move indoor-raised crops outside if the risk of frost has passed. Water the plants well and feed every other week with a balanced liquid fertilizer.

3 Container-grown crops are best harvested regularly as individual leaves, picked when young and tender. Leave the plants to grow on, but sow more seed to give a prolonged crop. Replace older plants every few weeks.

▶ SPINACH

Packed with vitamins, spinach is grown for its delicious leaves; smooth-leaved varieties can be eaten raw in salads, crinkled varieties are best cooked. Grow it in moist, rich soil, shaded from full sun, and keep it well watered at all times to prevent bolting. Sow seed direct outside, 2cm (¾in) deep, spaced 2.5cm (1in) apart, in rows 30cm (12in) apart. Thin to 7–15cm (3–6in).

Varieties to choose:
'Bordeaux' F1 • 'Crocodile' F1 • 'Emelia' • 'Ottawa' • 'Polar Bear' F1 • 'Triathlon'

◀ SWISS CHARD AND SPINACH BEET

The large, crisp leaves can be harvested young for salads or grown on for cooking. Grow in rich, moist soil; the plants are not as temperature-sensitive as lettuce, and less prone to bolting. Sow seeds outside in spring for a summer crop; mid- to late summer for a winter crop. Sow 2.5cm (1in) deep, 15cm (6in) apart.

Varieties to choose:
'Bright Lights' • 'Lucullus' • 'Perpetual Spinach' • 'Rainbow Chard' • 'Rhubarb Chard'

▶ CHICORY

Sugarloaf chicory and radicchio (red-leaved chicory) produce dense leafy heads in late summer, which are similar to lettuce but have a bitter taste. Sow outside, early to midsummer, 1cm (½in) deep in rows 30cm (12in) apart. Thin the seedlings to 23–30cm (9–12in) apart. Weed and water regularly and cut leaves from midsummer once the hearts have formed.

Varieties to choose:
Radicchio: 'Palla Rossa Bell' • 'Rossa di Treviso'
Sugarloaf: 'Borca' • 'Pan di Zucchero'

◀ CHINESE CABBAGE

Also known as Chinese leaves, this quick-growing crop is ready to harvest after 6–7 weeks. The cylindrical heads of densely packed leaves are good raw or stir-fried. Sow directly outside in succession from late spring onwards, 1cm (½in) deep, thinning to 30cm (12in) apart for large heads, 15cm (6in) apart for smaller ones.

Varieties to choose:
'Kasumi' F1 • 'One Kilo SB' • 'Richi' F1 • 'Wa Wa Sai' F1 • 'Wong Bok' • 'Yuki'

TOMATOES

Tomatoes are a popular crop, producing summer fruits in a wide variety of colours, shapes, and sizes. Depending on the type, they can be trained as cordons, left as bushes, or allowed to tumble from hanging baskets.

		SPRING		SUMMER		AUTUMN		WINTER
SOW/PLANT								
HARVEST								

Harvest fruits when fully ripe and evenly coloured.

HOW TO GROW

Tomatoes crop better under cover in a greenhouse in cool areas but there are varieties to grow outside. Sow seeds in modules or small pots indoors at a temperature of 18–21°C (64–70°F) in early spring. Pot into individual pots, 8cm (3in) in diameter, when large enough to handle, and harden off outdoor varieties once all threat of frost has passed. Plant outside into pots or growing bags, or into fertile, well-drained soil 75cm (30in) apart. If planting into greenhouse borders, space plants 60cm (24in) apart. Provide support, water regularly, and feed weekly once the first flowers appear in summer. Remove yellowing leaves as they appear and pinch out cordon varieties as needed.

TYPES AVAILABLE

Beefsteak tomatoes produce the largest fruit but can be slow to ripen and give fewer fruit per plant than other types. Best grown under cover.

Cherry tomatoes are very free-fruiting, producing long chains of berry-sized fruit. Some varieties are suitable for patio containers.

Plum tomatoes have larger, fleshier fruit than cherry types and a rich flavour. There are varieties suitable to grow inside or outdoors.

Heirloom varieties produce tasty fruit in a variety of shapes and colours, including striped forms. Most crop best under cover.

VARIETIES TO TRY

Tomatoes have either a bush (B), cordon (C), or tumbling habit (see *facing page*).

Cherry tomatoes:
'Balconi Red' (tumbling) • 'Chocolate Cherry' (C) • 'Gardener's Delight' (B or C) • 'Gold Nugget' (C) • 'Romello' (B) • 'Sungold' (C) • 'Tumbling Tom' (tumbling)

Plum tomatoes:
'Ailsa Craig' (C) • 'Crimson Crush' (C) • 'Moneymaker' (B) • 'Roma' (B) • 'Summer Sweet' (C)

Beefsteak tomatoes:
'Big Red F1' (C) • 'Beefeater' (C) • 'Marmande' (C) • 'Mountain Magic' (C) • 'Pink Wonder' (C)

Heirloom tomatoes:
'Green Sausage' (B) • 'Purple Russian' (C) • 'Antique Roman' (C) • 'Tigerella' (C)

Use tall garden canes or flexible strings for indoor cordon tomatoes.

TRAINING AND SUPPORT

Bush tomatoes, which are usually grown outdoors, are the simplest to support and train; insert canes around the plants and tie in the branches to help take the weight of the developing fruit. The bigger the crop, the more canes needed.

Cordon tomatoes are trained as single stems, and are usually grown under cover. To provide support, insert tall canes next to each plant, avoiding the roots, and tie in the stems at intervals as they grow. If using growing bags, attach the canes to the greenhouse frame to give extra support. Check and tie in plants every week, and pinch out

the main growing tips when they reach the top of the supports. Stop outdoor cordons once they have produced 4–5 fruit trusses.

To encourage cordons to fruit, and to limit their size, pinch out the sideshoots that develop in the joints between the leaves or flower trusses and the main stems. If these grow, they waste plant energy on unwanted growth, and also shade the fruit, preventing it from ripening. Bush and tumbling varieties do not need to be pinched out. As the plants grow, remove the leaves below the lowest truss of ripening fruit to promote airflow and reduce disease.

GROWING IN CONTAINERS

Tomatoes grow best in containers filled with new compost, or growing bags, as this reduces the risk of soil-borne disease. It also allows you to site plants in a warm and sheltered position.

If growing in pots, place crocks in the base of a 38cm (15in) diameter pot, fill it with good-quality compost, and plant one plant in each. If planting into a standard growing bag, make drainage holes in the bottom first then plant 2–3 tomatoes in each. To grow

tumbling varieties in hanging baskets, line the basket with pierced plastic to help retain moisture, and fill with compost. Position the plants near the edge so the stems can tumble over the sides. Hang the basket in a sheltered spot, out of the wind, and water every day.

▶ **Tumbling tomatoes** are ideal for small spaces. Baskets can be planted decoratively with flowers.

WATCH OUT FOR...

Tomato blight causes the leaves to discolour, dead tissue develops on the stems, and the fruit rots. Grow crops in greenhouses or use resistant cultivars. Do not replant in the same compost if growing in a greenhouse bed.

Blossom end rot causes the base of the fruit to turn brown, then drop off. It is commonly caused by erratic watering; destroy infected fruit, water regularly. (For more pests and diseases advice, see pp.356–369.)

FEEDING AND WATERING

Feeding and watering are the most important things to get right. Water regularly and evenly; allowing the plants to dry out then occasionally soaking them causes fruit to split, as well as blossom end rot (see left). Tomatoes are hungry plants and need weekly feeding with a high-potash liquid fertilizer as soon as the plants flower, and twice weekly once the first fruits appear. Follow the instructions on the packet. Liquid organic feeds are also available.

Irregular watering can cause cultural problems, such as split fruit and blossom end rot.

PEPPERS AND CHILLIES

These plants are closely related but choose carefully, as they have very different properties. Sweet peppers have a mild flavour and often a succulent texture, while chilli peppers are their fiery siblings with a spicy kick.

	SPRING	SUMMER	AUTUMN	WINTER
SOW/PLANT				
HARVEST				

HOW TO GROW

Pepper and chillies are best grown in containers under cover in a greenhouse or conservatory, or outside in a hot, sunny, sheltered spot. Buy pot-grown seedlings in spring or sow seed under cover, kept at 21–24°C (70–75°F). Pot on into individual pots when seedlings are large enough to handle. Repot when the roots fill the pot, and either grow on under cover or harden off to plant outside. Grow them on in containers or in sunny beds, spacing them 30cm (12in) apart, with 60cm (24in) between rows. Water regularly as the weather warms, and feed once a week with a high-potash tomato fertilizer. Pinch out and support tall plants with canes if necessary. Peppers change colour and flavour as they ripen; harvest when green for a milder flavour, or when red or orange for a richer taste (hotter in the case of chillies). Although ripe fruits have the best flavour, leaving them to fully ripen will result in a smaller harvest.

TYPES AVAILABLE

Sweet peppers are mild-tasting, and produce large, fleshy fruits that ripen from green to red. They can be grown inside or out.

Scotch bonnets are notoriously hot and are widely used in Jamaican cooking. They need a long hot summer under cover to grow well.

Jalapeno chillies are plump with thick flesh, and vary in spiciness according to variety. They crop best under cover but will grow outside.

Cayenne chillies are long, slender, thin-skinned and packed with seeds. They can be very fiery and are good for drying.

AUBERGINES

Also known as eggplants, aubergines are a mainstay ingredient in many cuisines. In cooler climates they are best grown under cover, but otherwise require little effort to give a rewarding crop.

	SPRING	SUMMER	AUTUMN	WINTER
SOW/PLANT				
HARVEST				

HOW TO GROW

Aubergines need warmth to fruit well and do best in a greenhouse or conservatory, but will crop outside in milder areas. Sow seed in early spring into pots or modules kept at 21–24°C (70–75°F). Pot on the seedlings and grow them under cover at 16–18°C (61–64°F) until late spring. To encourage bushiness and more flowers, pinch out the growing tips when the plants reach 30cm (12in) high. Harden off if growing outside, and plant out 60cm (24in) apart in a warm, sheltered, sunny spot in fertile, well-drained soil, after the last frosts. Outdoor plants can also be grown in large containers, stood in the sun. Plants under cover can be grown in large containers or growing bags, or planted into greenhouse borders.

Water plants more regularly as the temperatures rise and fruits appear, and feed every week with a high-potash tomato fertilizer. To encourage fewer, larger fruit, pinch out the first flower as it appears and thin fruits to three or four per plant. As the plants grow, support the main stems by tying them into canes or trellis. Harvest the fruits when full-sized and ripe. They are at their best when their full colour has developed and the skin is shiny. If the skin begins to dull, the plants have matured too much and will taste dry and bitter. After fruiting, discard all plant debris, including used compost from pots.

Aubergines grow well in containers indoors, or outdoors if given a sheltered spot. Keep them well watered and fed.

WATCH OUT FOR...

Glasshouse whitefly feed on plants, sucking their sap, spreading viruses, and reducing harvests. Leaves may start to yellow and feel sticky to touch. Hang sticky traps or use biological control.

Grey mould is most common in poor, wet summers and causes fluffy mould on leaves and flowers, reducing the crop. Remove infected growth and improve airflow.
(For more pests and diseases advice, see pp.356–369.)

Harvest young, rather than late. Older aubergines taste bitter and slow the growth of developing fruit.

CUCUMBERS

You have not experienced the true fresh, juicy flavour and crispy texture of cucumbers until you have grown your own. With varieties that can be grown easily inside or out, there's no reason not to give them a try.

	SPRING	SUMMER	AUTUMN	WINTER
SOW/PLANT				
HARVEST				

Harvest cucumbers by cutting them off using a knife or secateurs. Pick regularly to encourage new fruits.

HOW TO GROW

Cucumbers need a sunny position, with moist, fertile soil or compost, and are ideal for growing in containers or the soil. Sow seed under cover at 21°C (70°F) in small pots in early spring for indoor crops, mid-spring for outdoor varieties. Harden off cucumbers for planting outside when four weeks old, and plant out after the last frosts, putting supports in place first. Space the plants 45cm (18in) apart. Sow seeds direct in summer. Keep plants well watered, especially when in fruit, watering indoor plants daily in summer. Feed with a general liquid fertilizer every two weeks after the first flowers appear.

TYPES AVAILABLE

Ridge cucumbers are grown outside on the ground or trained up supports. They have tougher skins, which may have small spines.

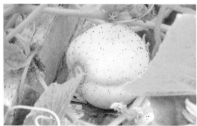

Heritage cucumbers are grown outdoors and generally produce smaller, rounded yellow or white fruit that are ideal for salads.

Greenhouse varieties produce long, smooth, thin-skinned fruit that need to be grown under cover to set reliably.

VARIETIES TO TRY

All-female varieties (F) are more expensive to buy than standard types, but produce better-tasting cucumbers (see right).

Greenhouse varieties
'Bella' F1 • 'Carmen' • 'Cucino' F1 (F) • 'Emilie' • 'Euphya' F1 (F) • 'Flamingo' • 'Louisa' • 'Passandra' F1 (F) • 'Socrates' • 'Telegraph Improved'

Outdoor varieties
'Burpless Tasty Green' • 'Bush Champion' • 'Long Green Ridge' 'Lungo Verde Degli Ortolani' • 'Marketmore' • 'Masterpiece'

Heritage varieties
'Boothby's Blonde' • 'Crystal Apple' • 'Crystal Lemon' • 'Miniature White' • 'White Wonder'

Providing support

Cucumbers can be left to trail along the ground but they crop better and take up less space if trained up a support. For outdoor plants, make a simple wigwam using 5–6 tall canes, tied at the top. In a greenhouse, insert one cane per plant, holding it upright by attaching it to the frame. To use all the space available, train plants along the inside of the greenhouse roof on long, sturdy wires and tie them in.

▶ **Cucumber plants** grow quickly so should be tied in regularly; the swelling fruit can become heavy.

▲ **Cane frames** provide an easy-to-make, robust support for outdoor crops.

Containers

Cucumbers thrive in containers and growing bags, inside or out. When planting containers, place crocks over the holes, use compost, and leave a large gap between the surface and the rim for easy watering. If you use growing bags, make several drainage holes in the bottom first, and insert the supports before planting.

▶ **Growing bags** are ideal for cucumbers and reduce the risk of soil-borne diseases affecting your plants.

"All-female" varieties

If modern indoor cucumbers are pollinated, the fruit that develops can be misshapen and bitter-tasting. Avoid this by growing "all-female" varieties or by removing any male flowers before they open.

◀ **Female** flowers are easy to spot as they have an immature fruit behind the petals.

WATCH OUT FOR...

Squash, cucumbers, courgettes, and pumpkins are related, and are affected by the same pests and diseases (see pp.221–223).

Cucumber mosaic virus causes mottled leaves, weak growth, and poor harvests. Destroy infected plants and grow resistant varieties.

Powdery mildew coats leaves in white fungal growth. Keep plants well watered and improve airflow. (For more pests and diseases advice, see pp.356–369.)

GROWING GHERKINS

Gherkins are immature cucumbers that are grown the same way as outdoor varieties. Sow seed under cover in pots, harden off, and plant out when the risk of frost has passed. Water and feed regularly and harvest the fruits when 2.5–7.5cm (1–3in) long. Harvest often and pickle fruits straightaway. Although cucumbers can be picked small as gherkins, specially bred varieties are more successful.

Varieties to try:
'Diamant' • 'Piccolo di Parigi' • 'Venio Pickling'

SWEET CORN

The minute a cob is picked, the sugar in the kernels starts turning to starch, reducing its tenderness and sweetness. When you grow your own and eat them fresh, you won't believe the difference in taste.

Fresh sweet corn is much sweeter than bought cobs.

	SPRING	SUMMER	AUTUMN	WINTER
SOW/PLANT				
HARVEST				

HOW TO GROW

Sweet corn requires a warm season to produce a good crop so plant in a sheltered, sunny site with well-drained soil. In colder areas, sow seed in spring under cover in a heated propagator, set to a minimum temperature of 16–21°C (61–70°F). Grow the seedlings on at room temperature and harden them off once the risk of frosts has passed. To produce full-sized cobs, the flowers must be fully pollinated, which is done by the wind. Help ensure this by growing the plants together in blocks (see below). It is best to sow seed under cover, even in mild areas, to deter mice. For a succession of crops, sow at two-week intervals into summer. Water in well and cover plants with fleece if cold nights are threatened. Plants do not need support, but if the stems are rocked by wind, earth them up. Water regularly once the plants start to bear crops.

As the cobs ripen in late summer the tassels darken and turn brown. Test if the cobs are ready (see right), then twist them from the plant. Leave late-season cobs to ripen as long as possible before the first frosts. The flowers of baby sweet corn don't need to be pollinated. Pick the fruits before the tassels darken.

Check if cobs are ready by exposing the cob and pressing a fingernail into a kernel. If it exudes milky sap, it is ready to harvest.

PLANTING OUT

1 To encourage good pollination, plant sweet corn in blocks, 45cm (18in) apart, so the pollen can be blown by the wind from plant to plant. Baby corn can be planted more closely, 15cm (6in) apart.

2 Sweet corn is slow to develop, and young plants cast only light shade. Take advantage of the space below them as they develop and underplant with a quick-growing catch crop, such as beetroot, radish, or kohl rabi.

VARIETIES TO TRY

"Super sweet" (S) hybrids produce sweeter kernels than traditional varieties; "Tender sweet" (T) are sweeter and more tender. They must not be pollinated by other varieties or their special qualities are lost.

'Incredible' (S) • 'Lark' (T) • 'Marshall's Honeydew' (T) • 'Mirai White M421' (S) • 'Prelude' (S) • 'Seville' (S) • 'Sundance' • 'Swift' (TS) • 'Minipop' (baby corn)

FLORENCE FENNEL

Attractive to look at as well as to eat, this lacy-leaved vegetable is grown for its aniseed-flavoured, slightly tender stem bases. It is prone to bolting and develops best in mild, warm conditions.

	SPRING	SUMMER	AUTUMN	WINTER
SOW/PLANT	■■	■		
HARVEST		■	■	

HOW TO GROW

This choice vegetable prefers a sunny, sheltered position and moist, rich soil, improved with lots of well-rotted organic matter – lesser conditions will cause the plants to bolt. Sow indoors into small pots to avoid disturbing the roots when transplanting, or sow outside when all risk of frosts has passed. Harden off indoor-grown seedlings and plant them out in late spring, spacing plants 30cm (12in) apart. Water well and regularly, especially during dry spells, keeping the soil permanently moist. Grow the plants early in summer and keep well watered to help prevent bolting. Weed often and earth up the stems as they grow to blanch them and make them sweeter. If nights turn cold, cover with fleece or cloches.

Florence fennel is ready to harvest about 12 weeks from sowing, when the stems are about the size of tennis balls. Don't allow them to grow larger or they will become tough. Unless you want the plants to resprout (see below) harvest by pulling the plants up whole.

▶ **Florence fennel** is attractive enough to grow as an ornamental and gives a good crop planted in containers. Resow regularly throughout summer for a steady supply.

RESPROUTING FENNEL

1 Cut the swollen stems off just above ground level with a sharp knife. Unless you need the space for other crops, leave the roots in the ground to regrow and produce a second crop of leaves.

2 Keep the stumps well watered and within two weeks the plant will produce new shoots. Although these won't grow into full-sized bulbs before autumn, the tasty, feathery leaves can be used fresh as a herb in soups and salads.

WATCH OUT FOR...

Rhizoctonia is a fungal disease that causes seedlings and mature plants to rot off at the base. There are no chemical controls. Rotate crops and don't grow lettuce or radish in the same soil afterwards.

Bolting, where plants quickly run to seed, is a common problem when growing Florence fennel. It is caused by stress. Transplant seedlings with care and keep them well watered, weeded, and fed. Once bolted, plants cannot be saved.

RHUBARB

Cooked like fruit and eaten in desserts, rhubarb is technically a vegetable because, like celery, it is the leaf stems that are eaten. It is very easy to grow, and mature plants crop from spring to summer.

	SPRING	SUMMER	AUTUMN	WINTER
SOW/PLANT				
HARVEST				

HOW TO GROW

Rhubarb is best planted in a sunny spot, although it does tolerate some shade, with well-drained, moisture-retentive soil that has been enriched with well-rotted organic matter. Plant bare-root plants while dormant, late autumn to early spring; container-grown plants can be planted any time if well watered. When planting container-grown plants, make sure the bud is at the same depth in the soil as it was in the pot, and position plants 90cm (3ft) apart. Water plants well during dry spells in the first year and mulch with well-rotted organic matter in spring, avoiding the crown itself. Cut the flowering stems that appear in summer, remove dead leaves in autumn, and mulch.

Stems are tender and ready to harvest when well coloured and just before the leaves unfurl, unless they are forced (see below). Crop as needed until early summer, then let the plant recover and grow on. Tug and twist the stems so they come away cleanly, rather than cutting them off. Do not harvest any stems from new plants in their first year, then harvest only lightly in their second.

▶ **Rhubarb leaves** are toxic – remove them from the stems before cooking. They are safe to add to the compost heap.

FORCING EARLY STEMS

1 For early, tender stems, cover the plant before it emerges with a large container to block out the light, such as a forcer (*above*) or a bucket weighed down with bricks. Check for slugs and snails first.

2 Remove the long stems as needed until mid-spring, then uncover the plant and allow it to grow naturally. To let the plant recover, do not force it the following year. For best results, apply this technique to early or forcing varieties.

CELERY

Versatile in cooking, celery is a fairly tricky vegetable to grow well and requires some effort. Novice gardeners should look for modern self-blanching varieties, which are easier to look after than trench types.

	SPRING	SUMMER	AUTUMN	WINTER
SOW/PLANT				
HARVEST				

HOW TO GROW

Celery prefers an open site with moist, rich, well-drained, slightly acid soil that has been improved with plenty of well-rotted organic matter, such as garden compost. Dig this into the soil in the season before you plan to grow.

Sow seeds (which can be slow germinating) under cover in early spring into modules or small pots. The seeds need light to germinate, so cover very lightly with compost, if at all. Keep the sown seeds at 15°C (60°F), then transfer seedlings into larger pots once they are large enough to handle. Grow them under cover at a temperature of 10°C (50°F) until all risk of frost has passed, then harden off and plant out in early summer.

Plant self-blanching varieties 23cm (9in) apart in blocks and trench celery 30–45cm (12–18in) apart in a prepared trench (*see right*). Water in well, keep the area free of weeds, and feed once a fortnight with a balanced liquid fertilizer throughout the growing season. Harvest celery after 4–8 months, when the heads are big enough to use. Trench celery is the hardiest and can be left to stand in the ground; self-blanching must be pulled before the first frost.

Blanching celery

Traditional trench celery needs earthing up to produce crisp, tender blanched stems. Dig a trench 30cm (12in) deep by 45cm (18in) wide, and spread well-rotted organic matter in the bottom, topped with soil. Space plants 15cm (6in) apart along the trench. When they reach 30cm (12in) high, wrap the stems with cardboard to keep the soil out and earth up against the sides. Do this two or three more times in summer, so only the leaves remain visible at harvest time. Alternatively, plant new self-blanching varieties, which, when planted in blocks, create enough shade to blanch the stems.

▶ **Blanching celery stems** makes them more tender to eat, but green stalks are more nutritious.

VARIETIES TO TRY

Traditional celery is grown in trenches; self-blanching types are easier to grow.

Trench celery
'Blush' • 'Ideal' • 'Giant Pink' • 'Giant Red' • 'Martine' • 'Pascal'

Self-blanching/naturally pale celery
'Crystal' • 'Green Utah' • 'Ivory Tower' • 'Loretta' • 'Tango' • 'Victoria'

COURGETTES AND MARROWS

The only difference between courgettes and marrows is their size. When harvested small, courgettes have a delicate flavour and tender skin; marrows develop a thicker skin over time. The edible flowers are a delicacy.

Courgettes form behind the female flowers.

	SPRING	SUMMER	AUTUMN	WINTER
SOW/PLANT				
HARVEST				

HOW TO GROW

Courgettes and marrows can be grown in beds or large containers, and need a warm, sunny spot with fertile soil. Sow seed under cover in early spring (see below), or outdoors under a cloche, 2.5cm (1in) deep, when the risk of frost has passed. Plant bushy varieties 60cm (24in) apart and trailing types, which can be trained up canes, 90cm–1.2m (3–4ft) apart. Water well and feed with a liquid fertilizer every week. Break the stems to harvest courgettes at 10cm (4in) long, or for marrows, thin the fruit to two or three per plant, and allow them to grow to 20–30cm (8–12in).

Pick courgettes young and tender but leave marrows to develop a thick outer skin.

VARIETIES TO TRY

Courgettes
Most courgettes are green but some are yellow (Y), which makes them easier to see when harvesting:
'Clarion' F1 • 'Defender' F1 • 'Gold Rush' F1 (Y) • 'Jemmer' F1 (Y) • 'Romanesco' • 'Supremo' F1 • 'Venus' F1

Marrows
Marrows are large courgettes but there are also varieties available that are particularly suited to growing as marrows:
'Badger Cross' F1 • 'Bush Baby' • 'Tiger Cross' F1

SOWING AND PLANTING

1 Sow seeds indoors, 2.5cm (1in) deep, into small pots to avoid disturbing the roots when planting them out later on.

2 Grow them on indoors in a greenhouse or on a bright windowsill. They will be large enough to plant out after 4–6 weeks, so don't sow too early.

3 Harden off and plant out once the risk of frost has passed. To avoid root damage, water the plants first, so they slide more easily from their pots.

4 Plant into containers or beds, and keep them well watered throughout the growing season. Larger containers retain moisture more effectively.

SUMMER SQUASH

Summer squashes are a lot like courgettes, in terms of growing, cooking, and eating, but they come in a much wider variety of shapes and textures. They are attractive plants and fun to grow.

	SPRING	SUMMER	AUTUMN	WINTER
SOW/PLANT				
HARVEST				

Summer squash can be grown amongst nasturtiums in the garden.

HOW TO GROW

Summer squashes prefer moist, rich soil, and crop better in hot summers. Sow seed under cover in early spring into small pots, harden off and plant outside into large containers or beds when all risk of frost is past. Plant bushy varieties 45cm (18in) apart and trailing types 90cm–1.2m (3–4ft) apart. Seed can also be sown outside under cloches at this time, 2.5cm (1in) deep. Water well, and when squash appear, feed with a high-potash fertilizer every week. Tie trailing varieties to supports and pinch the tips when they are 60cm (24in) tall. Harvest squashes while small for best flavour, cutting their stems at the base with a sharp knife. Watch your fingers – older stems may have needle-sharp bristles.

◄ **Train squashes up** supports or netting to save space and keep them clean.

WATCH OUT FOR...

Squash, cucumbers, courgettes, and pumpkins are related, and are affected by the same pests and diseases (*see p.215 and pp.222–223*).

Cucumber mosaic virus affects squash as well as cucumbers, causing the foliage to become yellow and mottled, weakening the plants, and reducing the crop. There is no cure for this disease, so any affected plants must be destroyed.
(*For more pests and diseases advice, see pp.356–369.*)

TYPES AVAILABLE

Patty pan squash have a flattened shape with a bumpy ring. The plants double as garden ornamentals when trained against fences.

Round squash are often highly decorative, producing fruits with colourful patterned skins that can be smooth or knobbly in texture.

VARIETIES TO TRY

Patty pans (P) are more decorative than plain round (R) varieties, although they taste similar when cooked.

'Custard White' (P) • 'Moonbeam' F1 (P) • 'Peter Pan' (P) • 'Scallop Yellow Bird' (P) • 'Summer Ball' (R) • 'Sunburst' F1 (P) • 'Tromboncino'

PUMPKINS

Pumpkins are a familiar sight at Halloween, carved into lanterns, and are more popular for decoration than as edible crops. However, they are easy to grow, fun for all, and spectacularly announce the onset of autumn.

		SPRING		SUMMER		AUTUMN		WINTER
SOW/PLANT								
HARVEST								

Pumpkins need time to develop and space to grow to a good size, in full sun.

HOW TO GROW

Pumpkins are a type of winter squash (see *facing page*), and require plenty of time to develop their bold colouring, as well as a lot of space. Sow seed indoors in mid-spring into small pots to help minimize root disturbance when planting out. Harden off the seedlings once the risk of frost has passed, and plant out 1–1.5m (3–5ft) apart in a sunny, sheltered spot, in well-drained, fertile soil that has been prepared with plenty of well-rotted organic matter, such as garden compost or manure. (If you're short of space, plant pumpkins directly into a well-rotted compost heap.) Water in and mulch well, covering with cloches or fleece during cold spells. Water regularly, particularly in hot, dry weather, and feed with a liquid fertilizer every other week. Lift trailing varieties off the ground with netting. If you want large pumpkins, thin the baby fruits, limiting each plant to bearing just two or three. For pumpkins to eat fresh, crop when they reach a good size. For large, decorative fruit, let them grow on and colour up, but pick them before the first frosts.

DRYING AND STORING

Pumpkins can be stored to eat later in the year but must be prepared properly. Leave the fruits on the plant to develop a thick skin, then cut them off leaving a long stalk (this delays rotting, which starts at the stalk end). "Cure" the pumpkins by leaving them outside in the sun for around ten days to dry. If rain is forecast, move them indoors or cover them. Turn them occasionally so that the whole surface dries. Once "cured", store the pumpkins in a dry, well-ventilated, frost-free space that is consistently cooler than 15°C (59°F). Check occasionally for signs of damage or decay.

▶ **Keep developing fruit clean** by raising them up with a thick mulch of chipped bark or straw, or with a brick.

VARIETIES TO TRY

'Atlantic Giant' • 'Baby Bear' • 'Becky' • 'Jack Be Little' • 'Jack of All Trades' • 'Mammoth' • 'Mars' F1 • 'Rouge Vif d'Etampes' • 'Sunshine'

WATCH OUT FOR...

Pumpkins, cucumbers, courgettes, and squash are related, and are affected by the same pests and diseases (see *pp.215, 221, and 223*).

Slugs will attack all parts of young plants, and may hide beneath the large leaves. Spread slug pellets, or use beer traps or biological control to keep them away from vulnerable crops. (*For more pests and diseases advice, see pp.356–369.*)

WINTER SQUASH

Closely related to pumpkins, their plump cousins, winter squashes produce smaller, tastier fruits, grown for their sweet, nutty flavour. They are also more decorative, developing interesting colours and shapes, and longer storing.

VARIETIES TO TRY

On smaller plots, make best use of the space and choose varieties with attractive fruit that can double as ornamentals (O).

'Butternut' • 'Crown Prince' (O) • 'Festival' (O) • 'Harlequin' (O) • 'Turk's Turban' (O)

	SPRING	SUMMER	AUTUMN	WINTER
SOW/PLANT				
HARVEST				

HOW TO GROW

Winter squashes require long, hot summers to ripen fully, and prefer a sunny, sheltered spot. They grow best in moist, fertile soil, improved with lots of rich, well-rotted organic matter, such as garden compost. Sow seed indoors during mid-spring into small pots to prevent disturbing the roots when planting out. Harden off seedlings once the risk of frost has passed, and plant out 1–1.5m (3–5ft) apart. Water in and mulch well, and cover with cloches or fleece if the weather is still chilly. Water plants regularly, particularly in hot, dry weather, and feed with a liquid fertilizer every couple of weeks. Squash are trailing plants that take up a lot of space but can be trained over supports, such as cane wigwams or trellis. Tie in trained stems regularly to help support the heavy fruit.

Squash are ready to harvest in late summer, when the fruit develops a hard skin and the stem starts to crack. If you want larger fruit, thin them out, leaving two or three per plant. Like pumpkins, winter squash can be stored for many weeks after harvesting if they have been "cured" first (see facing page). Leave them on the plants as long as possible but harvest before the first frosts.

'Turk's Turban' squashes are among the most distinctive and attractive. They can be enjoyed as decoration until used for cooking.

PLANTING OUT

1 Plant out squash seedlings when the risk of frosts has passed but before they become pot-bound or grow too large to handle easily. Squash germinate and grow quickly, so don't sow them too early.

2 Water the seedlings before removing the pots so they slip out easily, and plant the seedlings at their original depth. Water well and add a mulch of organic matter to feed them and to retain moisture. Sprinkle slug pellets lightly as a precaution.

WATCH OUT FOR...

Squash, cucumbers, courgettes, and pumpkins are related, and are affected by the same pests and diseases (see pp.215 and 221–222).

Glasshouse red spider mite can attack plants during hot summers, sucking sap, discolouring leaves, and seriously weakening plants. Spray with an appropriate insecticide (see p.359) when symptoms first appear. (For more pests and diseases advice, see pp.356–369.)

RADISHES

Crisp and peppery red-skinned radishes are a familiar summer
snack and salad ingredient that are quick and easy to grow.
However, there are also unusual oriental radishes to try,
as well as varieties to harvest in winter.

VARIETIES TO TRY

Summer radish
'Cherry Belle' • 'French Breakfast 3' •
'Marabelle' • 'Scarlet Globe' • 'Sparkler'

Winter radish
'Black Spanish Long' • 'Black Spanish
Round' • 'China Rose' • 'Mantanghong'

Mooli
'April Cross' • 'Minowase Summer
Cross' FI

	SPRING	SUMMER	AUTUMN	WINTER
SOW/PLANT				
HARVEST				

HOW TO GROW

All types of radish grow best in a sunny
spot, with moist, free-draining soil.
Avoid growing them in stony or recently
manured soil, as this causes the roots
to split or fork. Summer radish are very
quick growing, ready to pick in just
2–6 weeks from sowing. For an early
start, sow them indoors in modules in
early spring, 1cm (½in) deep, and plant
them out in late spring. Sow outdoors
from late spring to late summer in rows
15cm (6in) apart, and thin seedlings to
2.5cm (1in) apart. They can also be
grown successfully in containers. Best
pulled young, they become tough and
tasteless if left too long.

Winter radish are slower growing
than summer types, taking 8–10 weeks;
harvest in autumn when the size of
turnips. Sow seed in midsummer in
rows 30cm (12in) apart and thin to
15cm (6in) apart. Keep the soil moist to
encourage rapid growth and succulent
roots. Unless needed, leave mature
roots in the ground until midwinter,
then lift and store them undercover,
somewhere dry, well-ventilated, and
frost-free. Check the roots regularly
for signs of damage or decay.

Mooli radishes are grown in the
same way as winter types. Sow seed
directly in drills from mid- to late
summer, to harvest in autumn. The
roots can be left in the ground until
needed. Unlike summer radish, neither
these nor winter types are suitable
for containers.

WATCH OUT FOR...

Flea beetles eat small holes in the
leaves, which cause seedlings to die
off, and weakens growing crops. Sow
or plant out young plants under
garden fleece.

Cabbage root fly maggots burrow
into the radish, stunting their growth
and causing decay. Cover plants with
insect-proof netting.
(*For more pests and diseases advice,
see pp.356–369.*)

TYPES AVAILABLE

Summer radish are small, quick-growing, and are
eaten raw. They are the easiest to grow in small
gardens and there are lots to choose from.

Winter radish can be eaten raw, grated on to
salads, but their tougher flesh is best enjoyed
cooked. They have a mild flavour, not peppery.

Mooli is an oriental vegetable, rarely sold
in supermarkets. It can be eaten raw if finely
chopped and is commonly cooked in stir fries.

BEETROOT

Beetroot has recently been having a well-deserved comeback. Packed with antioxidants, these colourful roots, available in shades of orange, yellow, and white as well as red, are gracing plates and plots once more.

Beetroot 'Boltardy'

	SPRING	SUMMER	AUTUMN	WINTER
SOW/PLANT	███	██		
HARVEST		███	██	

HOW TO GROW

Beetroot prefer a sunny position with well-drained, fertile soil that has been improved with well-rotted garden compost or manure. If you have heavy soil, warm it in winter with cloches several weeks before sowing. Beetroot seeds are covered in chemicals that prevent them germinating, which should be removed by soaking them for an hour prior to sowing. Sow outdoors in early spring, 2.5cm (1in) deep, 10cm (4in) apart, in rows 30cm (12in) apart. Beetroot "seeds" are actually cases that contain a cluster of seeds, so thin out surplus seedlings as they appear, leaving only the strongest one. If you live in a colder area, protect germinating seeds with cloches or fleece.

Beetroots need regular watering throughout the growing season, particularly in dry spells, to prevent the roots becoming woody. Weed around them carefully by hand – a nick on the roots with a trowel or hoe will damage them and cause them to bleed. For the best flavour, pull roots when they are golf-ball sized, first loosening the soil with a hand fork. As an extra crop, you can also harvest the young leaves, but pick sparingly to avoid checking growth.

WATCH OUT FOR...

Aphids suck sap, weakening the plants and slowing growth. Crops can be delayed or reduced. Spray heavy infestations with a suitable insecticide (*see p.359 for further information*).

Leaf-mining fly larvae feed within the foliage, causing brown blotches. Remove infested leaves as there are no chemical controls available.
(*For more pests and diseases advice, see pp.356–369.*)

GROWING PATIO CROPS

1 Sow pre-soaked seeds sparingly into patio planters, cover them with 2.5cm (1in) of compost, and water them in well.

2 Beetroot seeds germinate about a week after sowing. Keep the compost moist, and site the container in a sunny position. Protect against slugs.

3 Depending on variety, harvest after 6–8 weeks and resow a second or third crop. Water regularly during summer to prevent them bolting (running to seed).

VARIETIES TO TRY

Traditional red beetroot varieties bleed easily, staining clothes and surfaces, so you may prefer other coloured forms that don't leave unwanted marks.

Red varieties
'Alto' F1 • 'Boltardy' • 'Boro' F1 • 'Cylindra' • 'Detroit 6 Rubidus' • 'Red Ace' F1

Other colours
'Albina Vereduna' (white) • 'Burpee's Golden' (orange) • 'Chioggia Pink' (pink)

CARROTS

In a large plot you can grow enough carrots to last for months, but even in small spaces you can produce a good crop, especially of the smaller varieties. Alternatively, try growing some with unusual shapes and colours.

Young roots are deliciously sweet.

	SPRING	SUMMER	AUTUMN	WINTER
SOW/PLANT				
HARVEST				

HOW TO GROW

Sowing early and maincrop varieties will provide you with carrots from summer until winter if you have the space. Carrots prefer a dry site with light, fertile soil that has not been manured in the last 12 months. Make sure there are no stones or clods of soil as this will produce forked or misshapen roots.

Sow early varieties in early spring under cloches, insect-proof mesh (see p.191), or fleece, and maincrops in the open or under mesh in mid-spring; sow seed in succession throughout the growing season. For a late crop, sow an early variety in midsummer. Sow at a depth of 1–2cm (½–¾in) about 2.5cm (1in) apart, and thin plants to 10cm (4in) apart as they grow. Allow 30cm (12in) between rows. Thinning releases scent from the foliage, which attracts carrot fly (see right). Thin in the evening to reduce the effect. Weed around the seedlings by hand. Full-sized carrots are ready for harvesting after 12–16 weeks, depending on the variety. Baby carrots are ready in 8–10 weeks.

◄ **Fine netting** prevents the female carrot flies laying eggs near your crop. The netting need only be 60cm (2ft) high as the flies stay close to the ground. Leave it in place all season.

WATCH OUT FOR...

Aphids attack the leaves, sucking sap and carrying viruses. Apply approved insecticides, or grow under very fine insect-proof mesh.

Carrot fly lay eggs near young plants, which hatch into maggots that burrow into the roots. Protect plants with fleece or fine netting. Avoid disturbing the plants during the day as this can attract the flies.
(For more pests and diseases advice, see pp.356–369.)

TYPES AVAILABLE

Rounded carrots produce short roots and are ideal for growing in containers or in gardens where the soil is thin and stony.

Finger carrots require deeper, finer soil to produce long, unforked roots, although they can be grown as baby carrots where soil is shallow.

VARIETIES TO TRY

Round varieties
'Atlas' • 'Early French Frame' • 'Parmex' • 'Rondo'

Finger varieties
'Adelaide' F1 • 'Autumn King 2' • 'Flyaway' F1 • 'Maestro' • 'Mignon' • 'Nantes 3' • 'Purple Haze' • 'Resistafly'

KOHL RABI

Kohl rabi produce striking stems and leaves, and would make an attractive addition to an ornamental display. Their swollen stems have a delicious nutty flavour, rather like a cross between celery and cabbage.

	SPRING	SUMMER	AUTUMN	WINTER
SOW/PLANT				
HARVEST				

HOW TO GROW

Kohl rabi are tolerant plants and will grow well in most garden soils, sandy or heavy, but will crop best in rich soil, improved with plenty of organic matter. When planting, avoid beds where traditional brassicas have been grown in the last three years to avoid clubroot (*see top right*); kohl rabi is a member of the brassica family.

For early crops, sow seeds under cover in modules and plant out in late spring after the frosts have passed. Sow outdoors in late spring to early summer when the soil has warmed up. Cold soil may cause plants to bolt (run to seed and spoil). Sow in rows 30cm (12in) apart, 2cm (¾in) deep, and 23cm (9in) apart. Kohl rabi is fast growing,

ready to pick when the stems reach golf-ball size, around 7–8 weeks after sowing. Crops left to grow longer become tough and tasteless. For a constant supply throughout the season, sow in repeated batches every two weeks throughout spring and summer. Water plants regularly to prevent roots becoming woody; they won't require additional feeding.

Kohl rabi can be grown successfully in containers, and repeated crops can be planted in the same compost all season; it may need refreshing after each harvest and should be discarded in autumn. Position in a sunny spot and keep plants well watered. Feed container-grown plants every other week using a balanced liquid feed.

As a bonus crop, when harvesting the mature stems also pick the young tender leaves and use them as summer greens.

TYPES AVAILABLE

Purple varieties can be slower to mature and hardier. Sow them later than white-skinned varieties for late-summer and autumn crops.

White varieties are a good choice for quick harvests, and can be sown as "catch-crops" while other vegetables become established.

POTATOES

The humble spud comes in myriad shapes and colours, and has many uses in the kitchen, from summer salads to all-season chips. Potatoes are easy to grow, even in small spaces and containers.

Potato 'Yukon Gold'

	SPRING	SUMMER	AUTUMN	WINTER
SOW/PLANT				
HARVEST				

HOW TO GROW

Potatoes need an open, sunny site with moist, well-drained, fertile soil, improved with plenty of well-rotted organic matter, such as garden compost. Sold as "seed" potatoes (small tubers), they are labelled as "earlies", "second earlies", or "maincrop", depending on when they are ready to harvest.

To suppress weeds, cover the planting area with sheet plastic and plant the tubers through it. Once "chitted" (see below), plant early potatoes in early spring; protect against frost by covering with fleece or drawing soil over tender shoots when frosty nights are forecast.

Plant second earlies in mid-spring, and maincrops from mid- to late spring. Plant tubers 10–15cm (4–6in) deep and cover the chits with 2.5cm (1in) of soil. Space them 30cm (12in) apart, with 60cm (24in) between rows for earlies, 75cm (30in) for maincrops. Keep plants well watered, weed regularly, and "earth up" (see facing page) as needed.

Harvest earlies in early summer, scraping away some soil first to see if they are large enough. Second earlies will be ready in midsummer, and maincrops from late summer to autumn. Unearth them with a fork, taking care not to spear them. Clear all plant debris from the soil.

VARIETIES TO TRY

First earlies
'Accent' • 'Concorde' • 'Epicure' • 'Foremost' • 'Pentland Javelin' • 'Red Duke of York' • 'Swift' • 'Vivaldi' • 'Winston'

Second earlies
'Belle de Fontenay' • 'Charlotte' • 'Estima' 'Kestrel' • 'Kondor' • 'Lady Christl' • 'Picasso' • 'Ratte'

Maincrops
'Desiree' • 'Golden Wonder' • 'King Edward' • 'Maris Piper' • 'Navan' • 'Nicola' • 'Picasso' • 'Pink Fir Apple' • 'Salad Blue' • 'Sarpo Mira'

GARDEN SPEAK

Chitting potatoes
Potatoes can be "chitted" before planting, which involves giving them an early start indoors. To do this, place the seed potatoes with their "eyes" facing upwards, in trays or egg boxes in a warm, light place so that short green shoots or "chits" appear. Once the chits are 5–10mm (¼–½in) long, the tubers are ready to be planted out. Chitting advances maturity so the potatoes can be harvested earlier, giving them some protection from slugs and blight.

PLANTING POTATOES

1 Chit early potatoes inside; second earlies and maincrop can be planted unchitted. Only plant undamaged tubers.

2 Tubers can be planted into individual holes if only growing a few, or in long trenches for larger crops. Plant the chits facing upwards.

3 Fill the holes or trench, covering the tubers with 2.5cm (1in) of soil. When planting chitted tubers, take care not to knock off the developing shoots.

Earthing up

When the developing stems reach 15cm (6in) tall, start "earthing up" by drawing up the surrounding soil to cover the shoots, burying them by half their height. Repeat every few weeks as the shoots grow. This prevents tubers being exposed to sunlight, which turns them green and makes them poisonous. It also helps stifle weeds and deters blight (*see bottom right*), and can protect early varieties from frost. Potatoes grown through black plastic sheeting don't require earthing up.

▶ **Earth up potatoes** carefully to avoid damaging the stems, which are brittle at the base and can snap. Earthing up also helps to control weeds.

Harvesting

If you're not sure when to harvest potatoes, look for tell-tale signs above ground. Early varieties are ready when their flowers begin to open or the buds drop. Maincrops are ready when their foliage yellows, although they can be left in the soil until mid-autumn to bulk up. Cut back stems 10 days before lifting.

◀ **Open flowers** mean that earlies are ready to lift, but maincrops still need time to grow.

Growing in containers

If you don't have much space, you can grow a decent crop of potatoes in a container or strong bag. Ensure that it is at least 30cm (12in) deep, with drainage holes, and half-fill it with compost. Place one or two potatoes on top and cover with 10cm (4in) of compost. Add compost to half-cover the shoots as they grow and water regularly. Harvest the potatoes as soon as they are ready. This method is suitable for all crops.

New potatoes are ideal for growing in strong plastic bags. Harvest the crop by tipping the potatoes out once they have matured.

Potatoes can be grown in any container that drains well and is deep enough for the tubers to develop fully, such as a dustbin.

Storing maincrop potatoes

Lift potatoes on a dry day and leave them to dry on the soil surface. Discard any that are diseased or damaged, and use smaller tubers fresh as they deteriorate sooner. Once the skins are dry, remove excess soil but don't clean them further, to avoid damaging the skins. Store the tubers in paper bags or in trays, somewhere dry, well ventilated, and frost-free. Check them often for damage or decay.

WATCH OUT FOR...

Potato cyst nematodes cause leaves to yellow and plants die off early, reducing the crop. There is no control. Rotate crops and use resistant varieties.

Potato blight causes dead patches on leaves and stems, and on tubers, which rot. It is prevalent in damp summers. Use resistant cultivars, or grow early varieties since blight occurs later in the season. Destroy infected plants. (*For more pests and diseases advice, see pp.356–369.*)

ROOT AND STEM CROPS

Roots are mainly long-term crops, best suited to larger plots where you can plant a worthwhile number and can leave them to grow undisturbed. Reliable to grow, they give a welcome feast when few fresh crops are available.

		SPRING	SUMMER	AUTUMN	WINTER
SOW/PLANT					
HARVEST					

Turnips can be harvested young.

HOW TO GROW

This group of vegetables needs an open, sunny site with deep, light soil, free from large stones. They will crop on heavy soil as long as it drains well; on shallow soils, choose varieties with shorter roots. Sow seed in spring, under cover for celeriac, directly outside in drills for the others, planting out or thinning to their preferred final spacings. Keep plants well weeded to reduce competition and water as required; avoid allowing the crops to become dry as the developing roots may then split when watered.

On smaller plots, interplant slower-growing parsnips and swedes (see p.200) with quicker crops, like radish and pak choi, sown directly, to make better use of the space. In milder areas, leave the roots in the ground in autumn and winter until needed. In colder, wetter areas, lift and store them.

▶ **Protect crops** stored in the soil over winter with a layer of straw or fleece.

WATCH OUT FOR...

Swede and turnips are brassicas and suffer similar pests and diseases (see pp.240–245).

Carrot fly maggots affect parsnip and celeriac, burrowing tunnels in the roots. Stored roots may rot. Protect plants in summer with fine mesh, 60cm (24in) high.

Parsnip canker is a fungal disease that causes brown or black growths on the roots, which may then rot. Destroy infected plants, grow resistant varieties, and rotate crops. (For more pests and diseases advice, see pp.356–369.)

SOWING AND GROWING

1 When sowing directly in the soil, sow seeds in small clusters spaced at the correct planting distance. After germinating, thin each cluster of seedlings, leaving the strongest. Water plants well as they grow.

2 Keep the seedlings weed-free, taking care not to damage the developing roots with the hoe; hand weed if possible. If intercropping, harvest and resow as soon as the catch crops are ready but avoid disturbing the main crop.

3 Harvest some roots as soon as they reach a usable size but leave others in the ground to grow on longer; avoid disturbing adjacent plants. Remove all plant debris after harvesting to prevent the build up of diseases.

▶ TURNIP

Turnips are quick growing and can be harvested as baby roots after 6–7 weeks, or left 11 weeks to grow larger. They prefer cool, moist conditions, and need a fertile soil, improved with well-rotted organic matter. For an early crop, sow seed under cover in spring in modules, and plant out when the seedlings have one or two leaves. Instead of thinning, they can also be grown as clusters.

Varieties to try:
'Armand' • 'Atlantic' • 'Golden Ball' • 'Manchester Market' • 'Purple Top Milan' • 'Primera' • 'Snowball'

◀ SWEDE

Swede is slow-growing, ready to harvest in winter after 20–26 weeks. It needs a sunny site with light soil that drains freely but doesn't dry out. Sow outside in late spring, in drills 2cm (¾in) deep. Cover with fleece or mesh to exclude cabbage root fly. Thin seedlings to 23cm (9in), and water and weed regularly. Harvest the roots when 10–15cm (4–6in) across and protect roots left in the soil in winter with a layer of straw.

Varieties to try:
'Brora' • 'Helenor' • 'Magres' • 'Marian' • 'Virtue'

▶ PARSNIP

Parsnips need an open, sunny site, with light soil that has been deeply dug to allow the roots to grow long and straight. Sow seeds direct in mid- to late spring, once the soil starts to warm; germination can be erratic. Thin seedlings to 10–20cm (4–8in) apart, depending whether you want smaller or larger roots. Water sparingly to encourage deep-rooting and harvest in late summer.

Varieties to try:
'Albion' • 'Countess' • 'Gladiator' • 'Panache' • 'Pinnacle' • 'The Student' • 'White Gem'

◀ CELERIAC

Although celeriac is commonly thought of as a root crop, it is the swollen stems that are eaten. It grows in sun or shade but prefers moist, rich soil improved with organic matter. Sow seed in spring in modules at 10°C (50°F), grow them on under cover, harden off, and plant out in late spring or early summer, 30cm (12in) apart, with the crowns showing above the surface. Water regularly in summer and harvest from early autumn to late winter.

Varieties to try:
'Brilliant' • 'Giant Prague' • 'Monarch' • 'Prinz'

ONIONS AND SHALLOTS

Easy to grow and indispensable in the kitchen, onions are a good crop for beginners. Try your hand at raising sweet-tasting shallots and red-skinned onions, as well as the more traditional garden varieties.

French shallots; easy to hold and slice.

	SPRING	SUMMER	AUTUMN	WINTER
SOW/PLANT				
HARVEST				

HOW TO GROW

Onions are undemanding to grow but prefer a sunny, sheltered spot, and well-drained soil, enriched with organic matter. They can be raised from seed sown in spring, or you can give yourself a headstart and buy "sets", which are small bulbs to plant out. Sow seed under cover into modules and harden off the seedlings before planting them out in late spring. They can also be sown directly outside in drills in late spring, once the soil has warmed up, giving a useful late summer harvest.

Plant onion sets directly outside from early to mid-spring, 5–10cm (2–4in) apart, in rows 30cm (12in) apart, pushing them into the soil with the tips uppermost until just protruding. Many shallots grow too slowly from seed, so plant sets from late winter to early spring, 15cm (6in) apart, in rows 30cm (12in) apart.

Onions and shallots need little attention except regular watering and weeding. Once the leaves start to turn brown, bend over the tops to help ripen the bulbs. When ready in summer, lift the bulbs with a fork, then dry and store (see *facing page*).

TYPES AVAILABLE

Red onions are generally smaller and sweeter than traditional brown-skinned onions and can be finely sliced and eaten raw.

Brown onions have the strongest, most pungent flavour, and there are many to choose from. Some can be harvested small for pickling.

Round shallots need a long season and grow as small clumps, not individual bulbs. They are richer and sweeter tasting than onions.

French shallots are similar in flavour and growth habit to the round types, but are easier to chop because of their elongated shape.

VARIETIES TO TRY

Brown onions
'Ailsa Craig' • 'Bedfordshire' • 'Golden Bear' • 'Setton' F1 • 'Sturon'

Red onions
'Hyred' F1 • 'Kamal' • 'Red Baron' • 'Red Brunswick'

Overwintering onions
'Radar' • 'Senshyu Semi-globe Yellow' • 'Shakespeare'

Round shallots
'Delvad' • 'Golden Gourmet' • 'Pikant' • 'Prisma' F1 (raise from seed) • 'Red Gourmet'

French shallots
'Jermor' • 'Longor' • 'Mikor' • 'Pesandor' • 'Vigarmor' • 'Zebrune'

GROWING ONION SETS

1 Plant onion sets pointed-end up, pushing them lightly into the base of shallow drills. They can also be planted in containers for a small crop.

2 Onions need little routine care during the growing season. Keep them well weeded but water only when established. Check them for signs of disease.

3 When the crop is ready to store, leave the bulbs on the soil surface to dry. Cover large crops if rain is predicted; small crops can be brought under cover.

4 Check stored onions for signs of disease or decay. Don't compost discarded bulbs as some diseases spread easily and are tricky to control.

Overwintering onions

Sometimes called Japanese or "overwintering" onions, these are hardy varieties that grow through the winter to harvest midsummer. Sow seed in late summer directly into a bed outside or plant sets mid- to late autumn into well-drained soil. Plant more closely than summer varieties as some will be lost during winter. Feed the plants twice in winter with a nitrogen-rich granular fertilizer, and thin them out in spring. This technique can only be used with hardy onions – others bolt in cold weather.

Plaiting onion bulbs together using their leaves is the traditional way to dry them and makes a decorative autumn feature.

Storing

Harvest onions and shallots when their leaves turn yellow and topple over; in midsummer for shallots, early to late summer for onions. Once lifted, lay the bulbs on the soil in the sun to dry out, ideally on wire mesh to allow air to circulate around them. If the weather is wet, dry the bulbs in a sunny, warm spot indoors. When the skins have turned papery, remove the leaves and any soil, and store them somewhere light and well ventilated. Lay them out in rows, plait them into ropes using their leaves, or store them in nets.

WATCH OUT FOR...

Onion fly larvae eat the roots and bulbs, causing plants to yellow, wilt, and even die. Rake soil to expose pupae to birds and cover young plants with garden fleece.

Onion white rot causes foliage to yellow and wilt, and white mould appears on the base of bulbs, which rot. Destroy infected plants and rotate crops.
(For more pests and diseases advice, see pp.356–369.)

GROWING SPRING ONIONS

Fast-growing spring onions are a staple of summer salads and Asian cooking, and are ready to harvest 4–6 weeks after sowing. They prefer fertile, well-drained soil and a sunny site. Sow successionally all summer from early spring, every month, into pots or shallow drills, 2cm (¾in) deep, 30cm (12in) apart, allowing 1cm (½in) between them. Weed regularly and water in dry conditions. Harvest when 15cm (6in) high and of your preferred thickness.

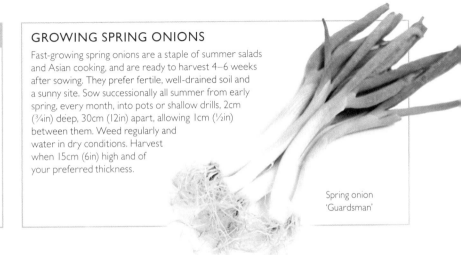

Spring onion 'Guardsman'

GARLIC

A member of the onion family, this versatile ingredient, highly valued for its culinary qualities, is extremely easy to grow. Although it takes time to mature, it grows through winter, takes up little space, and is good in pots.

	SPRING	SUMMER	AUTUMN	WINTER
SOW/PLANT				
HARVEST				

Garlic can be purple- or white-skinned.

HOW TO GROW

Garlic needs warmth to ripen and grows best in a sunny site with rich, moist, well-drained soil. Ideally, plant in autumn or early winter; spring-planted garlic will produce smaller bulbs because they have less time to mature. Separate the bulb into cloves and push the largest ones (discarding any tiny ones) into the soil with the points upwards; the tips should be just below the surface. Allow 10cm (4in) between cloves, and space rows 20cm (8in) apart. Keep the area around the plants free of weeds and the soil moist, particularly in dry conditions.

Check regularly to make sure birds have not pulled out the cloves; if so, push them back into the soil.

Garlic is ready to lift when the leaves turn yellow and wilt. Using a hand fork, lift the bulbs and lay them out to dry in the sun, ideally on wire mesh to allow good airflow. If the weather is wet, dry them indoors on trays, or hang them up in plaits. Once dried, garlic can then be stored in plaits or nets, somewhere cool and well-ventilated. If you prefer, harvest garlic while the stems are still green. This "wet" garlic has a milder flavour and should be used quickly as it will not store.

WATCH OUT FOR...

Onion white rot (see p.233) causes foliage to yellow and wilt and bulbs to become mouldy and rotten. This disease affects all members of the onion family, including garlic.

Rust causes orange patches on leaves, which wither and die, weakening the crop. Avoid planting in damp, shaded areas. There is no chemical control, so remove infected material and improve airflow.
(For more pests and diseases advice, see pp.356–369.)

PLANTING AND GROWING

1 Garlic needs a cold period to grow well, and is best planted in autumn or winter. Plant it in beds or in larger containers.

2 Control weeds during spring and summer and keep plants well watered. Even if plants bolt (run to seed), they still give a good harvest.

3 After harvesting garlic, don't grow other members of the onion family, including leeks and shallots, in the same soil to prevent the build up of diseases.

VARIETIES TO TRY

Supermarket garlic bulbs can be unreliable as they are grown in warmer regions and won't tolerate cool growing conditions. Bulbs supplied by nurseries are virus-free, and are bred to suit local conditions.

'Arno' • 'Californian Late' • 'Cristo' • 'Early Wight' • 'Germidour' • 'Early Purple Wight' • 'Solent Wight'

LEEKS

Although often thought of as a winter vegetable, leeks can be harvested from late summer to late spring, and can be grown with little effort. They store well outside to prolong the harvest.

	SPRING	SUMMER	AUTUMN	WINTER
SOW/PLANT				
HARVEST				

HOW TO GROW

Leeks need a sheltered, sunny site and fertile, well-drained, ideally slightly acid soil; preferably heavy and moisture-retentive. Dig over the bed the autumn before planting and incorporate plenty of well-rotted compost or manure. For an early start, sow seed under cover in late winter in trays or modules, to a depth of 2.5cm (1in). When risk of frost has passed, harden off seedlings when pencil-thick, and transplant them into deep holes, 15cm (6in) in depth, 15cm (6in) apart, with 30cm (12in) between rows. Water around the stems and allow the water to settle the soil around them, rather than backfilling and firming by hand. Seed can also be sown directly outside in drills from early to mid-spring. For a continuous crop, sow at regular intervals and transplant when seedlings are 20cm (8in) tall.

Once established, weed often, but water only in dry spells, and apply a high-nitrogen granular fertilizer in midsummer to late winter, for early to late crops. As the leeks grow, pile earth around the stems to exclude light ("earthing up"); this blanches the stems, making them white and sweet-tasting – deep planting is a good start to this process. Harvest as needed, late summer to late spring.

Storing leeks

To keep harvested leeks at their best, especially at the end of season when you need to clear the beds, bury the stems in shallow trenches. This keeps them fresh and frees up space for new-season crops.

◀ Heeled-in leeks stay fresh for a few weeks until needed, as long as the stems are covered with soil.

PLANTING OUT

1 Transplant from a seedbed or plant out leek seedlings in spring. Use a dibber to make deep individual holes, 15cm (6in) in depth.

2 Trim the roots with a knife or scissors so seedlings are easier to drop into their planting holes. This may slow growth but the roots soon grow back.

3 Water well, so the water washes the soil back into the deep planting holes without leaving large air pockets. This also prevents damage to the leek stems.

PEAS

Sweet, tender peas are well worth growing yourself for a taste that surpasses anything you can buy in the shops. If you don't fancy shelling peas, try mangetout and sugar snap peas, which can be eaten pod and all.

	SPRING	SUMMER	AUTUMN	WINTER
SOW/PLANT				
HARVEST				

HOW TO GROW

Peas grow best in rich, moist soil, improved with well-rotted organic matter, and a sunny spot that does not get too hot. Sow seed outside according to when you want your harvest, from early spring to early summer. Make a trench 5cm (2in) deep and 25cm (10in) wide, water well, then sow seeds at least 5cm (2in) apart, backfilling with soil. If you have space, plant another row 45–90cm (18–36in) away, depending on how tall the variety is, to allow space for picking and weeding. To gain a more continuous crop, sow at intervals when the preceding sowing is 5cm (2in) tall. For a head start, sow podded varieties indoors in late winter into long troughs or plastic guttering (see right), and plant out

in spring. Cover early sowings with fleece to protect plants against frost, and sow quick-growing mangetout and sugar snap peas in late spring and early summer.

Once sown, position supports along the row for the plants to climb. All peas need supports; twiggy sticks are ideal for dwarf or shorter varieties; taller varieties benefit from trellis, rows of bamboo canes, or netting. Keep plants well watered in warm weather; if planted into fertile soil, they won't require extra feeding. When the first pods are ready, pinch out the growing tips (which you can eat in salads). Peas are generally ready to pick about three months after sowing, and they are best harvested when small and tender.

Sow indoors into plastic guttering for an extra early crop. Plant out by sliding the pea seedlings out into a prepared trench.

TYPES AVAILABLE

Mangetout peas are eaten whole and should be picked just as the peas inside start to swell. Best eaten lightly steamed.

Sugar snap peas are allowed to develop for longer than mangetout; pick when the pods fill out but the peas are tiny.

Podding peas are traditional garden peas that are shelled before eating. Pick them young for the best flavour and texture.

BROAD BEANS

Not for nothing are these plants traditional favourites of the allotment; they are at their best when freshly picked. They are also easy to grow, producing good yields of tender crops in early summer.

		SPRING	SUMMER	AUTUMN	WINTER
SOW/PLANT					
HARVEST					

HOW TO GROW

In autumn, choose a sunny, sheltered spot with well-drained, fertile soil and dig in plenty of well-rotted organic matter such as garden compost or manure. For early crops, sow seed under cover in pots in late autumn, transplanting the seedlings outside in early to mid-spring. Sow seed outside in autumn in a sheltered site. Space seed 20cm (8in) apart in rows 45cm (18in) apart. For crops during summer, sow successively in early and mid-spring, when the previous sowing is 10cm (4in) tall. Support growing plants with twigs or bamboo canes, using smaller sticks for dwarf varieties. Mulch around the plants with compost, keep plants well weeded, and water regularly, especially when plants are in flower. Once the first pods have appeared at the base of each plant, pinch out the growing tips. This encourages the beans to mature more quickly and promotes a larger crop.

Harvest when the pods start to swell and the beans inside are thumbnail-size; they become tough and starchy if they are allowed to grow too large. Pick regularly, cutting the pods off, rather than pulling them, to prevent damage to the plants. Eat as fresh as possible.

▶ **Broad beans** mature from the bottom of the stem upwards. Each plant will crop over a few weeks as the pods develop.

▶ **Removing the tips** once the first pod sets encourages quicker ripening, and also deters blackfly which target the soft growth. The tips can be eaten.

FRENCH BEANS

Whether you grow dwarf varieties or climbers, French beans are the perfect crop for a small garden as just a few plants will keep you well stocked all summer. They're also a good choice for containers.

French beans can be dried as haricots.

	SPRING	SUMMER	AUTUMN	WINTER
SOW/PLANT				
HARVEST				

HOW TO GROW

French beans need a warm site, sheltered from the wind, and prefer well-drained soil, with organic matter dug in the autumn before planting (see below). Sow seeds in spring indoors in modules or deep pots, 5cm (2in) deep. When plants are about 8cm (3in) tall, harden them off and plant out once the frosts have passed. For a later crop, sow seeds outside when the soil is warmer.

Support climbing varieties with tall canes 15–20cm (6–8in) apart, one per plant. Plant dwarf varieties 15cm (6in) apart; they grow without support. Water frequently when in flower or cropping. Pick pods often while they are big enough to use but are still tender.

◄ **Encourage the plants** to twine around the supports and pinch off the tips as they reach the top of the canes.

WATCH OUT FOR...

French beans suffer many of the same pests and diseases as runner beans (see facing page).

Anthracnose causes red-brown spots on the pods, followed by pink slime in wet weather. No chemical controls; remove infected plants or grow resistant varieties.

Bean halo blight causes small spots with bright surrounding rings on leaves, which die, reducing yield. Remove and destroy infected leaves.
(For more pests and diseases advice, see pp.356–369.)

VARIETIES TO TRY

Climbing varieties give a good crop from a small space; dwarf beans do well in pots.
Climbing varieties
'Borlotto Lingua di Fuoco 2' • 'Cobra' • 'Hunter' • 'Pantheon' • 'Sultana'
Dwarf varieties
'Annabel' • 'Delinel' • 'Ferrari' • 'Purple Teepee' • 'Sonesta'

Digging a bean trench

To encourage the best crop, a traditional method is to dig a trench 60cm (24in) deep and as long as your planned rows of beans, the autumn before sowing. Loosen the soil at the base with a fork then pile up plant and vegetable waste (the sort normally destined for the compost heap). Backfill with soil and leave it to settle. By spring, the soil will be rich and moisture-retentive, ideal for French and runner beans (see right).

RUNNER BEANS

Worthy of the border as well as the vegetable patch, these climbing beans race up their supports in a flurry of lush growth, creating leafy columns of brightly coloured flowers. The beans are delicious and freely produced.

Runner beans mature in stages, so pick often.

	SPRING	SUMMER	AUTUMN	WINTER
SOW/PLANT				
HARVEST				

HOW TO GROW

Runner beans need a sunny, sheltered position, with deep, fertile soil, improved with organic matter the autumn before planting. They grow best in bean trenches (*see below left*). Sow seeds under cover in mid-spring in deep pots, harden them off, and plant out once the risk of frosts has passed. Provide support (*see below*), planting one plant per cane. Runner beans can also be sown outside in late spring. Sow two beans per cane, thinning to the strongest plant. Water the plants well, especially when in bloom or the flowers may drop off and won't mature into beans.

If planted into well-prepared soil, the developing beans won't need additional feeding.

Tie plants into their supports, pinching out the tips when they reach the top to prevent beans forming out of reach. Harvest the beans while they are young and tender, about 10cm (4in) long, and before the seeds start to swell. Surplus fresh beans can be frozen.

If you have found a variety you like, allow some pods to develop fully in late summer. Collect the beans and dry them on a sunny windowsill. Store them somewhere dry, cool, and frost free, and sow them again the following year.

WATCH OUT FOR...

Runner beans suffer many of the same pests and diseases as French beans (*see facing page*).

Blackfly can form large colonies quickly, sucking sap and weakening plants. Spray heavy infestations with a suitable insecticide.

Rust can occur in wet conditions. Leaves and stems develop orange or brown pustules, then wither and die. Dispose of infected growth, and improve air flow around plants.
(*For more pests and diseases advice, see pp.356–369.*)

VARIETIES TO TRY

Most runner beans have either white or red flowers and make an attractive feature in the garden before the beans form.

Red-flowered beans
'Achievement' • 'Celebration' • 'Enorma' • 'Hestia' (bicolour) • 'Lady Di' • 'Painted Lady' (bicolour) • 'Polestar' • 'Stardust'

White-flowered beans
'Desiree' • 'Moonlight' • 'White Apollo' • 'White Emergo' • 'White Lady'

Providing support

Runner beans are tall climbers and reliably produce heavy crops, so they need strong support. Put these in place before sowing directly or planting out. The supports should be about 1.8m (6ft) tall, and are most easily made from bamboo canes or bean poles. In smaller gardens, make individual frames using 5–6 uprights, or make a line of them (*see right*). Where space allows, or you are growing a large crop, make a linear support with two rows of uprights, linked together, with a cane along the top for added strength.

CABBAGES

One of the most popular of the brassica group of vegetables, cabbage has varieties to plant and harvest nearly all year. The selection includes textured savoys, sweet spring greens, and vibrant red-leaved varieties.

Savoy is a distinctive choice.

		SPRING	SUMMER	AUTUMN	WINTER
SOW/PLANT					
HARVEST					

HOW TO GROW

Cabbages grow in sun or partial shade and prefer moist, fertile, slightly alkaline soil that has been improved with plenty of well-rotted organic matter, such as garden compost. The soil should also be firm to help support the large heads, especially in winter. Depending on the type (see right), you can sow cabbage successively all year. Sow in early spring for summer cabbage; sow in late spring for autumn and winter crops, and sow mid- to late summer for cabbage the following spring. Sow seed 2cm (¾in) deep under cover in modules or outside in a seedbed,

and plant out or transplant the seedlings when they have 3–4 leaves. Keep plants well-watered until established, weed regularly, and remove any dead leaves. Harvest the cabbage when ready using a sharp knife, and clear away any plant debris.

WATCH OUT FOR...

All brassicas suffer similar pests and diseases (see pp.242–245).

Clubroot attacks brassica roots, stunting growth and killing plants. It can last in the soil for 20 years and there is no cure. Destroy infected plants, rotate crops, and lime the soil. Strong seedlings are less vulnerable. Some varieties show resistance, labelled (C) opposite.

Mealy cabbage aphids suck sap and weaken plants. They hide under the leaves. Spray with insecticide. (For more advice, see pp.356–369.)

◄ **Use collars** to protect young plants from cabbage root fly (see. p.244).

SOWING AND GROWING

1 Cabbages are hardy plants but for an early start, sow in spring under cover into trays or modules. This will help to produce stronger plants with greater resistance to clubroot.

2 When planting out, hold the cabbage by the leaves to avoid damaging the roots. Use a dibber to make planting holes about 15cm (6in) deep, water the hole before inserting the plant, then firm it in gently.

3 To harvest, use a sharp knife to cut the whole plant off at the base. Remove all debris to prevent the build-up of diseases, but don't disturb neighbouring plants. Stumps may resprout if left in the ground, especially if a cross is cut in the top.

▶ SPRING CABBAGE AND SPRING GREENS

For spring crops, sow seed in late summer and plant out in early to mid-autumn. Space plants 15cm (6in) apart for spring greens, 25cm (10in) for spring cabbage. Water well until established, then again only in dry spells. In winter, earth up the stems to help support the plants and remove any dead or yellowing leaves. In spring, harvest greens as individual leaves or cut the cabbages whole.

Varieties to try:
'Advantage' • 'Excel' F1 • 'Durham Early' • 'Frostie' F1 • 'Greyhound' • 'Spring Hero'

◀ SUMMER AND AUTUMN CABBAGE

Sow seed in succession, early spring to early summer, to give a harvest through summer and autumn. Make early spring sowings under cover into modules and harden plants off once they have 3–4 true leaves. Plant out 38–45cm (15–18in) apart, once hard frosts have passed; cover plants with fleece on colder nights. Apply a granular feed when adjacent plants start to touch across rows.

Varieties to try:
'Deadon' • 'Derby Day' • 'Golden Acre' • 'Hispi' F1 • 'Kilaton' F1 (C) • 'Kilazol' F1 (C)

▶ WINTER CABBAGE

For crops through winter, sow seed in batches from late spring to early summer. Plant out or transplant when seedlings have 3–4 leaves, spacing them 45cm (18in) apart. Apply a granular fertilizer when adjacent plants start to touch. Hardier varieties can be left in the soil in winter until needed, others should be cut and stored in nets; they will last 6–8 weeks if kept cool.

Varieties to try:
'Celtic' • 'Cordesa' (C) • 'Ormskirk 1' F1 • 'Rigoletto' • 'Savoy King' • 'Tarvoy' • 'Tundra'

◀ RED CABBAGE

Harvested in summer to autumn, sow seed for red cabbage from early to late spring; plant out or transplant the seedlings 45cm (18in) apart, once they have 3–4 leaves. Cover early crops with fleece to protect against frosts. Water well until established, weed regularly, and apply granular fertilizer when neighbouring plants start to touch. Harvest when the heads feel uniformly solid.

Varieties to try:
'Kalibos' • 'Lodero' (C) • 'Marner Large Red' • 'Red Flare' • 'Rookie' • 'Ruby Ball' • 'Ruby Perfection'

KALE

This goodness-packed vegetable fell out of favour for a while but is now hugely popular. It is a hardy and easy-to-grow plant, as architectural as it is flavoursome, and brings interest and sustenance to the winter garden.

	SPRING	SUMMER	AUTUMN	WINTER
SOW/PLANT				
HARVEST				

HOW TO GROW

Kale is a hardy crop and will survive outside in the worst winter weather. It tolerates most soil types, but prefers well-drained soil that has been improved with well-rotted organic matter, such as garden compost. It also benefits from firm, compacted soil, which helps support its tall stems. Sow seeds in mid-spring in pots or modules under cover, and plant out in late spring and early summer. Plant 45cm (18in) apart, taking care not to damage the roots. Firm the plants in well and water thoroughly. Continue to water only sparingly, except in dry conditions, in order to encourage tougher leaves for overwintering.

Keep plants well weeded, and remove yellowing leaves as they appear. If lots of the leaves start to turn yellow in early autumn, apply a high-nitrogen granular or liquid fertilizer to restore colour. If you are growing taller varieties, especially in exposed gardens, stake the plants before they are damaged by strong winds.

Harvest kale from autumn to spring, picking the tender leaves from the centre of the crown to encourage regrowth. Remove any flowers that appear but leave the older leaves in place to help protect the centre. Harvest until the plants flower; the leaves then turn bitter.

Kale can also be grown as a cut-and-come-again salad (see p.207). Harvest when 5–8cm (2–3in) high, or later at 15cm (6in).

Colourful kale varieties make an attractive winter feature in the garden. They are ideal for smaller plots, allowing you to incorporate vegetables into mixed planting schemes.

TYPES AVAILABLE

Curly kale varieties are sweeter-tasting and more tender than traditional smooth-leaved kale. They look attractive in the garden during winter.

Smooth-leaved kale is only grown for the tender leaves at the centre of the plant. Some varieties make handsome border plants.

VARIETIES TO TRY

Coloured (C) varieties are decorative as well as tasty.

Curly kale
'Dwarf Green Curled' •
'Redbor' (C) • 'Reflex' FI •
'Scarlet' (C) • 'Winterbor' FI

Smooth-leaved kale
'Black Tuscan'

BRUSSELS SPROUTS

Few vegetables provoke as strong a reaction as Brussels sprouts – people either love or hate them. Easy to grow, sprouts taste sweetest after a few hard frosts, and can be roasted and stir-fried as well as boiled.

	SPRING	SUMMER	AUTUMN	WINTER
SOW/PLANT				
HARVEST				

VARIETIES TO TRY

Most Brussels sprouts are green, although a few varieties produce red (R) ones. Being more colourful, they are a good choice for mixed planting schemes. Some varieties are resistant to clubroot (C).

'Abacus' F1 • 'Bosworth' F1 • 'Brodie' F1 • 'Clodius' F1 • 'Crispus' F1 (C) • 'Igor' F1 • 'Maximus' F1 • 'Montgomery' F1 • 'Red Bull' (R) • 'Trafalgar'

HOW TO GROW

Brussels sprouts prefer a sunny site, and neutral, moist, well-drained soil, improved with well-rotted organic matter. However, avoid very rich soils, which produce loose, open sprouts. They also benefit from a sheltered site and firm soil to prevent the laden stems being blown over in winter. Sow seeds in trays or modules under cover in early spring, or outdoors into a seedbed in mid-spring. Thin direct-sown seedlings to 7.5cm (3in); plant out indoor-sown plants in mid-spring, when 10–15cm (4–6in) high, spacing them 75cm (30in) apart. Plant deeply, with the first true leaves level with the soil surface to ensure the plants won't blow over when their crop develops. Water well during dry spells and cover with netting as the first sprouts form. Earth up around the stems to provide extra support, or stake plants growing on exposed or windy sites.

Start harvesting in autumn when the sprouts are firm, working from the bottom of the stem up, removing a few from each plant at a time. Alternatively, dig up the whole plant when it is covered in sprouts and hang the stem in a cold, frost-free place (or stand it in a bucket of water), and pick as required.

WATCH OUT FOR...

All brassicas suffer from similar pests and diseases (see pp.240–245).

Pigeons devour the leaves, weakening the plants, and may also damage young sprouts. Cover plants with netting in summer.

Caterpillars, especially those of cabbage white butterflies, eat the leaves, causing serious damage. Use fine netting to deter them. Check for eggs under the leaves, pick off caterpillars, or spray with insecticide. (For more advice, see pp.356–369.)

GROWING SPROUTS

1 Firm the soil around new plants to help support the tall stems as they grow. Attach plant collars to protect against cabbage root fly.

2 Support the plants as they grow by earthing up with soil. In more exposed areas, insert canes or stakes to prevent plants being rocked by the wind.

3 Use a sharp knife to harvest the sprouts or twist them off with your fingers. Cut sprouts soon spoil, so only harvest when needed. Cut stems last several days.

BROCCOLI

Packed with vitamins and highly ornamental, broccoli is an asset to any garden. Choose from white or purple winter sprouting types, which bear an abundance of tender stems, or the large domed heads of summer calabrese.

	SPRING	SUMMER	AUTUMN	WINTER
SOW/PLANT				
HARVEST				

Broccoli 'Early White Sprouting'

HOW TO GROW

Broccoli grows best in a sunny site, in rich soil that has been improved with plenty of well-rotted organic matter, such as garden compost or manure. The two types, sprouting and calabrese, are sown in different ways. Sow sprouting broccoli under cover into small pots or modules, in early spring for early varieties, midsummer for late crops. From mid-spring, it can also be sown directly outside in seedbeds and covered with cloches or fleece. Plant out or transplant seedlings into their final positions in late spring, once the frosts have passed, leaving 60cm (24in) between plants and rows.

Summer calabrese dislikes root disturbance, and should be sown outside where it will grow on in soil that has been raked to a fine tilth. Sow in drills 2cm (½in) deep, 30cm (12in) apart, with 45cm (18in) between rows.

Keep both types well watered in summer and cover with netting as the heads appear to protect against birds. The heads can become heavy, so support plants using canes or earth-up the base of the stems. Harvest summer or winter heads before the tiny flowers within the florets open. Pick sprouting broccoli often to encourage an extended crop; the more you pick, the more it crops. Cut calabrese heads in summer when less than 10cm (4in) across to encourage more flowering shoots; use a sharp knife to cut the florets, starting with the central head.

TYPES AVAILABLE

Calabrese is a quick-growing crop and is harvested the summer after sowing. Pick the heads while they are small for the largest harvest.

Sprouting broccoli is a winter staple and will crop for several weeks; harvesting the stems encourages growth.

VARIETIES TO TRY

Calabrese
Clubroot resistant varieties (C) are available.
'Apollo Brokali' F1 • 'Belstar' F1 • 'Fiesta' F1 • 'Monclano' F1 (C)

Sprouting
Different varieties of sprouting broccoli produce purple heads (P) or white (W).
'Claret' F1 (P) • 'Early White Sprouting' (W) • 'Rudolph' (P) • 'White Star' (W)

CAULIFLOWER

Cauliflowers can be harvested most of the year but they are sometimes challenging to grow. The extra effort is well rewarded however, with delicious homegrown curds, and coloured forms rarely seen in supermarkets.

	SPRING	SUMMER	AUTUMN	WINTER
SOW/PLANT				
HARVEST				

VARIETIES TO TRY

Clubroot-resistant types (C) are available.

Summer cauliflower
'Igloo' • 'Raleigh' FI • 'Snowball'

Autumn cauliflower
'Autumn Giant' • 'Clapton' FI (C) • 'Skywalker'

Winter cauliflower
'Boris' FI • 'Galleon' FI • 'Mayflower' FI • 'Medallion' FI

Coloured cauliflower
'Graffiti' • 'Romanesco' • 'Trevi'

HOW TO GROW

Cauliflowers can be grown year-round but sowing times differ for summer or winter varieties. All cauliflowers need fertile, well-drained soil that is firm enough to support the heads and has been improved with well-rotted organic matter. For early summer crops, sow seed under cover in autumn in small pots, or sow in midwinter for a slightly later crop. If you don't have much space, try growing miniature summer varieties, which can be grown 15cm (6in) apart.

For an autumn crop, sow under cover or outside under fleece in early spring. Harden off seedlings before they reach 5cm (2in) tall, then transplant outside, 60cm (24in) apart. For winter varieties, sow in late spring outdoors where they are to grow on, 75cm (30in) apart.

Keep the plants well watered as they grow, and feed them with liquid fertilizer in midsummer. If growing white varieties, shield the curds from the sun (see below). Harvest the heads while firm, cutting the stem with a sharp knife.

▶ Cauliflower 'Romanesco' is an unusual lime-green variety, with distinctive pointed curds. It is sometimes described as a calabrese but is really an autumn cauliflower.

BLANCHING THE HEADS

1 Cauliflower curds can discolour in bright sun. Prevent this by folding or tying 4–5 outer leaves over the centre. Make sure the curds are dry to prevent them rotting. Keep the leaves in place until harvest.

2 The curds are ready to pick when large enough to crop but still firm to touch. Do not harvest cauliflowers until you plan to use them; they soon deteriorate. When harvesting, cut the curd with some surrounding leaves to keep it fresh for longer.

WATCH OUT FOR...

All brassicas suffer from similar pests and diseases (see pp.240–245).

White blister is a disease that attacks all brassicas, and causes white blisters on the leaves and distorted growth. There are no chemical controls. Remove infected plants, improve airflow, and avoid wetting the leaves when watering.

Molybdenum deficiency causes leaves to become narrow and strap-like. Raise soil pH with lime.
(For further advice, see pp.356–369.)

GLOBE ARTICHOKES

The most elegant and statuesque of kitchen garden plants, globe artichokes wouldn't look out of place in an ornamental border. The huge flower buds are a delicious treat, expensive to buy yet very easy to grow.

		SPRING	SUMMER	AUTUMN	WINTER
SOW/PLANT					
HARVEST					

Globe artichokes can also be grown as ornamentals.

HOW TO GROW

Globe artichokes prefer a sheltered, sunny position in well-drained, moisture-retentive soil that has been enriched with well-rotted organic matter, such as garden compost. They are most commonly planted as young plants, bare-root from autumn to spring or as container-grown plants at any time if well watered afterwards. If you want several plants, sow seed under cover into pots in late winter or early spring. Harden the seedlings off and plant them out in early summer, 90cm (3ft) apart, with 90cm–1.2m (3–4ft) between rows. Water in well and regularly during dry spells and feed using a balanced general fertilizer in spring. To help new plants establish, remove any flowers produced the first year. In later years, the buds can be thinned to produce larger heads. When harvesting, timing is crucial; using secateurs, cut the flower buds when they reach golf-ball size but before the scales start to open. Cut heads last a few days but are best used quickly. Harvest too late and the heads are inedible.

Remove dead material when the plants die back in autumn, and if you live in a frost-prone area, protect the crown with a layer of straw over winter. Plants should be replaced every three years. Take offsets (young shoots) in spring from your existing plants and grow on.

JERUSALEM ARTICHOKES

Despite both being called "artichokes", globe and Jerusalem artichokes are not related. Globe artichokes are grown for their flower heads, while the Jerusalem type is a root crop, producing fleshy tubers in autumn that are eaten like potatoes and have a nutty flavour.

Related to the sunflower, Jerusalem artichokes are hardy perennials, and grow well even in poor sites. They grow to over 2m (6ft) tall and can be used as a windbreak, although will cast shade. The plants spread quickly and can be invasive if not harvested in autumn. Lift the tubers when the foliage dies back. Replant some tubers to grow on and harvest the rest. Use them fresh.

Globe artichokes are large perennials and grow best in rich soil. Mulch plants in autumn or spring with well-rotted organic matter.

WATCH OUT FOR...

Black bean aphids attack the stems and leaves, sucking sap, distorting growth, and weakening the plants. If severe, treat with a suitable insecticide (see p.359).

Petal blight is common in wet seasons and causes flowerheads to turn brown, then shrivel and develop fluffy mould. There are no chemical controls. Remove infected heads, avoid planting in shady sites, and keep plants healthy. (*For more pests and diseases advice, see pp.356–369.*)

VARIETIES TO TRY

If growing globe artichokes in smaller gardens, choose varieties with coloured heads (C) and plant in mixed borders. Look out for:

'Green Globe Improved' • 'Gros Vert de Laon' • 'Purple Globe' (C) 'Romanesco' (C) • 'Violetta di Chioggia' (C)

ASPARAGUS

These succulent spears appear only briefly in late spring, but once established, they crop for many years with very little maintenance. Tender spears appear in late spring and can be harvested for several weeks.

	SPRING	SUMMER	AUTUMN	WINTER
SOW/PLANT				
HARVEST				

The spears are delicious steamed.

HOW TO GROW

This perennial plant grows in the same spot for up to 20 years, so choose the site carefully. It prefers a sunny, sheltered position with well-drained soil, improved before planting with plenty of well-rotted organic matter. It is usually grown from young bare-root crowns, planted in spring (see below), or can be planted as container-grown specimens at any time of year if well watered. For the most productive plants, choose all-male varieties. If you want lots of plants, and are willing to wait for them to grow on, asparagus can also be grown from seed. Sow the seed under cover in late winter into modules, then plant out the seedlings in spring once they have been hardened off.

New crowns should be allowed to establish themselves for at least two years before harvesting (see below). Keep the plants well watered all summer, mulch with well-rotted organic matter in autumn, and apply a balanced granular fertilizer in spring, before and after harvesting. During summer, support the tall ferny growth with canes and keep plants well-weeded. At the end of summer, cut down the yellowing growth to 2.5cm (1in) above the soil and clear away all plant debris.

VARIETIES TO TRY

All-male asparagus hybrids (M) are the best choice as they don't waste energy producing seed, so give stronger crops. Most named varieties are sold as plants or as bare-root crowns.

'Ariane' • 'Backlim' F1 (M) • 'Connover's Colossal' • 'Gijnlim' (M) • 'Jersey Knight' • 'Pacific Purple' • 'Theilim' F1 (M)

PLANTING AND HARVESTING

1 Dig a trench, 20cm (8in) deep, add rich organic matter, and mound up the base. Position the bare-root crowns, spacing them 30cm (12in) apart, and spread out the roots. Cover them with soil and water well.

2 Mature plants, planted at least two years earlier, should be cropped as the new shoots appear in spring. Cut off the spears 2.5cm (1in) below soil level when they are about 20cm (8in) tall. Remove every spear to encourage more to grow.

WATCH OUT FOR...

Slugs and snails eat the emerging spears in spring and can be particularly damaging. Apply slug pellets, use beer traps, or use anti-slug nematodes as biological control.

Asparagus beetle larvae and adults feed on the spears and foliage, weakening the plants. Destroy them on sight. Spray badly affected plants with a suitable insecticide and burn all plant debris in autumn. (For more pests and diseases advice, see pp.356–369.)

ANNUAL HERBS

Fast-growing annual herbs are a must in the garden, even if you only have space for a few pots. They thrive in beds or containers, so plant them close to your kitchen door or barbecue area to pick fresh whenever needed.

	SPRING	SUMMER	AUTUMN	WINTER
SOW/PLANT				
HARVEST				

Thai basil has a subtly different flavour, making it an interesting variety to grow.

HOW TO GROW

Annual herbs are quick and easy to grow from seed, sown in batches from late spring to summer, to give a constant supply into autumn, or sown under cover in winter if given enough light and warmth. When they are large enough to plant out, they can be grown on outside in beds and containers in a sheltered, sunny site, in moist, well-drained soil or compost. When planting in beds, avoid very fertile sites; this promotes leafy growth that is poorly flavoured. Similarly, feed herbs planted in containers only sparingly. Watering is more important however, as coriander and dill are prone to suddenly bolting (running to seed) if plants become dry. Harvest the leaves and stems as needed, picking regularly to encourage new growth. Keep some for drying, freezing, or for making into pesto.

WATCH OUT FOR...

Aphids are attracted by the leafy growth, sucking sap and weakening plants. Avoid using insecticides; encourage natural predators such as ladybirds, blast the pests off with water, or use organic control.

Slugs and snails are major pests, spoiling leaves or eating whole plants. Apply slug pellets, or use nematodes as biological control.
(For more pests and diseases advice, see pp.356–369.)

◄ **Once in flower**, annual herbs are past their best, but grow them on to collect seed.

SOWING UNDER COVER

1 To avoid disturbing roots when planting out, sow basil and parsley into large-module trays that provide space for the seedlings to develop. Use a fine compost for sowing seeds.

2 Make hollows in the compost at the correct depths and sow seed into them. Cover with compost, water, and cover the trays with clear plastic to keep moist. Keep the trays at the required temperature.

3 Seeds germinate at different rates, so check often. As soon as seedlings appear, remove any covers and keep them warm. Thin them as they grow to leave the single strongest plant per module. Harden off and plant out.

▶ BASIL

This is a tender annual with aromatic leaves and stems. Sow seed under cover into module trays in spring, harden off, and plant out in a sheltered, sunny border or container, or grow on under cover. Pinch out regularly to encourage bushier growth. Container plants can be brought in and grown on over winter in a bright spot. There are many forms to choose, some quite decorative.

Varieties to try:
'Aristotle' • 'Genovese' • 'Lime' • 'Neapolitan' • 'Purple Ruffles' • 'Sweet Green' • 'Siam Queen' • 'Thai Sita'

◀ PARSLEY

This is a biennial herb, commonly grown as an annual for its tasty flat or crinkled leaves. Sow seed under cover in spring into modules to prevent root disturbance, which can trigger bolting; germination can be slow. Harden off and plant out into moist, well-drained soil, in sun or partial shade. Seed can also be sown outside in summer in drills. Keep plants well-watered during spring and summer and remove any flowers that appear.

Varieties to try:
'Envy' • 'Moss Curled 2' • 'Paravert' • 'Plain Leaved 2'

▶ DILL

This tall herb is grown for its mild-tasting leaves and seed, and makes a decorative addition to borders. Sow directly in spring in its final growing position, into moist, fertile soil. If transplanted, disturbed, or allowed to become dry, dill will bolt. Sow successively in batches until midsummer. Harvest the leaves before the plant flowers and use them fresh or dried. Collect the seeds as they turn brown and dry, then store them.

Varieties to try:
'Diana' • 'Dukat' • 'Tetra'

◀ CORIANDER

Coriander is a tall annual, grown for its tasty leaves and seed. Sow seed in regular batches, directly outside in their final growing positions from early spring to late summer. It prefers a moist, well-drained soil; grow in full sun for seed, partial shade for leaves. Keep plants well-watered to prevent bolting. Harvest and use the leaves fresh, and freeze any surpluses. Allow the seed to turn brown and dry before collecting it.

Varieties to try:
'Calypso' • 'Confetti' • 'Slow Bolt'

HARDY BORDER HERBS

Once established, hardy perennial and shrubby herbs provide a wealth of different flavours and scents year after year. Many form large clumps or bushes, so you won't need many plants to supply all your culinary needs.

	SPRING	SUMMER	AUTUMN	WINTER
SOW/PLANT				
HARVEST				

Sage and thyme like a sunny spot.

HOW TO GROW

Most perennial and woody herbs originate from the Mediterranean and prefer a hot, sunny position with poor, dry soil. Good drainage is essential, and if planting on heavy soil, first dig in some coarse grit and bulky organic matter, such as composted bark. Perennial herbs are normally sold container-grown, and are planted in spring and summer when in active growth. Some, like tarragon and mint, spread quickly and can be invasive, so should be planted into containers plunged into the soil to restrict their growth.

Hardy herbs are easy to grow, and often develop stronger scents and flavours when neglected slightly. In addition to watering in dry spells, support taller herbaceous herbs, like mint, in summer but cut all growth to the ground in autumn. They also benefit from being divided every couple of years (see p.332–333). Once established, shrubby herbs like sage and bay require only a light trim in spring to keep them in shape.

Many hardy herbs can also be grown in containers, provided they have good drainage. Plant into soil-based compost and site the pots in sunny, sheltered positions. Water regularly; feed herbaceous herbs monthly, shrubby ones annually.

WATCH OUT FOR...

Slugs and snails eat the softer leaves and stems, especially in spring. Herbaceous herbs are most affected. Apply slug pellets, use beer traps, or lay gritty traps.

Cats can be a particular problem on herb beds, which they often use as litter areas. Use cat repellent sprays or powders, or insert twiggy stems and netting to act as a barrier.
(For further advice, see pp.356–369.)

PLANTING A HERB BED

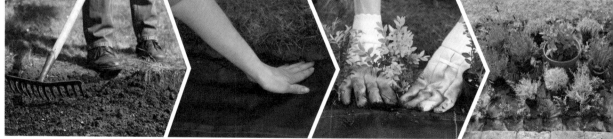

1 Choose a sunny spot and prepare the soil by adding grit to heavy soils or organic matter to lighter soil. Weed the area thoroughly.

2 Lay plastic membrane before planting the herbs to suppress weeds. This will help to warm the soil earlier in spring and retain moisture in summer.

3 Use a sharp knife to cut holes in the membrane and plant through it. For a formal design, consider edging the bed with a low hedge.

4 Choose a variety of herbs that enjoy the same growing conditions. Arrange them before deciding their final positions, allowing space for them to grow.

► **Mint** is a spreading perennial that can be invasive, so contain its roots. It needs moist, well-drained soil, and will tolerate some shade.

◄ **Rosemary** is an evergreen shrubby herb, best planted in poor, well-drained soil in a sunny site. Harvest the stems regularly.

► **Thyme** is a low-growing evergreen perennial that will form a dense carpet. It is ideal for patio containers and windowboxes.

◄ **Sage** is an evergreen shrubby herb, best grown in a sunny position in well-drained soil. It can be short-lived in cooler areas.

► **Bay** is a reliable, hardy evergreen shrub. It can be grown in large patio containers if clipped regularly.

◄ **Oregano** is a low-growing perennial herb, ideal for containers. It needs a sunny site and well-drained soil. There are many varieties.

► **Chives** This grass-like perennial will tolerate some shade, and forms a spreading clump. Its leaves and flowers can be eaten.

◄ **Tarragon** is a spreading perennial herb. There are two main types, Russian and French; French is more highly regarded for flavour.

FRUIT IN THE GARDEN

Growing your own fruit may conjure images of space-hungry orchards and strawberry fields, but with a bit of careful planning, fruit trees, bushes, and vines can be included in even the smallest garden schemes.

▲ DUAL-PURPOSE FRUIT

Although grown for their crops, many fruit trees and bushes are highly decorative. Spring-flowering apples and cherries are as attractive as many ornamental forms, with the bonus of fruit in summer and autumn. Fruit bushes, such as blueberries, give a good show, even in containers, easily rivalling conventional flowering shrubs.

► MIXED PLANTING

Rather than creating a fruit garden, plant fruit in mixed beds and borders. Most fruit trees can be underplanted with ornamentals, and some make attractive focal points, while many bushes make good bedfellows with border and patio ornamentals. You can even add delicious summer strawberries to your hanging baskets.

◄ PATIO CONTAINER

Containers offer a useful way to grow fruit in gardens where the soil is poor, the site is cold and exposed, or you don't have space in the borders. Some fruit, such as blueberries, need an acid soil and are usually grown in containers, as are tender crops like peaches, which can be moved to a sheltered spot when flowering. Most fruit can be grown in pots and will need regular feeding and watering during summer; some may need support.

▲ DWARF VARIETIES

If you don't have space for larger trees, or want to grow several on a smaller plot, choose dwarf or grafted varieties. The yield will be smaller than full-sized trees, but the quality and flavour are identical. Choose trees on rootstocks to suit your needs, whether growing them in pots or borders. Also consider family trees, with two or more varieties on one stem.

▲ WALL-TRAINED FRUIT

If you have a sunny wall, this is a spectacular and space-saving way to grow fruit. You can buy some plants already partially trained, or you can do the training yourself. Fruits such as peaches and nectarines thrive when grown this way, particularly on warm brick walls, and are easier to cover with fleece or netting to protect the blossom and fruit. A wide range of trees, from cherries to pears, are suitable for wall-training. Grapes are an obvious candidate. Wall-training requires some skill, which can be learned over a few seasons.

BUYING AND PLANTING FRUIT

When you have decided what crops you'd like to grow, you then need to decide how, where, and when to buy your plants; whether you need more than one; and the best way to plant them.

Container-grown plants can be planted at any time of year. Inspect them carefully before deciding which trees to buy.

BUYING NEW FRUIT PLANTS

Fruit plants are widely available in large garden centres, which offer a reasonable choice all year. Trees and plants are usually supplied in containers, and can be planted immediately. Specialist nurseries generally offer a wider selection of fruit, often supplied bare-root in winter, and often by post.

Container-grown plants

The advantage of container-grown plants is that they can be planted at any time of year, if well watered afterwards. You can also inspect plants for health and vigour before you buy them. When buying container-grown fruit, avoid those with weeds growing in the compost or bulging pots. Ease the plants from their pots and reject any that are pot-bound, which will root poorly. Plant as soon as possible; keep them watered if this isn't possible.

Bare-root plants

Lifted and sold when dormant, bare-root plants are available only from late autumn until spring. They are supplied without soil surrounding their roots, so should be planted straight away, or temporarily planted, "heeled in", to prevent them drying out. Bare-root plants are often cheaper than container-grown specimens, and the range available is larger. They are usually supplied by specialist nurseries, although garden centres may also sell some bare-root plants, such as raspberry canes.

FLOWER POLLINATION

The blossom of fruit trees and bushes is pollinated by insects, and many varieties must be cross-pollinated by another plant of the same species in order to set fruit. If you have limited space, buy self-fertile varieties; you will only need one plant, although trees do fruit better if cross-pollinated. Alternatively, find out what type of pollinator your tree needs before buying and check nearby gardens to see if there are suitable varieties.

For successful cross-pollination, compatible trees must flower together (be in the same "pollination group"). Some apples and pears are "triploids", meaning their pollen is sterile, and require two pollinators to set fruit.

PLANTING BARE-ROOT FRUIT

Plant bare-root fruit trees and bushes as soon as possible to prevent the roots drying out. The planting technique differs from planting container-grown plants (see p.121), as roots are exposed and can be easily damaged. Bare-root plants often establish more quickly than container-grown specimens, rooting directly into the new soil.

1 Dig a suitably large hole and lower the plant in place, using a cane to ensure the mark on the stem is level with the soil surface. Tease out the roots gently and spread them out evenly inside the planting hole.

2 Mix organic matter into the soil and backfill, working it gently in between the roots. Make sure the plant is planted upright, then water the soil every few spadefuls to ensure there are no air pockets trapped between the roots.

3 If planting trees or larger shrubs, support the main stems using stakes and adjustable ties that can be loosened as the plant grows. Support smaller shrubs using canes. Remember to check ties regularly for adjustment.

4 Once the tree or shrub is planted, and supported if necessary, water it thoroughly to help settle soil around the roots. Mulch around the plant to retain moisture, and water regularly during dry spells until established.

PLANTING WALL-TRAINED FRUIT

Training fruit against walls and fences is a useful way to use empty vertical surfaces for crops, but they must be planted correctly. The important thing is to provide basic support first, such as horizontal wires or trellis, so the plants can be tied in as they are planted. Additional supports can then be added as the plants grow on.

1 Horizontal wires, spaced 60cm (2ft) apart, are ideal for training fruit against walls and fences, and are easy to fix using vine eyes or screw eyes (above). Use strong, galvanized wire, which is very long-lasting.

2 If planting a row of wall-trained fruit, mark out the planting distances first, so they are evenly spaced. Cordon trees and soft fruits can be planted more closely than freestanding plants, as little as 30cm (12in) apart.

3 Once planted, train the stems and branches as required, whether vertical, angled or fan-trained, and tie them onto the wires with soft string. Use canes to hold young stems straight and remove them once mature.

4 Rain may have difficulty reaching the roots of wall-trained fruit, so plants should be watered frequently until well established. Mulch plants to help retain moisture and water mature fruiting plants well during dry spells.

A YEAR IN THE FRUIT GARDEN

Most fruiting trees and plants are perennials, so there is no need to sow or plant them every year. Because they are in the ground for many years, routine care is vital if good crops are to be produced. Fruit left to its own devices often produces poor yields, and can be prone to problems.

SPRING

Preparation
- **Early spring** is your last chance to spray trees with a winter wash to deter pests such as aphids.
- **Mulch around the base** of all fruit trees and bushes using well-rotted manure or compost.
- **Top-dress container-grown plants** and feed fruit trees and bushes with an appropriate fertilizer.
- **Water and feed plants regularly** as temperatures rise and the plants come into vigorous growth.

Sowing seed
- **Sow melon seeds** under cover in mid- to late spring in a heated greenhouse; sow in midsummer if your greenhouse is unheated.

Planting out
- **Plant strawberry runners** when the soil has warmed up and cover with cloches or fleece until after the last frosts. To help build up the plants, don't let them fruit in their first year. Pick the flowers off in mid-spring.
- **Plant bare-root trees** and bushes in early and mid-spring, as long as the soil is not frozen. This will be your last opportunity. (Container-grown types can be planted at any time of year.)
- **Finish planting raspberry canes** in mid-spring.

Routine care
- **Keep trees and plants well weeded**, taking care not to damage their roots.
- **Prune fan-trained** peaches and nectarines.
- **If frost protection is not already in place**, cover any tender plants with horticultural fleece to protect the blossom. Plum and cherry trees may also need protection.
- **Hand-pollinate** vines or trees that are growing under glass, which may not be accessible to insect pollinators.
- **In mid-spring**, prune and tie in fig trees.

- **In late spring**, train your grape vines, pinching out the vine shoots to leave two laterals (see p.275).
- **Prune out dead and damaged growth** from plum trees and remove any unwanted shoots on trained trees.
- **Tie blackberries**, loganberries, and tayberries into their supports if necessary.
- **Once flowers appear**, cover soft fruits with netting to protect the developing fruits from birds.
- **Apply a mulch of straw** around the base of strawberry plants to suppress weeds and keep the fruit clean.
- **Check regularly for signs of pests and diseases**, especially sawfly caterpillars, which may target gooseberry and currant bushes. Deal with them as they appear (see *individual fruit guides or pp.356–369 for further general information*).

Harvesting
- **Harvest any early gooseberries** that have been grown under cover.

Keep strawberries clean on a bed of straw.

SUMMER

Routine care

- **In early summer**, peg down or remove the runners from fruiting strawberry plants.
- **Thin out fruits** of apple, pear, plum, peach, apricot, and nectarine trees, and grape vines.
- **Net cherry trees** to deter birds.
- **Make sure plants are well watered** – especially those in containers – and mulch to conserve moisture and suppress weeds.
- **Feed plants** with high-potash fertilizer as the fruits develop.
- **Remove any dead and diseased shoots** and plants, and destroy them rather than composting.
- **Check for signs of pests and diseases** and take immediate action should any appear.
- **Continue to tie in trained plants** such as blackberries and other hybrid berries.
- **Prune currant bushes** and gooseberries.
- **In late summer**, prune fruited stems of apples and pears. Prune damsons and plums after fruiting.
- **Deadhead herbs** after flowering.

Harvesting

- **Harvest tree fruits as they appear**, and prune nectarines, apricots, and peaches once they have fruited.
- **Pick ripe currants** and gooseberries as they appear.
- **Blueberries, strawberries, summer-fruiting raspberries, and currants** should be ready for picking by midsummer.

Other tasks

- **Once strawberries have fruited**, remove old straw and leaves. Cut out fruited raspberry canes.

AUTUMN AND WINTER

Routine care

- **In autumn**, weed thoroughly around all plants and cut off and remove any damaged or diseased shoots.
- **Finish any summer pruning** of tree fruits and tie in any wayward shoots on trained plants.
- **Make sure stakes are secure** and firmly in the ground, and check the tree ties are in place.
- **Move any tender plants** such as citrus indoors.
- **Cut out old canes of blackberries** and hybrid berries after they have fruited.
- **In winter**, remove any netting from plants to prevent damage if snow falls.
- **Apply winter washes to trees and bushes** as needed. Apply a top-dressing of sulphate of potash to all plants.
- **Cover peaches, apricots, and nectarines** to protect their blossom from peach leaf curl and early spring frost, and wrap up containers to protect against frost damage.
- **Prune apples and pears** if frost is not forecast.
- **Prune autumn raspberries**, gooseberries, and currants.
- **Cover strawberries** with cloches or fleece.
- **Move container-grown plants under cover** to encourage an earlier crop.
- **Take precautions** against pests and diseases.

Harvesting

- **Pick autumn raspberries** until the first frosts and harvest any remaining perpetual strawberries.
- **Harvest the last ripening fruits** and store any gluts.

Other tasks

- **In autumn**, order any new bare-root trees or bushes and prepare the soil for them.
- **In winter**, plant bare-root plants as soon as they arrive if the soil isn't frozen.

Thin plum fruitlets to encourage full-sized fruit.

Prune pear and apple trees in winter for the best crop.

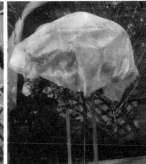

Use fleece to protect plants from frosts.

MANAGING A GLUT

For many fruit crops, even more so than vegetables, the harvest is fast and furious in summer and autumn, often presenting you with a glut. Fortunately, there are ways to even out the harvest, and by using simple preserving techniques, you need not waste a single berry.

▼ EVEN OUT THE HARVEST

All types of fruit have their own cropping periods, but with careful planning you can aim for a selection that gives a steady, mixed harvest, from gooseberries and strawberries in early summer to late apples and grapes in autumn. Most fruit is also available in early-, mid-, and late-season varieties, which extends their season by several weeks.

You can also extend the growing season of certain container-grown fruit, such as perpetual strawberries, by moving them under cover in spring or autumn.
Blueberries have a long harvest period, with early varieties ready in July and late ones cropping into September.

▼ STORE APPLES AND PEARS

Established apple and pear trees tend to be bountiful, and most likely to give you a surplus crop. Early-fruiting varieties should be eaten fresh but late croppers will last for weeks or months if stored correctly.

Harvest apples when they come away in your hand; pick the pears when still underripe. To store, select only unblemished fruit and place them in single layers in shallow containers or on shelves. Store the fruit in a cool, frost-free, well-ventilated position under cover, and check them regularly for signs of decay.
Apples and pears can be wrapped in tissue or newspaper. Store them in a container that allows air to circulate.

▼ FREEZING FRUIT

Freezing freshly picked fruit is the best way to preserve the flavours, colours, and textures while at their peak. All sorts of fruit can be stored this way, whether frozen whole like gooseberries, pitted like cherries, or first cut into usable slices, like apples and peaches.

Some soft fruits have a tendency to clump together when frozen, especially small berries, and are best frozen individually on trays. When frozen, they can then be decanted into smaller containers. You can also use this method to prevent sliced fruit sticking together when frozen. Date all frozen fruit and use within 3–6 months to enjoy it at its best.

Freeze small berries in a single layer on a baking tray before moving into labelled freezer bags or containers.

▶ PRESERVING

Bottling is a traditional method of preserving fruit (either whole or in large pieces) and can be used for a wide range of tree and bush fruit. There are various ways to bottle fruit, but all involve putting the fruit in bottles or jars with hot or cold sugar syrup, heating, then sealing with air-tight lids. Store in a cool, dark place, and use the fruit throughout autumn and winter.

Fruit can also be bottled in alcohol to produce flavoured spirits such as raspberry vodka, or steeped in wine or cider vinegar to make fruit-flavoured vinegars. Only bottle clean, undamaged fruit.

Sterilize all containers by washing thoroughly in hot, soapy water before drying completely in a warm oven.

▼ JAMS, SAUCES, AND CORDIALS

The traditional approach to preserving fruit is to boil it in sugar and water to make thick-set jams or syrupy cordials. This is a simple way of preserving many types of fruit, including currants, strawberries, gooseberries, blackberries, raspberries, apples, and plums, either as single or mixed flavours.

Jams will last for up to six months. Fruit sauces often contain spices, and are cooked until thickened but still runny. They keep for a few weeks. Cordials are strained to a thin syrup, which is then diluted with water to drink straightaway. The syrup will last a few days, or can be frozen in ice cube trays as individual portions.

Some soft fruits require additional pectin, which can be purchased, to produce a thick-set jam.

FRUIT CROP PLANNER

Use this table to check when to plant, prune, and harvest your fruit crops. The timings will vary for different climates, so adjust them according to your own site and weather conditions.

CROPS		J	F	M	A	M	J	J	A	S	O	N	D
Apples	SOW												
	PLANT	■	■									■	■
	HARVEST								■	■	■	■	
	PRUNE	■	■					■	■			■	■
Apricots	SOW												
	PLANT	■	■									■	■
	HARVEST								■				
	PRUNE			■	■		■	■	■				
Blackberries and hybrids	SOW												
	PLANT			■								■	
	HARVEST							■	■	■			
	PRUNE	■	■										
Blueberries	SOW												
	PLANT			■								■	
	HARVEST								■	■			
	PRUNE	■	■										
Cherries	SOW												
	PLANT			■								■	■
	HARVEST						■	■	■				
	PRUNE				■	■		■					
Currants – black-	SOW												
	PLANT	■	■								■	■	
	HARVEST							■	■				
	PRUNE	■	■									■	
Currants – red- and white-	SOW												
	PLANT										■	■	
	HARVEST							■	■				
	PRUNE							■	■				
Figs	SOW												
	PLANT			■								■	
	HARVEST								■	■			
	PRUNE		■	■			■	■	■				
Gooseberries	SOW												
	PLANT	■	■									■	
	HARVEST					■	■	■					
	PRUNE	■	■				■	■					

Key

▬▬▬	SOWN, PLANTED, HARVESTED UNDER COVER
▬▬▬	SOWN, PLANTED, HARVESTED OUTDOORS

CROPS		J	F	M	A	M	J	J	A	S	O	N	D
Grapes – outdoor	SOW												
	PLANT	▬	▬									▬	▬
	HARVEST									▬	▬		
	PRUNE		▬	▬	▬	▬	▬	▬	▬	▬			
Peaches and nectarines	SOW												
	PLANT	▬	▬									▬	▬
	HARVEST								▬	▬			
	PRUNE				▬	▬	▬	▬	▬				
Pears	SOW												
	PLANT	▬	▬									▬	▬
	HARVEST								▬	▬	▬		
	PRUNE	▬	▬					▬	▬			▬	▬
Plums, damsons, and gages	SOW												
	PLANT	▬	▬									▬	▬
	HARVEST								▬	▬			
	PRUNE						▬	▬	▬	▬			
Quinces	SOW												
	PLANT	▬	▬									▬	▬
	HARVEST										▬	▬	
	PRUNE	▬	▬									▬	▬
Raspberries – summer	SOW												
	PLANT	▬	▬								▬	▬	▬
	HARVEST							▬	▬				
	PRUNE								▬	▬	▬		
Raspberries – autumn	SOW												
	PLANT	▬	▬							▬	▬	▬	▬
	HARVEST								▬	▬			
	PRUNE	▬	▬										
Strawberries – summer	SOW												
	PLANT		▬	▬	▬				▬	▬	▬		
	HARVEST				▬	▬	▬	▬					
	PRUNE												
Strawberries – perpetual	SOW												
	PLANT			▬	▬	▬	▬	▬	▬	▬	▬		
	HARVEST								▬	▬	▬	▬	▬
	PRUNE												

APPLES

Apple trees can be grown in the smallest of spaces and can be trained into different forms, such as fans or cordons, to suit any site. As well as delicious fruits, they also provide spectacular displays of blossom in spring.

Worcester Pearmain is a dessert variety.

		SPRING	SUMMER	AUTUMN	WINTER
PLANT					
HARVEST					

HOW TO GROW

Plant apple trees in a warm, sunny position – although cooking varieties are more tolerant and can be trained on north-facing walls. All prefer free-draining, fertile soil, but will tolerate all but very wet or dry conditions. Bare-root trees can be planted late autumn to early spring; container-grown apples can be planted at any time, as long as you incorporate plenty of compost or manure. Freestanding trees require staking; trained forms such as fans and cordons need a system of posts and wires, or can be trained onto a fence or wall. Remove any fruit for the first two years to encourage the tree to establish fully and develop a branching structure.

Apple varieties, such as 'Golden Noble', can be bought on rootstocks of different vigour to suit your particular needs.

Pollination

Apple flowers must be pollinated to set fruit, and unless there are apple trees growing nearby, you'll need to plant at least two varieties from the same pollination group (trees are listed A to D: early to late) according to when they flower. Some are termed "self-fertile" but will crop better if cross-pollinated. Some, like 'Bramley's Seedling', are triploid. These need two pollinator varieties to bear fruit but cannot be used as pollinators themselves. Seek expert advice.

If you only have room for one tree and no pollinator, consider a "family tree", with two or more varieties grafted on to one plant.

Rootstocks

Apple trees are sold grafted onto rootstocks to control their size and vigour. Choose one that best suits your garden and your own needs.
M27 Most dwarfing, ideal for trees planted in containers. Trees grow to 1.5–2m (5–6ft).
M9 Dwarfing, needs good soil, but suitable for large containers. Trees grow to 2m (6ft).
M26 Semi-dwarfing, ideal for large containers, cordons, and fans. Trees grow to 2.5m (8ft).
MM106 Semi-vigorous, ideal for fans. Trees grow to 4.5–5m (12–17ft).
MM111 Vigorous, requires space. Trees grow to 5.5–6.5m (17–21ft).
M25 Very vigorous, suitable for large gardens. Trees grow to 8m (25ft).

VARIETIES TO TRY

Cooking varieties
'Bramley's Seedling' (triploid) • 'Golden Noble' (C) • 'Howgate Wonder' (C) • 'Lane's Prince Albert' (D)

Dessert varieties
'Court Pendu Plat' (D) • 'Discovery' (B) • 'Egremont Russet' (A) • 'Fiesta' (B) • 'James Grieve' (B) • 'Golden Delicious' (C) • 'Lord Lambourne' (A) • 'Pixie' (C) • 'Sunset' (B)

Fruiting types

Most apple trees are "spur-bearing", which means that their fruit is produced on short, stubby spurs that form on stems at least two years old. Over time more spurs form, giving more fruit, until they eventually become overcrowded and need thinning out in winter (*see right*).

Other varieties are referred to as "tip-bearing" and carry much of their fruit at the ends of stems that were produced the previous summer. When pruning these trees the aim is to remove stems and branches that have fruited, and to encourage new shoots that will fruit in following years. Before pruning your trees, make sure you know what type they are first.

Fruit thinning

In midsummer, after the "June drop", when the tree drops excess fruitlets, those that remain should be thinned to allow them to grow on to full size. When trees are left to overcrop, the apples are smaller and may not ripen fully, and the overladen branches can snap. Thin fruit clusters to one or two fruitlets per 10–12cm (4–5in) of stem on dessert apples, and single fruitlets every 15–20cm (6–8in) on cooking apples. Remove undersized, diseased, or damaged fruitlets first.

Pruning and training

All apples should be trained into shape when first planted. Established, freestanding trees need only basic pruning in winter. Trained trees are additionally pruned in summer.

Pruned growth

After planting, prune one- or two-year-old trees to 60–75cm (24–30in) high, leaving 3–4 lateral stems. Cut these back by two-thirds.

Prune spur-bearing trees to maintain an open centre. Prune strong new sideshoots back to 4–6 buds; reduce weaker growth by half. Thin out crowded fruiting spurs and remove dead wood.

Prune tip-bearing apples, cutting sideshoots over 30cm (12in) long back to a bud. Tip-prune the main branches. Maintain an open centre and prune dead or diseased stems.

Established cordons need little winter pruning, other than thinning congested spurs. In mid- to late summer, cut new shoots from the main trunk back to three leaves, and sideshoots from existing spurs to one leaf.

Established fans should be pruned as if each arm were a cordon. In summer, cut new shoots from the main arms back to three leaves and prune all sideshoots to one leaf each. Remove any shoots that appear from the main trunk.

Thinning Removing excess fruitlets in summer is essential to achieving a healthy crop of decent-sized fruit.

Store surplus apples during winter on shelves in a cool, dry, frost-free place, such as a garage. Check them regularly for signs of decay.

WATCH OUT FOR...

Apple sawfly lay eggs that hatch into tiny maggots that burrow into the developing fruit. Some fruit will fall as a result, others are left with unsightly scars across the skin. Dispose of fallen fruit; any that continue to ripen are safe to eat.

Codling moth caterpillars are another cause of maggoty apples. Control the larvae by spraying with an insecticide (*see p.359*) in June and again three weeks later.
(*For further advice, see pp.356–369.*)

PEARS

The buttery texture and delicious taste of pears make this fruit a must for any garden. They have a reputation for being tricky to grow but are as easy as apples, their only weakness being susceptibility to early frosts.

		SPRING	SUMMER	AUTUMN	WINTER
PLANT					
HARVEST					

'Concorde' is a tasty variety to eat fresh from the tree.

HOW TO GROW

Pears require a warm, sunny site, and should be planted away from frost pockets where their early spring flowers could be destroyed by hard frosts, resulting in little or no fruit at harvest time. The site should also be sheltered from strong winds that could damage blossom and cause fruit to fall early.

Pears prefer a rich, well-drained soil with lots of organic matter dug in, such as compost or manure. Bare-root trees should be planted while dormant, from late autumn to late winter, but container-grown pears can be planted at any time if kept well watered until established.

In smaller gardens, pears can be grown in containers or trained as space-saving espaliers, cordons, and fans against walls and fences, although they are too vigorous to grow as stepovers. Remove all fruit for the first couple of years after planting to allow the tree to establish a strong root system and a healthy framework of branches.

Pollination

Pear flowers must be pollinated to set fruit, so unless there are pear trees in neighbouring gardens, you must plant at least two varieties from the same pollination group. Trees are termed A to C (early to late), according to when they flower. Triploid pears need two pollinators and certain varieties do not have compatible pollen, so seek advice when buying them.

WATCH OUT FOR...

Scab causes corky patches on apple and pear fruits, which may shrivel and fall. Remove infected fruit (see p.359).

Pear midge lays eggs on the flower buds in spring. Maggots feed inside the fruitlets, causing them to blacken and drop. Destroy infested fruitlets.

Birds and wasps attack mature fruit, especially if the skin is damaged. Net small trees and hang wasp traps in the branches.
(For more pests and diseases advice, see pp.356–369.)

VARIETIES TO TRY

Dessert varieties
'Beurré Hardy' (pollination group B) • 'Beth' (C) • 'Concorde' (C) • 'Conference' (B) • 'Doyenné du Comice' (B) • 'Gorham' (C) • 'Louise Bonne of Jersey' (A) • 'Merton Pride' (triploid) • 'Williams' Bon Chrétien' (B)

Cooking varieties
'Black Worcester' (C) • 'Catillac' (triploid) • 'Vicar of Winkfield' (C)

Pear blossom is vulnerable to frost damage, so avoid planting in cold sites and frost pockets. At night, protect young trees with garden fleece.

Rootstocks

Pear trees are always supplied grafted onto quince rootstocks to restrict their size. Trees left growing on their own root system would become too large for most gardens.
Quince C – Semi dwarfing, suitable for trained specimens. Needs fertile soil. Trees grow to 3m (10ft).
Quince A – Vigorous and less fussy about soil conditions. Can be used for fans, cordons, and freestanding trees. Trees grow to 6m (20ft).

Fruit thinning

Fruitlets that have managed to avoid the spring frosts and "June drop" (*see far right*) will need thinning in midsummer to ensure they grow to their full potential. If allowed to overcrop, the fruit will be under-sized and may fail to ripen fully; overladen branches may snap.

Thin out pear clusters to one or two fruitlets every 10–12cm (4–5in) on freestanding trees, and to single fruitlets at the same spacing on cordons, fans, and espaliers.

▶ **When thinning fruitlets**, take the opportunity to remove any that are especially small and those that show signs of disease or damage.

"June drop" is a natural process in which trees shed overcrowded or damaged fruit in early summer, usually July. Wait until it has passed before thinning out the remaining fruitlets.

Pruning and training

Freestanding trees are pruned in winter the same way as apples (*see pp.262–263*). As their blossom is vulnerable to frost, they are often trained against walls as espaliers or fans.

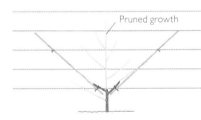
Pruned growth

Attach horizontal wires to a wall or fence, 30cm (12in) apart. Plant a branched, one- or two-year-old tree against them, pruning it to leave two branches 45cm (18in) above the soil. Train the branches laterally using canes.

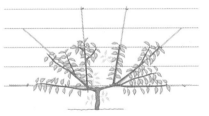

The first summer after planting, use canes to train new sideshoots that develop from the two main branches into a basic fan. Remove any that grow towards the centre of the tree or outwards from the wall. Tie young stems with soft string.

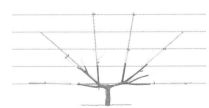

The first full winter after planting, prune the tips of all lateral branches back by one-quarter to one-third in length. Check all branches are securely tied in place. Remove any unwanted stems growing directly out from the main trunk.

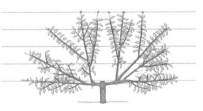

During the second summer, attach more canes and tie in additional sideshoots to form the ribs of the fan, creating a balanced shape. If required, remove congested growth by pruning long sideshoots on the main ribs back to three leaves.

Picking and storing

Judging when pears are ready to pick can be tricky, as culinary varieties only soften when cooked, and eating varieties should be picked when slightly underripe – the final ripening is done in the fruit bowl. To test if an early- or mid-season pear is ready, taste for sweetness – it should be still be firm. Once picked, late pears need storing to ripen, in a dry, dark, well-ventilated place such as a garage. Check them often as pears can quickly go from being under- to overripe in a matter of days. Take care when picking pears as the skin damages easily and the fruit will quickly spoil.

PLUM FAMILY

Plums are one of the easiest fruits to grow as they require little pruning and often crop heavily. Self-fertile varieties mean that only one tree is required, and there is a huge range of cooking and eating varieties to suit all tastes.

	SPRING	SUMMER	AUTUMN	WINTER
PLANT				
HARVEST				

Mouth-watering plums are a sure taste of summer.

HOW TO GROW

To give a good crop, plum trees need plenty of moisture, and require a moist soil that drains freely. They also prefer a sheltered site to protect their early spring flowers from damaging frosts. Bare-root trees should be planted in winter; those grown in containers can be planted at any time if kept well watered. Plum trees are too vigorous to train as cordons or espaliers but can be grown freestanding or as fans, or in containers if you choose trees grafted on to dwarfing rootstocks. Plums are prone to a number of diseases (see *facing page*) that can kill trees if infected growth isn't pruned out quickly. Check trees regularly.

Rootstocks

Plum trees are supplied grafted on rootstocks that restrict their size and encourage regular harvests. Two rootstocks are commonly used:
Pixy Semi-dwarfing, suitable for trees in containers. Trees grow up to 2.2m (7ft).
St Julien A Semi-vigorous. Trees grow up to 2.7m (9ft).

TYPES AVAILABLE

Plums are popular, with varieties suitable for cooking or eating fresh from the tree. A few are more versatile and can be used for both.

Gages have possibly the most delicious fruit within this group. They are usually sweeter and have a rounder shape than plums.

Damsons are smaller than plums and gages, and tend to have a darker skin and sharper flavour, making them excellent for cooking.

Bullaces bear the smallest, most abundant fruit of all, and are very hardy. They are only suitable for cooking due to their tart flavour.

VARIETIES TO TRY

Most plums are self-fertile (SF) but some need separate pollinators (see *opposite*).

Plums
'Avalon' (dessert; pollination group A) •
'Blue Tit' (cooking/dessert; SF) •
'Early Laxton' (cooking/dessert; B) •
'Marjorie's Seedling' (cooking/dessert; SF) • 'Opal' (cooking; SF) • 'Victoria' (cooking/dessert; SF)

Gages
'Cambridge Gage' (partly SF) •
'Denniston's Superb' (SF) • 'Golden Transparent' (SF) • 'Old Green Gage' (C)

Damsons
'Farleigh Damson' (C) • 'Merryweather Damson' (SF) • 'Prune Damson' (SF)

Bullaces
'Black Bullace' (SF) • 'Langley Bullace' (SF) • 'White Bullace' (SF)

Pollination

Self-fertile plums pollinate their own flowers, so you only need to grow one tree. Others need separate pollinators that flower at the same time. When buying plums, choose those from the same pollination group, labelled A to C (early to late) according to flowering time.

◄ **Plums flower in early spring** and are at risk of frost damage. Cover young and container-grown trees with garden fleece when frosts are predicted. Remove during the day to allow insects to pollinate. Young fruitlets are also vulnerable to frost.

Picking

Plums are ready to pick when slightly soft. They often ripen at different times on the same tree, so several pickings may be required. Plums and gages are ready mid- to late summer, damsons and bullaces towards autumn. Pick fruit with the stalk still intact.

Ripe plums don't keep long, so eat them soon after picking. Firm and slightly underripe plums will ripen in the fruit bowl over a couple of weeks.

WATCH OUT FOR...

Plum leaf-curling aphid suck sap from the leaves, causing them to curl and become misshapen. Treat with pesticides in midwinter and again at bud burst (see p.359).

Silver leaf enters wounds, causing a grey sheen on the leaves that may turn brown and fall. As the disease spreads, branches die back, until the whole tree dies. Prune infected material but sterilize tools between plants; silver leaf is easily spread.
(For further advice, see pp.356–369.)

Pruning and training

Plum trees should be pruned as little as possible to avoid silver leaf (see below) infecting the wounds. Only prune plums when in active growth in spring and summer.

Pruned growth

Prune new freestanding trees by removing the main stem above the uppermost sideshoots, and shorten 3–4 healthy branches by half or two-thirds to promote bushiness.

To prune established trees, thin congested stems to improve airflow between branches, take out weak or damaged growth, and remove overly vigorous upright new shoots.

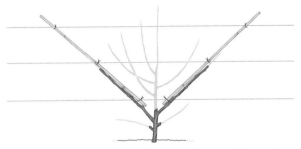

Prune new fan-trained trees by removing the main stem and leave only two branches 40cm (16in) long either side of the main stem, 25cm (10in) above the soil. Train the two fan arms using canes fixed to wires.

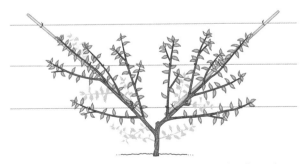

The first summer, select new sideshoots to train against the wires and tie in new growth. Cut back surplus shoots to one leaf, and any growing the wrong way or from below the fan arms. Repeat in following years.

CHERRIES

Modern cherry trees are ideal for smaller gardens as many are self-fertile, so you only need to grow one tree. Compact forms are available, and they give a fine display of spring blossom, as well as delicious summer fruit.

Picked fresh from the tree, cherries are a summer treat.

	SPRING	SUMMER	AUTUMN	WINTER
PLANT				
HARVEST				

HOW TO GROW

There are two types of cherries: sweet and acid. They are grown in different ways so be sure you know which you want. Sweet forms are the fussiest and need a sunny, sheltered site. In cooler areas, they are best grown trained against warm walls. Acid cherries are less demanding, and crop well even in cool, shaded positions. Bare-root cherries should be planted in winter; those grown in containers can be planted at any time. All prefer rich, free-draining soil, so add plenty of well-rotted compost when planting. They can tolerate slightly alkaline or acidic conditions, but avoid heavy soils as the shallow roots may rot. Cherries are prone to silver leaf disease (see p.267), so prune carefully.

Pollination

Many modern cherry varieties are self-fertile and will pollinate their own flowers, which means you only need to plant one tree. Others require cross-pollination in order to set fruit, so unless there are compatible varieties growing nearby, you'll need to plant two or more cherries from the same pollination group. These are listed A to D (early to late) according to flowering time.

◄ Cherry blossom can be pink or white, and is generously borne in spring.

Rootstocks

Cherries are naturally very large trees, too big for most gardens, and traditionally required long ladders to harvest the fruit. Modern trees are now supplied grafted onto rootstocks that restrict their size and make them more suited to domestic gardens. The most common rootstocks are:

Gisela 5 Dwarfing, suitable for trees in containers and wall-trained specimens. Requires good soil. Trees grow up to 2–3m (6–10ft).

Colt Semi-dwarfing, suitable for trees in large containers or fan-trained specimens. Any soil. Trees reach 4–5m (12–15ft).

TYPES AVAILABLE

Acid cherries are too sharp to eat directly from the tree but make great jam, sauces, or fillings for pies. They are the easiest to grow.

Sweet cherries are delicious eaten fresh from the tree, but can also be cooked. They require a warm, sheltered site to ripen fully.

VARIETIES TO TRY

Most cherries are self-fertile (SF) but some must be grown with other varietiess from the same pollination group. Self-fertile cherries will crop better if cross-pollinated.

Acid cherries
'Kentish Red' (SF) • 'Morello' (SF) • 'Nabella' (SF)

Sweet cherries
'Bigareau Napoleon' • 'Celeste' (SF) • 'Lapins' (SF) • 'Merton Glory' • 'Regina' 'Stella' (SF) • 'Summer Sun' (SF)

Pruning and training

To avoid silver leaf, a disease that can be fatal to some fruit trees, cherries are pruned only when in active growth. Prune young cherries in the same way as plums (see p.267); prune mature freestanding trees to create an open, balanced shape.

Pruned growth

Established acid cherry trees crop on wood produced the previous year. After picking, prune out fruited stems and thin congested growth (*above*). Sweet cherries need pruning in spring to remove dead or diseased growth.

To prune established acid cherry fans (not shown), remove old growth in spring to promote new stems, and remove any wayward shoots. After fruiting, cut back fruited stems, which will be replaced by the new growth.

Established sweet cherry fans are pruned by cutting sideshoots back (*above*) to 5–6 leaves in summer. New growth and uprights should be tied in horizontally. After fruiting, pruned sideshoots should be cut to three leaves.

Protection

Cherries flower in early spring, which means the blossom can be damaged by hard frosts. Unless planted in a sheltered site, protect young trees with garden fleece. Trees should also be protected against birds, which will quickly strip a tree of fruit. Net trees before the fruit starts to ripen, making sure birds can't sneak underneath.

WATCH OUT FOR...

Cherry slugworms are slimy sawfly larvae that leave skeletal patches on leaves. Spray with insecticide (see p.359).

Cherry blackfly sucks sap and causes leaf curling in early summer. Use an insecticide (see p.359) in spring when aphids first appear on the foliage.

Spotted wing drosophila lays eggs in developing cherries, spoiling the fruit with its larvae and the rot that follows. Use an insecticide (see p.359). (*For more pests and diseases advice, see pp.356–369.*)

Net your cherries before they ripen as birds won't wait. Secure any netting to the ground to prevent birds becoming trapped inside.

Picking and storing

Harvest cherries as soon as they are soft to the touch, picking them by the stalk to avoid damaging the skin. Use secateurs or scissors to remove them from the tree. Sweet cherries last a week after picking and can be frozen. Acid cherries require cooking to make them palatable.

Use scissors and snip fruit stems to avoid damaging the skins. This will make harvesting a slow process but fresh cherries are worth it.

PEACHES AND NECTARINES

Fuzzy peaches and their smoother cousins, nectarines, are delicious but can be a challenge to grow in cooler climates. Success comes with a bit of effort and the right conditions – few summer fruit crops are as rewarding.

	SPRING	SUMMER	AUTUMN	WINTER
PLANT				
HARVEST				

Freestanding trees need a very sheltered position.

HOW TO GROW

Peaches and nectarines are fully hardy but their early spring flowers are easily damaged by frosts, which prevents them fruiting; the young fruitlets are vulnerable too. To provide adequate protection, train them as fans and grow them against warm, sunny, south- or southwest-facing walls or

fences. Dwarf trees can also be grown freestanding in containers filled with soil-based compost, such as John Innes No. 3. Bare-root trees are planted in winter; container-raised trees can be planted any time if kept well watered afterwards. All varieties prefer rich, well-drained, slightly acidic soil, with a pH of 6.5–7.0. Prepare the ground before planting by digging in plenty of organic matter, such as garden compost. To prevent silver leaf infecting wounds (see p.267), prune only when the trees are in active growth during spring and summer.

◀ **Juicy peaches** may be tricky to grow but they are deliciously rich and tasty. A fruiting tree also provides a real talking point in the garden.

Protection and pollination

During late winter the trees need protection from rainfall to help prevent peach leaf curl, and in spring, protection from frosts. Container-grown trees can be brought under cover. Outdoor, fan-trained trees should be covered with bubble insulation or plastic sheeting and garden fleece. When the flowers start to open, remove the covers on bright, dry days to allow insects to pollinate them, which is essential for fruiting. If the weather remains wet, you'll need to pollinate the flowers by hand using a soft brush.

Good airflow is important for preventing diseases, so don't wrap trees completely and remove covers when the weather allows.

VARIETIES TO TRY

Some peach varieties show good disease resistance (DR) to peach leaf curl (see right for more information). Nectarines are a more reliable crop.

Peaches
'Avalon Pride' (DR) • 'Garden Lady' (dwarf) • 'Peregrine' • 'Rochester' • 'Red Haven'

Nectarines
'Early Rivers' • 'Fantasia' • 'Lord Napier' • 'Nectarella' • 'Pineapple'

WATCH OUT FOR...

Peach leaf curl causes red blisters on the leaves, which drop, weakening the tree. Spores enter the buds in late winter, carried by rainfall. Cover the tree with plastic sheeting in winter, remove infected leaves, and pick up all fallen leaves in autumn.

Glasshouse red spider mite causes fine mottling on the foliage and early leaf fall, especially on trees in sheltered spots. Introduce a predatory mite, *Phytoseiulus*, to control the pest.
(For further advice, see pp.356–369.)

Pruning and training

To provide a sheltered spot, peaches and nectarines are usually trained against walls on lateral wires. They are pruned twice a year in spring and summer.

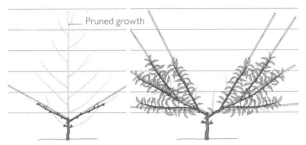

Pruned growth

The first spring after planting a one- or two-year-old tree, cut the main stem, leaving one branch each side, 25cm (10in) above the soil. Cut the branches to 35cm (14in) and tie them horizontally on canes.

The first summer, as sideshoots grow, select three each side, one below the branches, two above, and train them on canes. Cut other shoots to one leaf. In spring, cut back the ribs by a quarter.

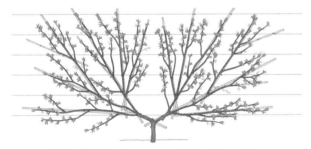

Prune established fans in spring to remove dead or damaged growth and wayward stems. On each rib, choose two sideshoots to grow on and remove the others. After harvesting, cut back fruited stems to make way for those left to grow on.

Prune established freestanding trees by removing one-quarter of the stems that fruited last year, cutting back to healthy, pointed buds. Remove any dead or damaged wood, and thin out old branches that have stopped bearing fruit.

Thinning

Developing peach and nectarine fruitlets need thinning in early summer to allow the remaining fruits to ripen fully and reach their optimum size. This process also helps to prevent laden branches snapping and damaging the tree. Thin to one per cluster, at a spacing of 10cm (4in) apart, when the fruitlets are the size of hazelnuts, then to 20cm (8in) when they reach walnut-size.

◄ **Harvest fruit** when they are slightly soft near the stalk, cupping and twisting them off. Fresh fruit won't keep long so eat them soon.

GROWING APRICOTS

Apricots are closely related to peaches and are grown in the same way, most commonly as fans on south-facing walls. Dwarf varieties can also be grown in containers. They are less susceptible to peach leaf curl than peaches and nectarines, and modern varieties, like 'Flavorcot' and 'Tomcot', flower later so are less prone to frost damage. Protect the developing fruit from birds. Apricots are ready for picking when they start to soften in summer and pull easily from the tree.

Apricots to try include: 'Alfred' • 'Flavorcot' • 'Goldcot' • 'Moorpark' • 'New Large Early' • 'Petite Muscat' • 'Tomcot'

◄ **Apricots fruit** on stems produced the previous year. Trees are pruned in spring and summer to promote new growth and replace fruited stems.

QUINCES

These trees are an asset in any garden with their fragrant, pale pink spring blossom, gnarled bark, and large, attractive, unusual autumn fruit. Slow ripening, the fruit is best eaten cooked in jams and pies.

		SPRING	SUMMER	AUTUMN	WINTER
PLANT					
HARVEST					

Ripening fruit make a colourful feature.

HOW TO GROW

These trees are easy to grow and need little care once established. They require a warm, sheltered site and prefer deep, fertile, free-draining, acidic soil (pH of 6.5). Bare-root trees should be planted in winter; container grown trees can be planted at any time if kept well watered afterwards. Dig in plenty of organic matter when planting, such as well-rotted garden compost, and mulch annually in spring with more of the same material.

Autumn fruits should be left to ripen as long as possible, but watch out for frosts.

Picking and storing

Quinces rarely ripen fully in cool climates and should be left as long as possible before picking. Even so, they are still likely to be too hard and sour to eat fresh from the tree. To promote ripening indoors, store unblemished fruit over winter in a frost-free, ventilated place. Check regularly for damage or decay.

◄ **Spring colour** Quince flowers are highly attractive, and give a good show in spring.

Rootstocks

Quinces are often grown on their own root system but may be grafted to restrict their size, making them more suitable for a small garden. Two rootstocks are commonly used.
Quince C Suitable for small gardens. Trees grow to 3m (10ft).
Quince A Suitable for larger plots. Trees grow to over 4m (12ft).

VARIETIES TO TRY

When choosing varieties, you'll often find quinces listed under their botanical name, *Cydonia oblonga*. This is not to be confused with Japanese quince (*Chaenomeles*).

'Champion' • 'Lusitanica' •
'Meech's Prolific' • 'Vranja'

Pruning and training

Quinces are normally grown as freestanding trees, and are pruned in winter. They are too vigorous to train or to grow against walls.

Pruned growth

To prune established trees, cut back strong sideshoots to 30cm (12in) and tip-prune the main branches in winter. Keep an open centre.

FIGS

Native to the Mediterranean, figs are easy to grow and ideal for planting in containers. Unlike most fruit trees, they are not too fussy about soil conditions and will fruit in poor, shallow soil, as long as it drains well.

		SPRING	SUMMER	AUTUMN	WINTER
PLANT					
HARVEST					

In cold areas, pack trees with straw in winter.

HOW TO GROW

Figs need a warm, sunny site, and do best trained on a south- or southwest-facing wall, where they can be easily protected with nets and fleece from pests and frosts. Figs fruit best with restricted roots, so plant in a "fig pit". Plant bare-root trees in winter, and container-grown trees at any time, if well watered. Figs set fruit in late summer; they will overwinter and ripen the following summer. Remove any figs bigger than peas in late autumn, leaving only tiny embryo fruits at the tips to over-winter.

Make a fig pit using 30cm (12in) concrete slabs, sunk into the soil to form a box. Line the bottom with a few inches of hard core or crocks.

Picking and storing

It's time to pick the figs once they are fully coloured, slightly soft, and the stalks start to bend. Look for drops of nectar appearing at the base of the fruit but don't pick too early as they won't ripen further. Gather them when ripe and consume immediately.

VARIETIES TO TRY

'Brown Turkey' • 'Brunswick' • 'Rouge de Bordeaux' • 'White Marseilles'

Pruning and training

Whether trained against a wall or grown freestanding, figs should be pruned in spring to remove old growth, and again in summer to encourage the formation of fruitlets. Fig sap can irritate skin, so wear gloves when pruning trees.

To prune freestanding trees, in spring select long, old stems that only fruit at the tips and cut them back to within 5–8cm (2–3in) of the trunk or branch. Remove congested growth from the centre and any dead or diseased wood. Also cut back frost-damaged shoots to healthy growth. In summer, pinch out growing tips once they have 5–6 leaves to stimulate new fruit production. This will also let in the sun to ripen last year's fruit.

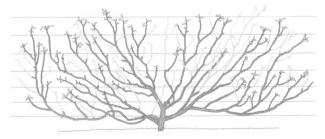

To prune established wall-trained trees, in late spring cut back old, unproductive main branches to one bud. Prune half of all sideshoots growing from the trunk and branches back to one bud. Remove any dead or diseased growth, any crossing branches, and any wayward shoots. Tie in new growth. In summer, pinch out sideshoots once they have 5–6 leaves to encourage fruit formation. Tie in new growth to the wires.

GRAPES

Wine grapes can successfully be grown outdoors in most cool climates, and many modern varieties are also sweet enough to eat, at least when cooked. True dessert grapes grow best under cover but you will need space.

	SPRING	SUMMER	AUTUMN	WINTER
PLANT				
HARVEST				

Ripening grapes should be watered well.

HOW TO GROW

Grape vines are fully hardy but prefer a sheltered site, away from strong winds and frost pockets. They need full sun to ripen the fruit, and are best planted against south-facing walls or fences. Grape vines will grow in a wide range of soils, including chalk, sand, and clay, and will tolerate poor, shallow conditions. Bare-root vines should be planted in winter; container-grown vines can be planted at any time. They need little additional feeding once established, as their long roots dig deep. Being climbing plants, grapes need support, and can grow quite large. The simplest way is to grow them as cordons (see *facing page*). They can be allowed to clamber over pergolas but will fruit poorly.

Container-grown grapes are widely available in garden centres, but contact specialist nurseries for the best selection.

Indoor grapes

Certain dessert grapes require long, warm seasons to ripen fully, and can only be grown successfully in large greenhouses or conservatories. Growing grapes indoors requires year-round care, so consider carefully before planting.

Growing under cover allows you to grow a wider range of dessert grapes as long as you have plenty of space available.

TYPES AVAILABLE

Wine grapes are commonly grown outside, although the fruit is often too sour to eat fresh. Use them for cooking or wine-making instead.

Dessert grapes are delicious fresh from the vine and can be grown outside if you choose the right varieties. Others must be grown indoors.

VARIETIES TO TRY

Grapes ripen green, referred to as white (W), or red (R), depending on variety.

Outdoor wine grapes
'Bacchus' (W) • 'Brant' (R) • 'Chardonnay' (W) • 'Dornfelder' (R) • 'Phönix' (W)

Outdoor dessert grapes
'Black Hamburg' (R) • 'Boskoop Glory' (R)

Training techniques

Grapes are vigorous climbers and must be trained on a system of horizontal wires in order to give a good crop. There are two different techniques commonly used:

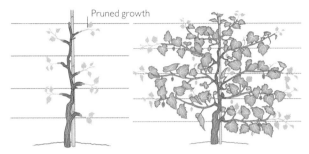

Pruned growth

The single cordon system, often used indoors, involves a single, 2m (6ft) tall stem that is permanently trained upright and pruned to develop a system of fruiting spurs.

In summer one new shoot is allowed to develop per spur. New growth is trained on wires and bears fruit. Fruited stems are pruned out in winter.

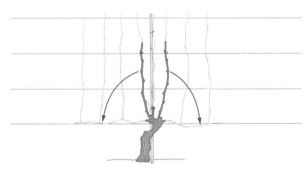

The double guyot system, most commonly used for outdoor grapes, involves keeping only three stems and removing the rest in winter. The centre stem is pruned to 3–4 buds, the outer two should be carefully bent out horizontally and tied to the wires to grow on in summer.

In summer, new stems develop from the horizontal limbs and bear fruit. At the same time, three new shoots are allowed to develop from the central stem but are not allowed to flower. In winter, when all fruited growth is removed, these three stems are left to start the cycle again.

Thinning and harvesting

As fruit clusters develop in summer, they should be thinned to promote healthier, full-sized fruit. Left unthinned the grapes will be undersized and will not ripen fully. They will also be prone to disease, which could spread to other clusters. To give time to establish, vines should not be allowed to bear fruit for their first two years.

In summer use a pair of secateurs, or round-tipped scissors, to carefully thin individual berries. Avoid damaging remaining fruit.

Continue thinning until the bunch is reduced in size by a third. Take the opportunity to remove weak or damaged fruit.

Grapes are ready when they are soft, taste sweet, and their skin has taken on a translucent quality. Remove them by cutting through the stem with secateurs.

WATCH OUT FOR...

Birds and wasps may target outdoor vines as the fruits are ripening. Use wire or plastic netting to deter birds, and hang wasp traps nearby.

Grey mould, also known as botrytis, causes fungal growth on stems, leaves, and fruit. Fruit often decays before ripening. Destroy all infected material and prune congested growth to improve air circulation. (*For more pests and diseases advice, see pp.356–369.*)

STRAWBERRIES

Every garden has room for strawberry plants, which give a sweet, succulent crop planted in pots, baskets, and growing bags, as well as in traditional beds. Pick the right varieties and enjoy them from spring to autumn.

Snap the stems to pick fruit.

		SPRING	SUMMER	AUTUMN	WINTER
PLANT					
HARVEST					

HOW TO GROW

Strawberries need full sun to ripen completely, and prefer free-draining, fertile, acid (pH 6.0–6.5) soil. They also grow well in raised beds, and especially in containers and baskets, which suits their trailing habit. Plant in spring or summer, depending on type, 45cm (18in) apart, in rows spaced at 75cm (30in). To avoid soil-borne diseases, don't plant in beds recently used for tomatoes, potatoes, or chrysanthemums. After cropping, cut back old leaves to expose the crown to sunlight, as this will encourage better fruiting the following year. Replace plants grown in the soil every four years, and those in containers every two years.

Strawberries are self-fertile but need insects or wind to transfer the pollen to the stigma.

TYPES OF STRAWBERRY

Traditional strawberries are either "summer-fruiting", which are the tastiest, or "perpetual", which crop over a longer period.

Alpine strawberries are perennial plants and crop for many years. Although their fruits are small, they are sweet and flavoursome.

VARIETIES TO TRY

Summer-fruiting strawberries crop from early to midsummer. Perpetual-fruiting types crop in early then late summer and into mid-autumn. Replace plants annually. Alpine varieties fruit freely throughout summer.

Summer-fruiting
'Alice' (early) • 'Cambridge Favourite' • (mid) • 'Elsanta' (mid) • 'Honeoye' • (early) • 'Pegasus' (mid) • 'Symphony' (late)

Perpetual-fruiting
'Albion' • 'Buddy' • 'Flamenco' • 'Mara des Bois' • 'Ostara'

Alpine strawberries
'Alexandria' • 'Baron Solemacher' • 'Mignonette' • 'Rugen'

Containers

Strawberries can be grown in almost any type of container with adequate drainage holes, including hanging baskets, stackable towers, traditional strawberry planters, and growing bags. All will need watering at least once a day during the growing season, and should be fed weekly with a high-potash tomato fertilizer. Turn containers often to avoid fruit being left in the shade.

Keep the fruit clean

Strawberries grow on the ground, and to keep them clean they are best lifted off the soil. Straw mulch is commonly used; barley straw is considered the best as it is softer. Fibre mats slipped around each plant are also popular and easy to use. You can also plant through black plastic stretched over a slightly raised bed. As well as keeping fruit clean, this warms the soil, retains moisture, and supresses weeds.

▲ **Cover fruit** with netting to protect them from birds. Always replace it after harvesting.

PROPAGATING

To maintain a good crop, strawberry plants should be replaced at least every two years. It's well worth propagating your own, so you have a constant supply of replacement plants. This is easy to do because strawberries naturally produce "runners", which are little plantlets that you can grow on. Propagate only healthy runners and remove the rest to encourage plants to concentrate their energy on producing fruit.

1 When runners start to develop in summer, and the young plantlets have strong leaves, lift them from the soil but leave them attached to the parent plant.

2 Sink small pots filled with potting compost into the soil. Plant one plantlet per pot, pegging them in place with bent wire staples. Keep them well watered.

3 After 4–6 weeks, the plantlets will develop roots of their own and can be separated from the parent. Grow them on, potting up and planting out as necessary.

Forcing strawberries

Strawberries can be encouraged to crop at least one or two weeks early by placing a cloche over them in spring. Container-grown plants can also be moved into an unheated greenhouse in spring to fruit earlier. In autumn, move perpetual varieties under cover to prolong their fruiting season. Make sure plants are stood in the sun to help ripen the fruit.

▶ **Check the fruit** every day. Strawberries ripen quickly in summer and soon spoil.

WATCH OUT FOR...

Grey mould, or botrytis, enters through the flowers and remains dormant until the fruit matures. Destroy all infected plant debris.

Vine weevil grubs destroy the roots, particularly on container-grown plants. Adults chew notches from the leaf margins but the white grubs cause more serious damage. Control with nematodes in late summer. (*For more pests and diseases advice, see pp.356–369.*)

RASPBERRIES

The rich scent and taste of raspberries is the very essence of summer, and they are very easy to grow. Plant summer- and autumn-fruiting types and enjoy a plentiful harvest from high summer to the first frosts.

	SPRING	SUMMER	AUTUMN	WINTER
PLANT				
HARVEST				

Ripe berries leave the core when picked.

HOW TO GROW

Raspberries prefer a moist, slightly acid soil, with a pH of about 6.0. They need a sunny site for the fruit to ripen, although they will tolerate some shade. Raspberries are leggy plants, so put a support structure of posts and wires in place before planting. Plant bare-root canes (*see right*) from late autumn to late winter; container-grown plants can be planted at any time if kept well watered afterwards. Canes should be planted 40cm (16in) apart, in rows spaced at 2m (6ft) intervals. Plant them shallowly to prevent the roots rotting, and cut the tops of the canes back to 20cm (8in) immediately after planting. When the canes start to send out new shoots, the original cane can then be cut down to ground level. Raspberries need watering regularly during dry periods. Feed them in early spring with a rose fertilizer containing iron and magnesium, or apply a mulch of well-rotted organic matter, such as garden compost, spread around the base of the canes.

◀ **Water canes** at cool times of day, using a can or hose to direct water at the base.

Bare-root canes

Bare-root raspberries are usually sold during autumn and winter in bundles of 10–20 canes. This is a cheap way to buy a lot of plants but they should be planted as soon as possible. To prevent damaging the roots, and to reduce planting stress, stand the bundle in water for an hour before unwrapping it.

TYPES AVAILABLE

Summer-fruiting raspberries come into fruit mid-season and usually crop for about three weeks, depending on the variety grown.

Autumn-fruiting raspberries crop from late summer to the first frosts. Like summer varieties, their berries can be red or yellow.

VARIETIES TO TRY

Summer-fruiting
'Glen Ample' • 'Glencoe' • 'Malling Jewel' • 'Octavia' • 'Tulameen'

Autumn-fruiting
'All Gold' • 'Autumn Bliss' • 'Autumn Treasure' • 'Joan J' • 'Polka'

Support

Raspberries are tall plants with a lax habit, and need support throughout the growing season. For a single row of canes, tightly stretch three wires horizontally, spaced 75cm (30in), 1m (3ft) and 1.5m (5ft) above the ground, between two 2.5m (8ft) posts. For a double row (see below), use two parallel wires, supported by cross-members, spaced 1m (3ft) and 1.5m (5ft) above the ground, and pulled taut between upright posts.

Summer-fruiting raspberries are tall plants and must be given adequate support.

Pruning and training

It's important to know what sort of raspberries you have before pruning them. Summer-fruiting varieties crop on canes produced the previous year; autumn types fruit on canes produced during the current year. Mix them up and you might remove fruiting stems by mistake.

Prune summer-fruiting raspberries in late summer, cutting all fruited canes to the ground. This allows light and air into the remaining canes produced during the current year, helping to prevent disease.

Tie in new-season summer-fruiting canes to their wire support after pruning out old fruited growth in late summer. Space canes 10cm (4in) apart and loop taller stems over the top wire. In spring, prune to 15cm (6in) above the top wire.

Prune autumn-fruiting raspberries in spring by removing all the canes to ground level. Tread carefully to avoid damaging any new shoots that may be appearing from the soil. Rake up fallen leaves to keep the site clean.

New autumn-fruiting raspberry canes can be grown without supports, but bear a better crop, that is easier to pick, if gathered up with string. Support may be needed in exposed sites. Remove any weak, diseased, or damaged stems.

BLACKBERRIES AND HYBRIDS

Blackberries can be picked from hedgerows but garden varieties generally have bigger, juicier fruit. You can also choose from several hybrid forms, which are just as easy to grow but offer something slightly different.

VARIETIES TO TRY

Some blackberry varieties are thornless (TL), making them easier to harvest.
'Fantasia' • 'Helen' (TL) • 'Loch Ness' (TL) • 'Oregon Thornless' (TL) • 'Silvan'

	SPRING	SUMMER	AUTUMN	WINTER
PLANT				
HARVEST				

HOW TO GROW

Blackberries and their hybrids are vigorous climbing plants, and prefer a sheltered site. Blackberries will tolerate light shade and poorer soil, while the hybrids need full sun and richer growing conditions. Bare-root canes should be planted in winter, when all stems should be cut back to healthy buds 20cm (8in) above the soil. Container-grown plants can be planted all year round if kept well watered. Enrich the soil prior to planting by digging in well-rotted organic matter. Feed annually with rose fertilizer or apply more organic matter in spring, and water plants well, especially when in fruit.

▲ **Successful pollination** is essential for the fruit to develop fully and to reach full size.

▶ **Harvest regularly**, as blackberries and the hybrids ripen over several weeks, and it will take several sessions to pick the whole crop.

HOW TO PROPAGATE

1 Blackberries and hybrids can be easily propagated in late summer by bending a new stem to the ground and burying the tip to a depth of 10cm (4in). Firm it down, water well, and leave it attached to the main plant.

2 The stem will have rooted by the following spring, when it can be lifted from the ground and either potted up or transplanted. Keep the young plant well watered until it establishes fully and don't allow it to fruit for the first two years.

WATCH OUT FOR...

Blackberry cane spot causes grey or purple spotting on the canes, which die back. Infected canes should be destroyed immediately.

Raspberry beetle may also affect crops (see p.279).

Raspberry spur blight causes purple-grey areas around buds on the canes. The following year, canes produce weak growth, and may wither and die. Cut out and destroy any infected canes.
(For further advice, see pp.356–369.)

Pruning and training

Blackberries and the hybrids are grown against wires, and can be trained in several ways (*below*). Fruit is produced on canes formed the previous summer, so the aim is to separate these canes from new growth that will fruit next year. Wear gloves as blackberries can be very thorny.

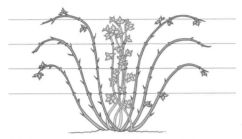

The upright fan method of training blackberries and hybrids involves cutting all fruited canes to the ground in autumn, and tying in the current year's growth either side to form a fan. The year-old, fan-trained stems will fruit the following year, with new stems trained up the centre until autumn. The whole process is then repeated each year.

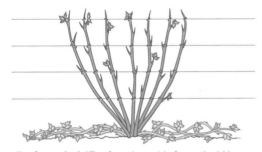

The trailing fan method differs from the upright fan method. Here, fruited stems are also removed in autumn and year-old growth is tied in to form a fan. The difference is that the new growth is trained across the ground then trained up to the wires in autumn to replace the fruited growth. This method suits bigger gardens with ground to spare.

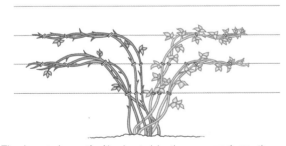

The alternate bay method involves training the new season's growth on the opposite side to where the fruiting stems, produced last year, are trained. In effect, the fruiting side of the plant alternates left or right from one year to the next. Fruited stems are removed in autumn. This method is a good choice for smaller gardens.

HYBRID BLACKBERRIES

These hybrid berries are mostly the result of cross-breeding between raspberries and blackberries, and have similarities to both parents. Each hybrid has its own eating qualities. All are vigorous climbers.

Boysenberry

This is a cross between a loganberry (*below*) and a blackberry. It crops for 3–4 weeks in midsummer and produces a large crop of succulent, dark-purple fruit. They look much like blackberries but are larger, and their flavour is considered superior. Naturally thornless forms are available from specialist suppliers.

Loganberry

A cross between blackberries and raspberries, the sharp-tasting fruit most resemble the latter and are best eaten cooked. The loganberry is naturally spiny, but thornless forms are also available from specialist suppliers. Allow the fruit to ripen fully and turn dark red before picking from mid- to late summer.

Tayberry

Resulting from a cross between blackberries and raspberries, the rich red berries are larger and sweeter than loganberries and appear in midsummer. Allow the fruit to turn dark red before picking. They are sweet enough to eat fresh from the plant but are best when cooked for jams and pies.

Japanese wineberry

While this is a separate species rather than a hybrid it is very similar, producing bright red, raspberry-like berries in mid- to late summer. Its stems are covered with attractive red bristles, and it is often grown partly as an ornamental. This dual purpose makes it a good choice for smaller gardens.

BLACKCURRANTS

One of the easiest fruit bushes to grow, blackcurrants even do well in containers, producing healthy berries, packed with vitamins. They can be eaten fresh but taste far better in jams, pies, and summer cordials.

		SPRING	SUMMER	AUTUMN	WINTER
PLANT					
HARVEST					

Fruits are a magnet for birds; net them (*see right*).

HOW TO GROW

Blackcurrants require moist, fertile soil and prefer full sun but will also ripen, albeit later, in some shade. Plant bare-root shrubs in winter; container-grown plants can be planted at any time if well watered. Dig in well-rotted organic matter and plant deeply (*see below*). Blackcurrants grow well in containers filled with soil-based compost. Before the fruit is ready to harvest, from mid- to late summer, cover plants with netting to deter birds. Water well during dry periods, and feed in spring with granular fertilizer or well-rotted organic matter, such as garden compost.

Support fruiting plants with string and canes to prevent branches laden with fruit from drooping and snapping off.

PRUNING AND TRAINING

Blackcurrants fruit on one-year-old wood. They should be pruned in winter (*below*) to encourage new fruit-bearing shoots. Plants can also be pruned in summer to allow light in to ripen the fruit and to improve air circulation between branches, which helps to deter disease.

Pruned growth

In winter, prune established shrubs by cutting a third of the oldest branches off at ground level, and removing dead, damaged, or diseased wood. Horizontal branches that are lying close to the ground should also be removed. Don't prune healthy young stems.

HOW TO PLANT

1 Dig a hole deeper than the rootball is tall and fork some well-rotted garden compost into the base.

2 Check the level and ensure that the crown of the plant is positioned in the hole slightly below the soil surface.

3 Backfill the hole with soil and water the plant in well. New stems will develop from below soil level.

VARIETIES TO TRY

Modern varieties have been bred for improved disease resistance. These are often denoted by 'Ben' in their names.

'Baldwin' • 'Ben Connan' • 'Ben Gairn' • 'Ben Hope' • 'Ben Lomond' • 'Ben Sarek' • 'Big Ben' • 'Ebony' • 'Titania'

RED- AND WHITECURRANTS

With a slightly tart taste, these colourful berries are the basis of many sauces and desserts. They are very easy to grow, and can be trained or grown in pots, depending on how much space you have available.

	SPRING	SUMMER	AUTUMN	WINTER
PLANT	■			■
HARVEST		■	■	

HOW TO GROW

Red- and whitecurrants prefer fertile, well-drained, acid soil with a pH of 6.5–7.0. They need a warm, sunny position, but will tolerate some shade. Bare-root shrubs should be planted in winter; container-grown shrubs may be planted at any time if well watered. The shrubs are usually grown as bushes on a short stem or "leg" 15cm (6in) tall. Alternatively, they can be trained as fans, cordons, standards, or stepovers. Like most soft fruits, they require protection from birds as the fruit starts to develop. Feed plants in spring with a granular fertilizer or well-rotted organic matter. Plant shrubs in containers into a soil-based compost, such as John Innes No. 3.

Redcurrants fruit on buds at the base of last year's wood and also on old spurs. They should be pruned hard in winter to encourage new spurs, similar to gooseberries (see p.284).

Net all currants before they ripen to prevent birds stripping the plants bare.

Pick fruit as "strings" when all the berries have turned red and look slightly opaque. Replace netting after each harvest.

◄ **Whitecurrants are sweeter** than redcurrants but don't have such an attractive, jewel-like appearance.

GOOSEBERRIES

These very hardy fruit bushes are a good choice for cold, exposed gardens. Firm, tart, and juicy, gooseberries are especially good cooked; their old-fashioned appeal is becoming more widely appreciated.

		SPRING	SUMMER	AUTUMN	WINTER
PLANT					
HARVEST					

Some varieties ripen green, others dark red.

HOW TO GROW

Gooseberries require a moist, fertile soil and will tolerate some shade. Commonly grown as freestanding bushes, they are usually planted on a short 15cm (6in) stem, called a "leg". Where required, they can also be trained as stepovers, cordons, and standards, or as fans on north-facing walls. Bare-root shrubs should be planted in winter; container-grown can be planted at any time of year if well watered. Dig well-rotted organic matter into the planting hole. Space bushes 1.2m (4ft) apart and cordons 35cm (14in) apart. Thin the fruit from early summer, removing alternate berries, which can be used in cooking. This encourages full-sized fruit, which can be harvested once ripe from midsummer onwards. Net young fruit to protect it from birds. Take care when harvesting as the bushes have long, sharp thorns.

Water plants well during dry spells, and feed in spring with a granular fertilizer or well-rotted organic matter. Freestanding shrubs may need support with canes in summer to prevent laden branches from collapsing or snapping.

◄ **Ripe fruit** is best eaten fresh but can also be stored in the fridge or frozen.

VARIETIES TO TRY

Dessert varieties (D) can be eaten raw; culinary fruit (C) are best for cooking; dual types are suitable for both uses (C/D).

'Captivator' (C) • 'Careless' (C/D) • 'Greenfinch' (C) • 'Invicta' (C/D) • 'Leveller' (D) • 'Whinham's Industry' (C/D)

Pruning

Established gooseberry bushes are pruned winter and summer. The main aim is to create an open, airy centre and to keep older fruiting wood productive.

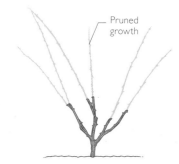

Pruned growth

In the first winter after planting, choose 4–5 healthy stems and cut them back by half to three-quarters. Remove all other stems and shoots coming from the "leg" at the bottom.

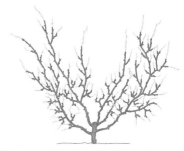

To winter-prune established shrubs, tip-prune main stems and cut back sideshoots to 1–4 buds. The centre of overgrown shrubs should be thinned by a quarter. In summer, prune sideshoots to five leaves.

Cordon-trained plants can be grown much closer together than freestanding shrubs, which is ideal for smaller gardens.

BLUEBERRIES

Native to North America, these delicious berries need minimal pruning and training, and grow well in patio containers. The sweet, summer fruit is packed with goodness and tastes even better when cooked.

	SPRING	SUMMER	AUTUMN	WINTER
PLANT				
HARVEST				

Fruit ripens throughout summer, so harvest regularly.

HOW TO GROW

Blueberries need moist, acid soil with a pH of 4.0–5.5. They prefer full sun but will tolerate some shade. Plant bare-root shrubs in winter; plant container-grown shrubs at any time if well watered. Add leafmould of composted pine needles to the planting hole to maintain acidity, and mulch in spring with more of the same. Space blueberries 1.2m (4ft) apart, water well during dry spells, and net developing fruit against birds. Blueberries are partially self-fertile, and can pollinate their own flowers, but they crop better if other varieties are planted nearby. Don't allow pot-grown plants to dry out and feed regularly, especially when in fruit.

Unless your soil is acid, grow blueberries in large containers filled with lime-free, ericaceous compost, available from garden centres.

◀ **Cross-pollination** is essential for fruit formation and is ensured by planting two or three varieties that flower at the same time.

VARIETIES TO TRY

'Berkley' • 'Bluecrop' • 'Bluetta' • 'Coville' • 'Duke' • 'Earliblue' • 'Herbert' • 'Patriot' • 'Spartan' • 'Top Hat'

WATCH OUT FOR...

Birds can strip plants of berries in a matter of hours. Net bushes before the fruit starts to ripen and secure it at ground level so birds can't sneak underneath.

Blueberry stem blight is a fungal disease that enters the plants through wounds and pruning cuts. It causes the leaves to brown and die, weakening the plant and reducing the crop. Remove and destroy all infected growth.
(For further advice, see pp.356–369.)

Pruning and training

Blueberries are pruned from late winter to early spring, when the swelling buds show which parts of the plant are alive. Avoid pruning stems with lots of healthy fat buds, as these will bear fruit in summer.

▶ **To prune established shrubs**, prune out a few of the oldest stems, leaving 4–6 main shoots. Tip-prune stems that fruited last year, cutting back to strong buds. Remove lateral branches growing too close to the base, and thin the centre of overgrown shrubs. Never remove more than a quarter of the shrub at once.

CARE FOR YOUR GARDEN

The essence of good gardening is care and maintenance, and
a little bit of know-how and some expert tips can go a long
way. This chapter equips you with key techniques such as
propagation and pruning as well as advice on tools, timing,
feeding, and watering to help you make a success of
everything you do in the garden.

EARLY TO MID-SPRING

After the long autumn, the first hint of spring in the air means that it's time to start tidying and preparing the garden for the warmer months to come. You'll still need to watch out for frosts, but look ahead and start planning your spring and summer borders.

▶ PROTECT AGAINST FROST

March and April can still be frosty, especially at night, so keep an eye on the weather forecast and protect tender plants if a frost threatens. Cloches, horticultural fleece, or even cut-down plastic bottles will give frost protection. You can also use cloches on areas of bare earth to warm up the soil ready for sowing.

▼ TRANSPLANT SEEDLINGS

If you come across any self-sown annual or biennial seedlings in your beds and borders, pot them up or transplant them to a more permanent growing position if necessary. You can begin to harden off seedlings raised in pots under cover, but do not plant them on outside until the threat of frost has completely passed.

▲ FEED FISH

March is the time to start feeding fish in your ponds. Take stock of your plants: marginals may need trimming and aquatics may need moving or dividing. Pond pumps can now be taken out of storage, checked over, and replaced in the pond.

▶ TIDY LAWNS AND BORDERS

Spruce up your lawns and borders for spring. Start by mowing the lawn after its winter break, then trim and tidy any ragged edges by hand. Inspect the lawn, checking for perennial weeds (see pp.352–353) and reseed any bare patches (see p.93). In borders, keep an eye out for germinating weed seedlings, and remove them with a hoe when you spot them. Once your beds and borders are tidy, mulch them with a thick layer of organic matter to suppress weeds.

◀ GUARD AGAINST SLUGS AND SNAILS

Young growth is particularly vulnerable to attack from slugs and snails, so protect it using nematodes as a biological control, or scatter organic slug pellets.

▲ PROTECT FRUIT BLOSSOM

Late frosts can still fall in early spring, so take care to protect fruit blossom and young fruitlets until there is no further threat. The buds and flowers of peaches, nectarines, and cherries open up early and are prone to frost damage. Protect wall-trained and free-standing trees with fleece.

▲ PLANT TREES

Take your last chance to plant bare-root trees in March, while they are still in a near-dormant state. If you have missed out on bare-root stock, container-grown trees can be planted throughout spring and will be available from garden centres. If you plant young fruit trees and bushes, pinch out any flowers this year to encourage a good root system.

LATE SPRING TO EARLY SUMMER

June is the month when the garden is at its peak – borders look perfect and summer vegetables and soft fruit are flourishing. Keep an eye out for pests over the summer months, and water plants regularly but wisely during drier spells.

▶ PROTECT PLANTS FROM SLUGS

Slugs and snails are especially fond of young growth, particularly that of delphiniums and hostas, and can attack young buds before they have even emerged from the soil. General controls, such as organically approved slug pellets, can be very effective, but other organic methods such as beer traps are also worth trying. Microscopic nematodes can be purchased and watered in and will infect slugs, helping to control them in spring and summer. Another way to try and stop these pests in their tracks is to use a physical barrier such as eggshells or a layer of coarse grit.

▲ PLANT OUT VEGETABLES

Vegetables sown earlier in the year, such as globe artichokes, leeks, and celery, can be planted out in May once they are robust enough. Tender marrows and courgettes can also be planted out once the threat of frost has passed.

▶ MOVE POTS OUTSIDE

Any tender or exotic plants, such as citrus trees, that you have brought indoors over winter can now be moved back into the garden after a gradual acclimatization to outdoor temperatures (the shock of a sudden change can cause leaves to drop).

◄ KEEP WATERING

As temperatures start to rise, it's important to keep plants well watered, especially those that have just been planted out. As plants become established and develop bigger and more effective root systems they will need watering less frequently. Established plants only need a good soaking in dry conditions if they show signs of wilting.

▲ HARVEST FRUIT

Remove cloches from strawberries now to let the fruit ripen in the summer sun, ready for imminent picking. Tuck straw under the developing fruits to keep them dry and away from the soil. Keep all fruit well watered in dry spells to ensure a good crop of quality fruits throughout summer.

▲ PLANT SUMMER BEDDING

Beds and borders planted with spring bedding can be cleared now as summer approaches, ready for tender summer bedding plants, such as *Bacopa*. A wide selection will be on show at nurseries and garden centres, and can be safely planted out from May into June.

▲ TRIM HEDGES

Formal evergreen hedging that is free of nesting birds should be lightly trimmed by hand now. Hand shears will give a better result than a mechanical hedge trimmer, which can bruise leaves instead of cutting them cleanly, resulting in brown and unsightly foliage. It's much better to trim a formal hedge regularly to keep it in shape. Use a length of taut garden twine or a cane as a guide to help you keep the line straight as you work.

MIDSUMMER

Now's the time to relax and enjoy your garden, as all the hard work you invested in sowing and planting earlier in the year starts to pay off with borders and beds looking their best for the long summer evenings. Devote your energies to keeping the garden well watered in hot weather.

▶ SUPPORT YOUNG PEAS

Sweet peas and peas have rather straggly growth and like to be supported. Twiggy sticks are a good way to do this, and strong, straight prunings from other shrubs in the garden will also work well. The tendrils of the peas will cling to the sticks.

▼ HARVEST EDIBLE FLOWERS

Nasturtiums and other edible flowers, such as violas and roses, make delicious and eye-catching additions to summer salads. Gather the flowers as required, choosing flawless, pest-free blooms wherever possible.

▶ PICK RASPBERRIES

Summer-fruiting raspberries should ripen this month. The "plug" or core will remain behind on the bush, and the berries should come away easily when ripe. If they don't, they're not ready to be picked. Pick ripe fruits regularly so that they are not allowed to rot on the bush.

◄ DEADHEAD FLOWERS

Removing faded blooms will prevent plants from setting seed and keep roses coming for the rest of the summer. An easy way to deadhead straggly plants such as pansies and petunias, which have smaller flowers and are more fiddly to trim, is to cut them back with secateurs or shears.

▼ CARE FOR BASKETS

Colourful summer hanging baskets will be at their best now with their profusion of plants, but will need daily watering and regular feeding in the hot weather. If they start to flag and droop, unhook the baskets and plunge them into a bucket of water to revive the plants.

◄ WATER FOR BIRDS

During hot, dry summer spells, water for birds will be scarce, so provide pools, ponds, and baths for them wherever possible. As well as a continuous supply of drinking water, water for bathing is also important and helps to keep birds' feathers in good condition.

◄ PLANT OUT LATE BEDDING PLANTS

To ensure that any late summer bedding plants such as *Petunia*, *Alyssum*, and *Nemesia* have enough time to settle in and flower for the rest of the summer, plant them out as soon as possible in baskets, containers, and borders. Replace any tired-looking plants in your borders with healthy new specimens, and fill gaps to keep your garden looking lush throughout the season.

LATE SUMMER TO MID-AUTUMN

Flower borders may be starting to fade, but late summer is a time of "mellow fruitfulness" in the garden. Most summer crops can be gathered in with tomatoes, peppers, sweet corn, and squash reaching their peak. Use the warm days for cleaning and tidying tasks too.

▲ FEED TOMATOES

Continue to feed tomato plants with a high-potash feed applied weekly. Water plants every evening if possible. If you have green tomatoes towards the end of the season, bring them indoors to ripen on a sunny windowsill or in the fruit bowl. Remove any yellowing and old leaves and thin any foliage clustered around the trusses of fruit. As well as allowing more light to reach the fruits and ripen them, this will improve air circulation around the plants and reduce the possibility of botrytis, also known as grey mould.

▶ HARVEST APPLES AND PEARS

The first apples and pears in the garden should be ready to pick from August onwards. When you see one or more apples on the ground, this is a sure sign that the fruit is ready to harvest. If you cup an apple in your hand and gently twist it, a ripe fruit should part effortlessly from the tree, stalk intact. If it does not come away easily, leave it on the tree for a few more days before testing again. Pears should be harvested slightly underripe, and ripened indoors (see p.265).

▲ FIX GREASE BANDS

Female winter moths are unable to fly, so will climb apple and pear tree trunks to lay their eggs during winter. To catch them, fix sticky grease bands around the trunks. Use the bands on stakes too, to prevent moths from reaching the trees via tree ties.

▼ LIFT ONIONS

When the foliage collapses, onions are ready to harvest. On a dry day, gently ease the onions out of the soil and leave them out to dry. To ensure that they store well and do not rot, they must be completely dry – if the weather turns wet, cover them with a sheet of polythene or move them indoors.

▲ NET PONDS

Leaves will start to fall as autumn approaches, so ensure that you cover your pond with specialist netting to prevent dead leaves from falling in and affecting the water quality. Nets will also protect your fish from herons and other predators.

◄ RAKE LEAVES

Fallen leaves will collect on your lawn in autumn and can kill off the grass if left in a thick layer, as well as encouraging slugs and snails if left lying over and around plants. Rake leaves up regularly and use them to make leafmould (see pp.22–23).

▲ PRUNE LAVENDER

Once your lavender plants have flowered and started to fade, go over the plants with a pair of secateurs, cutting them back. This will encourage side shoots to grow and give plants a bushier, more compact habit. Rambling roses should also be pruned after flowering (see pp.318–319).

LATE AUTUMN TO WINTER

Although flowers can be scarce in the garden over the winter months, berries, evergreen foliage, and trees with decorative bark will cheer up the garden and add interest. Take stock of the gardening year as it ends, and use the time to begin planning your spring displays.

▶ BRING HERBS INDOORS

Most container herb plants are too delicate to survive the winter outdoors, so bring them under cover in their pots for the colder months before temperatures begin to drop. This will ensure a steady supply to liven up your winter dishes when other produce is thin on the ground. Position pots on a windowsill to catch as much winter sunshine as possible, and pinch out growing tips when necessary to promote a bushy habit.

▲ LEAVE SEEDHEADS

Many grasses, such as the huge range of *Miscanthus* varieties available, have attractive seedheads that can be left on the plants over autumn and winter. Their dry plumes look attractive, especially when dusted with winter frost.

▶ PLANT FRUIT TREES

Now's the time to order and plant bare-root trees. Prepare the ground first by digging in plenty of well-rotted organic matter to improve the soil structure. A feed of general fertilizer will also help to get your trees off to a good start.

◄ WINTER-PRUNE SHRUBS

February is the month to prune many woody plants, including winter-flowering shrubs such as *Hamamelis*, once their flowers have faded. Summer-flowering shrubs, such as the butterfly bush (*Buddleja davidii*), that flower on new wood later in the summer can be cut right back, using loppers if necessary. The twiggy prunings can be used as plant supports elsewhere in the garden, or shredded to be added to the compost heap or to make a mulch that can be applied in spring when the ground is a little warmer.

◄ FEED THE BIRDS

Food for birds is in short supply over the colder months, so put food out for them on a regular basis; different mixes are available for feeders and for bird tables and ground feeding. Clean out bird boxes of old nesting material to encourage birds to nest in them again next year. Birds will be looking for winter roosts, so do this as soon as possible. If they are already familiar with a box by spring, they are more likely to select it as a nesting site.

▲ STORE WINTER SQUASHES

Pumpkins and winter squashes can be left on the plant during autumn to reach their maximum size and develop brightly coloured skins. Do not leave on the plant over winter as they may rot or be eaten by pests. Once "cured" in the sun for ten days, they can be stored. Keep them in a dry, well-ventilated, frost-free place, checking regularly for damage or decay.

▲ CLEAN TOOLS AND EQUIPMENT

Take advantage of the quieter winter months in the garden to check over and clean all your garden equipment before storing it. Clean or discard any old pots and trays that you're not intending to reuse, as well as checking tools and getting the lawnmower serviced and sharpened. You won't need to mow the lawn itself over the winter – just avoid walking on it in frosty weather to try to prevent damage.

Water individual pots regularly in dry conditions and when growing under cover. Use a rose to prevent displacing soil in small pots.

REVIVE A WILTED BASKET

If a summer hanging basket begins to flag, plunge it into a sink, bowl, or bucket of water. Once the compost is moist, remove it and let excess water drain away. Replace dead plants and trim damaged growth.

Restore baskets by immersing them in water and leaving them there for a little while. They will draw up the moisture they need through their roots.

HOW TO WATER

To ensure your plants thrive rather than wilt or struggle to survive, it's important to water them efficiently. If you understand the needs of different plants, you can use techniques that deliver water where it is needed most.

EFFICIENT WATERING

Adequate water and sound watering methods are essential for healthy plant growth. Poor watering does more harm than good: drenching plants with abandon can leave roots exposed if compost is washed away or soil is eroded by the fast flow of water. If there is puddling on the soil surface and the ground becomes waterlogged, roots may rot.

Water is a valuable resource, both in environmental terms and to your pocket, if you are on a water meter. The aim of effective watering techniques is to reduce the need for watering and use water effectively and economically when you do water.

To reduce moisture loss through evaporation, water plants in the cool of the evening or early in the morning. This ensures water reaches roots with minimum wastage. Timing is critical. Although it may occasionally be necessary to water in the heat of day, avoid it if you can.

If beds, borders, or vegetable patches need watering, avoid the temptation to freshen them up by sprinkling water lightly over a wide area. Light watering won't penetrate the soil and may encourage roots to develop closer to the surface. This makes plants more susceptible to drought and in need of repeated watering. Instead, give individual plants a thorough soaking by watering directly above the root area. Let the water soak in before applying more.

Needy plants

Start with seedlings newly planted out, then established plants. Close attention needs to be paid to newly sown lawns or recently planted beds and borders, plants in pots, and most fruit and vegetables. Elsewhere, keep an eye on plants growing beneath

To reduce water wastage, water directly at the base of individual plants so that moisture gets straight to the roots.

Thoroughly water young plants individually as you transplant them. Continue to water regularly while they become established.

Get up early and water plants at the very beginning of the day when the sun is not at its hottest – this way you'll lose less to evaporation.

trees and hedges, along with those planted in a rain shadow, perhaps trained against a wall or fence. Generally, established plants growing in soil do not require watering, but their growth is usually improved by watering in drought conditions.

Watering baskets and containers

Summer rainfall seldom keeps hanging baskets and containers moist; the foliage will often act like an umbrella, keeping the compost beneath dry. To ensure plants in pots thrive, water regularly and thoroughly, especially over summer. When planting up containers, leave a 5cm (2in) gap between the top of the compost and the lip of the container to act as a well for water to gather and then filter down to the roots of the plants.

To water baskets, remove the rose from a watering can and pour water slowly beneath the foliage, directly on to the compost. Place trays under patio containers to act as a reservoir in summer. Although plants in pots are at their most demanding while in active growth, they also need occasional watering in dry spells over winter.

EASY WATERING

Watering cans are probably the only watering equipment you'll need for a small patch, but a hose is a better option for a large plot and will make life easier. Instead of attaching a hosepipe to a tap indoors, install an outdoor tap (new taps must legally be fitted with a device that prevents contaminated water being siphoned back into the drinking-water supply). There are many devices available to improve the efficiency of watering and make life easier; a long-handled lance can be fitted to a hosepipe to reach individual plants, or a timer can be fitted to a tap to deliver water via a seep hose or an automatic irrigation system.

Sprinklers release a huge amount of water. They are best used only on newly laid lawns in dry conditions. Always check for watering restrictions in case of drought.

Drip feeders along a length of hose can be used to water at intervals along a bed or in pots.

Low-level watering systems attached to buried hoses will deliver water close to the roots.

Hosepipes will avoid a lot of time spent carrying watering cans round the garden.

Timer systems enable you to water at optimum times of day, even when you are not around.

Seep hoses on the soil surface or buried around perennials put water where plants need it.

Extended watering heads mean you can water plants directly from a distance.

SAVING WATER

Conserving water is essential if you have a meter, but there are other incentives. Climate change, urban spread, and the expense of processing tap water make it increasingly important to use water wisely.

An old barrel makes an attractive feature as well as serving a practical purpose. Make sure it is watertight and position it under a downpipe.

USING GREY WATER

Waste water from the sink, bath, and washing machine can be recycled in the garden. Avoid polluting it with detergents by using environmentally friendly products, and dilute this "grey water" before using it.

Don't pour waste water down the sink – water your ornamentals with it instead. Avoiding using grey water on edible crops.

WISE WATERING

Most rainwater washes down the drains; reduce waste by ensuring as much as possible reaches plants. When planning a garden, ensure that the direction of the slope over a path, patio, or drive directs water to lawns or beds. Lawns are particularly resilient, and in temperate climates rarely need special watering once established. Build in ways to collect and store rainwater, and add moisture-retaining mulches to soil.

Collecting rainwater

Although underground rainwater harvesting systems can be installed, it is far cheaper and easier to use water butts. These can be sited to collect rainwater from any roof with gutters

Attach butts to downpipes by the house or by a shed or greenhouse to catch rainwater. Keep a lid on to prevent evaporation and mosquitoes.

and downpipes, and come in all shapes and sizes from huge tanks to slimline models ideal for small gardens. To plumb in a water butt, remove a lower section of downpipe so it empties into a butt placed beneath it, then add an overflow pipe to take away excess water. Alternatively, stand the butt next to the downpipe and link them with a diverter kit.

Mulching

Covering the soil surface with mulches, such as gravel, leafmould, garden compost, composted bark, or well-rotted manure helps to reduce water evaporation, and also stifles weeds that compete for moisture. Mulches are best applied from mid- to late spring and in autumn,

Drainage pipes from a raised patio can provide an additional water source for flower beds situated below them at a lower level.

when the soil is moist and warm. Avoid mulching in winter and early spring, as the soil is cold and the mulch may slow it warming up. Mulching retains moisture most effectively if applied to damp soil, so unless it has rained recently, water the area well first and allow the surface to drain. Spread the mulch 5–7.5cm (2–3in) thick over the soil, taking care not to pile it up against stems or smother low-growing plants. On new beds and borders, consider laying a permeable membrane before mulching to protect against weeds (see p.350). Plant through slits and cover the membrane with mulch.

DROUGHT-LOVERS

Acanthus spinosus (Bear's breeches)

Cistus x lenis 'Grayswood Pink' (Rock rose)

Elaeagnus angustifolia

Eryngium x oliveranum

Euphorbia myrsinites

Foeniculum vulgare 'Purpureum' (Bronze fennel)

Iris unguicularis

Lavandula (Lavender)

Salvia officinalis (Common sage)

Salvia rosmarinus (Rosemary)

Sempervivum arachnoideum (Houseleek)

Stachys byzantina (Lambs' ears)

Stipa tenuissima (Feather grass)

Camouflage unattractive sheets of permeable membrane with gravel or fine bark chippings. This will give the area a neat, weed-free finish.

Gravel laid around the base of individual plants is enough to keep in moisture around the roots. Water the plants well first to be most effective.

HOW TO WATER POTS LESS

Plants in containers dry out faster than those in the ground. To keep watering to a minimum, don't over-plant, ensure plants are not pot-bound, and use large pots, which hold more compost and retain moisture better. Loam-based compost retains moisture well; multi-purpose composts are easy to rewet if they dry out.

Choose your material carefully. Plastic pots hold moisture more effectively than porous terracotta. If you grow plants in metal pots, avoid placing them in full sun to keep the compost and roots cool.

Group plants in containers together so they shade each other, and stand them on saucers that will act as a reservoir for excess water. Cover the compost surface with finely chipped bark, gravel, garden compost, or a decorative material to reduce evaporation.

A mulch of bark chippings or other biodegradable material will hold in moisture.

Add water-retaining crystals to compost before planting. These may release water as needed.

Terracotta pots look beautiful but do not retain water as well as plastic containers.

Group pots together and the plants will shade each other, keeping their roots cool.

Fit pots with individual drip attachments from a hosepipe, operated by a timer switch.

Larger plastic containers retain moisture well, and are suitable for thirsty plants and crops.

Soluble fertilizer is easy to apply to plants, and can be mixed and applied with a watering can. Check the packet for dilution rates first.

FEEDING FACTS

It's important to get feeding just right. Too little results in weak growth, while too much promotes soft sappy shoots that attract the attention of aphids, become vulnerable to frost damage, and may need support.

A careful look at a plant should tell you if it is lacking an essential nutrient. Leaves that yellow at the edges and between the veins show signs of iron deficiency.

HOW TO FEED

Ensure your garden is full of flourishing plants by providing them with the correct nutrients as and when they need them. Get the feeding right and they will respond with healthy leaf, fruit, and flower growth.

FEEDING TECHNIQUES

There is a wide range of plant foods available, from manure and compost to liquid, granular, and powdered feeds. Some are inorganic – man-made; others are organic – derived from plant and animal waste.

Some feeds have equal proportions of the three major plant nutrients (nitrogen, phosphorus, and potassium, represented by the symbols N, P, and K), which promote all-round healthy growth. Others have a higher percentage of a particular nutrient; these are designed to encourage root, foliage, or fruit development. Specialist feeds and tonics are also available for specific plants or purposes, such as orchid, tomato, citrus, and bonsai fertilizer, and sequestered iron and ericaceous fertilizers.

Dry fertilizers

Granular or powdered fertilizers are mainly used to feed established plants in beds or borders, or to boost soil fertility before planting. Apply in early spring, scattering it around established trees, shrubs, and perennials, or broadcasting it over the soil and working it in. If you need to treat a large area of your garden, divide it into square metres (yards) with canes for more even distribution. Always wear gloves when handling dry fertilizer.

Slow-release fertilizers

Added to the soil or mixed into compost in powder or granular form, these fertilizers feed plants gradually over time. They are particularly useful if you are short of time, as only one application is needed. Follow the packet

Granular fertilizer can be scattered on the soil around the base of the plant, and will deliver nutrients straight to roots as it is washed in.

Bulky organic fertilizers are invaluable, feeding plants by boosting the soil's nutrients while also improving its structure.

instructions for the correct application, and wear gloves when handling it.

Liquid fertilizers

Fast-acting liquid fertilizers can be applied to soil or compost, once diluted, or added to a sprayer and used as a foliar feed. Liquid feeds that are high in potash are ideal for improving yields of plants such as tomatoes, peppers, and strawberries, or to extend the display of flowering annuals. Liquid seaweed is a good organic fertilizer for garden plants. Dilute concentrated feeds according to the instructions on the packet, or use the more expensive ready-mixed feeds. Yellowing leaves (chlorosis) can be a sign of nutrient deficiency. Liquid feeds can offer a quick fix, but first be sure that the symptom does not have another cause, such as poor drainage or disease.

Manure

Simply adding bulky farmyard manure into the soil improves its structure and water-retaining ability, encourages beneficial organisms, and adds nutrients. Ideally, apply well-rotted manure in the autumn, either as a 5–7.5cm (2–3in) deep mulch to established beds or dug into large areas being prepared for planting in the spring.

Liquid fertilizers act quickly once diluted in water, and when applied to the soil or leaves will soon revitalize flagging plants.

Plants in pots need more feeding than those in the ground. Top-dressing large containers with a balanced fertilizer helps them to thrive.

Well-rotted manure is best applied in late winter, so it can gradually rot into the soil, nourishing it ready for spring growth.

Making garden compost

Making your own compost is easy, and makes sense economically and environmentally too. Fill your bins with a mixture of green and brown waste. Green waste includes lawn clippings, annual weeds, plant trimmings, and other soft material that rots down quickly, bringing nitrogen and moisture to the mix. Shredded cardboard and dead leaves are good brown-waste materials – they are dry, rich in carbon, and give compost structure. Green materials rot to a smelly sludge, but brown materials balance out the compost to produce a rich, crumbly texture. Do not add animal waste, meat, cooked food, diseased plants, or fresh perennial weeds.

1 Choose a compost bin to suit your needs and position it in the garden where it can be easily accessed and tended.

2 Add uncooked kitchen waste as well as healthy plant materials and grass clippings to your heap. Pick out any perennial weeds or diseased plants.

3 Build up your heap in layers of green and brown material to blend the materials and give the finished compost a good structure and texture.

4 Turn the heap periodically with a garden fork to mix up all the rotting materials and aerate the heap; this also helps the mixture compost more thoroughly.

CONTAINER GROWING

There are thousands of plants that will thrive in containers – in fact you can grow just about anything in them, from trees to miniature bulbs, fruit and vegetables, and aquatic plants such as water lilies.

Containers make the perfect home for many plants, and are an ideal solution if you have limited space or want herbs or plants to hand.

PLANTING POTS

Whether you want to create a vibrant display of summer colour or just a focal point, the key to success with containers is to make sure all the plants' needs are met.

Pick containers that suit your plants and style of garden. Good-quality terracotta suits a formal, classic space, while galvanized steel cubes, cylinders, or conical pots look good in a more contemporary garden. Black or white terrazzo (faux marble) oozes sophistication and suits many garden styles. If you have a balcony or roof garden, use lightweight pots.

The size of the pot you need depends on the plant. Make sure it is large enough for the rootball, with space around the sides and base for the roots to grow. Use large pots for trees, shrubs, or groups of plants, while smaller containers can house herbs, bulbs, or perennials.

Using the correct compost is vital. Shrubs, trees, and other perennials growing permanently in pots grow best in a soil-based compost as it retains moisture well and is fairly

Planting a patio pot

Patio containers are easy to plant up, but it's worth spending a few minutes preparing pots before you start. Choose a pot with a drainage hole that will accommodate the plants easily with room for growth. Fill with compost to within 5cm (2in) of the rim. Once you have planted up, keep this gap between the surface of the compost and lip of the container to prevent water spilling over the edges when watering. Stand containers on pot feet to allow excess moisture to drain away. This prevents moisture building up at the base of pots, and subsequent waterlogging and root damage. Pools of water may stain the ground and the container, and encourage roots to grow out of the base of the pot, which can look untidy.

1 If you are using terracotta pots, prepare them for planting by first giving the insides a good soaking using a watering can or hose.

2 If the pot is large, cover the base with polystyrene or rubble to avoid using more compost than you need. This also prevents compost washing out of the drainage hole

3 Fill the pot with compost, leaving a gap at the top to allow for watering. Mix a controlled-release fertilizer into the soil according to the instructions on the packet.

4 Position plants in the pot, leaving enough space between them to allow for growth. Gently firm down the soil around the roots and water in well.

heavy, preventing pots toppling over. Multi-purpose compost is ideal for temporary displays of annual plants or vegetables. Once planted up, add a decorative mulch over the surface of the compost. It looks good, stifles weeds, and locks in moisture.

Group pots together to create an interesting display. Use a few different styles of pots, but keep it simple for a unified look.

A simple pot supporting a well-shaped plant can create a focal point in a garden, or can be used to draw the eye to what lies beyond it.

TOP-DRESSING

Plants that are permanently grown in pots can run out of steam and should be given a boost in spring. Top-dressing is simply removing the top layer of compost and replacing it with fresh material mixed with an appropriate fertilizer.

Top-dress containers with fresh compost, then cover with a mulch of bark chips or decorative pebbles to keep the moisture in and prevent weeds germinating.

Planting a hanging basket

Hanging baskets can be planted up for all-year interest or to provide a blast of colour in specific seasons. Baskets are available in a wide range of sizes and styles, and have either solid or open sides. Those with open sides require liners to retain the compost; choose one the right size, made of cardboard, plastic-backed jute, coconut fibre, or artificial moss. To make planting up easier, sit your basket in a large pot or bucket to prevent it moving around. Fill it using specially formulated hanging basket compost, or make your own blend using multi-purpose compost mixed with controlled-release fertilizer granules and water-retaining crystals.

1 If your hanging basket is not already lined, cut your preferred lining material to size and press it into place. Cut planting holes in the sides.

2 Half-fill the basket with a mix of multi-purpose compost, fertilizer, and water-retaining granules. Insert the plants into the compost through the side holes.

3 Add more compost to the basket once all the side plantings are in place, then position the plants to grow on the top of the basket or to tumble down.

4 Firm down plants then give the hanging basket a good watering using a fine rose. Leave the basket to drain in the pot or bucket before hanging in position.

Encourage a good display from your plants by removing spent flowers, which may promote new flowering stems.

A GOOD DISPLAY

Every gardener wants a great display of colour in the garden, and it's not hard to achieve with good plant care. There are a few simple tricks that will help you keep ornamental plants flowering better, and for longer.

PROLONGING FLOWERING

Deadheading spent flowers, pinching out growth, and dividing crowded bulbs and perennials are effective techniques used to encourage plants to perform at their best. They are carried out at different times of year, and all are simple to do.

Deadheading

Most plants divert their energy into producing seeds when their flowers start to fade, but you can encourage them to continue flowering longer by regularly removing spent heads. Dying flowers on soft-stemmed plants can be snapped off with your thumb and forefinger; use secateurs for thicker stems or where accurate pruning is needed, such as on roses. This technique can be used on many shrubs, perennials, and annuals.

A small number of plants are sterile and don't set seeds, which means they will continue to flower even if you don't remove the dead heads. You may still wish to remove dying flowers, however, to improve the plant's overall appearance, and to reduce the risk of disease or rotting in damp weather. In contrast, some plants are prolific self-seeders, such as annual poppies, and can become a nuisance in the garden. In this situation, deadheading before seeds are produced will prevent unwanted seedlings appearing everywhere.

Pinching out

Left to their own devices, some perennials, bedding plants, and flowering pot plants produce thin, spindly shoots, leading to a disappointing display of colour.

STAKING PLANTS

Weak-stemmed or top-heavy perennials need supports in summer, which should be put in place in early spring. Use link stakes to surround large clumps, and wire-mesh rings on legs for multi-stemmed perennials.

Help plants to hold their heads high for all to see in summer by putting supports in place before they get too big.

Removing spent flowers not only makes the plant look better, but also encourages the plant to direct its energy into making new blooms.

Pinching out the growing tips "stops" vertical growth and encourages the growth of stems lower down, creating a bushier plant.

However, by pinching these shoots back early in the season you can encourage plants to produce bushier growth from lower down, which will give the plant a more balanced shape. It also creates more robust plants that are less likely to collapse, while also encouraging the production of more flowers. Some plants, like annual sweet peas, only need pinching out once, but others, such as fuchsias and petunias, need regular attention during summer.

Generally, plants need pinching out when they are about a third of their ultimate height; aim to remove around 2.5–5cm (1–2in) of growth.

Thinning overcrowded bulbs

Over a number of years, most bulb species form clumps that gradually become so overcrowded that the plants stop flowering – described as becoming "blind". To rejuvenate them, carefully lift the clumps with a fork as the leaves die down in autumn, and divide them into separate bulbs. Remove any dead, diseased, or unhealthy bulbs, and replant the rest into well-prepared soil. Most bulbs will need thinning every three to four years, but be guided by flowering performance; lift and divide bulbs when the flowering season deteriorates.

Established bulb colonies can be difficult to lift from the soil in one piece, so work from all sides and lift smaller, individual clumps.

PLANT LIST

Perennials that benefit from occasional division
Achillea (Yarrow)

Astilbe

Coreopsis (Tickseed)

Helenium (Helen's flower)

Hylotelephium spectabile (Ice plant)

Iris

Monarda (Bergamot)

Rudbeckia (Coneflower)

Stachys byzantina (Lambs' ears)

Perennials that resent disturbance
Anemone x hybrida

Aquilegia (Columbine)

Crocosmia (Montbretia)

Dierama (Angel's fishing rod)

Helleborus

Hemerocallis (Day lily)

Lamprocapnos spectabilis (Bleeding heart)

Paeonia (Peony)

Lifting and dividing perennials

Many perennials outgrow their allotted space or lose vigour with age, forming unproductive mounds of foliage that are shy to flower. Others form unsightly rings of plants around a bare centre. Revive plants by dividing them when dormant, either in late autumn or early spring – plants split early in the year establish better as the soil is damp but quickly warms up. Most perennials need dividing every two or three years, but some grow more vigorously than others, requiring frequent division, while others flower better when congested, are slower growing, or resent disturbance. Dividing perennials is a useful way to propagate them (see p.332).

1 Carefully lift the plant, using a fork. Take care not to damage the roots as you do so. Gently shake off excess soil as you remove the clump.

2 Separate plants by inserting two spades back-to-back in the centre of the clump and pushing them away from each other to split the mound.

3 Divide the larger clumps into smaller, more manageable pieces using your hands. Discard any unhealthy-looking sections, and pull out any weeds.

4 Replant the newly divided sections into their new positions, at the same depth as before. Firm the soil around the roots well.

TENDER PLANTS

During colder months, plants are vulnerable to frosts, low temperatures, biting winds, and excessive rain. Losing a few plants is inevitable in a very hard winter, but you can reduce the risk with protective measures.

Mature tender plants may be too large to bring under cover during winter, so you will need to protect them where they grow.

MOVING UNDER COVER

If you are overwintering crops, extending the growing season, or making early or late sowings in the ground, use polythene tunnels, cloches, or fleece to protect plants from hard frosts and excessively wet conditions.

A simple cloche provides enough protection for young plants in mid-spring when there is still risk of frost.

WINTER PROTECTION

A sudden cold snap will take its toll on tender plants, so don't be caught out. Wrap up plants well in advance and prepare them for the worst weather to help them get through the winter unscathed.

While tender bulbs and tubers are best lifted from the ground, vulnerable shrubs, climbers, and other plants can be protected from the elements *in situ* with hessian, horticultural fleece, and straw. Wrap plants in late autumn, or before the first frosts. Protect branches of shrubs such as *Cestrum*, fuchsia, and *Clerodendrum* with a sheet of horticultural fleece held in place with twine. Encase the lower stems of tender climbers with dry straw wrapped with hessian.

Tender architectural plants need extra cosseting. Place straw in the crown of tree ferns and palms, then gather up the fronds and wrap in fleece. To protect bananas, cut off the leaves and encircle the trunks with chicken wire. Stuff this with straw and cover it all with plastic sheeting to keep out the rain – loosen the covers during milder weather to allow air to circulate.

Plants in containers

Plants in pots are particularly vulnerable to cold weather, and a sudden cold snap or a prolonged period of icy weather can cause damage to roots or tender shoots. Move plants to a cool conservatory, porch, or frost-free greenhouse if possible; dormant plants that don't

Keep roots of container-grown plants frost-free outside in winter by wrapping the pots with bubble plastic or hessian, secured with twine.

Tender blossom on wall-trained fruit trees can be protected *in situ* from frost damage over winter by covering with horticultural fleece.

need light, such as fuchsias, can also be moved into garages and sheds. If you don't have space or the pots are too heavy to move, take other precautions.

Keep the roots protected from frost by wrapping the outside of the container with bubble plastic, hessian, or fleece, and tie it securely in place with garden twine. Alternatively, push pots up against the wall of the house, where it is slightly warmer, and pack them together tightly so they help to insulate each other. Protection material can then be wrapped around the whole group. Sheets of fleece can also be wrapped around the tops of plants to protect foliage, buds, or early flowers, particularly on fruit trees.

Excessive moisture caused by winter rain can also cause problems for container-grown plants. Wet compost or puddles building up at the base of pots can starve roots of oxygen and they may then rot,

causing the plant to die. Reduce problems by moving pots into a rain shadow or sheltered spot, and raise containers off the ground on pot feet to allow excess moisture to drain and air to circulate around the roots.

Tropical plants, such as bananas (*above*) and palms, are vulnerable to frost. If you can't move them under cover, mulch them well with straw.

TENDER PLANTS
Bougainvillea
Brugmansia
Callistemon (Bottlebrush)
Canna (Indian shot plant)
Clerodendrum bungei (Glory flower)
Cordyline australis (New Zealand cabbage palm)
Dahlia
Dicksonia antarctica (Tree fern)
Eucomis (Pineapple lily)
Fuchsia
Galtonia
Gladiolus
Hedychium (Ginger lily)
Leonotis leonurus (Lion's tail)
Melianthus major (Honey bush)
Musa basjoo (Japanese banana)
Pelargonium
Punica granatum (Pomegranate)
Tigridia (Tiger flower)

Lifting and storing tender bulbs and tubers

Unless you have a mild winter climate and well-drained soil, lift your tender bulbs and tubers and store them under cover during winter to prevent them rotting in damp soil, or being damaged or killed by penetrating ground frost. Dahlias, *Eucomis*, cannas, gladioli, *Tigridia*, *Galtonia*, and other summer-flowering species should be lifted during the

autumn once the foliage starts to die back. Lift the bulbs and dry off completely to prevent them rotting, then store under cover in a garage, shed, or any dry, frost-free place. Label them before storing for easy identification when they are planted outdoors again in spring. Check bulbs occasionally for signs of decay.

1 Lift bulbs out of the soil in autumn using a fork, being careful to avoid damaging them with the prongs. Discard any damaged bulbs.

2 Remove soil, trim off dying top growth and lay the bulbs out on a wire rack. Once they are dry, store the bulbs in boxes or trays of sand in a frost-free place.

1 Lift tubers out of the ground during autumn using a fork, digging around the edge of the clump to prevent damage to the roots.

2 Shake off excess soil, trim away any dying foliage and stems and let the tubers dry out completely. Once dry, dust off the remaining soil and store the tubers.

Many trees benefit from regular pruning to control their size and produce an attractive shape. It also promotes strong new growth.

PRUNING

You can influence the way plants grow through pruning, which will also increase their production and ensure they look their best. Knowing when and where to prune, and which technique to use, will help your plants to flourish.

WHY PRUNE?

Pruning plants worries some gardeners, but armed with the right tools and a little knowledge, you can improve the look and vigour of your plants without them coming to harm.

Hard pruning results in more vigorous growth further down the plant. At the end of each shoot is a terminal bud that is stronger than those along the sides, which grow to form side shoots. Cutting off the terminal bud directs the plant's energy to the side buds, resulting in a bushier, fuller plant.

There are many reasons why you might need to prune plants in this way. Left to their own devices, some

plants become an unsightly tangle of overgrown branches, promoting conditions ripe for pests and diseases. Overgrown plants also tend to be less vigorous, resulting in a poorer display of flowers, or the production of fewer fruit.

Pruning helps to maintain an attractive shape and prevents plants suffocating compact neighbours, especially in small gardens where space is at a premium. Many beautiful effects can be achieved by careful pruning. Cutting some plants back hard will result in foliage that is larger and brighter than mature leaves, while cutting back the shoots of plants grown for winter stem colour encourages a

PINCH PRUNING

You will need pruning tools to make a clean cut to woody or thick branches, but soft and sappy growth can be pruned by hand. Pinch off this growth with your thumb and forefinger to encourage a bushy plant.

Young, fresh growth can be pinched out neatly between thumb and forefinger, without causing damage.

Make an angled cut downwards on stems that bear alternate buds along their length. Select a healthy bud and prune just above it.

On plants with opposite buds on their stems, prune just above a pair of healthy buds, making a clean, straight cut.

Choosing and using the right tools for the right job is essential to prevent damaging plants, which in turn can lead to infections.

PRUNING TOOLS

To prune properly you need a small selection of good-quality tools. It is important that they are maintained well so that they make clean cuts that do not damage plant growth.

Different tools are needed for different jobs. Choose secateurs for the accurate pruning of stems up to 1.5cm (½in) in diameter and keep them sharp and clean. Hand-held pruning saws are ideal for thicker branches. Telescopic loppers are used for cutting stems up to 2.5cm (1in) thick, growing above head height. Hand-held shears are best for topiary, while electric and petrol hedge trimmers are useful for cutting most hedges.

Long-arm loppers make trimming stems above head height easier and safer and dispense with the need for ladders.

flush of bright new shoots. Regular pruning to remove diseased or damaged material also keeps plants in good health. Pruning needs depend on the type of plant, and for some, a light trim is all that is necessary to maintain a good display.

WHEN TO PRUNE

The timing of pruning is important: if you prune at the wrong time you might remove flower buds or leave plants vulnerable to damage by frost. A good rule of thumb for any shrub or climber is to prune lightly shortly after flowering as the blooms start to fade – an exception is forsythia, which can be pruned hard to control its size. If the plant flowers after the longest day, you can usually prune quite hard in spring. Of course, there are exceptions to this rule (such as mophead and lacecap hydrangeas, which have their flowerheads left in place through winter and are then pruned lightly in spring), so research specific plants. Evergreen shrubs are usually pruned between late spring and autumn. Soft growth is vulnerable to frosts, so prune to allow plenty of time for regrowth to toughen up before cold weather arrives.

To prune back stems and branches, you only need a pair of sharp secateurs.

Remove thicker stems of large shrubs and trees with a sharp-toothed pruning saw.

A bow saw is ideal for removing branches of 15cm (6in) or more and cutting them into logs.

Loppers make it easier to cut woody stems of 1cm (½in) thick, especially where access is tricky.

Electric hedge trimmers make light work of cutting and shaping long or tall hedges.

Shears are invaluable for trimming smaller hedges, but also for cutting long grass.

Prune little by little if you are unsure of how much of the stems' length to remove. You can always prune a little more if necessary.

PRUNING SHRUBS

To keep shrubs looking their best, prune them regularly to keep them within bounds and maintain a well-balanced structure. Pruning at the right time will keep them healthy and encourage masses of flowers.

WHY PRUNE SHRUBS?

Most shrubs will grow happily without intervention, but unless you prefer a natural look, unpruned plants look out of place in traditional gardens. Annual pruning will keep shrubs at a size suitable for your garden, will prevent them muscling out other plants, and stop them spreading onto pathways.

Pruning also improves the flowering or fruiting performance of shrubs. Older wood is less vigorous than younger shoots, and removing this material encourages plants to be more productive. Timing is key to avoid mistakenly removing developing flower buds.

Although some shrubs respond to hard pruning with a flush of new growth, others are slower growing and only require minimal pruning to keep a balanced shape.

Routine tasks

To ensure healthy plants, remove dead, diseased, or dying growth as you notice it. If left, diseased portions can spread into other parts of the plant. Either cut out the damaged branch or cut back to healthy wood.

Pruning early-flowering shrubs

Shrubs that flower in spring and early summer on wood formed the year before, such as *Philadelphus*, *Weigela*, *Kerria*, *Forsythia*, *Buddleja alternifolia*, *Kolkwitzia*, and *Deutzia* should be trimmed when blooms fade. This will encourage a flush of new branches and the production of flowers closer to the ground, where they are easier to enjoy. If left, plants will become lanky and the flowers will be held higher up the plant. To improve their appearance and keep them under control, remove thin and wispy growth, then cut back branches that held flowers to strong side branches, aiming to maintain an open, balanced framework.

1 As soon as *Philadelphus* has finished flowering, cut back about a quarter of the oldest flowering stems to 15cm (6in) above the ground.

2 First remove any dead, damaged, or diseased stems, cutting them back to the base of the plant using sharp, clean secateurs.

3 Prune out stems of the previous year's growth, cutting them back to about 2 or 4 buds from the old wood. This will encourage a new flush of growth.

4 Finally, trim the tips of any strong young stems that are already present in the plant. This encourages them to branch further down, resulting in more flowers.

Some shrubs grow unevenly, spoiling the symmetry of the plant; if a plant has developed more growth on just one side, lightly prune the stronger shoots on the bushy side and hard prune the weaker ones to restore balance.

Congested branches reduce airflow and light to the centre of the plant, which can result in disease. Thinning out growth and removing crossing or unwanted branches will improve the resilience of the plant.

A shrub that looks out of shape and unbalanced should be pruned to give it more structure and create a healthier framework.

Once pruned, the plant puts on a whole new flush of vigorous growth and begins to take on a more attractive shape.

ALSO RECOMMENDED

Shrubs pruned in summer after flowering:

Buddleja alternifolia

Deutzia

Exochorda

Kolkwitzia

Philadelphus

Photinia villosa

Ribes sanguineum

Syringa

Weigela

Shrubs pruned in spring:

Buddleja davidii

Caryopteris x clandonensis

Cotinus

Forsythia

Fuchsia

Hibiscus syriacus

Hydrangea

Lavatera

Perovskia

Pruning late-flowering shrubs

Shrubs that flower on the current season's growth (wood), such as lavender, roses, *Spiraea japonica,* fuchsias, *Caryopteris,* and buddleja should be pruned in early spring. This gives them plenty of time to form vigorous new branches to carry blooms in summer. There are a number of ways to prune these plants: *Leycesteria, Perovskia,* and those that do not produce a woody framework can be pruned to almost ground level, while others can be allowed to develop a permanent framework with the branches cut back each year to maintain their shape. After pruning, give plants a boost by scattering a general granular fertilizer over the soil.

1 Prune late-flowering shrubs such as *Hydrangea paniculata* in the dormant season well after flowering.

2 Using a sharp pair of secateurs, begin by removing dead, diseased, and damaged wood, cutting back to healthy growth and stem joints.

3 Cut out up to one-fifth of the oldest wood all over the plant, reducing stems to within 5–8cm (2–3in) of the ground. It is easiest to do this with a pruning saw.

4 Remove any weak or twiggy growth, too, and cut out any crossing or straggling stems to create a well-balanced shrub with an open centre.

PRUNING FOR A PURPOSE

Some shrubs are grown for their foliage or for their colourful stems, which are at their best after leaf fall. By pruning these plants hard early in the year, you can create magical effects in the dark, cold winter months.

The **flame-red stems** of dogwood provide a much-needed splash of colour in winter. This annual spectacle is maintained by hard pruning.

SPECIAL EFFECTS

It might look brutal at first, but many shrubs respond positively to hard winter pruning by rewarding you with a mass of fresh, new, colourful stems, or by developing leaves that are much bigger, are a better shape, or are more colourful than those produced by unpruned plants.

A number of shrubs will become quite large if left to their own devices, but by cutting them back hard annually in spring, or at least once every few years, you can contain their size and also encourage healthy, decorative leaves.

Avoid pruning plants in autumn, because decay fungi might enter the pruning cuts and cause damage or even death.

Before you start, check that specific plants will respond well to hard pruning. Remember that although cutting back will improve foliage or stems, it might also mean a loss of flowers for that season. Not all plants will tolerate hard pruning, and some may not survive such treatment.

Coppicing and pollarding

Shrubs grown for their winter stems tend to merge into the background for

Pruning for colourful winter stems

Dogwoods, willows, and ornamental brambles are prized for their colourful winter stems, which emerge as their leaves fall in autumn. To ensure a great display each year, these plants need pruning annually, once established, in early spring to encourage a flush of new stems. Known as coppicing, this pruning technique aims to create a permanent low, stubby framework close to the ground. After they have been cut back, new, vibrant shoots will grow vigorously in time for winter. If you are worried about the vigour of your plants, for example for some variegated shrubs, prune more lightly, to encourage new growth. This will also keep the shrub at a larger size.

1 Just before growth commences in early to mid-spring, cut out old, stray stems using secateurs to give the plant some shape.

2 Cut away last year's shoots and all non-woody growth to within 7.5cm (3in) of the main stems, to get better access to the centre of the plant.

3 Once you have clear access to the main stems, cut back hard all shoots to 5–8cm (2–3in) from the base of the plant, cutting just above the join with the main stems.

4 Once you have finished pruning, feed plants with fertilizer and give the area around their roots a good mulch with compost or well-rotted manure.

SPECIAL PRUNING

Plants that respond well to pruning

Acer negundo 'Winter Lightning'

Catalpa bignonioides
(Indian bean tree)

Cercis siliquastrum
(Judas tree)

Cornus species
(Dogwood)

Cotinus species
(Smoke bush)

Davidia involucrata
(Handkerchief tree)

Eucalyptus gunnii
(Cider gum)

Rubus species
(Ornamental bramble)

Salix species
(Willow)

Sambucus nigra 'Aurea'
(Elder)

much of the year, only coming into their own in autumn after the leaves fall. If left, their stems appear dull and tatty and lose their vibrancy of colour, but cutting them back annually, or at least every other year, will promote a flush of new colourful shoots.

Willows and dogwoods can be pruned using a technique known as coppicing, which encourages a mass of colourful winter stems. Begin training plants just after planting by pruning back all shoots hard, close to their base. The following spring and in subsequent years, prune the tree in the same way to produce a stumpy framework.

Pollarding (see *p.321*) is another method used for pruning dogwoods and willows to produce spectacular winter stems. Instead of being pruned back close to the ground, plants are pruned above a clear trunk. The branches are cut back to previous cuts on the top of the trunk to leave a lollipop shape. After cutting back plants hard, feed around the roots and mulch.

PRUNING FOR FOLIAGE

Some shrubs are pruned hard to produce winter stems, and others can be given similar treatment to encourage more eye-catching foliage. The Indian bean tree (*Catalpa bignonioides*), Judas tree (*Cercis siliquastrum*), foxglove tree (*Paulownia tomentosa*) and others respond by producing larger leaves than those on unpruned plants. Cider gum (*Eucalyptus gunnii*) has curved, oval leaves when mature. If cut back hard, it responds by producing attractive juvenile leaves.

The foliage of many deciduous variegated shrubs is far more vibrant if pruned annually. The usual techniques for these plants are pollarding and stooling, which should be carried out between late winter and early spring, before leaves appear. To stool plants, cut back stems to within 5–7.5cm (2–3in) of the ground. To grow as a pollard, cut back shoots to within 5–7.5cm (2–3in) of the trunk. Apply a balanced granular fertilizer at 70g per sq m (2oz per sq yd) to assist new growth after pruning.

▲ **Prune back hard** in spring for a more impressive display. Certain plants produce their most attractive foliage with juvenile leaves.

◀ **Pollarding** trees and shrubs encourages them to bear their most eye-catching young growth, raised above ground level.

Variegated plants can quickly become overrun by non-variegated shoots, so prune them out on sight to maintain interesting foliage.

A little judicious pruning will give you walls of colour throughout the seasons, and even a seemingly informal garden requires a little work.

PRUNING CLIMBERS

Climbing plants and wall shrubs provide vertical colour and interest, but if neglected they will soon grow out of bounds, becoming shy to flower or casting unwanted shade. Pruning once a year will keep them at their best.

BASIC CLIMBER PRUNING

Without a helping hand, some plants will romp away, outgrowing their allotted space and becoming an unsightly tangle of shoots. Others will lose vigour and produce few flowers, berries, or fruit.

Annual pruning helps keep climbers attractive, productive, and in check, but you can make life easier by selecting plants that suit your garden, along with their allotted space or support. This reduces the need to prune too often, making it easy to keep your climbing plants under control.

Whether you're growing self-clinging climbers (see p.144) or those with lax stems that need training against supports to flourish, your aim is to create a well-balanced framework that clothes the area. Remove any weak or damaged shoots and prune wayward growths to encourage branching. As the climbing plant matures, older, woodier stems will need pruning to promote more vigorous shoots.

Types of cut

Plants that have a network of woody stems are easily pruned using secateurs

Pruning honeysuckle

Honeysuckles are prized for their highly scented flowers and will happily scramble over supports. However, they can break ranks and invade the space of other plants or cause damage to overburdened supports or structures. Pruning and training in spring will help to keep them in check as well as productive and healthy.

1 To encourage even coverage, cut out old woody stems at the base or just above a point where strong growth is emerging.

2 Remove unwanted new shoots as they grow to keep plants within bounds. Cut away these wayward stems close to the main framework and tie them into their supports.

Pruning ivy

Ivy's vigorous and dense growth means it must be pruned regularly to stop it becoming a nuisance. Plants can be pruned in late spring or early summer to reduce the height, width, and density of growth; they can also be sheared or cut back hard. Check plants before pruning to avoid disturbing nesting birds.

1 Ivy can be an irritant, so wear gloves to prune it. Peel away and cut off all unwanted ivy. Check for dead, damaged, or diseased growth and then prune that too.

2 Ivy will attach itself to most surfaces and cling on. If it has strayed into territory where it is unwanted or might cause damage, peel it away from the wall by hand.

to ensure accurate cuts and a tidy finish. If growth is needed to fill a certain area, pruning cuts can be made above outward-facing buds pointing in the direction needed. Pruning like this would be a chore on those plants that form a dense

If your climber needs drastic pruning, cut away all the unproductive material beneath the foliage using a pair of hand shears.

mass of spindly growth, so prune these stems en masse with shears or secateurs. Wall shrubs, and climbing plants with evergreen foliage, can be clipped tightly with shears to keep them neat and bushy.

When to prune

The timing of pruning is generally the same for climbers as it is for other shrubs. Evergreen climbers grown for their foliage can be pruned in spring, while those grown for their flowers need pruning at specific times to avoid removing flower buds. Early-flowering plants that flower on the previous season's wood should be pruned after flowering, while those that flower in mid- to late summer on the current season's growth can be pruned in winter or early spring. Clematis fall into three pruning groups and are categorized according to when they flower (see p.149).

PRUNING WALL SHRUBS

Unlike true climbers, which are largely self-clinging, wall shrubs have no natural means of supporting themselves vertically, so branches are usually tied into a network of wires, trellis, or other supports. Like all other shrubs, these need pruning annually to keep them within bounds, to prevent them becoming too heavy and falling away from supports, and, if grown for their flowers, to encourage a good display.

Start by pruning horizontal branches to reduce the width, then cut taller vertical stems to reduce the height. Foliage plants can be pruned in spring, but for others, their pruning depends on their flowering times (see pp.312–13).

Prune back wall shrubs such as this *Euonymus fortunei* in late spring to shape them and keep them contained. Pruning by hand with secateurs creates a neater finish.

WISTERIA

Wisteria will grow rampantly if left to its own devices, producing masses of leafy growth at the expense of flowers. Pruning diverts the plant's energy from making leaves to producing flower buds, while

reducing the mass of whippy shoots helps light reach the network of branches inside. Although wisterias can cover a large area, don't trim them back quickly with a pair of shears; precise pruning twice a year with secateurs yields better results.

In summer, prune back vigorous shoots and long, whippy stems to about four or six leaves from the main stem, creating shoots that are 15cm (6in) long.

In winter, cut back all the stems you shortened in summer to about two or three buds, or so that they are approximately 8–10cm (3–4in) in length.

Cut away horizontal stems first on large-growing shrubs such as *Garrya elliptica* in spring, then reduce the height to the required level by cutting off vertical stems.

PRUNING ROSES

Roses are among our best-loved plants, valued for their scent, variety, colour, and multiple uses in the flower garden. They are relatively easy to train and prune to ensure a great display each year.

New buds are a useful clue to the direction in which a new shoot will grow. Prune back to an outward-facing bud to avoid congestion.

HOW TO PRUNE ROSES

Roses need pruning for a variety of reasons. Left to grow as they please, they will flower for a few years but then begin to produce weak stems that carry fewer blooms. The plant is likely to develop a mass of congested stems, which reduces the amount of light and air reaching its centre. These unhealthy conditions weaken new growth and provide the kind of conditions that encourage pests and diseases to prosper. Choose a pruning technique that suits the type of rose you are growing. For most pruning

work secateurs are fine, but thicker branches should be removed with a pruning saw.

Climbing and rambling roses (see facing page) need trimming to keep them within the bounds of pergolas, arches, and fences. Bush roses, which include hybrid tea and floribunda varieties, are usually grown in beds and borders. After removing dead, diseased, and dying growth, hybrid teas should be pruned back in early spring, reducing healthy main stems by a quarter to encourage plenty of well-placed flowering shoots. Aim

Pruning shrub roses

Early spring is the best time to prune shrub roses, starting with any dead, diseased, or dying material. Your aim is to create a strong, open framework with a good airflow to prevent fungal diseases. Cut a few of the oldest stems back to the ground, then reduce healthy main stems by a quarter. Use a slanting cut, directly above an outward-

facing bud, and snip sloping away from the bud. As well as pruning these roses annually, keep the floral show going longer by deadheading flowers as they start to fade. Despite their slow-growing nature, patio roses are pruned in the same way to keep them compact and flowering freely.

1 Prune roses between late autumn and early spring, before leaves appear. First remove any dead or damaged stems from the plant.

2 Prune any over-vigorous shoots by shortening them to about half their original length using secateurs. You may want to wear gloves to do this.

3 Cut back any other stems by about half if they look as though they will affect the balance of the shape of the plant when growth begins again in spring.

4 Once you have finished pruning, apply fertilizer around the roots of the plant and add a layer of mulch, keeping it clear of the main stem.

for a strong, open structure that is uncluttered in the centre.

Less vigorous floribundas are not pruned so hard. Cut back shoots to

Crossing and rubbing branches will cause damage to the plant, which can lead to disease. These stems should be removed as they appear.

within 15–20cm (6–8in) of the base of the plant, leaving a framework of 6–8 of the strongest stems.

Lightly prune miniature roses in spring, cutting wayward branches back by a third and pruning to shape. Patio roses also need pruning to boost flowering, and the shoots of ground-cover roses need to be cut back to keep them within bounds; remove thicker branches on old plants to stimulate new growth.

Aftercare

After pruning, water roses well and apply a granular rose fertilizer over the root area. Finish by mulching plants, leaving a gap between the mulch and the stems. During summer, you can extend flowering by deadheading flowers that are within reach all over the plant to encourage more to develop. Use your fingers to snap off fading blooms at the slightly swollen section of the stem just below the flower, or use secateurs.

REMOVE ROSE SUCKERS

Grafted roses often produce unwanted, vigorous, less ornamental stems from their roots. Remove these by twisting them off at the base. Avoid cutting them at ground level, as this promotes regrowth.

Rose suckers are easy to spot at the base of plants. They detract from the plant's appearance and sap its resources.

Pruning rambling roses

Rambling roses generally need less pruning than climbers, but if their allocated area or supports have been covered, you may want to prune back the stems to regain control and improve their flowering. Ramblers should be pruned in late summer once they have finished flowering.

1 Remove one in three of the oldest stems entirely using loppers, cutting the stems back to just above the soil surface.

2 Cut back any stems that have flowered or are making the plant look unruly, then shorten sideshoots by about two-thirds of their length using secateurs.

Pruning climbing roses

Climbing roses are not self-clinging and need their shoots to be tied to supports. They are best pruned in late autumn after the flowers have faded or in winter. Remove dead, diseased, or dying branches, and cut out any old branches if the plant is heavily congested, to promote fresh new growth.

1 Spur-prune last season's flowering stems back to two or three healthy buds to encourage them to produce more flowering stems.

2 Train any straggling new and old stems to fill gaps in the allocated framework for a neat finish. Tie them into their supports using garden twine.

PRUNING TO RENOVATE

Many woody plants become an unsightly mass of congested branches if irregularly pruned, but few are beyond salvation. Most plants can be restored using some drastic but essential pruning techniques.

Neglected shrubs, or those that have seen better days, should be cut back hard as an alternative to digging them up.

SHAPING UP

Regular pruning helps to maintain the appearance and health of shrubs, but if plants have been neglected or have grown too large, or you have inherited a garden with out of control plants, more drastic action may be required.

Overgrown plants are unlikely to flower well, and new growth tends to be weak and less vigorous than in well-tended plants. Apart from becoming an eyesore and losing their attractive shape, neglected plants can also cast unwanted shade in a garden, restricting the growth of other plants, and preventing you from planting perennials, bulbs, or other plants to make the most of your space. Pests and diseases are also more prevalent among unpruned plants due to their weaker growth, a build-up of dead stems and plant debris, and the reduced light levels and air circulation passing through the crown.

The key to dealing with overgrown shrubs is to cut them back hard,

Using the three-cut pruning method

Sometimes trees require more radical pruning than just trimming a few unwanted branches or shoots. If a branch has become diseased, damaged, or unsafe, it is often better to remove it altogether. Or it may be that you want to improve the tree's overall shape and appearance. If you are removing a whole branch, it needs to be done in stages rather than with one cut near the trunk. This will prevent any damage to the tree should the heavy branch break mid-cut, taking with it the bark on the trunk. Such damage can expose the trunk and the whole plant to serious infections, such as silver leaf (see p.368), which may prove fatal.

1 Using a pruning saw or secateurs (depending on the width of the branches), first remove sideshoots and the end of the branch.

2 Using a pruning saw in one hand and holding the branch close to the trunk, make a cut under the branch further along, then cut through from above.

3 Holding the stump steady, make the final cut to remove the branch just outside its "collar", cutting through from above with a pruning saw.

4 Make sure the final cut leaves a clean wound; if there is any damage, neaten up the cut. You do not need to apply any wound paint to the stub.

usually to bare stumps, which should be carried out in late spring or summer, after the plants have finished flowering. Feed well to promote regrowth. Many plants respond well to this treatment, throwing out a flush of new growth, and soon start to earn their place again. Regard this as a last-ditch attempt to save the plants however, because although this technique works well with many plants, some may not recover, and so may need to be dug up and replaced.

Hard-pruning evergreens

Many evergreen shrubs can be hard-pruned if necessary. Bushy plants with lots of branches at ground level, such as mahonia (see below), can be pruned to leave just a cluster of stumps. Plants that grow from single trunks, such as camellia, should be reduced to around 60cm (24in) high, with side stems cut close to the main

branch. Despite looking severe, a flush of young stems will appear from this stump, although it may take several years for the plant to reach flowering size again. *Aucuba japonica* (spotted laurel), escallonia, *Prunus laurocerasus* (cherry laurel), and *Viburnum tinus* can all be pruned in this way.

Stems and sideshoots of some deciduous shrubs can be pruned back hard in spring to improve their overall appearance.

POLLARDING

Dogwoods and some willows, along with eucalyptus and other trees and shrubs, are valued for their juvenile, colourful winter stems. The best displays come from plants that have been heavily pruned or pollarded.

To produce colourful winter stems, all previous stems need cutting back hard in spring to encourage vibrant, new shoots.

Pruning mahonia

Mahonia is a statuesque shrub grown for its attractive evergreen foliage and its winter and spring flowers, many of which are highly scented. You can keep mahonias short and bushy by pruning plants immediately after flowering, cutting them back to healthy new shoots. Over time however, plants can become quite large, with dense

growth that will cast unwanted shade and muscle out any less robust plants growing nearby. To restore the shape of plants or to keep them within bounds, prune them hard from midwinter to early spring, when flowers have faded. Only overgrown mahonias need this treatment.

1 First remove all the stems from the tops and sides of the plant using a pruning saw. Cut them back close to the main stems.

2 Once you have cut back the tall growths, remove any damaged, diseased, or crossing stems and old growth to leave five or six strong stems.

3 Once the upper stems have been removed, cut back all the stems to about 90–120cm (3–4ft) high, or to 60cm (2ft) if you want a smaller plant. Feed the plant well.

4 By summer, the plant will have recovered and produced many fresh new stems and leaves from the stumps. It will not require such drastic pruning again for years.

HOW TO CUT A HEDGE

Hedges are invaluable for dividing a garden, for use as a windbreak or boundary, or to provide background to a border, but, unlike fences, they need regular care to keep them healthy, neat, and looking their best.

Formal hedges and topiary rely on a neat, well-maintained shape for impact. Trim them as necessary to keep them looking tidy.

SHAPING UP

An attractive hedge can become an unshapely mess if neglected, so make sure it is trimmed regularly – whether this is just once a year or several times during the growing season, as is necessary with certain fast-growing conifers. Sections of hedge may die if uncared for, and the hedge overall can begin to lose its function. Low growing hedges or short runs can be kept in shape easily with a pair of sharp hand shears; an electric, cordless, or petrol-powered trimmer will make light work of larger hedges. Use secateurs to prune hedges planted with large-leaved evergreens, such as laurel, to prevent leaving tattered leaves.

Formal and informal hedges

Hedges generally fall into two categories – formal and informal – both of which can make excellent windbreaks, barriers, or partitions. Formal hedges are clipped tightly to maintain a geometric shape. Hornbeam, beech, privet, holly, laurel,

Cutting an evergreen hedge

Evergreens, such as yew (*Taxus baccata, shown below*), make excellent dense hedges and are often planted as a boundary, to divide up a garden, or as a dark backdrop to herbaceous perennials. Unlike most conifers, they respond well to hard pruning and can be trained to any height or shape. Aim to maintain a fairly narrow hedge. You may wish to trim so that the base is slightly wider than the top, so that, in winter, snow will fall down the sides rather than accumulate. Plants can put on around 30cm (12in) of growth each year, so keep them in shape by pruning in late summer. Although neglected hedges can be restored, they tend to billow outwards over time.

I Decide how much you want to remove when trimming. If you want straight edges, stretch a string along the top to act as a guide.

2 Using a powered hedge trimmer and safety equipment, trim the sides in sweeping movements, keeping the blade parallel to the hedge.

3 Standing on a properly supported platform, use the hedge trimmer to cut along the top of the hedge, keeping the blade flat to create a straight edge.

4 Brush away all hedge trimmings from the top and sides of the hedge once you have finished trimming. Remove them, along with any at the base.

yew, and Leyland cypress are often used for this style. Formal hedges will need trimming every 4–6 weeks in summer, to keep a neat shape with slightly tapered sides.

Informal hedges are left to grow more naturally and suit a relaxed style of garden. Because they are not clipped hard, the plants flower or fruit, and are usually pruned back into shape once the display is over. Forsythia, escallonia, berberis, hawthorn, and spindle are suitable for this kind of hedge. These hedges often attract wildlife, such as birds, so trimming should be avoided at nesting time, which can last well into the summer.

DISEASE CONTROL

Reduce disease problems by removing any hedge trimmings immediately after cutting. Rake up material left at the base and flick hedges with a cane to dislodge loose clippings. Make the job easier by placing sheets below the hedge before trimming to catch clippings.

Formal hedges make beautiful features, either as a focal point or a backdrop to other plants. They need regular attention to look their best.

Informal hedges are well suited to more relaxed garden schemes with a natural feel. They also require less precise pruning.

Compost any disease-free hedge trimmings but destroy any that show signs of pests or disease.

Renovating a hedge

If you've inherited a hedge that is too wide or overgrown, you can restore its shape with some hard pruning, carried out in stages over a two-year period. In the first year, trim the hedge as normal, then cut one side back hard. The following year, if growth has been vigorous on the side that's been hard pruned, trim this side as normal and cut back the other side hard. If there is poor growth on the side that was hard pruned, feed and mulch well and wait a further year. Although drastic, many plants respond well to this technique, including beech, hornbeam, yew, holly, cotoneaster, and pyracantha. Always seek advice, as some plants, including most conifers, resent this treatment.

I Carry out major renovation work on deciduous hedges in winter, and evergreens in late winter, while they are dormant.

2 After trimming, cut the branches of the hedge back to the main stems. Set sticks along the length to guide you and help create an even surface.

3 Continue to cut along the length of one side of the hedge to the end. Cut back along the top to create a straight line as you work along.

4 In the winter of the following year, if the hedge has responded to trimming, do the same work to the other side of the hedge to create an even and balanced shape.

Neatly clipped pieces of topiary make an elegant feature on patios, on either side of a doorway, or as focal points in the garden.

STERILIZING TOOLS

Be vigilant when trimming plants, especially if they are showing signs of pest or disease damage. Clean all tools with a garden disinfectant and water, and collect up all trimmings to reduce the risk of infection.

Clean tools as you move between plants by spraying them with a disinfectant solution and wiping the blades clean.

BASIC TOPIARY

If you believe topiary is just for skilled experts or, at best, an expensive purchase, think again. Many simple shapes are easy to establish from scratch and with regular care make attractive features that last for years.

SHAPING UP

Manicured topiary balls, cones, cubes, lollipops, and spirals, or cloud-pruned trees provide sculptural shapes, structure, and a dash of elegance, in pots or in beds and borders.

Box, holly, yew, Portuguese laurel, *Phillyrea*, bay, and many other evergreen and deciduous plants respond well to being closely clipped. Box is prone to the disease box blight (see p.365); be vigilant if choosing this shrub. Partially and completely trained specimens are available, but a cheaper alternative is to create topiary shapes from scratch using untrained plants.

Before clipping, gather together the right tools. You need a pair of good-quality shears for cutting large plants and hand-held clippers for detailed work or cutting smaller

pieces of topiary. Use secateurs to snip off thicker branches or remove any that spoil the shape. While working, regularly dip cutting tools into a bucket of water to prevent sap building up on the blades.

Making a standard tree

A traditional lollipop-shaped standard, where a rounded head of foliage perches above a clear, straight stem, makes an elegant, vertical feature. Bay, Portuguese laurel, holly, myrtle, and hornbeam are easily manipulated in this way.

Pick a plant with a single, strong central leader that will act as your main stem and tie it to a cane or stake. Gradually clear the lower stem of shoots, then nip back the leader to encourage bushy growth to develop, and clip to a rounded shape.

If you want to create a lollipop shape, prune back the topmost stems to create a loose ball. Clip to define the shape as the plant grows.

To create a strong supporting stem, tie the main stem into a cane with twine and clear it of all sideshoots and foliage.

Maintaining a shape

To ensure the crisp silhouette isn't lost under shaggy new growth, clip plants regularly. It's easy to restore them by eye following the contours of the shape, or make a template or use a cane as a cutting guide. Step back often to check your work. Tidy up in early summer and again in late summer for a crisp winter outline. Yew only needs pruning once, in summer, while fast-growing shrubs such as box may need trimming more regularly, but avoid trimming evergreens late in the season, otherwise the new growth that is stimulated will not have time to harden off before the first frosts.

If you don't feel confident about pruning topiary by eye, the best way to get the shape right is to use a template.

Once you have trimmed an approximate ball, make future prunings by eye, stepping back from time to time to check your progress.

PLANT LIST

Topiary-friendly plants:

Carpinus betulus
   (Common hornbeam)

Cryptomeria japonica

Fuchsia varieties

Ilex crenata
   (Box-leaved holly)

Juniperus chinensis
   (Chinese juniper)

Myrtus communis subsp.
   tarentina (Tarentum myrtle)

Phillyrea latifolia

Pittosporum tenuifolium

Prunus lusitanica
   (Portuguese laurel)

Quercus ilex (Holm oak)

Salvia rosmarinus 'Miss
   Jessopp's Upright' (Rosemary)

Santolina chamaecyparissus
   (Cotton lavender)

Viburnum tinus

Creating a topiary cone

Cone shapes are among the easiest to create and maintain. Yew, bay, box-leaved holly, and many other plants with dense foliage are ideal and shapes are best started on bushy, untrained plants. If you want a tall cone, choose a substantial plant with a strong central leader. You can use very young plants, but bear in mind these will take several years to reach a good size. Cone shapes can be created by pruning by eye, or you can use guides. Rest three canes on the sides of the cone, pushing them into the ground. Secure them at the top and bind the sides together with garden wire to make an evenly shaped wigwam, then prune around it.

1 To create a topiary cone, take a healthy, bushy, previously untrained plant. Remove some of the untidy straggler stems first.

2 Stand above the plant, looking down on it, and prune in an outward direction using shears, working your way around the sides of the plant.

3 Still using large shears, go back around the plant, neatening the sides. Stand back and look at the shape a few times as you work, to make sure it is balanced.

4 To keep your topiary cone at its best, trim whenever it begins to lose shape. Stop pruning in early autumn to reduce the risk of frost damage to new growth.

PROPAGATING PLANTS

New plants can be raised easily using simple techniques that include growing from seed, taking cuttings, or dividing existing plants. This is a rewarding and inexpensive way to increase your plant stocks.

Raising your own plants from seed or cuttings is very rewarding, and is an economical way to fill your beds, borders, and containers.

Most plants can be propagated in several ways, but some methods are more successful for certain plants. Raising plants from seed may be the only option if you want to grow a rare or unusual variety that is not readily available in nurseries; it can be more economical too. Taking cuttings is an ideal way to increase your stock of plants, such as shrubs, perennials, or succulents, and there are several methods for doing this, associated with different times of the year. Clump-forming perennials, including alpines and many herbs, can be propagated by dividing their crowns in spring and autumn.

Propagating outdoors

Plants can be propagated both indoors and out. In the garden, seeds of hardy vegetables or annuals can be sown directly into the soil where they are to grow. Apart from some exceptions, most are best sown in spring after all danger of frost has passed. Hardwood cuttings of trees and shrubs, taken during the dormant season, can be inserted in the ground in a warm, sheltered part of the garden, then carefully dug up and planted out into their final positions when roots have formed.

Propagating under cover

Plants can be propagated throughout the year if you have a greenhouse, as the staging allows plenty of room for plants to develop. The warmth and shelter they offer means you can sow flowering or edible plants earlier than usual – later sowings or cuttings often catch up in here too, because of the improved growing conditions. You will need good ventilation and some form of shading to shelter plants from the scorching sun in summer. An unheated structure or simple cold frame provides some warmth and extra protection. In

COLLECTING SEED

An inexpensive way to get new plants is to collect seed. Many annuals can be easily grown this way; seed from shrubs and perennials may need special care to germinate.

Collect seeds in late summer and autumn as the seedheads become brown and dry. Shake the heads into a paper bag.

Hardy seeds can be sown outdoors in spring as the soil warms up, without being started under cover. Others must wait until after the frosts.

Taking cuttings from plants will give you identical versions of your favourite plants with minimal effort.

Cold frames allow for earlier sowing, and can be used to acclimatize plants grown indoors to outside temperatures in late spring.

Cloches are perfect for protecting young plants or those that are borderline hardy until the last of the frosts have passed.

PROPAGATION MATERIALS

To make propagation easy, put together a simple kit of essential tools and materials to keep near your potting area. A selection of different-sized pots, seed trays, and cell trays with clear plastic lids, along with compost, are useful for all types of propagation. Use a sharp knife or secateurs for taking cuttings. A dibber allows you to insert them into pots smoothly and without damage; it can also be used to prick out seedlings. Cover seeds with vermiculite or perlite, or a fine layer of compost sieved through a metal riddle. Use a small watering can with a rose fitted to water seedlings without damaging them. Keep plant labels and a pencil or waterproof pen handy.

many cases, heat is only needed in the early stages of propagation, whether it is to germinate seeds or root cuttings. Additional heat is usually not necessary once plants start to grow.

You can also raise seeds or take cuttings early in the year in a conservatory or on a windowsill, as long as there is plenty of light. You don't even need a propagator. Small pots can be covered with a clear plastic bag held in place with an elastic band. The bags can then be removed as soon as seeds have germinated or cuttings have formed roots and started to grow.

Many plants can be raised successfully in a light place indoors. A bright kitchen windowsill is ideal, or place them on a table, or close to a window in a conservatory. Avoid placing them in shady corners, though, as plants will not grow.

It's always useful to have propagating equipment to hand for when you need it. Label plants as you prepare them, to save confusion later.

A windowsill in a sunny, draught-free position is a good alternative if you do not have room for a greenhouse in your garden.

Mini-greenhouses are useful for protecting plants and seedlings at key times of the year, and can be dismantled when not needed.

A propagator tray with a lid is a really useful piece of kit. The warmth generated gets seeds off to a great start. Make sure the lid has an adjustable vent to allow air to circulate.

GROWING FROM SEED

Watching plants grow from seeds you have sown yourself is a magical experience. You can raise just about any plant from seed: annuals, perennials, and vegetables – and even trees.

Watching seedlings germinate and develop can be very satisfying. Keep them well watered.

WHAT SEEDS NEED

Most seeds are easy to germinate if they are given the right combination of water, air, dark, and warmth. Some seeds require light to germinate and are sown on the surface of compost without covering.

For best results, use good-quality seeds and clean equipment to avoid diseases. Seeds sown indoors require a fine compost that is capable of easily drawing up moisture – it should be firmed, rather than compacted, which inhibits the take-up of water. If you are sowing seeds in the ground, weed first, remove stones, and create a soil texture that almost resembles fine breadcrumbs.

F1 and F2 hybrids

Many annuals, perennials, and vegetables are classed "F1 hybrids". These have been bred for uniformity, health, vigour, and, in the case of vegetables, high yields. They are more expensive due to the breeding work that has gone into their development, but offer more consistent results. They won't breed true from their own seeds, so don't bother collecting their seeds to use the following year. F2 hybrids are the progeny of self- or

Sowing seed indoors

Prior to sowing, make sure your container is large enough for your chosen seeds and that it is scrupulously clean, to avoid spreading soil-borne diseases. Fill it with fresh multi-purpose or, ideally, seed-sowing compost. If you are using seed trays, firm down the compost gently with a piece of flat wood; use the base of another pot if sowing in traditional round containers. After sowing, place pots in a place where the seed can germinate. Some will benefit from a heated propagator, or a simple cover of glass, a clear plastic bag, or clingfilm. After germination, water carefully with a watering can fitted with a fine rose. To avoid displacing plants or compost while watering, start by pouring the water away from the container, then move the spout methodically over the plants.

1 Take a clean seed tray which has holes in the bottom for drainage and fill it with compost. Gently firm down the compost.

2 Carefully scatter the seeds over the surface of the compost, following the instructions on the packet for sowing depth and distances.

3 If necessary, cover the seeds with a thin layer of compost, sieving it over to gently cover but not smother seeds. Alternatively, cover with a thin layer of vermiculite.

4 Water the soil and seeds gently, taking care not to displace the compost or seeds. Use a fine rose on a watering can to help you do this carefully.

Sow seeds outside in drills at the depth and spacings specified on the seed packet. Use a cane in the drill to keep them in straight lines.

Thin out seedlings grown in pots or trays to prevent overcrowding; this will also inhibit the spread of any diseases such as damping off.

To prevent patchy germination of seedlings, rather than even distribution across the container, always firm and level compost carefully prior to sowing, and take care to sow the seed evenly across the surface of the compost.

Seedlings can sometimes become leggy, but to avoid this, remove them from heated propagators as soon as they have germinated and place pots in a well-lit place. This should ensure growth remains even. If seedlings appear to become lopsided, rotate the pot daily so they are evenly exposed to light.

Overwatering is one of the most common causes of seeds not growing well, while underwatering can cause them to wither; try to get the balance right.

cross-pollinated F1 plants. F2 seeds are seldom sold, but may occasionally be superior to open-pollinated seeds, while cheaper than F1 hybrid seeds.

Hardening off

Plants that are raised indoors but are destined for the garden will need to be hardened off to help them cope with lower temperatures and air movement. Acclimatize them to life outdoors two to three weeks before

Move plants outside into sheltered spots on warmer days and bring them in at night to start getting them used to outside temperatures.

they are due to be planted out by placing them in a cold frame. Keep vents open during the day, but close them at night. If you don't have a cold frame, take trays outside during the day and bring them in at night.

Inducing germination

Some seeds have hard shells or a chemical inhibitor in their seed that air and moisture cannot easily penetrate, making them difficult to germinate. Among them are beetroot, cotoneaster, euonymus, morning glory, and laburnum. You can help the process along by softening seed coats by soaking them in warm water, scratching them with sandpaper, or nicking them with a knife – this process is known as scarification.

Most sowings are successful but problems can arise if you use old seeds or those that have been stored incorrectly, which may fail to germinate. Follow the sowing dates on seed packets and keep your seeds in a cool, dry, dark place until you are ready to sow them.

DAMPING OFF

Seedlings are vulnerable to damping off, a disease that can run riot and cause the stems to collapse at soil level. To prevent this, start with clean pots, sow thinly, and always use fresh compost and tap water, rather than rainwater.

Once it sets in, damping off will tear through trays of seedlings, leaving no option but to start from scratch with new seeds, fresh compost, and a clean tray.

Taking cuttings is an excellent way to get new stock from favourite plants that need replacing, or as an insurance for tender ones over winter.

TAKING CUTTINGS

Cuttings can easily be taken from many plants and will readily form roots if grown in the right conditions. For best results, select strong, healthy shoots and use sharp secateurs or a knife when preparing them.

TYPES OF CUTTINGS

Taking cuttings is one of the most widely used forms of propagation because it ensures the new plants created have the exact physical characteristics of the parent. Many popular trees, shrubs, fruit bushes, climbers, conifers, herbs, perennials, and tender house plants can be propagated in this way.

Cuttings can be taken at different times of the year at different stages of the plants' growth. Softwood cuttings are taken from spring to early summer using very new growth and have the highest potential of taking root. However their young leaves are at risk from dehydration, which means they need care and attention.

Semi-ripe cuttings are taken in late summer using growth that has started to harden. These cuttings root more slowly than softwood cuttings, but are easier to care for and less likely to dry out.

Hardwood cuttings are taken in winter from deciduous shrubs and trees and are quite straightforward, requiring low levels of aftercare.

HARDWOOD CUTTINGS

Some woody plants can be propagated in winter, when dormant. Cut pencil-thickness stems into 15cm (6in) lengths and insert them into pots or in the ground, leaving 2.5cm (1in) of stem showing.

Take hardwood cuttings by trimming off lengths, cutting one end at an angle so that you can identify the top and the bottom.

Taking semi-ripe cuttings

Semi-ripe cuttings are taken in late summer, when stems start to harden and growth slows. At this stage, stems have food reserves that will help them to survive. Cuttings do not need heat to form roots, but do prefer high humidity. Once potted up, put them in an unheated propagator or cover with a clear plastic bag. Place on a windowsill or in an unheated greenhouse or cold frame.

1 Select from the parent plant (such as Box, shown) a healthy stem that is young and vigorous but is beginning to harden and is not floppy.

2 Cut off a piece of stem about 10cm (4in) long using clean secateurs. Keep the cuttings in a plastic bag while you gather the rest.

3 Remove the leaves from the lower two-thirds of the stem. Pinch out the sappy tips. Once planted, it will start to grow within a few weeks.

Softwood and semi-ripe cuttings are inserted into pots filled with moist, well-drained cutting compost to root, while hardwood cuttings can be placed in pots or directly into soil in a warm, sheltered site outdoors. The latter can take many months to form roots, so choose a planting spot where the cuttings can be left undisturbed. The cuttings should have formed roots by the following autumn, when they can be transplanted to their final position.

Although not usually needed, some cuttings can be encouraged to form roots more quickly by dipping the bottom end in a specialized rooting hormone liquid. Shake off the excess before planting as normal in soil.

PLANT LIST
Hardwood cuttings
Buddleja (Butterfly bush)
Chaenomeles (Japanese quince)
Cornus alba (Dogwood)
Sambucus (Elder)
Ribes (Flowering currant)
Salix (Willow)
Softwood cuttings
Fuchsia
Hydrangea
Pelargonium
Salvia (Sage)
Solenostemon (Coleus)
Semi-ripe cuttings
Buxus (Box)
Lavandula (Lavender)
Lavatera
Philadelphus
Pyracantha
Viburnum

Rooting hormones can help cuttings to put on roots, particularly semi-ripe or hardwood ones. Gently dip the rooting end in before planting.

Stem cuttings can be left to root in compost in individual pots, seed trays, or positioned around the edges of one pot.

Taking softwood cuttings

Softwood cuttings are usually taken between mid-spring and early summer on young growth that has been produced in the current year. Many house plants, perennials, and shrubs can be propagated using this technique. Cuttings readily form roots if placed in a heated propagator, which will keep their bases at a temperature of between 21–24°C (70–75°F). However, their immature leaves dry out quickly, so it's important to keep material damp when collecting cuttings (place them in a moist bag) and to keep the humidity high inside the propagator until they have rooted. Open vents daily to reduce condensation, and keep light levels high.

1 Select healthy, very young growth at the end of stems (*from plants such as Cotton lavender, shown*). Cut lengths between 5–8cm (2–3in) long.

2 Using a clean penknife or sharp blade, cut the stem just beneath a leaf joint. Do this carefully and cleanly – torn stems attract disease.

3 Any leaves left below the surface of the soil are likely to rot, so trim the cutting carefully to remove them, leaving just a few leaves at the top.

4 Place the cuttings carefully into a seed tray of compost or into pots. Make sure the leaves are clear of the surface of the compost by not planting cuttings too deeply.

Dividing plants by pulling them apart or cutting them into pieces is a very simple way of creating lots of new plants from a single specimen.

LAYERING AND DIVIDING

Propagating plants by layering and division are simple techniques that enable you to make more of your favourite plants, while controlling their spread and keeping them healthy and vigorous.

CREATING NEW PLANTS

While some propagation methods require careful attention or the use of shelter or heat to induce plants to root, others require minimum effort and are almost foolproof.

Division is probably the easiest of all propagation techniques, as plants are simply split into smaller pieces and replanted outdoors. Layering is useful for shrubs and climbers that are not easily propagated by cuttings – rather than remove a portion of growth, as in taking cuttings, shoots are induced to form roots while still attached to the parent plant.

Dividing perennials

Herbaceous perennials that spread to form clumps are easily propagated by division in spring or autumn. To do this, lift plants from the ground with a fork, taking care not to damage the roots. Lightly rooted plants can simply be divided by pulling them apart by hand, while those with sturdier root systems,

LAZY CUTTINGS

Some plants are easy to propagate by hand, and require no tools or specialist equipment. Gently tease apart sections or individual shoots, keeping plenty of root attached, then plant into pots or in the ground.

Plants such as Sedum, Saxifraga, Sempervivum, and other creeping plants are ideal candidates for this type of easy division technique.

Root cuttings

A number of perennials and shrubs can be propagated from pieces of root lifted from the ground between November and late February, such as tree poppy (*Romneya*), *Catalpa*, *Paulownia*, oriental poppies, Japanese anemones, and *Verbascum*. For best results, plant roots of pencil thickness, but if using finer roots, lay them on the soil surface and cover with a thin layer of compost.

1 Lift plants from the ground using a fork, avoiding damaging the roots. Gently tease apart the clump with your hands.

2 Shake off excess soil carefully and select a few healthy roots that are of pencil thickness from the clump.

3 Cut lengths 5cm (2in) long and insert them into pots filled with compost. Place in an unheated greenhouse or cold frame.

such as *Hemerocallis*, will need splitting with a spade or a knife. Those with fibrous roots, such as *Achillea*, are best divided using two garden forks – place them back-to-back in the centre of the plant and prise apart the clump by pushing the forks away from each other. Whichever method you use, discard any dead material and replant portions as soon as possible in well-dug soil to prevent the roots drying out. Division helps to rejuvenate congested plants.

Dividing bulbs

Many bulbs increase readily during the growing season, forming new bulbs from the parent plants. To propagate your favourites and to keep clumps floriferous, divide them every few years.

Divide bulbs before growth begins in spring, prising clumps from the ground with a fork. Replant larger bulbs in the ground and grow smaller bulbs in pots for several years until they are large enough to plant out.

Runners and suckers

Although you have to actively propagate some plants, many are self-propagating, naturally producing runners or suckers. *Tetrapanax*, *Rhus*,

Divide small clumps as you would larger ones, by inserting two forks into the middle of the clump and pushing them away from each other.

Kerria, *Ajuga*, *Aralia*, *Euonymus fortunei*, and strawberries can all be propagated this way. These growths can be carefully removed from the parent plant, along with a portion of roots, and planted elsewhere. Removing runners and suckers also helps you control the spread of plants.

You can grow new strawberry plants from old by rooting their self-propagating runners. Simply peg them to the soil and let them root.

Layering shrubs and climbers

This simple technique can be used to propagate many shrubs and climbers, some of which, such as rhododendrons, may be difficult to propagate by other methods. A shoot is encouraged to form roots while still attached to the parent plant by bending it down and burying it in the soil. After the layer has rooted (usually after about a year), it can be detached from the parent and planted on where it is to grow.

1 Select a flexible, healthy stem and make a slanting cut on the underside of it, at the point where the stem will reach the ground.

2 Make a shallow trench in the soil about 10–15cm (4–6in) away from the parent plant and bend down the shoot, positioning the cut on the soil surface.

3 Peg the layer in place with a loop of wire, then tie the tip of the shoot to a cane in the ground to encourage it to grow upwards.

PLANT LIST

Plants for division
Achillea
Aster
Festuca
Hemerocallis (Day lily)
Hosta
Hylotelephium (Ice plant)
Ophiopogon
Paeonia (Peony)
Pulmonaria
Thalictrum

Plants for layering
Camellia
Clematis
Jasminum (Jasmine)
Lonicera (Honeysuckle)
Magnolia
Rhododendron
Wisteria

Lawns are the ultimate outdoor carpet, providing a multi-purpose surface, suitable for relaxation or play in any garden.

CHOOSING TURF

Turf can vary in quality, so buy from a reputable supplier and check it for weeds. Meadow turf is cheap, but often of poor quality, while domestic turf is hard-wearing and best for family lawns. Fine turf is ideal for a showpiece lawn.

Always check turves before you buy. Reject any with weeds and bare patches, as well as yellowing edges that suggests they are long overdue planting.

LAWNS

Nothing sets off a garden scheme like a verdant blanket of grass. Whether you're looking for a hard-wearing family lawn or a manicured showpiece to complement your plants, lawns are easy to begin from scratch.

NEW LAWNS

Technically, you can create a new lawn at any time, but it is more likely to succeed if started at the right time of the year. Lawns sown in autumn tend to establish quickly as the soil is still warm, and the wet weather prevents it drying out. The next best time is in spring, although seedlings will have to cope with frosts, cooler soil temperatures, and competition from weeds.

Turf is generally laid between early autumn and late winter, and although it is possible to create both turf and seed-sown lawns during summer, they will require copious watering to help them establish.

After laying or sowing a lawn (see pp.92–93), you will need to give it close attention until it has established and is ready for use. Grass seed will germinate within 7–21 days, and you should ensure that the soil does not

dry out during this time. If the weather is dry, use a sprinkler to keep the ground moist. Hungry birds can disturb seeds, so cover the newly sown area with horticultural fleece held down with tent pegs or large stones. When the grass is about 6cm (2½in) high, give the lawn its first cut. Use a rotary mower with the blades set high to avoid dragging the delicate seedlings out of the ground. Repeat several times during the growing season, but avoid any other traffic on the lawn for at least ten weeks after sowing to allow the grass to develop a strong root system.

Turf is easier to establish. After laying the turves, keep them well-watered, especially during dry weather. When the grass shows signs of new growth, cut it with a mower set on a high setting. Wait at least six weeks before using the turf, and then avoid anything but light traffic. When

Starting from scratch is sometimes the only option but you may have to wait a little time before your lawn is ready to be used.

Wildflower meadows give a natural look and need less routine care. They should be mowed in a particular way and at certain times of year.

the turves have knitted together without any gaps, your new lawn is ready to be used (fill any gaps that do appear with soil).

Low maintenance

Although newly created lawns need careful attention, you don't need to be a slave to an established lawn. Allowing the grass to grow longer and raising the height of the cut means you will mow less often, and the lawn should be able to cope better in drought situations.

An alternative to a traditional lawn is a wildflower lawn. Lay special turves containing native flowers, such as yarrow, ragged robin, and cowslip, and a mixture of ornamental and native grasses that can be left to grow long.

Old, tired lawns

If you inherit a neglected lawn, you may be able to restore it with a programme of renovation starting in spring. Mow on a high setting, then feed with a general-purpose spring feed. Ten days later, apply a lawn weedkiller. Level out bumps and hollows, and reseed any bare patches. Keep the lawn well watered during dry periods. If the lawn has more weeds than grass, it may be better to start again from scratch.

LAWN-CARE TOOLS

You only need a few tools to keep your lawn in good shape; a mower, rake, edging tool, and shears are sufficient, although other pieces of kit may be necessary depending on the size or state of your lawn. By far the most important lawn-care tool is a mower. Choose carefully: manual mowers, hover mowers, or compact cordless mowers suit small lawns, while a cylinder mower fitted with a rear roller is the best option for creating perfect stripes on a larger lawn. Mulching mowers reduce maintenance as clippings are shredded and returned to the lawn. Ride-on mowers are ideal for those with more than half an acre.

A mower is an indispensable piece of lawn machinery. Choose one that is right for your size of lawn and will fit into the storage that you have when not in use.

A spring-tine rake is useful for removing any moss and debris clogging up your lawn.

If your lawn suffers from compacted soil, literally breathe life into it using an aerator.

Neat edges define a lawn, and hand-held edging tools will give a crisp edge.

If there are more weeds than grass, it may be time to start again, or treat lawns with weedkiller and reseed bare patches.

Edging shears trim grass at the edges without damaging plants in borders.

Strimmers are ideal for the bits mowers can't reach, or for small areas that can be cut by hand.

Push-along seed dispensers can also be used to spread lawn fertilizers. Hire one if necessary.

The perfect lawn demands tender loving care, and a few tricks to get the lush, verdant look just right. You will also need the right tools.

MOWING SAFETY

To prevent accidents, always ensure mowers are turned off when you are cleaning or otherwise maintaining them. Do not put hands or feet near blades when the mower is in use.

CARING FOR YOUR LAWN

If you are aiming for an immaculate lawn you need to do a little more than mow it every few weeks. Regular feeding, watering, weeding, and trimming are necessary to give you a lawn to be proud of.

HOW OFTEN TO MOW

There are no hard-and-fast rules about how often you should mow, so be guided by the rate of growth of your lawn and the type of finish you require. Unless the weather is extremely mild, your lawn is unlikely to need cutting over winter, but it will need regular trimming from early spring until the autumn.

Hardwearing family lawns will need cutting once a week, while those maintained for their ornamental looks may need trimming up to three times a week at the height of their growing season. Start with the blades on their highest setting, then reduce the height of the cut as the season progresses; an eventual height of 2.5cm (1in) is ideal for domestic lawns, while 2cm (¾in) is suitable in gardens where a more manicured look is required.

Stripes and edges

Alternating dark and light green stripes gives a smart finish to a formal lawn. To achieve this you need a mower with a rear roller. Mow in parallel rows, with each row in the opposite direction to the next. The stripes are most obvious from a distance, especially from above.

After mowing, put the finishing touches to your lawn by trimming the edges. Use a pair of long-handled edging shears to remove any overhanging grass. Edges can become uneven over time, so redefine them with a half-moon edging tool. Use a piece of timber as a straight-edged cutting guide. Remove all cuttings and trimmed turf.

Watering and feeding

Recently created lawns will require regular watering in order to thrive, but once established, lawns are remarkably tolerant of drought.

Electric mowers should always be turned off at the mains before you inspect or replace cutting blades.

Apply special lawn fertilizers in liquid or granular form during spring and autumn to give lawns the nutrient boost they require.

Collect grass cuttings after mowing and add them to your compost heap, preferably in layers with brown material (see p.303).

Although grass may turn brown in extended dry periods, the damage is largely superficial and the grass will bounce back when the rain returns. Longer grass deals better with drought, so raise the blades of your mower to their highest setting. This encourages plants to become deeper rooted and avoids the risk of scalping the surface, which will pull out dry grass by its roots, leaving ugly bald patches in the lawn.

Most lawns will do well if fed twice a year. Give them a quick boost in spring with a liquid or granular formulation high in nitrogen, then strengthen up the roots for winter with an autumn feed. Avoid using spring feeds later in the year as this can result in soft sappy grass, vulnerable to frosts.

Rolling a lawn

A heavy roller, which can be hired if necessary, is traditionally used in spring to resettle the surface of the lawn after winter, especially if autumn-laid turf was lifted by frost. However, rolling is not essential and can cause problems. The heavy weight may compact the soil, impeding drainage and leading to the conditions favoured by moss.

Keep lawn edges defined and crisp-looking by trimming them with edging shears. Trim the wispy grass and avoid cutting into the lawn.

If the edge of the lawn or a path begins to look uneven or has lost its definition, carefully go around it with a half-moon edging tool.

Bare patches of lawn can be easily restored by raking the soil and sowing new seed. Apply fertilizer and water well for quicker growth.

Get ready for winter

Autumn is a good time to carry out maintenance to your lawn, to get it in shape to cope with winter. A layer of dead grass and other material, known as thatch, can build up on the surface of the soil, impeding drainage, encouraging moss, harbouring fungal diseases, and preventing the strong growth of grass. This can be removed by scarifying it – vigorously raking it with a spring-tine rake or using an electric scarifier. Wet weather can make lawns boggy, so relieve compaction caused by heavy foot traffic, by aerating with a fork or hollow tine machine. This helps to improve drainage and prevents the conditions favoured by moss.

1 Clear any leaves or other debris from the lawn in autumn. Rake the lawn surface firmly to remove any embedded debris or moss.

2 Using a garden fork or a special aerator (as shown here), spike holes into the lawn all over the surface to aerate it and improve drainage.

3 Brush dry fine sand into the holes created to prevent them closing up, allowing air and water to pass freely into the root zone. Only use horticultural grade sand.

4 Spread dry top-dressing over the surface to help improve drainage and to level out hollows. Use a brush or the back of a rake to work it into the grass evenly.

Most lawns suffer from minor problems, especially if they are used as a family play space. The majority are easy to fix with a little care.

LAWN PROBLEMS

Almost every lawn shows problems from time to time, often after a long period of drought, or a wet winter when moss takes hold. Most can be remedied and there are useful quick fixes for untidy edges and bare patches.

UNEVEN SURFACE

Lumps and bumps often become noticeable in spring after a winter of little attention, or in summer when anthills cause bare patches in the grass. Bumps make mowing the lawn difficult as they tend to be scalped by the mower. You can deal with them by raising the height of cut, but the better solution is to make a quick repair.

Very small bumps can be levelled by removing cores of soil with a hollow tine aerator. To repair larger bumps, you need to cut a cross over the lump using a half-moon edger, then peel back the four corners of turf. Remove some of the soil, smooth the soil surface, then fold back the turf into place carefully.

Making repairs

Like lumps, hollows in the ground look ugly and are likely to contain longer grass that the mower cannot reach. Small depressions can be repaired gradually by filling them with a sandy top dressing, adding 1cm (½in) at a time. (See facing page for advice on larger depressions.)

Edges may crumble or break, because of wear and tear and also as a result of mowing. To repair these, carefully cut out a rectangle of turf including the broken edge. Cut precisely, with sharp vertical edges and right-angled corners. Turn the piece of turf around so that the good edge is on the outside. Keep the broken part within the lawn, fill it with topsoil, and then resow it with some grass seed. The combination of new seed and regular mowing will encourage the lawn to spread and fill the patch.

Damaged patches within a lawn are equally easy to repair. Remove a rectangular piece of turf by cutting

WET LAWN DAMAGE

Rain can cause problems on compacted or poorly drained lawns. Waterlogging starves roots of oxygen, and moss and damp-loving weeds will prosper in these conditions.

Leaves and other debris make lawn turf slippery underfoot, causing skidding and damage to the grass.

Adjust the height of your mower's cut to avoid damaging bumpy surfaces; raising it in dry conditions helps grass survive drought.

Mossy hollows can develop in lawns where the soil has been compacted by frequent footfall. Consider installing stepping stones.

around the damage with a half-moon edger – use a straight-edged piece of timber as a cutting guide. Put the blade of a spade under the turf, keeping it parallel with the surface and digging down to as shallow a depth as possible. Remove the damaged piece, rake over the exposed soil, then cut an identically shaped piece of turf and plug the gap. Alternatively, prepare the soil, resow with seeds, and cover it with netting to protect it from birds. Avoid walking on resown patches until they are established.

Stepping stones

If your lawn suffers in wet weather or needs protection from heavy traffic, try laying stepping stones through it to reduce wear on the grass. Space slabs, stones, or circles of wood on the grass, making sure they are evenly spaced and checking the distance between them to make sure they are a comfortable step apart. When happy with the pattern, cut around them with a half-moon tool and lift the turf beneath

Remove soil to the depth of the stepping stone, along with an extra 5cm (2in). Level the base and add a 5cm (2in) layer of compacted sand. Place the stepping stones on top, keeping them level with the lawn so you can mow across them.

Stubborn perennial weeds or those with deep tap roots can be treated with weedkiller or dug out by hand with a fork or kitchen knife.

Repair worn edges by removing turf and turning it around so the good edge is on the outside. The inner bare patch will grow over.

Rake out thatch and other debris that clogs up the lawn. Moss, combined with other materials, competes with the grass and hinders its growth.

Filling a large depression in a lawn

Over time, lawns can develop lumps and bumps as parts sink or endure heavy traffic. If larger hollows are causing problems with the mower, it makes sense to try to fill them, which means lifting the grass and adding more soil to level it. To repair these bumps, cut a cross through the hump with a half-moon edging tool, then carefully fold the four flaps back, taking care not to break the turf. Add some soil, then replace the turf. If the hollow is still visible, repeat until it appears level. When you are satisfied with the appearance of the lawn, replace the corners and firm the grass back into place with the back of a rake.

1 Cut through the surface, making a cross shape on the grass. Using a spade laid parallel to the soil, slide it under one corner of turf.

2 Repeat, lifting the four corners of the turf and gently folding them back onto the soil surface, taking care not to break any of them as you do so.

3 Add some soil to the hollow, using your hand to fill the dip and level off the surface of the soil. Add more topsoil as necessary until it is quite level.

4 Replace the turves and firm back into place with the back of the rake. Brush some more topsoil in between the cracks to help the turves knit together.

MINI MEADOWS

Wildflower meadows are an attractive alternative to a traditional lawn, and will attract wildlife and provide vibrant colour for many weeks. They can be time-consuming to establish but are simple to maintain.

Long, waving grasses are reminiscent of summer meadows, and work well as a natural lawn, or when used to edge a formal one.

MEADOW OPTIONS

A meadow will add a naturalistic touch to a garden and there are many exciting seed mixes available, along with plants that will add a bold splash of colour from spring to summer. To make a meadow that will return year after year, use perennial seeds or plants. For a one-off spectacular, or to fill a bare patch with a splash of colour, sow a mixture of annual varieties.

An existing lawn or patch of grass can be turned into a meadow, but you will have better results if you start with a bare piece of ground. Wildflower turf is available for those who are pressed for time and want to create a meadow quickly.

Let it grow

The simple way to create a meadow look is to allow your lawn to grow long and let the grass flower. To add extra colour, plant wildflower plugs in groups amongst the grass, along with small bulbs. Plant in autumn after cutting the grass short. To keep fertility low, which will encourage wild flowers, do not use lawn fertilizers and always remove clippings so nutrients cannot re-enter

Sowing a wildflower meadow

The best way to establish a wildflower meadow is to sow seeds onto bare soil in spring or autumn at a rate of 5g per square metre (¼oz per 10sq ft). Spring-sown seeds will germinate easily, but those sown in autumn can rot over winter if your soil is heavy and wet. Start preparing the site about six weeks before sowing. Strip away all vegetation and weeds, then remove all of the topsoil from the area to be sown, replacing it with less-fertile subsoil. Finally, prepare the bare soil as you would for sowing a new lawn (see p.93). Replacing the soil is not feasible over a very large area, so reduce fertility by sowing nutrient-hungry crops for a season.

1 Wildflower seed mixes are sown in small quantities; to make it easier to see where you have sown, mix the seeds first with silver sand.

2 Prepare the soil to be sown by digging it over and removing any large stones or debris. Then firm it down and rake the surface to give a fine, even texture.

3 Mark out evenly sized squares over the area to be sown using bamboo canes. This makes it easier to sow the right amount of seed evenly.

4 Rake the seed into the soil very lightly using a spring-tine rake. Water the seed in well using a fine spray. Cover the area with fleece to ward off birds.

Paths mown through long grasses make a lovely natural feature as well as a practical solution to navigating your mini meadow.

Annual flowers add a glorious splash of colour through long grass. You can choose your favourite flowers or sow mixed packets of seed.

the soil. It can take several years to establish a balance between grass and wildflowers.

Wildflower meadow mixes

There are many types of seed mixes available that contain different varieties, colour blends, or suit a specific soil type or location. Perennial meadow mixes tend to prosper in low-fertile soil. Where soil fertility is too high, for example in an existing border, sow a cornfield annual mix that includes plants such as cornflower, corn poppy, corn marigold, and corncockle. Barley and wheat seed add an authentic touch. Perennial wildflowers tend not to flower in their first season, so to ensure interest in the first year, choose a mix that contains some faster-growing annuals.

Cutting your meadow

Although meadows do not require as frequent cutting as traditional lawns, they do need mowing occasionally. Meadows that flower in summer are generally cut from early autumn to early spring, while those designed for spring colour should be cut from midsummer. If you have a mixture of flowers that appear at different times, cut once a year in early autumn. The height of cut should be no lower than 8cm (3in). Remove all clippings to keep soil nutrient levels low.

MEADOW PLANT LIST

Centaurea nigra
  (Common knapweed)
Daucus carota (Wild carrot)
Galium verum
  (Lady's bedstraw)
Leucanthemum vulgare
  (Ox-eye daisy)
Malva moschata
  (Musk mallow)
Plantago lanceolata
  (Ribwort plantain)
Prunella vulgaris
  (Selfheal)
Rumex acetosa
  (Common sorrel)
Salvia pratensis
  (Meadow clary)
Sanguisorba minor
  (Salad burnet)
Silene dioica (Red campion)

HERB LAWNS

Chamomile and thyme lawns are attractive alternatives to a traditional lawn, although they also need considerable upkeep. They suit areas that receive only light foot traffic.

To establish a herb lawn, prepare the site as you would for sowing a new lawn in spring (see *page 93*). Choose a ground-hugging variety of thyme or a non-flowering chamomile, such as *Chamaemelum nobile* 'Treneague', and plant plugs or plants at 10–25cm (4–10in) intervals, depending on the size of plant. Water the plants in well and keep the site weed-free until established. Do not walk on the lawn for 12 weeks after planting, and allow only light traffic over it for its first year.

Thyme plants make a lush, aromatic lawn, spreading to create a pretty, edible carpet studded with pink flowers in summer. Use several varieties for a patchwork effect.

Chamomile is a classic alternative lawn. It is a more fussy plant to establish than thyme, but in light, moist soils it will form a pretty, fragrant carpet of low-growing plants.

PONDS AND WATER

Whether you have a large pond or a simple bubble fountain, water in any form will add interest to your garden, creating sound and movement, attracting wildlife, and enabling you to grow aquatic plants.

There is a water feature to suit any garden. If you have the space, a large wildlife pond makes an attractive garden asset.

CLEAN POND PUMP

Streams, fountains, waterfalls, and other features rely on pumps to keep water moving. To ensure they continue to work properly, remove pumps from ponds in early winter, to check and clean them.

To prepare ponds for winter lift pumps out of the water and give them a good clean, removing weed and debris, then dry carefully before storing until spring.

ROUTINE CARE

The aim of most water gardeners should be to have a healthy pond or water feature, where plants and creatures thrive in a body of clear water. However, this cannot be achieved by leaving the pond to its own devices. Without intervention, a pond can become engulfed by plants, while a build-up of algae or pond weed can lead to unsightly murky water. To keep ponds and water features in good shape, you have to maintain them year round.

A key task is to remove plant debris as it appears. Deadhead marginal or aquatic flowers and remove dying or unhealthy foliage to prevent it rotting in the water.

To keep the surface of ponds clean, remove excess amounts of floating weeds. Use a net to scoop out mats of tiny-leaved duckweed and twirl hair-like blanketweed from the surface with a stick or garden cane. Before putting weeds on the compost heap, place them at the edge of the pond overnight so any creatures you have unwittingly removed can return to the water. Check around the edge of the pond and among marginal plants for any traditional garden weeds, too, and tug them out.

Over a hot summer, the level of ponds can drop as water evaporates, leading to a reduced surface area and less oxygen available to fish. Keep ponds at the right level by topping them up once a week with rainwater from a butt, if possible. If you don't have a water butt, use water from a mains supply, topping up little and

Marginal and aquatic plants in baskets need repotting when roots burst through baskets. Check them in spring and pot on if necessary.

Plant marginal plants at the edge of ponds in baskets or mesh pots to prevent them taking over and crowding out other plants.

often to prevent the shock of the colder water disturbing fish.

Leaves can fall for many weeks over autumn; stretch wire netting over the surface to catch them until nearby trees and shrubs are bare, or rake leaves from overhung ponds regularly.

Pond equipment is expensive to install and needs maintenance, so remove and clean lights, filters, and pumps annually.

Maintaining water quality

The importance of water quality can vary depending on the style of pool or pond. Crystal-clear water is usually required for formal features, while slightly cloudy water can be overlooked if you have a wildlife pond. However, your aim should be to keep your water as clean as possible with good hygiene practice.

There are hundreds of different types of algae that can cause problems in ponds, from those that cause a "pea soup" effect in the water, to others that form a dense mat of growth on the surface.

Use rainwater to top up ponds if possible as it is very low in nutrients, so does not encourage algae. Consider adding a UVC filter, which binds any algae particles together in the water and then filters them out.

Filters help keep the water clean; a mechanical filter will sit on the pond floor, while a biological filter must be placed at the highest point. These types contain beneficial bacteria that convert organic waste into useful nutrients.

Another option is to use natural filtration to keep ponds clean. For example, in swimming ponds about fifty per cent of the total area is taken up by aquatic plants, which remove nutrients from the water to prevent algae forming. Alternatively, consider using barley straw, which releases hydrogen peroxide as it rots, suppressing algae (see *below left*).

Basic pond-care equipment

To maintain your pond you will need a hand net, a cane for removing blanket weed, netting to cover the pond in autumn, and a selection of mesh baskets for plants.

To operate ponds with moving water you will need a pump. A submersible pump is sufficient for gently moving features, but a more powerful surface version will be needed for fast-flowing streams, waterfalls, or fountains.

WATER FEATURES

While ponds, pools, and rills are generally better suited to a larger garden, even a smaller plot can accommodate a water feature. If you have an outdoor electricity supply, a wall-mounted fountain, where water trickles from a spout into a pool below, is a great way to use vertical space, while a bubble fountain or pebble pool can transform an awkward corner. For a simple pond, fill a low barrel with tiny aquatic plants (see p.97), or use a shallow container that can double as a bird bath.

A pretty terracotta pot with a bubbling fountain makes an attractive and soothing focal point in a small garden if you don't have space for a larger pond.

Barley straw can be used to suppress algae. Add it in spring, and remove it once once it turns black, usually within about six months.

Keep pond surfaces clear of blanket weed, which can quickly overrun a pond. Twirl the weed around a stick for easy removal.

Create a miniature water garden by standing marginal plants such as marsh marigolds, *Sagittaria*, and *Butomus* on stacked bricks within a barrel pond.

MAINTAINING POND PLANTS

Aquatic plants need less maintenance than many plants growing in beds and borders, but to keep them looking good they need attention during the growing season so that the pond continues to be attractive.

The best displays in ponds and water rely on a balance between well-maintained aquatics and oxygenating plants, kept in careful check.

ROUTINE CARE

Most pond plants are fairly vigorous and after a few years of growth, begin to outgrow their allotted space and need to be divided and thinned out. Submerged oxygenating plants such as hornwort, whorled milfoil, and water crowfoot can quickly become a dense mass of growth that gets entangled with other plants. These plants should be thinned out in spring or autumn by lifting baskets out of the pond and trimming back growth. Do not remove too much growth because you will expose the surface of the pond to sunlight, creating the right conditions for algae to grow.

Some aquatics, especially marginals, form dense clumps that need to be divided to provide a good floral display, and to prevent them crowding out neighbouring plants. Irises, Japanese rush, dwarf reed, flowering rush, water mint, marsh marigold, and many others should be lifted in spring, split into smaller sections, and replanted.

Dividing and planting irises

Irises growing in containers will eventually become a mass of congested shoots and pot-bound roots. At this stage they will become shy to flower and plants will lose vigour. Check whether plants need dividing in late spring or early autumn, lifting containers out of the pool to see whether there is a mass of roots poking through the mesh at the sides and bottom. Most irises can be divided by hand by tugging them apart gently, but if roots are held tightly together, they should be divided with a knife. Repot divisions individually and return them to the pond. This basic technique can be used to propagate and rejuvenate many clump-forming aquatics.

1 Dig the clump out of the pond using a spade or fork, taking care not to damage the roots or disturb the pond too much.

2 Place the clump on the ground and divide it using a spade. Separate out these smaller clumps into individual plants for replanting.

3 Choose the healthiest-looking divisions, discarding any past their best, and, taking one plant at a time, lower them into an empty aquatic planting basket.

4 Once the plant is in position in the middle of the new basket, start to fill around it with garden soil or specialist aquatic compost. Firm down and put grit on the surface.

Most pond plants do not need feeding, but water lilies need plenty of nutrients to do well. Feed plants when just coming into growth in spring. Push sachets of aquatic fertilizers into the container, next to the crown of the plant, and cover with pea gravel.

Remove all flowers on aquatic plants as they start to fade, to prevent them rotting and discolouring the water. This also prevents them forming seedheads and colonizing neighbouring baskets. At the same time, trim off any dead, dying, or diseased growth, including lily pads.

Planting aquatic plants

Aquatics are usually grown in mesh containers, which are available in many sizes to suit different plants. These pots allow water to flow freely in and out, enabling the plant to take up nutrients from the water while preventing the roots spreading out of bounds. Growing in baskets also makes it easy to move plants around to change the display or to remove them if they need dividing.

First, line your basket with a piece of hessian or plastic mesh. This prevents the soil escaping through the sides and clouding the water. If planting very tall marginals, place a brick or stone in the base to keep it stable and prevent it blowing over in wind. Fill the basket with garden soil or a specialist aquatic compost, leaving a 2.5cm (1in) gap between the soil surface and the rim of the pot. Soak the soil with a watering can, then make a hole large enough to accommodate the roots of the plant. Place the plant in the hole, cover the roots with more soil and firm into place. Cover the surface with a 1cm (½in) layer of pea gravel to stop the surface being washed away. Water again to remove any air pockets. In shallow ponds, baskets can easily be lowered in by hand, but if the water is deep you may need to thread heavy duty string through the sides of the basket and lower it in.

Oxygenating plants are often sold in bunches and do not need any preparation before planting. Simply push them into a basket of soil, making sure they are firmed in well to prevent them floating free. If you have a pool with a soil bottom, they can be planted into the base instead. Floating aquatics can simply be placed on the surface of the water.

The rounded leaves of duckweed are a common sight on ponds, and need to be skimmed off the surface to keep them in check.

Cover the soil surface with grit before submerging aquatic plants in baskets. It prevents the soil escaping.

AQUATIC INVADERS

Some fast-growing plants should be avoided as they escape from ponds and colonize waterways. Culprits include water lettuce (*Pistia stratiotes*), and Canadian pondweed (*Elodea canadensis*).

Parrot's feather (*Myriophyllum aquaticum, above*) is a pernicious, invasive weed that will quickly overrun your pond or pool unless it is removed.

FISH AND WILDLIFE

A pond stocked with fish or one that provides a natural habit for a community of native creatures adds interest and beauty to your garden. Ensure your pond teems with life by creating ideal conditions for its occupants.

Dragonfly nymphs, along with newts and frogs, will soon colonize a natural pond and are fascinating for children and adults to observe.

CARING FOR FISH

Fish are very easy to look after, but if you want a thriving population you will need to care for them. Choose fish varieties that are suitable for the size of your pool; use a maximum of 50cm (20in) of fish body length, when fully grown, per square metre of water surface as a guide. Rather than stocking a pond in one go, introduce fish in two lots, about ten weeks apart; if too many are added at once there will be a build-up of excrement that will pollute the water and will be detrimental to the fish's health.

Fish are best introduced during the warmer months of the year to prevent them becoming almost dormant in cooler water. Do not pour fish in bags straight into the pond, but add them gradually so they can acclimatize (see below).

Although fish will feed on insects and plants in the pond, they still need extra food pellets or flakes. Ensure that you add the correct amount based on the size of your pond and the number of fish in it, following the instructions on the packet. The amount fish eat largely depends

DETERRENTS

Given the opportunity, herons will make a bid for your fish. Stretch heron netting over the water or create a low fence around the perimeter using wire to keep them at bay.

Installing a decoy heron close to a pond is believed to discourage the real birds from visiting to steal fish. Herons will revisit ponds repeatedly, taking every fish.

Introducing new fish

If you are stocking a new pond or adding new fish to an existing community, do this during the warmer months to avoid stressing the fish with a drop in temperature. At first, keep your fish in their transfer bags of water, floating the bag unopened on the surface of the pond. When the temperature of the water inside and outside the bag is more or less the same, release the fish into the pond.

1 Fish are usually sold in bags with their own water. Add a little of the pond water to that in the bag and reseal the bag.

2 Float the unopened bag on the surface of the pond until the temperature of the water in the bag matches that of the pond.

3 When the water in the bag has cooled sufficiently, open the bag and allow the fish to swim free into the pond.

If you want to encourage specific wildlife into your pond, find out what sort of habitat is preferred and include the right elements.

Frogs feast on all sorts of pests, especially slugs. You can watch their life cycle from spawn to tadpole to frog played out in your pond.

PREPARING FOR WINTER

Ponds are vulnerable during winter weather. Expanding ice can cause concrete liners to crack and water to seep out. Fish also suffer, because the water's surface can freeze over in severe weather, due to the narrow gap of air between the surface of the water and ice being replaced by gases produced by decaying vegetation. In ponds with concrete liners, floating a small ball on the surface of the pond in winter is most effective; not only will this keep a patch free of ice, but it will absorb the pressure and prevent fractures. To create a ventilation hole for fish, either add a floating electric pool heater or melt a 45cm (18in) wide patch with boiling water.

on the temperature of the water; in winter they eat less, but get hungrier as the water warms up in summer. Generally, give them high-protein food in summer, and a low-protein formulation in winter.

Keep an eye out for diseases so you can nip problems in the bud and prevent them spreading to other fish. Fungal growth, cuts, ulcers, missing scales, lumps, and infected eyes are all possible signs of problems, as is a change in behaviour, such as refusing to feed. If you are concerned, consult a fish care book to see if you can diagnose the disease and find a suitable cure. Herons are the greatest predator of pond fish and suitable deterrents should be put in place (see *facing page*). To protect fish from cats, fill the marginal shelf with plants so they cannot get close to the water.

Caring for wildlife

The success of a pond in attracting wildlife largely depends on its design. If you are creating a pond from scratch, aim to design it with a simple shape, along with a ramp, peninsula, or inlet to encourage wildlife to enter. A good way to do this is to

build a pebbly beach on a sloping side using large and small pebbles. Use larger stones around the edge of the pond and grade their size as you work up the slope. Continue building beneath the surface of the pond to create a ramp down to the floor of the pond. Native aquatic plants are loved by indigenous wildlife, so include some of these along with more vibrant exotics. Surround the pond with plenty of plants to provide cover, enabling visiting creatures to feel protected. Avoid adding fish to a wildlife pond as they are voracious predators of some smaller creatures.

Observe wildlife in the pond, but try not to disturb surroundings and water habitats, which may frighten away shy animals. Wildlife ponds do not need cleaning as often as formal features, but whenever thinning out oxygenators or removing other plants from a pond, place them on the side for a day or so to allow any creatures that have been accidentally removed to find their way back in. Do this in spring, rather than in the autumn, when pond creatures may be going into hibernation.

Hold a saucepan of boiling water against the pond's surface to melt a breathing hole if a thin layer of ice has formed.

Float a tennis ball on the surface of the water as temperatures drop. If the surface ices over, it can be removed to leave a hole.

HELP AND ADVICE

Even the most careful gardener will occasionally find plants that are flagging or a crop overrun with a troublesome pest. No garden is immune from pests and diseases, and recognizing the symptoms and finding appropriate controls is your best defence. This section will help you identify and tackle the main culprits.

Mulch around ground-cover plants to provide extra protection against weeds.

CONTROLLING WEEDS

Weeds can colonize any garden quickly, and while weeding can be time-consuming, it is a necessary job. However, there are ways to prevent weeds taking hold.

DESIGNING OUT WEEDS

Weeds need space to grow, so try to keep bare soil to a minimum when designing and planting your garden. Choose vigorous perennials and shrubs that can compete against weeds, and plant them closely, so new weeds can't get a foothold. Before planting, weed the area thoroughly, being sure to remove perennial weed roots, and water new plants well to ensure they establish quickly.

Regularly weeding new plantings from the outset will give your plants an advantage over emerging weeds, when new growth appears the following spring.

An alternative approach is to learn to live with the more attractive annual weeds and only control problem perennials. Use the chart on page 352 to help identify them. Alternatively, keep planting to a minimum and grass over large areas.

WEED-PROOF MEMBRANES

Laying permeable, weed-proof membrane around your plants is the most effective way to deter weeds, and is most easily installed on new beds and borders. Water still penetrates to plant roots but weed shoots and seedlings are unable to break through, and eventually die. The membrane also retains moisture in the soil, further benefiting your plants, and can be disguised with attractive gravel mulch or chipped bark.

1 To prepare a weed-free border, cultivate the soil first, digging in organic matter, removing any weeds, and laying down weed-proof membrane. Anchor the membrane's edges or dig it into the soil, and lay out your plants on top.

2 When you have decided where to place your plants, use a sharp knife to cut crosses in the membrane, then fold the flaps open to create planting windows. Dig planting holes in the soil, and sink your plants in.

3 Firm the plants in, water well, and fold the membrane flaps around the plant. Lay gravel or bark over the membrane to a depth of about 10cm (4in). Keep plants well watered and top up the mulch every year or so.

GROUND-COVER PLANTING

When planted together, vigorous, low-growing plants can be used as a living mulch, suppressing weeds by absorbing water and nutrients, blocking out light, and forming a physical barrier. Evergreen shrubs and perennials are the most effective, and give year-round protection. Deciduous plants can also be used, although you may need to weed between them in spring and autumn, until new growth appears. If you only need temporary cover, plant bushy annuals such as *Tagetes* (French marigold) close together, or choose a trailing type such as *Tropaeolum majus* (nasturtium). For extra protection, mulch between ground-cover plants, especially while they establish.

Evergreen climbers will also blanket the soil.

Trailing conifers make excellent ground cover.

Flowering herbs provide colour and deter weeds.

WEEDING MANUALLY

Pulling weeds by hand or using a hand fork is the best way to remove them from small beds or confined areas, where you risk damaging adjacent plants. Pulling them out by hand allows you to work between plants without disturbing them; loosen the soil with a fork to release deep-rooted weeds. You may have to gently untangle plants from creeping or climbing weeds such as bindweed.

Cutting weeds off at the base with a hoe is the best way to tend larger, more accessible areas. It is most effective when done in dry weather, so the weed seedlings wilt and die quickly without a chance to recover. Annual weeds are easily hoed off; perennial weeds are best dug out or, if necessary, treated with a systemic weedkiller.

USING WEEDKILLERS

For large areas infested with perennial weeds, weedkillers may be necessary as a last resort. Choose a "systemic" type, which is absorbed by the plant, killing it completely – although several applications may be needed for tough weeds such as ground elder. "Contact" weedkillers kill the leafy growth quickly and are best reserved for annual weeds only.

Ready mixed weedkiller sprays can be used on their narrowest "jet" setting to spot treat weeds.

TROUBLESOME WEEDS

Weeds can develop unnoticed in the garden, giving them time to establish and spread. This can spoil the appearance of your borders and give your plants unwelcome competition. Use this guide to identify weeds and nip them in the bud.

ANNUAL AND PERENNIAL WEEDS

Some annual weeds set seed within weeks, and there can be several generations in a single year. Remove them before they flower; more seed means more weeds. Perennial weeds are easy to remove when young but the longer they are left, the harder it becomes. To control them effectively, be persistent and thorough.

Annual meadow grass This annual grass forms small tufts, often in the gaps between paving stones where it can be difficult to remove. It is common in borders and containers.

Bindweed This perennial weed is a vigorous climber, and can quickly smother border plants. Use canes to train it away from your plants and spray it with a suitable weedkiller.

Brambles Spreading by roots, suckers, and seed, these woody climbers can form an impenetrable barrier. Regular digging will help to keep them under control, or use an appropriate weedkiller.

Chickweed This annual appears quickly whenever the soil is cultivated, and forms a spreading mat. Late plants overwinter until spring if left; it sets seed in just six weeks.

Couch grass This perennial grass grows in beds and lawns, where its tough roots spread among neighbouring plants and make it hard to control. It spreads easily by root fragments.

Dandelion Most commonly seen in lawns, this perennial weed spreads via wind-borne seeds. Although deep-rooted, dandelions are easy to dig out. Mowing lawns helps to control them.

Fat hen This is a slower-growing annual weed, producing one generation per year. It flowers from midsummer onwards and produces masses of seed that last for years in the soil.

Ground elder This is a low-growing, perennial weed that often spreads among border plants, making it difficult to dig up or spray. It will resprout from tiny root pieces.

Groundsel With its fluffy seedheads, this annual weed spreads quickly and in large numbers. It will grow anywhere and can easily smother young seedlings. Weed it out by hand.

Hairy bitter cress This annual weed grows very quickly, and is often brought into gardens with container-grown plants from nurseries and garden centres. Weed by hand before it flowers.

Japanese knotweed A very vigorous perennial that is hard to control once established. It resprouts from small root pieces. It is vital to control it so it is not a nuisance elsewhere.

Oxalis Several species of this bulb-forming perennial are garden weeds, and spread by tiny bulbils that are buried deeply and are difficult to remove completely. Treat with weedkiller.

Shepherd's purse This upright, wiry weed is more common on the vegetable bed than in borders, but will grow anywhere. It flowers from midsummer, producing masses of seeds.

Stinging nettles More common on new or neglected sites, this perennial weed forms large clumps with thick mats of roots. It can be controlled by digging and cultivating the soil.

Willowherb Forming tall, upright spikes, this perennial spreads by creeping underground roots, as well as by seeds that are freely spread by the wind. Remove plants before they flower.

Rhododendrons are an example of a plant that requires specific growing conditions. Without them, plants will soon deteriorate.

DIAGNOSING PROBLEMS

Understanding why plants are unhealthy can be tricky because different problems can cause similar symptoms. The trick is to pinpoint the likely cause by a process of elimination, although there can often be more than one.

All plants need some care, even established trees and shrubs, and it doesn't take long for neglected plants to suffer. Plants that aren't looked after are likely to have weak or congested growth that is prone to pests, diseases, and physical damage. Although they may flower, the display will be disappointing. As a first step, research what care your plants require, and see where you might be going wrong.

Wilting leaves can indicate various problems.

SOIL, SITE, AND ASPECT

All plants have preferred growing conditions, but some may tolerate a wide variation. It helps to know what these are, so check when you buy new plants. Those on lighter soils often succumb to nutrient deficiencies and wilting, while plants on heavier soils risk rotting off in prolonged wet weather, especially in winter. Some plants thrive in full sun, while others can be scorched, needing cooler corners. Sun-lovers perform poorly in shade, leading to spindly growth and few flowers.

Growing conditions also change through the year, which can affect plant health. Frost and sun-scorch are seasonal risks, but changing wind patterns, lengthening shadows, lower light levels, and cooler soils are also factors to consider.

Unexpected frosts can kill tender plants.

Bright sun can scorch plant leaves.

Waterlogging causes plant roots to rot.

Shade weakens plants that prefer full sun.

Common nutrient deficiencies

Plants need nutrients for healthy growth, but they must be in balance. Even well-tended soils can lack specific nutrients, causing poor displays or yields, and leaving plants prone to pests and diseases. Changes in leaf colour can help diagnose which nutrients are in short supply.

Nitrogen Foliage turns pale green, and yellowing young leaves are seen in spring. Overall growth is weak, and plants spindly. Apply a high-nitrogen fertilizer. Mulch helps to stabilize nitrogen levels.

Iron Plants develop yellow on edges of young leaves, spreading between the veins. Growth is weak. Most common on alkaline soils. Apply a product containing chelated iron around the roots.

Magnesium Older leaves turn yellow, with red or brown coloration spreading between veins. Most common on light, sandy soils; apply a fertilizer containing magnesium.

Calcium Present in the soil, calcium is not taken up by plants that are too dry; keep them moist. It causes distorted leaves, cracks, and spots on fruit, and bitter pit and blossom end rot (shown).

Other deficiencies

Boron Affects many crops and ornamentals; growing tips die, growth is stunted, fruit and leaves distort. Apply 'Borax' (sodium borate) to the soil, although be sure to use the correct dose: excess boron also causes problems.

Manganese Similar symptoms to iron deficiency; young leaves turn yellow or pale green, but veins remain green. Affects many plants, often acid-lovers grown in alkaline soil. Spray plants with manganese sulphate or apply to the soil.

Molybdenum Occurs on acid soil and affects brassicas, causing the leaves to turn yellow and become stringy. Apply fertilizer containing sodium molybdate or lime the soil to raise pH.

Potassium Leaves turn blue or yellow, with brown blotches or leaf edges. Leaves may roll inwards, and flowering and fruiting is weak. This affects many plants; apply a high-potassium feed.

OTHER FACTORS

There are lots of factors that affect how well your plants grow, some more obvious than others. If you have ruled out issues with soil, site, care, and pests and diseases, consider what else has changed in the area that could affect plants. For instance, are they more shaded than before due to neighbouring plants, or could they be suffering from competition? Have there been any building works nearby that could change aspect or soil drainage? Another consideration is the plant itself. All plants have a lifespan, and yours may well be declining due to old age. Some shrubs live less than ten years; some trees less than 40.

Poor plant health can be difficult to diagnose, and can be the result of many different causes. Consider the plant's overall growing conditions, and seek advice from your local nursery.

CONTROLLING PESTS AND DISEASES

Plants are naturally attacked by pests and diseases, and while the vast majority will thrive, there are some that will succumb. There are several practical steps you can take before reaching for a chemical solution.

Plants are not helpless, and have their own natural defences to help them fend off and recover from pests and diseases. The trick is to help your plants help themselves. Keeping them growing strongly is the best defence: give them sufficient moisture and feed to encourage healthy growth. Avoid high-nitrogen feeds, or feeding in late summer, however, as this encourages soft, sappy growth that attracts pests and diseases and is prone to frost damage. Prune plants regularly to promote strong growth, and remove weak or diseased material each year.

For long-term health, give your plants the best possible growing conditions, choosing the right plants to suit the site. Make sure they establish fully and don't compete with each other for moisture and nutrients. For an added advantage, seek out resistant varieties, especially of edible crops.

Water well, as stressed plants are easy targets.

PEST-PROOF PLANTING

Invertebrates are adept at locating specific plants to feed on; many do this by identifying volatile chemicals (odours) given off by plants. These are undetectable to humans, but easily sensed by insects from some distance away. Once the insects are nearby they also use sight and taste to determine if a plant is suitable. However, insect-damaged plants give off different odours to undamaged plants, and natural enemies use these odours as a way to locate their prey.

To combat and make use of these natural processes, try mixed growing, such as adding fruit trees and bushes in borders and vegetables among summer bedding. This can lead to less pest damage than growing crops in large groups and conventional rows. A variety of plants often has a greater diversity of predators and prey, leading to a better balance and reduced damage.

Nasturtiums climb or trail along the ground, and can easily be accommodated in vegetable beds.

French marigolds can help protect plants from root nematodes, and are attractive in beds.

TAKING SIDES

Gardens are mini ecosystems with an ongoing battle being fought between predator and prey. Take advantage of the fact that the pests that feed on your plants are all prey to other organisms, and encourage these predators in your garden. These allies need somewhere to live, so provide basic habitats for them. Create a pond for slug-eating amphibians; provide nest boxes for birds; and supply winter shelter for beneficial insects, such as ladybirds. Beneficial predators also need food, so don't rush for the pesticides when pests first appear. Leave them to build up and wait for your allies to find them.

This approach will not eradicate pests, but will help to balance their numbers. It best suits the relaxed gardener, who is happy for nature to take its course.

Food and water tempts beneficial insects, birds, and animals to your garden, helping to reduce the number of unwanted pests.

Hoverflies Many of these wasp and bee mimics feed on aphids as larvae, and are valuable garden pollinators. Encourage them by planting lots of colourful, nectar-rich flowers.

Ladybirds These insects feed eagerly on aphids as larvae and adults. They are among the earliest predators to appear, emerging in spring as the temperature rises.

Birds Many species play an important role in eating pests throughout the year, picking off aphids or larger pests, like slugs and caterpillars. Provide nest sites and drinking water.

Amphibians Frogs and toads scour the garden at night, looking for slugs, insects, and other prey. If you don't have room for a pond, provide cool damp areas where they can shelter.

Ground beetles Several species of beetle feed on slugs, and often shelter in the cool, shaded spots slugs prefer. Place large stones on the soil for them to hide under undisturbed.

Hedgehogs Although rarely seen, hedgehogs are an ally, eating slugs, snails, and other invertebrates from spring to autumn. Provide habitats and summer drinking water, and a winter nest area.

CHECK FOR PROBLEMS

It isn't often possible to prevent pests or diseases from attacking your plants, but you can reduce the damage caused. Your best defence is to check plants regularly and act quickly. Symptoms of plant diseases are often easy to spot, so look out for weak growth or discoloured or distorted leaves, flowers, and fruit.

Pests may be less obvious as they are mobile and can hide on or around the affected plant. Sometimes there are tell-tale signs, such as slug trails, but others are harder to identify. Check plants at night, when many pests are active, and look under leaves or around the base of plants for likely culprits.

Check plants carefully and regularly. Pests may be nocturnal or very small, and can hide in nooks and crannies between leaves or in the soil.

USE BARRIERS AND TRAPS

Physical barriers and traps are increasingly important methods of controlling pests in the garden, particularly on fruit and vegetable crops. They simply prevent pests from accessing plants, which removes the need for pesticides. Tree and shrub guards will protect young trees and shrubs from larger pests, such as deer and rabbits, while nets can exclude birds from fruit and vegetables. A very fine mesh netting will keep harmful insects away from vulnerable crops and root collars can be placed around the base of plants in the cabbage family to exclude cabbage root fly. Traps can be used to lure pests away from plants, or at least monitor their activity. For example, pheromone traps can be used against codling moths on apple trees, and bottle traps can be used to catch nuisance wasps feeding on fruit.

BIOLOGICAL CONTROLS

Instead of pesticides, biological controls are a way to tackle certain pests by using natural enemies. They are often bought by mail order. Most commonly they are used to protect indoor plants, although they can also be used outside. The technique involves introducing a beneficial predator, such as a parasitoid wasp, to feed on the pest. To be effective, there must be sufficient prey and the conditions must be suitable.

Bottle cloches are impenetrable to slugs and crawling insect pests, and promote growth.

Suspended traps filled with sugary water are irresistible to wasps, which meet a sticky end.

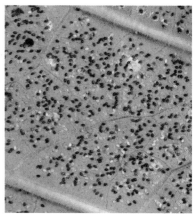

Encarsia formosa is a parasitic wasp, often used to control whitefly in greenhouse crops.

OTHER CONTROLS

Synthetic insecticides and fungicides can be effective at treating plant problems but they should only be used as a last resort. Many pests move on in time, or are eaten by predators, and many diseases can be avoided by keeping plants strong and healthy. When plants are clearly suffering however, pesticide control can be an option, although it is important to use an appropriate treatment and to apply it correctly. Always check product packaging and seek advice if necessary.

Fungal diseases, such as rose blackspot, can be difficult to control once established.

Insecticides

There are two basic categories of insecticide used to kill insects. "Contact" insecticides are sprayed directly on to pests, or kill pests that touch treated surfaces. They must be applied thoroughly, soaking the plant's leaves. "Systemic" insecticides are absorbed and travel through plant tissues and kill insects that feed upon them. Be aware that insecticides are indiscriminate and also kill beneficial insects; apply them sparingly and never to plants in flower to protect pollinating insects.

Fungicides

Used to treat fungal diseases (not bacterial or viral), fungicides are most effective when used to prevent infection rather than cure it. Once plants are infected, the best strategy is to remove all affected growth and to treat new shoots as they appear. Depending on the product used, the fungicide should be reapplied at recommended intervals, and may be required throughout the season.

If plant disease is a recurrent problem, try to improve plant health as a long-term solution, or consider growing different plants. Fungicides are a short-term treatment.

Using pesticides safely

Follow the instructions on the packaging carefully when you apply garden chemicals. Don't be tempted to increase the dose – you risk harming yourself and your plants. Avoid spraying on windy days, to prevent drift, and in full sun, which could scorch plant foliage. Aquatic life is very sensitive, so never spray near ponds or streams.

To store pesticides, keep them in their original packaging and keep them in a frost-free place, away from children and pets. Dispose of surplus treatments carefully, and never use out-of-date pesticides.

Ready mixed insecticide sprays are convenient to buy and use. They also reduce the risk of overdosing your plants. Gloves are a wise precaution when spraying pesticide.

Fungicides available to gardeners only treat some fungal diseases, such as powdery mildew (*above*). Remove growth affected by bacterial or viral diseases, and burn to destroy the infection.

Store garden chemicals in a safe place, clearly labelled, and away from children. Safely dispose of those that are no longer recommended or licensed for use; it is illegal to keep or use them.

A–Z OF COMMON PESTS

APHIDS

Plants affected: *various.*
Also known as green- or blackfly (but can be other colours), these insects feed in large colonies on plants, often on softer new growth. Severe infestations weaken plants, distort growth, and may reduce yields. They also spread viruses, and their sticky excretion, "honeydew", allows the growth of black sooty mould. Spray severe attacks with insecticide.

ASPARAGUS BEETLE

Plants affected: *asparagus.*
Adults and larvae attack plants, eating the leaves and outer surface of the stems, defoliating plants. Stems may die, weakening plants and reducing future yields. There are two generations a year, in late spring and summer. Pick off the black, red, and yellow adults and cream-coloured larvae or spray with organic insecticide.

BIRDS

Plants affected: *various.*
Many species attack plants, pecking the leaves, flowers, and fruit. The damage is usually annoying rather than harmful, although birds will strip fruiting cherry, raspberry, and strawberry plants. Install scarers or net plants, especially those in fruit.

CABBAGE ROOT FLY

Plants affected: *all brassicas.*
The maggots eat the roots, stunting growth, and causing plants to wilt in dry spells. Young plants can be killed; adult plants may produce smaller harvests. Protect young plants with collars around their bases to prevent adult flies laying their eggs, plant out stronger seedlings that will fend off attack, or cover plants with insect-proof netting.

CAPSID BUG

Plants affected: *various.*
These small, green, sap-sucking insects attack tender plant shoots and flower buds, secreting a toxin that kills plant cells. As the shoots develop, the emerging leaves are peppered with holes; affected flowers may abort or open deformed. Most common in late spring to late summer; spray with insecticide.

CARROT FLY

Plants affected: *carrot, celery, parsnip, and parsley.*
Carrot fly maggots tunnel into the taproots, forming holes just under the skin that collapse, leaving the roots prone to secondary infections. Stored roots are also prone to decay. There are two or three generations a year from late spring to autumn. Sow during midsummer to avoid the first generation, grow resistant varieties, grow under insect-proof mesh, or cover plants with fleece.

CHERRY AND PEAR SLUGWORM

Plants affected: Chaenomeles, *cherries,* Crataegus, *pears, plums, and* Sorbus.
These caterpillar-like larvae, which have a slimy, slug-like appearance, graze on the upper surface of leaves from late spring to mid-autumn, causing the remaining tissue to dry up and turn brown. There are two or three generations a year.

CODLING MOTH

Plants affected: *apples and pears.*
Small caterpillars tunnel into the fruit, feed in the core, then tunnel out,

Aphids attack many plants, usually the new growth.

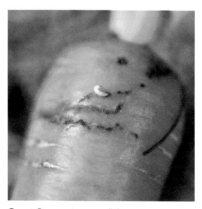
Carrot fly maggots can spoil the crop.

Codling moth caterpillars can ruin mature fruit.

leaving the mature fruit unpalatable. Use pheromone traps to capture adults and to indicate when spraying is needed. Use a suitable insecticide in late spring and early summer to kill the caterpillars as they hatch out.

CURRANT BLISTER APHID

Plants affected: *currants.*
This sap-sucking pest feeds on the leaves at the shoot tips in spring, distorting growth and causing a blistered appearance that is unsightly but not damaging.

CUTWORMS

Plants affected: *various.*
These are the soil-dwelling caterpillars of various moths that eat roots, causing plants to wilt and die and damaging tubers. At night they feed above ground, eating plant leaves. Check the soil around plants for caterpillars, control weeds, and cultivate the soil regularly. There are no pesticide controls.

FLEA BEETLES

Plants affected: *brassicas, potatoes, and many ornamentals.*
These tiny beetles eat holes in the leaves, which may turn brown and die. Seedlings can be killed by severe attacks, and mature plants can be checked. There are many species, which attack a wide range of plants from mid-spring to late summer. Sow under fleece or plant out seedlings under fleece in good weather to encourage rapid growth.

GLASSHOUSE RED SPIDER MITE

Plants affected: *various.*
These tiny mites form huge colonies, sucking sap and causing the foliage to become dull and mottled, often with a silvery sheen. Fine webs may also appear between leaves and stems. Most common on indoor plants, these mites occur outside in warm summers and can seriously weaken plants. Use biological control or spray plants using a suitable pesticide.

GLASSHOUSE WHITEFLY

Plants affected: *various.*
These sap-sucking, white-winged insects are most common on indoor plants but also occur outside in warmer summers. They quickly breed and infest plants, weakening them, and encourage sooty mould with their sugary secretions. Hang sticky yellow traps near plants to monitor numbers of whitefly. For indoor crops, use *Encarsia formosa*, a parasitic wasp, as a biological control. Alternatively, or for outdoor plants, treat using a suitable insecticide.

GOOSEBERRY SAWFLIES

Plants affected: *gooseberries, red- and whitecurrants.*
Plants are rapidly and severely defoliated by caterpillar-like insects in late spring and summer, and are often reduced to bare stems by the time crops are ready in early summer. Check plants from mid-spring and remove by hand.

LARGE AND SMALL WHITE BUTTERFLIES

Plants affected: *mainly brassicas.*
The caterpillars of large and small white butterflies eat holes in the outer leaves and crowns, causing damage to crops and reducing yields. There are two generations a year from spring to autumn. Cover plants with fine insect netting or 4mm (⅛in) mesh butterfly netting to deter adults, check plants often and pick off caterpillars, or spray with insecticide.

LEAF MINERS

Plants affected: *various.*
These are the larvae of various flies, moths, sawflies, and beetles that burrow into the leaf tissue, forming obvious tunnels. The damage is unsightly but is usually harmless. Protected inside the leaf, the insects are difficult to control. On smaller plants, pick off badly affected leaves.

Flea beetles disfigure leaves and weaken plants.

Gooseberry sawflies will also attack currants.

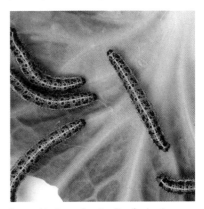
Large white butterfly caterpillars feed on leaves.

LEATHERJACKETS

Plants affected: *various.*
Crane fly (daddy long legs) larvae; these pests live in the soil, eating plant roots. They can cause brown patches on lawns, and kill seedlings and young plants, including vegetables, from late winter to midsummer. Use nematodes as biological control.

LILY BEETLE

Plants affected: *lilies and fritillaries.*
Both the bright red adults and excrement-covered, maggot-like larvae eat leaves and flowers, and can ruin plants quickly. Active from spring to autumn. Check plants and pick them off by hand, or spray with insecticide.

MEALYBUGS

Plants affected: *various, mainly indoor plants.*
Covered with white, waxy fluff, these sap-sucking pests are more common on house plants. Forming colonies in leaf joints and other inaccessible places (root mealybugs attack roots), they are hard to control. Spray with insecticide or use biological control.

MEALY CABBAGE APHID

Plants affected: *all brassicas.*
Forming large colonies on the undersides of leaves from mid-spring to mid-autumn, these grey-white aphids suck sap, causing yellowing leaves and distorted growth. Heavy attacks can kill shoots, causing multi-headed plants. Mealy cabbage aphid damage is usually superficial but heavily infested plants can be treated with a suitable insecticide.

MOTHS

Plants affected: *various.*
Moth larvae can occasionally be a significant pest to crops. Look out for the tomato moth on tomatoes and peppers in late summer. Most moth species are host-specific. Pick off larger moths by hand (they are most active after dark). Look under leaves for eggs, or spray with a suitable insecticide.

ONION FLY

Plants affected: *onions, leeks, shallots, and garlic.*
White maggots eat the roots in early summer, causing plants to collapse. In late summer maggots may also tunnel into bulbs, causing rot to set in. Destroy infested plants; there are no pesticide controls. Plant onion sets, which are not as vulnerable as seedlings, and cover plants with fine insect-proof netting.

PEAR MIDGE

Plants affected: *pears.*
Young fruitlets become blackened in early summer, spreading up from the eye at the base, then fall from the tree; inside are small white maggots. The entire crop can be lost. Destroy infested fruit before the maggots leave.

PLUM LEAF CURLING APHID

Plants affected: *plum trees.*
This aphid forms large colonies on the undersides of plum leaves, sucking sap and causing the leaves to curl inwards, in spring and early summer. The damage is mainly superficial, and new leaves will develop.

POTATO CYST NEMATODES

Plants affected: *potatoes and tomatoes.*
Leaves yellow and die from soil-level upwards in mid- to late summer, killing the plants. Small white or brown cysts can be seen on the roots. Nematodes build up and persist in the soil for many years, preventing a worthwhile crop. No pesticide controls; rotate crops or plant resistant varieties.

RASPBERRY BEETLE

Plants affected: *raspberries, blackberries, and hybrids.*
The grubs feed inside the fruits, causing dried patches near the stalk

Glasshouse whitefly are found on indoor plants.

Glasshouse red spider mite is hard to control.

Lily beetle adults are easy to spot on plants.

end, and can often be seen crawling in the bowl after fruits have been picked. Raspberries should be sprayed with insecticide as the fruit turns pink, and hybrid berries when the petals fall.

ROOT APHIDS

Plants affected: *beans, carrots, lettuce, parsnips, roses, and pinks.*
These sap-sucking pests feed on the roots, weakening plants and causing them to wilt in sunny weather; crops are reduced. They are difficult to control as they are protected by the soil; keep plants well watered in dry spells and rotate crops.

SAWFLIES

Plants affected: *various.*
There are many types of sawfly, mostly plant-specific. The caterpillar-like larvae feed on young fruit, or eat or tunnel into the leaves, sometimes causing distorted growth. Depending on the type, damage can be rapid and extensive. Control with insecticide, or pick off and destroy infested fruit and leaves.

SCALE INSECTS

Plants affected: *various.*
These sap-sucking insects resemble small shields stuck to the leaves and stems, and attack indoor and outdoor plants. There are many species with varying lifecycles, and they feed on a range of host plants. They weaken the plants and can reduce harvests, and also attract sooty mould with their sticky excretions. Spray when nymphs are present with insecticide.

SLUGS AND SNAILS

Plants affected: *various.*
Not all slugs and snails damage plants, but those that do attack a wide range of plants, eating leaves, stems, and fruit. They are most active in cool, wet weather, and feed throughout the year, especially at night, as long as the temperature is above 5°C (40°F). They can never be eliminated from a garden, so focus on protecting vulnerable plants. Apply slug pellets sparingly, or use beer traps or biological control.

VINE WEEVIL

Plants affected: *various.*
The slow-moving, black adult beetles eat leaf margins, making distinctive notches, but the white larvae cause most damage. These eat roots, causing plants to wilt and often killing them. They also tunnel into tubers, leaving them prone to other infections. Container-grown plants are most at risk, especially those with fleshy roots, although even woody shrubs can be attacked. Pick off adult beetles, drench potting compost with pesticide, or apply a biological control.

WIREWORMS

Plants affected: *various.*
These are the larval stage of click beetles and live in the soil, eating the roots of seedlings and tunnelling into root crops. They are most common where new beds have been cut into lawns, and fall in number after a few years of cultivation. There is no pesticide control. Dig root crops early to reduce damage.

Plum leaf curling aphid affects all forms of plum.

Apple sawfly larvae spoil the appearance of fruit.

Vine weevil larvae eat roots, killing plants.

A–Z OF DISEASES AND DISORDERS

APPLE SCAB AND PEAR SCAB

Plants affected: *apples, pears.*
Caused by closely related fungi, these diseases are most prevalent in damp conditions. Fruit are affected by dark, scabby marks; these often just affect the skin, but severely affected fruit may crack. Leaves develop dark blotches and may fall, and blisters may form on twigs. Remove affected growth and fruit, and dispose of fallen leaves. Prune in winter to improve air flow. Olive, pyracantha, willow, and some other trees and shrubs can also be affected by scab diseases.

BACTERIAL CANKER

Plants affected: Prunus *species.*
Most common in wet seasons, this disease causes sunken areas of bark to develop on branches and stems, which ooze yellow sticky resin as they develop. Buds may fail to open and leaves die back; eventually whole branches die and plants may be killed. Prune and destroy infected growth as soon as it appears, and grow resistant varieties.

BEAN CHOCOLATE SPOT

Plants affected: *broad beans.*
Brown spots develop on upper leaf surfaces with dark streaks on the stems, flowers, and pods, which may spread and join up. Yield is reduced and severely affected plants may die. This is a fungal disease, most common in damp conditions, and can be seed-borne. Grow on well-drained soil, avoid high-nitrogen fertilizers, and space plants widely.

BEAN HALO BLIGHT

Plants affected: *French and runner beans.*
This is a bacterial disease, causing water-soaked dead areas with a yellow rim to develop on leaves. The leaves then yellow and may die, weakening plants and reducing yield. Stems and pods can also be affected. It is spread by overhead watering. Destroy infected plants in autumn and grow resistant varieties.

BITTER PIT

Plants affected: *apples.*
Apple fruits develop small, sunken, brown spots, spoiling their appearance, and the flesh may taste bitter. Large fruits and heavy cropping trees are most susceptible. Bitter pit is caused by calcium deficiency, brought on by the tree being too dry. Water well and spray with calcium nitrate.

BLACKCURRANT REVERSION DISEASE

Plants affected: *blackcurrants.*
Plants affected by this virus problem have smaller leaves with a change of leaf shape and number of veins. They flower weakly, and produce small crops. They may show swollen buds ("big buds"), which is not a symptom of the virus, but of the mite that transmits it. There is no cure. Destroy infected plants and only buy certified disease-free plants.

BLOSSOM END ROT

Plants affected: *tomatoes, peppers.*
This condition causes dark sunken patches on the base of fruit, making them inedible. It is caused by dry soil conditions, leading to calcium deficiency. Water plants regularly and remove affected fruit.

Bacterial canker can kill infected plants.

Bean chocolate spot causes brown leaf marks.

Bitter pit can be avoided by watering apples well.

BLUEBERRY STEM BLIGHT

Plants affected: *blueberries.*
This fungal disease infects wounds, cuts, and damaged areas, causing clusters of leaves to turn brown and die, staying attached to the plant at first and falling off later. Infection spreads quickly and whole stems die back. Prune out affected growth.

BLACKBERRY CANE SPOT

Plants affected: *blackberries, hybrids.*
This is a fungal disease that causes silver-grey spots with purple margins on stems and leaves in early summer. In severe cases individual canes die back, reducing yield. Remove infected canes and destroy.

BLOSSOM WILT

Plants affected: *apples, pears, cherries, plums, apricots, and peaches.*
Fruit tree flowers wilt and turn brown but stay attached to the plants; the disease may also spread to leaves and fruiting spurs, killing them. It is most common in damp weather. Prune out affected shoots and dipose of any rotten fruit.

BOX BLIGHT

Plants affected: *box and related species.*
Fungal disease that defoliates plants, particularly during wet weather and in sheltered spots. Leaves turn brown and fall causing bare patches; stems are streaked with black and young stems die back. In wet weather, white fungal material is visible beneath infected leaves. Control is difficult, so avoid buying any plants with signs of blight. Cut back mildly affected plants and dispose of potentially diseased fallen leaves and adjacent topsoil. Protect recovering foliage with fungicides. In severe cases remove affected plants, replanting with another species.

BRASSICA RING SPOT

Plants affected: *brassicas.*
This fungal disease causes dark angular spots, often with yellow edges, on the leaves and stems. Leaves may yellow and fall, weakening plants. It is most common in cool, wet conditions. Remove infected leaves, clear plant debris, and grow resistant varieties.

CANKER

Plants affected: *apples, pears, mulberry, and many ornamentals.*
Caused by fungi, cankers can affect a wide range of woody plants. Common symptoms are raised or sunken areas of dead bark, which spread and cut off the sap, causing buds, leaves, and branches to die back. Cut out any infected growth.

CLEMATIS WILT

Plants affected: *clematis.*
This is a fungal disease affecting certain large-flowered hybrid clematis varieties. It causes leaves and stems to suddenly wilt and collapse, dying back to the base. Established plants will resprout but younger specimens can be seriously weakened. Remove all infected growth. Note that wilting in clematis often has other causes, such as pest, weather, or physical damage.

CLUBROOT

Plants affected: *all brassicas.*
This is a serious disease that distorts roots, causing the foliage to become pale and pink-tinted, with the stems and leaves wilting even when plants are well watered. Yield can be seriously reduced and plants may even die. Destroy all infected material, increase soil drainage, and raise pH using lime. Plant out large healthy seedlings and grow resistant varieties.

CORAL SPOT

Plants affected: *various broadleaved trees and shrubs.*
This fungal disease causes woody stems to die back and bright orange pustules to develop on the dead bark. It is carried by water splashes and pruning tools, and enters plants via open wounds. It is most damaging to plants that are already under stress from other problems. Destroy infected material, cut back to healthy growth, and clean pruning tools.

Canker can kill branches and whole trees in time.

Clubroot affects brassicas, stunting their growth.

Damping off can decimate young seedlings.

CROWN ROT

Plants affected: *various, mainly bulbs and perennials.*
Caused by fungal or bacterial infections, leaves and stems wilt and die, and the base of the plant rots away and may smell unpleasant. Remove infected material, which often means the whole plant. Avoid wounding stems, planting too deeply, or mulching close to stems.

CUCUMBER MOSAIC VIRUS

Plants affected: *many vegetable crops and ornamentals.*
Plants are stunted, and the foliage may be distorted with yellow mottling. Flowering may be reduced and flowers discoloured, and the fruit of any affected cucurbits can be distorted, discoloured, and inedible. The virus is easily spread between plants, often by aphids, and there is no cure. Control aphids, avoid handling plants, grow resistant varieties, and destroy infected specimens quickly.

DAMPING OFF

Plants affected: *various.*
This disease kills seed and seedlings, causing stems to collapse and roots to rot. Prevent it by using sterile compost and trays, sowing thinly, and watering using tap water.

DOWNY MILDEW

Plants affected: *various.*
This disease, most common on plants in damp conditions, causes discoloured patches on the upper leaf surfaces, with fuzzy white, grey, or purplish mould below. These spread, killing leaves and weakening plants. Remove infected material, improve air flow, and avoid overhead watering.

FIREBLIGHT

Plants affected: *some members of the Rosaceae family, including apples, pears, and* Pyracantha.
Flowers, leaves, and stems wilt, and branches may die back rapidly. Bark sinks inwards and sticky ooze may be secreted. This bacterial disease is most common in warm, wet weather; prune and destroy infected material, and sterilize pruning tools.

FUSARIUM WILT

Plants affected: *various.*
This fungal disease causes plants to wilt and die, and older leaves appear scorched. Cutting into stems may reveal reddish-purple streaks. There is no cure. Destroy infected plants, clear plant debris, and avoid planting the same species in an affected patch of soil for several years.

GREY MOULD

Plants affected: *various.*
This fungal disease is prevalent in cool, damp conditions, especially on plants overwintered under cover. Fluffy mould appears on leaves, flowers, and fruits, and whole stems may wilt and die. Remove infected growth and all debris, and improve air flow around plants under cover.

HONEY FUNGUS

Plants affected: *various trees, shrubs and perennials.*
Affected plants can die suddenly, or may die back over a number of seasons; the leaves discolouring and wilting, or failing to emerge in spring. Infected plants develop white, mushroon-smelling, fungal mycelium under the bark of the stem base and roots. Black, bootlace-like strands may also be found in the surrounding soil. Dig up and destroy infected plants, removing as much root as possible. Plant less susceptible species.

LEAF SPOTS

Plants affected: *various.*
Round or irregular spots, sometimes surrounded by a yellow halo, can be caused by various bacterial or fungal infections. Spots may join and some leaves may die but the damage is usually minor; it can be a sign of poor plant health. Remove infected

Downy mildew causes discoloured patches.

Grey mould thrives in cool, damp conditions.

Onion white rot can destroy a crop in summer.

leaves, rake up any that have fallen, and improve plant health.

LEEK RUST

Plants affected: *various members of the onion family.*
Outer leaves develop small, bright orange pustules, and may die off, weakening the plants. Inner leaves are rarely affected and crops are still edible if affected leaves are removed. Most common in damp conditions. Clear plant debris after harvest, space plants widely, and grow resistant cultivars.

ONION WHITE ROT

Plants affected: *onions, shallots, garlic, and leeks.*
This serious disease causes leaves to yellow and wilt, and white fluffy mould appears around the base of developing bulbs. There is no cure, and the soil where affected plants have been grown will be contaminated for many years. Remove and dispose of affected plants, and avoid moving contaminated soil around.

PARSNIP CANKER

Plants affected: *parsnips.*
This disease causes dark, cankered areas on the roots. It is caused by a number of different fungi, some of which can also cause leaf spotting. Points of root damage are frequently colonized by the canker, including feeding damage from carrot fly larvae. There are no chemical controls of parsnip canker. Grow resistant varieties, and sow closely in late spring to produce smaller roots, which are less susceptible.

PEACH LEAF CURL

Plants affected: *peaches, nectarines.*
New leaves in spring are puckered and blistered, turning red before dropping off. A second flush of leaves may develop; these are unaffected, but trees can be weakened if attacked over several years. Remove infected leaves quickly, and feed and water plants well. Cover the tree with clear plastic in late winter and spring to provide shelter from rain, which is necessary for infection.

PHYTOPHTHORA ROOT ROT

Plants affected: *various.*
This damaging desease causes the roots and stem base of affected plants to rot, and overall growth is weak. Foliage is sparse and may become discoloured, stems die back, and the whole plant may be killed. If the bark is removed at the base of the main stem, the tissues below are stained reddish-brown. It is most common on poorly drained soil. There is no cure; destroy infected plants and remove the soil.

POTATO BLIGHT

Plants affected: *potatoes, tomatoes.*
This disease is most common in warm, wet seasons. It causes brown patches on leaves that wither and die. Stems develop dark patches and collapse, and infected tubers have orange-brown discoloured flesh, and usually rot. Destroy infected growth, earth up to protect tubers, and grow resistant varieties.

POTATO COMMON SCAB

Plants affected: *potato, beetroot, radishes, swedes, and turnips.*
This is a bacterial disease that causes rough, corky patches on the skin of tubers. Yield isn't reduced and the unsightly scabs can be removed when peeling the tubers. It is most common in hot, dry summers. Improve the soil with organic matter, water well, and grow resistant varieties.

POWDERY MILDEW

Plants affected: *various.*
This common disease causes white fungal growth on leaves, stems and fruit. Growth can become yellow and distorted; affected fruit (such as grapes) can split. Affected plants are unsightly and may be

Peach leaf curl weakens plants and reduces yields.

Potato blight is most common in wet seasons.

Powdery mildew affects a very wide range of plants.

weakened, but are rarely killed. Remove infected growth, water plants well, and improve air flow around each plant.

QUINCE LEAF BLIGHT

Plants affected: *quince trees.*
Numerous small dark spots appear on the leaves and commonly merge together. Leaves yellow and fall, fruit may be spotted and misshapen, and shoot tips may die back. This fungal disease is most common in wet weather. Remove and destroy infected growth, and clear plant debris in autumn.

RASPBERRY SPUR BLIGHT

Plants affected: *raspberries, hybrids.*
Dark patches appear on the leaves in summer, and purple areas form on the stems around the buds. The affected areas turn a grey or silver colour during autumn and winter. The following spring the new shoots wither and die, and crops are heavily reduced. It is most common in wet seasons. Remove and destroy all infected stems, and thin out canes.

RED CORE

Plants affected: *strawberries.*
This uncommon disease causes stunted growth in late spring and early summer, when leaves turn

orange or brown. Berries are small and ripen early. The disease is worse on heavy, wet soils and persists for years. Destroy infected plants and replant elsewhere.

ROSE BLACK SPOT

Plants affected: *roses.*
This fungal disease causes purple-black spots on leaves that usually yellow and drop. The spots disfigure plants, which are weakened by the repeated leaf fall. Remove infected leaves and growth, clear away all autumn debris. Resistant varieties are available but resistance may not last the lifetime of the plant. Fungicides can also be applied as a preventative measure.

REPLANT DISEASE

Plants affected: *most commonly roses and fruit trees.*
Newly planted roses and fruit trees fail to thrive and may die back, but there are no obvious cultural problems, such as over- or under-watering. Replant disease commonly occurs where the same species has been grown before; the full cause is not known, but is thought to be various soil-borne pests and pathogens attacking the roots. Plant something else instead or remove as much soil as possible before replanting.

RUST

Plants affected: *various.*
Most common in wet conditions, this disease is caused by various fungal species, many of them host-specific. It commonly causes orange or brown pustules on the leaves and stems, which may yellow, wither, and die. Severe attacks can weaken and kill plants. Remove infected material, improve air flow around plants, and grow resistant varieties. If necessary, treat ornamental plants with fungicide.

SILVER LEAF

Plants affected: *plums, cherries, apples, and some other woody plants.*
Leaves develop a silver sheen, and if affected branches over 2.5cm (1in) in diameter are cut across, brown staining can be seen inside. Stems and branches die back, and established trees may be killed. It is caused by a fungal infection that enters plants through wounds and pruning cuts. There is no cure. Prune and destroy infected growth, cutting stems to 15cm (6in) beyond where staining is visible. Prune trees in summer when infection is less likely, and plant resistant varieties and rootstocks.

SCLEROTINIA ROT

Plants affected: *various.*
This disease causes the basal leaves of plants to wilt and yellow, and a rapidly

Rose black spot spoils the appearance of plants.

Rust affects many crops and ornamental plants.

Silver leaf infects through pruning wounds.

spreading brown rot appears on the stems. Large amounts of fluffy white fungal growth often develops, and black, seed-like structures appear. It is most common in cool, damp conditions. There is no cure. Destroy all infected material as soon as possible.

SOOTY MOULD

Plants affected: *various.*
This is black or grey mould that forms on the surface of leaves, growing on the sugary excretions ("honeydew") produced by sap-sucking insects, such as aphids. Although it doesn't attack the plant, it prevents light reaching the leaves, and can reduce vigour. It is also unsightly. In some cases it may be possible to control the pest producing the honeydew. The mould growth can be wiped or washed off.

TOMATO BLIGHT

Plants affected: *tomatoes, potatoes.*
Caused by the same pathogen as potato blight, this disease causes dark patches on the leaves, which die back, and lesions on the stems, which usually collapse. Infected fruit turn brown and eventually decay. It is most common on outdoor-grown plants, especially in wet summers. Destroy infected material as soon as symptoms appear. If indoor crops are affected, wash out the greenhouse

thoroughly after the plants are removed. Effective resistant varieties are now available.

TURF RED THREAD

Plants affected: *lawn grasses.*
Patches of turf turn reddish or become bleached, then characteristic, small, pinkish-red, thread-like growth develops. Grass is rarely killed but becomes unsightly. It is most common on poorly fed and aerated lawns. Scarify the grass, feed with a nitrogenous fertilizer, and aerate the lawn.

VERTICILLIUM WILT

Plants affected: *various.*
Symptoms of this fungal disease are most prominent during hot, dry conditions. Leaves on affected branches discolour, turning brown or yellow between the veins, wilt, and die, although not all branches will be infected at the same time. Branches may die back, and if cut open, there will be brown or purple-brown streaks inside. There is no chemical control. Destroy infected plants, including the roots, and remove the surrounding soil. Conifers and grasses are immune to the disease.

VIOLET ROOT ROT

Plants affected: *various.*
Plants are stunted with yellowing leaves, and when lifted, the roots

are covered with a dense network of purple fungal strands. It is most common on wet, acid soils, and persists for several years. Remove infected plants before they disintegrate, and improve drainage.

VIRUSES

Plants affected: *various.*
There are many viruses that affect plants, although most cause yellowing leaves, often in a mottled or mosaic pattern. The method of spread varies according to the virus. Insect transmission (such as by aphids) is common; handling or propagating from infected plants is another cause. Viruses weaken plants, and commonly reduce flowering and lower yield. There is no cure and infected plants should be destroyed to prevent the virus spreading.

WHITE BLISTER

Plants affected: *vegetable brassicas, honesty, and some other ornamentals.*
Shiny white fungal pustules develop on the undersides of leaves, singly or in rings. The affected leaves become puckered and distorted, and the upper surface forms sunken yellow pits. This disease is most common in damp conditions and may persist in the soil. Remove infected leaves and heavily affected plants, and grow resistant varieties.

Tomato blight is most common on outside crops.

Verticillium wilt attacks a wide range of plants.

Viruses cause a wide range of debilitating symptoms.

PLANT CHOOSER

This gorgeous catalogue of plants is designed to help
you find the perfect plant for every corner of your garden.
Search by type, whether you're looking for an autumn
shrub, a summer climber, or a spring perennial, or browse
through the problem-solver pages to find something to
cover shady ground or to thrive in a sun-baked border.

ANNUALS, BIENNIALS, AND BEDDING

Antirrhinum majus 'Liberty Yellow' (Liberty Classic Series)
Bearing distinctive yellow, freesia-like blooms all summer, these snapdragons are perfect for summer bedding and for cutting.
↕ 45cm (18in) ↔ 30cm (12in) ☼ ◊ ❋

Calendula officinalis
The bright orange-yellow, daisy-like flowers of the pot marigold are produced from summer through to autumn. Deadhead to keep the show going.
↕ 75cm (30in) ↔ 45cm (18in) ☼ ◊ ❋❋❋

Cosmos bipinnatus Sensation Series
This popular annual cosmos produces large pink and white flowers on elegant thin stems above the fine, feathery leaves throughout summer.
↕ 90cm (36in) ↔ 60cm (24in) ☼ ◊ ◐ ❋❋❋

Digitalis purpurea Camelot Series
This is one wonderful foxglove among many. Tall spires of freckled, bell-like flowers are produced in shades of white, pink, lavender, or cream.
↕ 1.2m (4ft) ↔ 60cm (24in) ☼ ☀ ◐ ❋❋❋

Eschscholzia californica
The California poppy is a low-growing annual for the front of a sunny border. The bright orange and yellow flowers are very attractive against the ferny foliage.
↕ 30cm (12in) ↔ 15cm (6in) ☼ ◊ ❋❋❋

Felicia amelloides 'Santa Anita'
This delicate subshrub has bright green foliage. Large, daisy-like flowers, with blue petals and bright yellow centres, open from late spring to autumn.
↕↔ 60cm (24in) ☼ ◊ ❋

Hibiscus trionum
Flower-of-the-hour produces a succession of stunning cream flowers with burgundy centres from summer to early autumn. Each flower lasts only for a single day.
↕ 60cm (24in) ↔ 30cm (12in) ☼ ◊ ❋

Lantana 'Radiation'
Vibrant yellow and red flowerheads are produced throughout summer above the wrinkled, dark green leaves of this tender subshrub.
↕ 45cm (18in) ↔ 25cm (10in) ☼ ◊ ☖

Limnanthes douglasii
This low-growing annual, known as the poached egg plant, bears masses of cup-shaped, white flowers with yellow centres throughout summer.
↕ 15cm (6in) ↔ 10cm (4in) ☼ ◊ ❋❋❋

❋❋❋ FULLY HARDY　　❋❋ HARDY IN MILD REGIONS/SHELTERED SITES　　❋ PROTECT FROM FROST OVER WINTER　　❋ NO TOLERANCE TO FROST

☼ FULL SUN　　☀ PARTIAL SUN　　❋ FULL SHADE　　◊ WELL-DRAINED SOIL　　◊ MOIST SOIL　　◊ WET SOIL

Nemesia strumosa 'KLM'
Named for the Royal Dutch Airlines, this bushy annual with toothed and slightly hairy leaves is covered in masses of tiny blue and white flowers in summer.
‡ 30cm (12in) ↔ 15cm (6in) ☼ ◊ ◊ ❋

Nicotiana 'Domino Salmon-pink'
During mid- to late summer this tobacco plant is clothed with star-shaped, salmon-pink flowers, which open up in the early evening and emit a delicate scent.
‡ 45cm (18in) ↔ 40cm (16in) ☼ ☀ ◊ ◊ ❋

Nigella damascena Persian Jewels Group
Mixed shades of blue, pink, and white add charm to this old cottage-garden favourite, love-in-a-mist. Both flowers and seedheads are good for cutting.
‡ 40cm (16in) ↔ 23cm (9in) ☼ ◊ ❋❋❋

Osteospermum 'Buttermilk'
Sun-loving Cape daisies are mainly grown for their bright and cheerful flowers; these are borne from spring to autumn, but close in dull conditions.
‡ 60cm (24in) ↔ 30cm (12in) ☼ ◊ ❋❋

Papaver rhoeas
Field poppies are ideal for creating a splash of colour in a sunny area of the garden. Various flower colours are available, from white to red and mauve.
‡ 60cm (24in) ↔ 15cm (6in) ☼ ◊ ❋❋❋

Viola 'Bowles's Black'
A pretty annual viola with dainty, midnight blue-black flowers. Perfect for rockeries and containers or for growing between the cracks in paving stones.
‡ 15cm (6in) ↔ 8cm (3in) ☼ ◊ ❋❋❋

Zinnia marylandica Zahara Coral Rose (Zahara Series)
Zinnias produce an abundance of bright summer flowers; this variety bears pink pompon blooms.
‡ 30–45cm (12–18in) ↔ 30cm (12in) ☼ ◊ ❋

ALSO RECOMMENDED

Ageratum houstonianum 'Blue Danube'

Campanula medium 'Bells of Holland' (Canterbury bells)

Cerinthe major 'Purpurascens'

Clarkia amoena (Satin flower)

Convolvulus tricolor 'Blue Flash'

Eustoma grandiflorum

Gaillardia pulchella Lollipop Series

Helianthus annuus 'Music Box' (Sunflower)

Iberis umbellata Fairyland mixture (Common candytuft)

Lathyrus annuus (Sweet pea)

Lobularia maritima 'Snow Crystals'

Lunaria annua (Honesty)

Nemophila menziesii (Baby blue eyes)

Omphalodes linifolia (Venus's navelwort)

Sanvitalia procumbens (Creeping zinnia)

Sutera cordata Snowstorm Series Giant Snowflake ('Danova906')

Tagetes patula 'Naughty Marietta'

Tropaeolum majus Alaska Series

PLANTS FOR SUMMER CONTAINERS

Agapanthus praecox subsp. orientalis
The sky-blue tubular flowers of this tall
perennial are borne in clusters at the top of
strong stems that rise from clumps of broad,
dark green leaves.
‡ 1m (3ft) ↔ 60cm (2ft) ☼ ◊ ◑ ❀

Ageratum 'Adriatic'
From summer until the first frosts, this plant
produces small mid-blue flowers in dense
clusters above downy green oval leaves.
Water well in containers.
‡ 20cm (8in) ↔ 30cm (12in) ☼ ◊ ◑ ❀

Argyranthemum 'Jamaica Primrose'
The soft yellow daisy flowers of this
easy-going plant are beautifully
complemented by the ferny, deeply
divided mid-green leaves.
‡↔ 1m (3ft) ☼ ◊ ❀

Brachyscome iberidifolia
The blue, violet or white daisy-like flowers
of this bushy annual appear from mid- to late
summer, held above deeply divided
grey-green foliage.
‡↔ 45cm (18in) ☼ ◊ ◑ ❀

Calibrachoa Cabaret Series
From summer to autumn, this mound-
forming, trailing plant bears bright pink,
trumpet-shaped flowers in profusion. They
are set against dark green leaves.
‡ 13cm (5in) ↔ 45cm (18in) ☼ ❀ ◊ ❀

Dianthus 'Becky Robinson'
The pretty semi-double flowers of this
compact perennial are clear pink, bordered
with deep red. Cut or dead-head them to
prompt repeat flowering.
‡ to 45cm (18in) ↔ 40cm (16in) ☼ ◊ ❀❀❀

Fuchsia 'Celia Smedley'
An upright fuchsia bearing deep red flowers
and pink sepals from midsummer, 'Celia
Smedley' will give its best display if given
well-fertilized loamy compost.
‡ 1.5m (5ft) ↔ 1m (3ft) ☼ ❀ ◊ ◑ ❀

Gazania Talent Series
Providing a vivid splash of yellow in a
container display, the open, daisy-like
flowers appear over a long period. The
leaves are felted and greyish-green.
‡↔ 25cm (10in) ☼ ◊ ❀

**Impatiens walleriana
'Tempo Lavender Butterfly'**
The strong lavender-pink flowers of this busy
lizzie are long-lasting and provide a bright
display from summer to autumn.
‡↔ 25cm (10in) ☼ ◊ ◑ ❀❀

Ipomoea tricolor 'Heavenly Blue'
A fast-growing climber with twining stems, this variety of morning glory bears sky-blue funnel-shaped flowers with white centres throughout the summer.
↕ 3m (10ft) ☼ ◊ ❀❀

Lobelia erinus Cascade Series
This trailing lobelia bears masses of tiny dark blue flowers from summer through to mid-autumn; they last better if given a position in partial shade.
↕↔ 15cm (6in) ☼ ☀ ◊ ❀

Pelargonium 'Caligula'
This miniature zonal pelargonium has dark green leaves and bright scarlet double blooms. Deadhead regularly to prolong their season until the first frosts.
↕ 12cm (5in) ↔ 10cm (4in) ☼ ◊ ❀

Petunia Surfinia Pink Vein
With large pink flowers veined and centred with a deeper hue and vigorous growth, this trailing petunia makes a strong display in a container. Deadhead regularly.
↕ 40cm (16in) ↔ 90cm (36in) ☼ ◊ ❀

Ricinus communis 'Impala'
Suitable for a large container, this tall, fast-growing shrub has deeply divided bronze leaves up to 30cm (12in) across. The small red flowers are followed by red seedheads.
↕ 1.5m (5ft) ↔ 1m (3ft) ☼ ◊ ❀

ALSO RECOMMENDED

Aloysia triphylla
  (Lemon verbena)

Argyranthemum 'Vancouver'

Begonia Nonstop Series

Bidens ferulifolia

Brugmansia x *candida*
  'Grand Marnier'

Campanula isophylla
  (Falling stars)

Canna 'Assaut'

Chrysanthemum 'Mary Stoker'

Cosmos bipinnatus
  Sensation Series

Fuchsia 'Thalia'

Gazania Mini-Star Series

Limnanthes douglasii
  (Poached egg plant)

Matthiola incana Cinderella
  Series (Gillyflower)

Narcissus 'Tête-à-Tête'

Nemesia strumosa 'KLM'

Nerium oleander (Oleander)

Pelargonium 'Happy Thought'

Petunia 'Purple Wave'

Prostanthera rotundifolia
  (Round-leaved mint bush)

Rosa 'The Fairy'

Tropaeolum majus
Nasturtiums are popular for their bright yellow, orange, or red flowers. Both the flowers and pale green leaves are edible, adding colour and flavour to salads.
↕ 30cm (12in) ☼ ◊ ◊ ❀

Verbena 'Sissinghurst'
Large round clusters of bright magenta flowers are borne from summer to autumn, providing bold colour against the dark green leaves of this easy-to-grow plant.
↕ 20cm (8in) ↔ 1m (3ft) ☼ ◊ ◊ ❀❀

SPRING-FLOWERING BULBS

Anemone blanda 'White Splendour'
The white daisy-like flowers of this anemone are held on upright stems above the deeply toothed leaves, making a prolific display in spring.

‡ 10cm (4in) ↔ 15cm (6in) ☼ ◊ ✽✽✽

Camassia leichtlinii
The leafless stems of this striking plant bear dense spikes of star-shaped white or blue-violet flowers with six petals. Long, slim leaves grow at the base of the stems.

‡ 1.5m (5ft) ↔ 30cm (12in) ☼ ☀ ◊ ◖ ✽✽

Convallaria majalis 'Albostriata'
This variegated lily of the valley bears spikes of white, sweetly scented flowers in late spring, surrounded by handsome gold-striped, broad green leaves.

‡ 20cm (8in) ↔ 30cm (12in) ☀ ◊ ◖ ✽✽✽

Crocus chrysanthus 'E.A. Bowles'
The rich yellow of the goblet-shaped flowers of this crocus is emphasized by the purple feathering on the outer petals and the dark green, white-striped leaves.

‡ 8cm (3in) ↔ 5cm (2in) ☼ ◊ ✽✽✽

Cyclamen coum subsp. coum f. coum Pewter Group
This cyclamen has dark green leaves with a pewter sheen. The flowers appear from late winter to early spring and range from white to crimson.

‡↔ 10–12cm (4–5in) ☀ ◊ ✽✽✽

Erythronium dens-canis
With heavily marked green leaves and dainty nodding flowers in colours from white to pink, this dog's-tooth violet makes a pretty display in early spring.

‡ 15–25cm (6–10in) ↔ 10cm (4in) ☀ ◊ ✽✽✽

Fritillaria meleagris
A native of English grasslands, the snake's head fritillary is stunning planted in grass. The pink-purple or white flowers have a distinctive chequered pattern.

‡ 30cm (12in) ↔ 8cm (3in) ☼ ☀ ◊ ◖ ✽✽✽

Galanthus nivalis
The fragrant white flowers of the common snowdrop are a classic sight in early spring. Given the right conditions, it will self-seed easily to make spreading colonies.

‡ 15cm (6in) ↔ 8cm (3in) ☀ ◊ ◖ ✽✽✽

Hyacinthus orientalis 'City of Haarlem'
In late spring, this hyacinth produces a dense spike of intensely fragrant primrose-yellow flowers. The leaves are bright green and lance-shaped.

‡ 25cm (10in) ↔ 8cm (3in) ☼ ◊ ✽✽✽

✿✿✿ FULLY HARDY ✿✿ HARDY IN MILD REGIONS/SHELTERED SITES ✿ PROTECT FROM FROST OVER WINTER ✿ NO TOLERANCE TO FROST

☼ FULL SUN ☼ PARTIAL SUN ✸ FULL SHADE ◊ WELL-DRAINED SOIL ◊ MOIST SOIL ◖ WET SOIL

Iris 'George'
This vigorous dwarf iris flowers in early spring, producing fragrant, deep violet-purple flowers up to 8cm (3in) across, with bright yellow markings on the falls.
‡ 10cm (4in) ↔ 1m (3ft) ☼ ☼ ◊ ◖ ✿✿✿

Leucojum aestivum 'Gravetye Giant'
Resembling a giant snowdrop, the summer snowflake bears nodding white flowers with green tips in spring. Narrow green leaves provide a subtle backdrop.
‡ 90cm (36in) ↔ 8cm (3in) ☼ ◖ ✿✿✿

Muscari armeniacum
Grape hyacinths bear upright spikes of fragrant, bell-shaped, deep blue flowers with pale blue or white rims, surrounded by narrow, mid-green leaves.
‡ 20cm (8in) ↔ 10cm (4in) ☼ ◊ ◖ ✿✿✿

Narcissus 'Ceylon'
This large, very vigorous daffodil has showy, long-lasting flowers with deep yellow petals and orange-rimmed cups. The strap-shaped leaves are dark green.
‡ 40cm (16in) ↔ 12cm (5in) ☼ ◊ ✿✿✿

Puschkinia scilloides
Slender bell-shaped flowers in pale blue with a fine deeper blue line down the centre of each petal make a pretty display on compact stems in early spring.
‡ 15cm (6in) ↔ 5cm (2in) ☼ ☼ ◊ ✿✿✿

Scilla bifolia
Particularly attractive naturalized in grass or beneath deciduous trees, this early-blooming plant bears blue-violet star-shaped flowers on one side of the stems.
‡↔ 15cm (6in) ☼ ◊ ✿✿✿

Tulipa 'Spring Green'
With a feathery green flash on each ivory petal, this Viridiflora Group tulip is a cool and elegant presence in a mixed or colour-themed border. It flowers in late spring.
‡ 40cm (16in) ☼ ◊ ✿✿✿

ALSO RECOMMENDED

Allium acuminatum

Allium aflatunense

Anemone tschernjaewii

Calochortus luteus
  (Yellow mariposa)

Chionodoxa 'Pink Giant'

Colchicum luteum

Crocus 'Blue Pearl'

Ferraria crispa

Fritillaria imperialis 'Lutea'
  (Crown imperial)

Fritillaria verticillata

Hyacinthoides non-scripta
  (English bluebell)

Hyacinthus orientalis
  'White Pearl'

Iris 'Natascha'

Ixia viridiflora

Leucojum vernum
  (Spring snowflake)

Muscari botryoides 'Album'

Narcissus 'Silver Chimes'

Ornithogalum magnum

Ornithogalum oligophyllum

Scilla siberica 'Alba'
  (Siberian squill)

Sparaxis tricolor

Tulipa 'Giuseppe Verdi'

SUMMER AND AUTUMN BULBS

***Allium hollandicum* 'Purple Sensation'**
The deep purple, spherical flowerheads of
this early summer-flowering, stately allium
look stunning when planted with silver-
leaved, shorter plants.
‡ 80cm (32in) ↔ 7cm (3in) ☼ ◊ ❋❋❋

Allium sphaerocephalon
Known as the roundheaded leek, this plant
produces ovoid, 2.5cm (1in) wide flowerheads
in midsummer. They are rich purple and are
a magnet to bees.
‡ 90cm (36in) ↔ 5cm (2in) ☼ ◊ ◐ ❋❋❋

***Alstroemeria ligtu* hybrids**
These midsummer-flowering perennials
bear sprays of delicate flowers in a wide
variety of colours, from white to shades
of pink, yellow, and orange.
‡ 50cm (20in) ↔ 75cm (30in) ☼ ☀ ◊ ◐ ❋❋❋

***Canna* 'Striata'**
A statement plant with rich green leaves
striped with yellow, and bright orange
flowers, carried on dark red-purple
stems in midsummer.
‡ 1.5m (5ft) ↔ 50cm (20in) ☼ ◊ ❋

Colchicum autumnale
Autumn crocuses flower when least
expected, their large pale lilac blooms
suddenly appearing in autumn before the
leaves emerge in spring.
‡ 10–15cm (4–6in) ↔ 8cm (3in) ☼ ◊ ◐ ❋❋❋

Crinum x powellii
A very decorative plant, this lily produces
flared trumpet blooms, up to ten at a time, at
the top of tall, rigid stems from late summer
to mid-autumn.
‡ 1m (3ft) ↔ 60cm (24in) ☼ ◊ ◐ ❋❋

***Crocosmia masoniorum* 'Firebird'**
This dazzling, bright red crocosmia makes a
fabulous mid- to late-summer display, when
its spikes of vivid flowers arch over the fans
of bright green leaves.
‡ 80cm (32in) ↔ 45cm (18in) ☼ ◊ ◐ ❋❋❋

Cyclamen hederifolium
Fluted pink flowers are carried above the soil
surface in autumn before the foliage appears.
The heart-shaped leaves are dark green with
silver patterning.
‡ 10cm (4in) ↔ 15cm (6in) ☼ ☀ ◊ ❋❋❋

***Dahlia* 'Bishop of Llandaff'**
The vivid red flowers of this dahlia look
dramatic against the black-red foliage,
making it a striking addition to a late
summer border.
‡ 1m (3ft) ↔ 45cm (18in) ☼ ◊ ◐ ❋❋

✤✤✤ FULLY HARDY   ✤✤ HARDY IN MILD REGIONS/SHELTERED SITES   ✤ PROTECT FROM FROST OVER WINTER   ✤ NO TOLERANCE TO FROST

☼ FULL SUN   ☼ PARTIAL SUN   ✲ FULL SHADE   ◊ WELL-DRAINED SOIL   ◗ MOIST SOIL   ◆ WET SOIL

Dierama pulcherrimum
The delightful name of angel's fishing rod perfectly suits this airy perennial, whose pink bell flowers move gracefully on long stems in the slightest breeze.
↕ 1.5m (5ft) ↔ 60cm (24in) ☼ ◊ ◗ ✤✤

Fritillaria imperialis
Stately and strong-growing, the crown imperial stands regally within a border. Clusters of orange flowers radiate from the top of tall stems in early summer.
↕ 1.5m (5ft) ↔ 30cm (12in) ☼ ◊ ✤✤✤

Gladiolus murielae
Fragrant, pure white flowers, with deep burgundy centres, are carried on the tall, arching stems of this exotic gladiolus during late summer and into autumn.
↕ 1m (3ft) ↔ 5cm (2in) ☼ ◊ ✤✤

Iris pallida 'Variegata'
The long, tapering, yellow-striped leaves of this elegant iris surround a succession of showy, scented blue flowers in early summer. A perfect plant for a hot border.
↕ 1.2m (4ft) ↔ indefinite ☼ ◊ ✤✤✤

Lilium regale
The large, white, trumpet-shaped flowers of the regal lily are purple on the outside and held in clusters on tall stems, creating an eye-catching display in midsummer.
↕↔ 2m (6ft) ☼ ◊ ✤✤✤

Nectaroscordum siculum subsp. bulgaricum
The flowers on this onion relative are green, white, and burgundy. Grouped in sprays on top of tall stems, they are a pretty sight in early summer.
↕ 1.2m (4ft) ↔ 45cm (18in) ☼ ✲ ◊ ✤✤✤

Nerine bowdenii
South Africa has given gardeners many spectacular plants, and this is no exception. Stems of vivid pink, spidery flowers appear from bare soil in autumn.
↕ 60cm (24in) ↔ 15cm (6in) ☼ ◊ ✤✤

ALSO RECOMMENDED

Summer-flowering
Allium 'Gladiator'

Alstroemeria 'Moulin Rouge'

Cardiocrinum giganteum
  (Giant lily)

Dahlia 'Hillcrest Royal'

Dichelostemma congestum

Ismene x spofforthiae
  'Sulphur Queen'

Lilium 'Starfighter'

Polianthes tuberosa 'The Pearl'

Ranunculus asiaticus var. flavus
  (Persian buttercup)

Watsonia meriana

Zantedeschia elliottiana
  (Golden arum lily)

Autumn-flowering
Acis autumnalis
  (Autumn snowflake)

Amaryllis belladonna 'Hathor'

Colchicum bivonae

Cyclamen mirabile

Scilla scilloides

Nerine bowdenii 'Alba'

Nerine 'Orion'

Zephyranthes grandiflora

SPRING AND EARLY SUMMER PERENNIALS

Anemone ranunculoides
With small, bright yellow five- or six-petalled flowers, this spring-flowering plant resembles a buttercup. It is ideal for naturalizing in a woodland garden.
↕↔ 20cm (8in) ☀ ◐ ◑ ❀❀❀

Aquilegia vulgaris 'Nivea'
Clusters of white flowers borne on upright stems with grey-green divided leaves make this plant a pretty addition to a border, especially in a shady spot.
↕ 90cm (36in) ↔ 45cm (18in) ☀ ◐ ◐ ❀❀❀

Bergenia ciliata
In spring, this evergreen perennial bears small white flowers ageing to pink. Its large, round, hairy leaves make it attractive outside the flowering season too.
↕ 30cm (12in) ↔ 45cm (18in) ☀ ◐ ◐ ◑ ❀❀❀

Brunnera macrophylla
A clump-forming perennial excellent for ground cover, this plant produces slender sprays of star-shaped flowers resembling forget-me-nots in early spring.
↕ 45cm (18in) ↔ 60cm (24in) ☀ ◐ ◑ ❀❀❀

Digitalis grandiflora
This species of foxglove produces its pale yellow flowers in early summer. It is a short-lived, clump-forming perennial ideal for an informal border.
↕ 1m (3ft) ↔ 45cm (18in) ☀ ◐ ◑ ❀❀❀

Eranthis hyemalis
In early spring, winter aconites produce bright yellow, cup-shaped flowers from deeply divided, green bracts; naturalized in grass, they make a pretty carpet.
↕ 10cm (4in) ↔ 10cm (4in) ☀ ◐ ◑ ❀❀❀

Euphorbia polychroma
The yellow flowers of this bushy, rounded perennial provide bright colour over several weeks in spring, set against mid-green leaves.
↕↔ 50cm (20in) ☀ ◐ ◑ ❀❀❀

Geranium cinereum 'Ballerina'
One of the earliest hardy geraniums to bloom, this variety has cup-shaped purplish-pink flowers with purple veins and dark centres, carried in profusion.
↕ 10cm (4in) ↔ 30cm (12in) ☀ ◐ ◑ ❀❀❀

Geum rivale
A native of waterside locations, water avens is ideal for a bog garden or a site beside a pool. In late spring it produces nodding, bell-shaped, deep pink flowers.
↕↔ 60cm (24in) ☀ ◐ ◑ ❀❀❀

❀❀❀ FULLY HARDY ❀❀ HARDY IN MILD REGIONS/SHELTERED SITES ❀ PROTECT FROM FROST OVER WINTER ❀ NO TOLERANCE TO FROST

☼ FULL SUN ☀ PARTIAL SUN ❀ FULL SHADE ◊ WELL-DRAINED SOIL ◗ MOIST SOIL ◆ WET SOIL

Helleborus argutifolius
Given the right conditions, this hellebore puts on a profuse display of pale green flowers with bold stamens, held above its sometimes prettily marbled leaves.
‡ 60cm (24in) ↔ 45cm (18in) ☼ ☀ ◗ ❀❀❀

Iris sibirica 'Butter and Sugar'
In early summer, this Siberian iris produces abundant large flowers with creamy-white standards and butter-yellow falls veined with green.
‡ 1m (3ft) ↔ indefinite ☼ ◗ ❀❀❀

Lamprocapnos spectabilis
The main charm of this plant is in the pretty pink heart-shaped flowers held on arching stems in spring, but the deeply divided leaves are also very attractive.
‡ 75cm (30in) ↔ 50cm (20in) ☀ ◊ ◗ ❀❀❀

Lupinus 'Chandelier'
From early to midsummer this lupin bears spires of bright yellow pea flowers. If deadheaded, it may sometimes bloom again in early autumn.
‡ 90cm (36in) ↔ 75cm (30in) ☼ ☀ ◊ ❀❀❀

Maianthemum racemosum
From late spring to midsummer, this plant bears conical spires of small, slightly scented white flowers on tall stems, followed by red berries.
‡ 90cm (36in) ↔ 45cm (18in) ☀ ❀ ◗ ❀❀❀

Paeonia cambessedesii
This peony bears single, deep rose-pink flowers in mid-spring, above attractive foliage; dark green above with purplish-red veins, stalks and under-surfaces.
‡↔ 55cm (22in) ☼ ◊ ❀❀

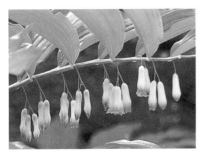

Polygonatum x hybridum
Small white tubular flowers hang from elegantly arching stems with glossy green oval leaves. This Solomon's seal is a superb plant for shady gardens.
‡ 1.2m (4ft) ↔ 1m (3ft) ❀ ◊ ❀❀❀

Primula x bulleesiana
A lovely hybrid candelabra primula, this plant produces flowers that are mainly terracotta in colour but may range from greyish-yellow to maroon.
‡↔ 60cm (24in) ☀ ◗ ❀❀❀

Pulmonaria 'Diana Clare'
A vigorous, densely clump-forming hybrid, 'Diana Clare' has beautiful silver-flushed lance-shaped foliage and bright purple-blue flowers.
‡ 30cm (12in) ↔ 45cm (18in) ☀ ❀ ◗ ❀❀❀

SPRING AND EARLY SUMMER PERENNIALS *CONTINUED*

Pulsatilla vulgaris
In spring, pasqueflower bears nodding
cup-shaped flowers in purple, pink or white
with bright yellow centres, held above
feathery, light green leaves.
↕↔ 23cm (9in) ☼ ◊ ❀❀❀

Rhodanthemum hosmariense
The yellow-centred white daisy flowers of
this subshrub make a great show from spring
through to autumn, growing from mounds of
ferny silver-grey leaves.
↕ 10–30cm (4–12in) ↔ 30cm (12in) ☼ ◊ ❀❀

***Saxifraga* Southside Seedling Group**
This mat-forming evergreen saxifrage
produces arching spires of white blooms
with strong red markings in late spring and
early summer.
↕ 30cm (12in) ↔ 20cm (8in) ☼ ◊ ❀❀❀

***Symphytum* x *uplandicum* 'Variegatum'**
Clump-forming, variegated comfrey is good
for ground cover in wild gardens, and has
large leaves with cream margins, and blue
or purple-blue tubular flowers.
↕ 1m (3ft) ↔ 60cm (24in) ☼ ◐ ◖ ❀❀❀

Tanacetum parthenium
Fast-growing feverfew is a short-lived
bushy perennial. It produces white flowers
in summer on upright stems, held above
richly aromatic foliage.
↕↔ 45cm (18in) ☼ ◊ ❀❀❀

ALSO RECOMMENDED

Achillea 'Fanal'

Anchusa azurea
  'Loddon Royalist'

Asphodeline lutea
  (Yellow asphodel)

Convallaria majalis
  (Lily of the valley)

Diascia personata

Epimedium 'Amber Queen'

Erysimum cheiri 'Blood Red'

Geranium macrorrhizum
  'Ingwersen's Variety'

Geum 'Bell Bank'

Heuchera species

Leucanthemum x *superbum*
  'Aglaia'

Lupinus 'The Chatelaine'

Meconopsis grandis
  (Himalayan blue poppy)

Papaver orientale
  (Oriental poppy)

Primula veris (Cowslip)

Ranunculus aconitifolius

Salvia x *sylvestris* 'Mainacht'

Trillium grandiflorum
  (Wake-robin)

Viola x *wittrockiana*
  Ultima Series

***Thalictrum aquilegiifolium* 'Thundercloud'**
From rounded leaflets of ferny foliage rise
tall stems with clusters of tiny mauve-pink
flowers in summer. The seedheads are
also attractive.
↕ 1m (3ft) ↔ 30cm (12in) ◐ ◖ ❀❀❀

***Trollius* x *cultorum* 'Alabaster'**
The globe-shaped, rich cream flowers of this
plant are borne on slender, upright stems in
spring above attractive, deeply divided
mid-green foliage.
↕ 60cm (24in) ↔ 45cm (18in) ☼ ◐ ◖ ◖ ❀❀❀

SUMMER AND AUTUMN PERENNIALS

Acanthus spinosus
This handsome clump-forming perennial makes a striking architectural presence in a border, with tall spikes of purple-hooded white tubular flowers.
‡ 1.2m (4ft) ↔ 60cm (24in) ☼ ◊ ✿✿✿

Achillea **'Paprika'**
A vigorous, tough variety of yarrow, this plant produces flat clusters of striking red flowers with yellow centres, held above the feathery mid-green leaves.
‡↔ 60cm (24in) ☼ ◊ ◑ ✿✿✿

Agapanthus **'Blue Giant'**
With exceptionally large flowerheads, 'Blue Giant' makes a strong statement with its deep blue, bell-shaped blooms held on tall, stiff stems in late summer.
‡ 1.2m (4ft) ↔ 60cm (24in) ☼ ◊ ✿✿

Anemone x hybrida
This group of Japanese anemones encompasses single, semi-double and double forms in white or pink; 'Honorine Jobert' is a popular single white.
‡ 1.2–1.5m (4–5ft) ↔ indefinite ☼ ◑ ◊ ✿✿✿

Aster amellus **'King George'**
From late summer to late autumn, this bushy perennial bears a profusion of large, daisy-like, violet-blue flowers with yellow centres, held in loose clusters.
‡↔ 50cm (20in) ◑ ◊ ✿✿✿

Astrantia major
Small greenish-white or pink-tinged flowers, produced over a long season, make a pretty display above massed divided, mid-green leaves.
‡ 60cm (24in) ↔ 45cm (18in) ☼ ◊ ✿✿✿

Delphinium **Blue Fountains Group**
These dwarf delphiniums form clumps of dark green divided foliage, from which rise dense spires of white-eyed flowers in shades of blue from pale to dark.
‡ 1m (3ft) ↔ 60cm (24in) ☼ ◊ ✿✿✿

Dianthus **'Bovey Belle'**
The bright pink double flowers of this modern pink are good for cutting as well as for colour in the border, offering a fragrance of cloves as a bonus.
‡ 45cm (18in) ↔ 40cm (16in) ☼ ◊ ✿✿✿

Echinops ritro **'Veitch's Blue'**
Round purplish-blue flowers resembling those of thistles are borne on tall stems in summer, with architectural interest provided by the spiny grey-green leaves.
‡ 1.2m (4ft) ↔ 75cm (30in) ☼ ◊ ✿✿✿

SUMMER AND AUTUMN PERENNIALS CONTINUED

Echinacea purpurea 'Magnus'
The purple-pink flowers of 'Magnus' have orange centres with the raised shape that gives the common name of coneflower to this genus of late-summer perennials.
↕↔ 60cm (24in) ☼ ◊ ◊ ✿✿✿

Eryngium x oliverianum
Large, rounded thistle-like heads in lavender blue are borne in late summer, a striking sight against the jagged-edged, mid-green leaves.
↕ 1m (3ft) ↔ 60cm (2ft) ☼ ◊ ✿✿✿

Geranium 'Nimbus'
This hardy geranium is prolific in flower, with large, violet-blue, saucer-shaped blooms produced all summer. It is compact, with finely divided foliage.
↕ 1m (3ft) ↔ 45cm (18in) ☼ ☀ ◊ ✿✿✿

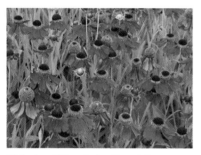

Helenium 'Moerheim Beauty'
The rich coppery-red daisy flowers of this plant appear in late summer, a time when the garden may begin to lack colour. Deadhead to prolong flowering.
↕ 1m (3ft) ↔ 60cm (2ft) ☼ ◊ ✿✿✿

Hemerocallis 'Buzz Bomb'
This lovely daylily has broad-petalled tawny flowers with yellow throats, appearing throughout the summer. The foliage is thick and strap-like.
↕↔ 60cm (24in) ☼ ◊ ◊ ✿✿✿

Kniphofia 'Bees' Sunset'
Tall spires of pale orange, tubular flowers rise from slender foliage, and bloom over a long season. This red hot poker is excellent for bold borders.
↕ 1m (3ft) ↔ 60cm (2ft) ☼ ☀ ◊ ◊ ✿✿✿

Monarda 'Cambridge Scarlet'
Like all bergamots, 'Cambridge Scarlet' is attractive to bees. It has vivid red spidery flowers and aromatic toothed foliage; given the right conditions, it spreads fast.
↕ 1m (3ft) ↔ 45cm (18in) ☼ ◊ ✿✿✿

Papaver orientale 'Cedric Morris'
This Oriental poppy bears large soft pink flowers with black centres above the grey divided leaves in May or June; many bloom again later in the summer.
↕↔ 90cm (36in) ☼ ◊ ✿✿✿

Penstemon 'Stapleford Gem'
One of the hardiest penstemons, this has multi-coloured flowers in pastel shades of pink, mauve, and purple, blooming from midsummer through to early autumn.
↕ 60cm (24in) ↔ 45cm (18in) ☼ ☀ ◊ ✿✿

❊❊❊ FULLY HARDY   ❊❊ HARDY IN MILD REGIONS/SHELTERED SITES   ❊ PROTECT FROM FROST OVER WINTER   ❊ NO TOLERANCE TO FROST

❊ FULL SUN   ❊ PARTIAL SUN   ❊ FULL SHADE   ◊ WELL-DRAINED SOIL   ◑ MOIST SOIL   ● WET SOIL

Perovskia 'Blue Spire'
With profuse spires of violet-blue flowers on white stems and aromatic, grey-green foliage, this is a beautiful subshrub that can find a place in many colour schemes.
‡ 1.2m (4ft) ↔ 1m (3ft) ❊ ◊ ❊❊❊

Persicaria bistorta 'Superba'
This vigorous, rapidly spreading plant produces tall spikes of small, tightly massed soft pink flowers, standing above clumps of broad green leaves.
‡ 75cm (30in) ↔ 60cm (24in) ❊ ❊ ◊ ◑ ❊❊❊

Phlox paniculata 'Eva Cullum'
Dense clusters of bright pink flowers with magenta eyes are produced on upright stems in midsummer; their strong fragrance is an added attraction.
‡ 1.2m (4ft) ↔ 60cm (2ft) ❊ ❊ ◊ ◑ ❊❊❊

Rudbeckia fulgida var. sullivantii
'Goldsturm' Bearing golden flowerheads with conical black centres on tall stems in late summer and autumn, 'Goldsturm' provides valuable colour in a border.
‡ 75cm (30in) ↔ 30cm (12in) ❊ ❊ ◊ ◑ ❊❊❊

Salvia x jamensis 'Hot Lips'
The showy red and white flowers of this variety provide bright colour through the summer. The small oval foliage is aromatic and may turn red in autumn.
‡↔ 75cm (30in) ❊ ◊ ❊❊

ALSO RECOMMENDED

Actaea simplex 'James Compton'

Agapanthus inapertus subsp. *pendulus* 'Graskop'

Anaphalis triplinervis 'Sommerschnee'

Aster x *frikartii* 'Mönch'

Centaurea pulcherrima

Cosmos atrosanguineus (Chocolate cosmos)

Galega x *hartlandii* 'Lady Wilson'

Gaura lindheimeri

Helianthus 'Lemon Queen'

Impatiens tinctoria

Kniphofia 'Percy's Pride'

Kniphofia 'Royal Standard'

Ligularia 'The Rocket'

Linaria triornithophora (Three birds toadflax)

Lobelia cardinalis 'Queen Victoria'

Persicaria amplexicaulis 'Firetail'

Potentilla 'Arc-en-ciel'

Romneya coulteri (Tree poppy)

Salvia patens

Thalictrum delavayi 'Hewitt's Double'

Verbascum 'Cotswold Queen'
This is a short-lived perennial that forms rosettes of grey-green foliage; tall stems bear soft apricot-buff flowers with a purplish eye throughout the summer.
‡ 1.2m (4ft) ↔ 30cm (12in) ❊ ◊ ❊❊❊

Verbena bonariensis
Though this is tall, the minimal presence of its slender stems and tiny blue-purple flowers make it ideal for the front of a border, framing smaller plants behind.
‡ 1.5m (5ft) ↔ 60cm (24in) ❊ ◊ ❊❊

PERENNIALS FOR WINTER INTEREST

Anaphalis triplinervis
Pearl everlasting bears clusters of tiny flowers in midsummer with papery white bracts. The flowers and foliage persist into winter and are good for drying.

↕ 90cm (36in) ↔ 60cm (24in) ☼ ❋ ◐ ◊ ❀❀❀

Arum italicum 'Marmoratum'
A truly exotic-looking plant whether in leaf, flower, or fruit. The glossy green leaves are veined with white, and spears of red berries appear in late autumn.

↕ 25cm (10in) ↔ 30cm (12in) ❋ ◊ ◐ ❀❀

Bergenia 'Ballawley'
This vigorous evergreen has large, dark green leaves flushed with red in winter. In spring, clusters of bright crimson flowers appear at the top of strong stems.

↕↔ 60cm (24in) ☼ ❋ ◊ ◐ ❀❀❀

Bergenia cordifolia 'Purpurea'
During late winter this bergenia bears magenta flowers. Its round green leaves turn reddish-purple in winter; the colour is most intense in very cold weather.

↕↔ 50cm (20in) ☼ ❋ ◊ ◐ ❀❀❀

Cynara cardunculus
The cardoon's silver, thistle-like foliage and purple flowerheads add a theatrical touch to the border; leave them on the plant for a structural feature over winter.

↕ 2m (6ft) ↔ 1m (3ft) ☼ ◊ ❀❀❀

Dianthus gratianopolitanus
A delightful perennial for the rock garden, the Cheddar pink forms an evergreen mat of grey-green leaves, and has scented flowers in early summer.

↕ 15cm (6in) ↔ 30cm (12in) ☼ ◊ ❀❀❀

Eryngium giganteum
Miss Willmott's ghost makes a dramatic addition to a sunny border with its ruffs of silver bracts. Its architectural flowerheads remain attractive into early winter.

↕ 1.2m (4ft) ↔ 30cm (12in) ☼ ◊ ❀❀❀

Helleborus niger
The Christmas rose has leathery, dark green leaves that remain green over winter. Large, white flowers appear in early winter and remain until early spring.

↕↔ 30cm (12in) ❋ ◐ ❀❀❀

Heuchera 'Plum Pudding'
Evergreen heucheras are useful for year-round foliage interest. This cultivar has purple leaves and its small white flowers are held aloft on thin stems in late spring.

↕ 50cm (20in) ↔ 30cm (12in) ❋ ◊ ❀❀❀

✷✷✷ FULLY HARDY   ✷✷ HARDY IN MILD REGIONS/SHELTERED SITES   ✷ PROTECT FROM FROST OVER WINTER   ✷ NO TOLERANCE TO FROST

☼ FULL SUN   ☼ PARTIAL SUN   ☀ FULL SHADE   ◊ WELL-DRAINED SOIL   ◑ MOIST SOIL   ◆ WET SOIL

Iris foetidissima
This iris really comes into its own when the seed pods ripen in autumn and split to reveal glistening orange seeds that remain in place until winter.
↕ 90cm (36in) ↔ indefinite ☼ ☀ ◊ ✷✷✷

Liriope muscari
Lily turf is a neat, spreading perennial that flowers from late summer to late autumn. The evergreen foliage makes good ground cover that endures the winter.
↕ 30cm (12in) ↔ 45cm (18in) ☼ ☀ ◊ ◑ ✷✷✷

Miscanthus sinensis 'Gracillimus'
This elegant grass has narrow arching leaves and silky flowerheads that turn from white to purple-brown; it retains a graceful presence throughout winter.
↕ 1.2m (4ft) ↔ 45cm (1½ft) ☼ ◊ ✷✷

Monarda 'Beauty of Cobham'
Flowering during late summer and early autumn, this bergamot bears crowded heads of pink flowers, with purple bracts that turn a warm brown in winter.
↕ 90cm (36in) ↔ 45cm (18in) ☼ ☀ ◊ ◑ ✷✷✷

Ophiopogon planiscapus 'Nigrescens'
Few plants are as deeply coloured as this small evergreen, black-leaved perennial. It provides a useful contrast in schemes where grasses predominate.
↕ 23cm (9in) ↔ 30cm (12in) ☼ ☀ ◊ ◑ ✷✷✷

Phlomis russeliana
The pale yellow, hooded flowers of this sage-like plant appear throughout summer. During winter the tall stems carry dense brown, spherical seedheads.
↕ 1m (3ft) ↔ 60cm (2ft) ☼ ◊ ✷✷✷

Sedum 'Matrona'
Purple leaves and dark red stems form a backdrop to the flattened heads of tiny pink flowers in summer. The dried flowerheads add structure to the winter garden.
↕ 75cm (30in) ↔ 45cm (18in) ☼ ◊ ✷✷✷

Viola x wittrockiana Universal Series
Winter pansies are among the most prolific of all winter-flowering plants. The colour range includes yellow, blue, mauve, maroon, red, and white.
↕ ↔ 20cm (8in) ☼ ◊ ◑ ✷✷✷

ALSO RECOMMENDED

Achillea filipendulina
  (Fern-leaf yarrow)

Chasmanthium latifolium
  (Northern sea oats)

Dianella caerulea Cassa Blue

Echinops ritro (Globe thistle)

Helleborus x hybridus
  (Lenten Rose)

Helleborus odorus

Iris unguicularis

Ophiopogon japonicus (Lily turf)

Stipa tenuissima (Feather grass)

WATER AND BOG PLANTS

Astilbe 'Willie Buchanan'
This cultivar produces a haze of pink in
midsummer, when its tiny white flowers with
red stamens are borne on fine, branching
flower stems.
‡ 30cm (12in) ↔ 20cm (8in) ☼ ◐ ❀❀❀ ∼

Butomus umbellatus
The flowering rush has narrow leaves that
are bronze when young. Pink, fragrant late-
summer flowers are borne on long stems.
‡ 1m (3ft) ↔ indefinite ☼ ❀❀❀ ≈
⊥ 5–15cm (2–6in)

Caltha palustris
Marsh marigolds bring colour to pond
margins with intense yellow, cup-shaped
blooms in late spring. Grow in baskets.
‡ 60cm (24in) ↔ 45cm (18in) ☼ ◐ ❀❀❀
≈ ⊥ at water level

Darmera peltata
The umbrella plant bears heads of white to
pink flowers on long stems in late spring. The
large, round leaves gradually turn red in
autumn before dying down.
‡ 1.2m (4ft) ↔ indefinite ☼ ◐ ❀❀❀ ∼

Euphorbia palustris
This spurge makes an unusual waterside
plant. Strong stems are covered with narrow,
lime-green leaves, topped in early summer
by clusters of light green flowers.
‡↔ 90cm (36in) ☼ ❀❀❀ ∼

Filipendula rubra 'Venusta'
The meadowsweet needs space to spread.
Green jagged leaves sit below wiry stems
bearing a frothy display of deep rose-
pink flowers in summer.
‡ 2.5m (8ft) ↔ 1.2m (4ft) ☼ ◐ ❀❀❀ ∼

Glyceria maxima var. variegata
A handsome perennial grass, suitable
for the water's edge, with strap-shaped,
cream-striped leaves that are tinged shades
of pink in spring and autumn.
‡ 80cm (30in) ↔ indefinite ☼ ❀❀❀ ∼

Iris sibirica 'Perry's Blue'
The mid-blue flowers with rust-coloured
veins of this traditional cultivar appear in
early summer and brighten the edges of
small ponds and damp borders.
‡ 1m (3ft) ↔ 60cm (24in) ☼ ❀❀❀ ∼

Ligularia 'The Rocket'
A plant of contrasts with jet black flower
stems and bright yellow flowers that emerge
through a carpet of leaves in late summer; a
must for larger gardens.
‡ 2m (6ft) ↔ 1.1m (3½ft) ☼ ◐ ❀❀❀ ∼

❋❋❋ FULLY HARDY　　❋❋ HARDY IN MILD REGIONS/SHELTERED SITES　　❋ PROTECT FROM FROST OVER WINTER　　❂ NO TOLERANCE TO FROST

☼ FULL SUN　　◑ PARTIAL SUN　　● FULL SHADE　　~ BOG PLANT　　≈ MARGINAL PLANT　　≋ AQUATIC PLANT　　⊥ PLANTING DEPTH

Myosotis scorpioides
The tiny blooms of the water forget-me-not have white, pink, or yellow eyes and appear in early summer.
‡ 45cm (18in) ↔ indefinite ☼ ◑ ❋❋❋ ⊥ at water level

Nymphaea 'Froebelii'
Tiny burgundy-red flowers with golden stamens open amid dark green leaves; a perfect water lily for small ponds.
↔ 75cm (30in) ☼ ❋❋❋ ≋
⊥ 30–45cm (12–18in)

Pontederia cordata
The pickerel weed is a pretty plant with bright green, lance-shaped leaves and spikes of starry blue flowers in summer.
‡ 0.9–1.3m (3–4½ft) ↔ 60–75cm (24–30in)
☼ ❋❋❋ ≈ ⊥ 30cm (12in)

Primula beesiana
A semi-evergreen candelabra primula with vivid, magenta spherical flowerheads that appear at intervals up the light green stems during summer.
‡↔ 60cm (24in) ◑ ❋❋❋ ~

Rodgersia pinnata 'Superba'
The young bronze leaves of this plant mature to dark green with distinctive veins. In late summer, clusters of bright pink flowers reach above the foliage.
‡ 1.2m (4ft) ↔ 75cm (30in) ☼ ◑ ❋❋❋ ~

Typha minima
Ideal for small ponds, this perennial has narrow leaves, which are joined in late summer by cylindrical flower spikes.
‡ 75cm (30in) ↔ 45cm (18in) ☼ ❋❋❋
⊥ 30cm (12in)

Zantedeschia aethiopica
The arum lily brings style to bog gardens. Large pure white flowers, which gleam against the green foliage, open from late spring through to midsummer.
‡↔ 90cm (36in) ☼ ❋❋ ≈ ⊥ 15cm (6in)

ALSO RECOMMENDED

Actaea simplex
 (Atropurpurea Group) 'Brunette'

Aruncus dioicus 'Kneiffii'
 (Goatsbeard)

Astilbe 'Fanal'

Cardamine pratensis
 (Lady's smock)

Eupatorium purpureum
 (Joe Pye weed)

Gunnera manicata

Hottonia palustris (Water violet)

Hydrocharis morsus-ranae
 (Frogbit)

Iris sibirica 'Butter and Sugar'

Kirengeshoma palmata

Matteuccia struthiopteris
 (Ostrich fern)

Nymphaea '**Gonnère**' (Water lily)

Nymphaea 'Marliacea
 Chromatella' (Water lily)

Nymphoides peltata (Water fringe)

Primula alpicola

Primula 'Inverewe'

Rheum palmatum
 'Atrosanguineum'

Sanguisorba canadensis
 (Canadian burnet)

PLANTS FOR SCENT

Cosmos atrosanguineus
The chocolate cosmos is a beautiful spreading perennial that bears cup-shaped, chocolate-scented, dark maroon velvety flowers in late summer.
‡ 60cm (24in) ↔ 45cm (18in) ☼ ◊ ◖ ❀❀

***Daphne* x *burkwoodii* 'Somerset'**
A small semi-evergreen shrub, this daphne bears clusters of highly scented, white and pink flowers in late spring, and sometimes again in autumn.
‡↔ 1.5m (5ft) ☼ ◊ ❀❀❀

***Dianthus* 'Becky Robinson'**
This modern pink bears clove-scented, red-bordered, rose-pink blooms above strappy grey-green foliage in summer. Deadhead regularly to promote flowering.
‡ to 45cm (18in) ↔ 40cm (16in) ☼ ◊ ❀❀❀

***Erysimum cheiri* 'Orange Bedder'**
Wallflowers are short-lived evergreen perennials. This variety flowers from late spring to midsummer, bearing brilliant orange, scented flowers.
‡↔ 30cm (12in) ☼ ◊ ❀❀❀

***Hamamelis* x *intermedia* 'Arnold Promise'**
In late winter, this witch hazel is a welcome sight with a profusion of spidery, yellow, fragrant flowers blooming on its bare, upright branches.
‡↔ 4m (12ft) ☼ ☀ ◊ ◖ ❀❀❀

***Jasminum officinale* 'Argenteovariegatum'**
This climbing jasmine has cream-edged, green leaves. The sweetly scented, pure white flowers appear in clusters throughout the summer.
‡ 12m (40ft) ☼ ☀ ◊ ❀❀

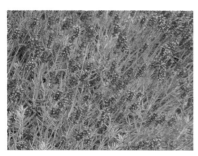

***Lavandula angustifolia* 'Hidcote'**
This compact lavender with thin, silvery-green leaves and spikes of dark purple, fragrant flowers in summer is an evergreen shrub that is useful for edging.
‡ 60cm (24in) ↔ 75cm (30in) ☼ ◊ ❀❀❀

***Lilium* 'Star Gazer'**
Both the colour and the perfume of this Oriental lily attract attention. The upward-facing, pink and white flowers with speckled petals appear in summer.
‡ 1–1.5m (3–5ft) ↔ 25cm (10in) ☼ ◊ ❀❀❀

***Lonicera periclymenum* 'Belgica'**
Early Dutch honeysuckle is a vigorous climber that bears fragrant, tubular flowers in spring and again in summer, followed by bright red berries in autumn.
‡ 7m (22ft) ☼ ☀ ◊ ◖ ❀❀❀

✹✹✹ FULLY HARDY   ✹✹ HARDY IN MILD REGIONS/SHELTERED SITES   ✹ PROTECT FROM FROST OVER WINTER   ✹ NO TOLERANCE TO FROST

☼ FULL SUN   ◐ PARTIAL SUN   ✴ FULL SHADE   ◌ WELL-DRAINED SOIL   ◖ MOIST SOIL   ◗ WET SOIL

Mahonia x media 'Charity'
A beautiful architectural shrub with spiny, dark green leaves. From late autumn to early spring it bears spikes of strongly fragrant, lemon yellow flowers.
‡ 5m (15ft) ↔ 4m (12ft) ☼ ◌ ✹✹

Melissa officinalis 'Aurea'
Lemon balm is a perennial with small white flowers that are attractive to bees. The leaves are splashed with gold and smell strongly of lemons when crushed.
‡ 1.2m (48in) ↔ 45cm (18in) ☼ ◌ ✹✹✹

Philadelphus x lemoinei
The arching shoots of this mock orange are smothered in small, deliciously fragrant, creamy-white flowers from early to midsummer.
‡ 1.5m (5ft) ↔ 3m (10ft) ☼ ◌ ✹✹✹

Rosa Gertrude Jekyll
This hardy shrub rose is grown for its deep pink flowers, which are extremely fragrant and start to appear in early summer. Deadhead regularly.
‡ 2m (6ft) ↔ 1.2m (4ft) ☼ ◌ ◗ ✹✹✹

Sarcococca hookeriana var. digyna
Winter-flowering Christmas box has slender, evergreen leaves, and is prized for its honey-scented, white flowers, which are followed by black fruit.
‡ 75cm (2½ft) ↔ 1.5m (5ft) ◐ ◗ ✹✹

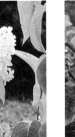

Syringa vulgaris 'Madame Florent Stepman' An upright lilac with heart-shaped, dark green leaves, which bears spikes of large, sweetly scented, single white flowers in late spring.
‡↔ 6m (20ft) ☼ ◌ ✹✹✹

Viburnum x burkwoodii 'Anne Russell'
This semi-evergreen shrub bears clusters of intensely fragrant white flowers from mid- to late spring. Plant it near to a pathway to make the most of its scent.
‡↔ 1.5m (5ft) ☼ ✴ ◌ ◗ ✹✹✹

ALSO RECOMMENDED

Azara microphylla

Chimonanthus praecox
   (Wintersweet)

Galium odoratum
   (Sweet woodruff)

Hemerocallis lilioasphodelus
   (Day lily)

Hyacinthus orientalis

Jasminum humile
   (Yellow jasmine)

Lathyrus odoratus (Sweet pea)

Lavandula stoechas subsp.
   stoechas f. *rosea* 'Kew Red'
   (French lavender)

Lonicera etrusca 'Michael Rosse'
   (Etruscan honeysuckle)

Matthiola incana (Gilliflower)

Mentha suaveolens 'Variegata'
   (Pineapple mint)

Narcissus tazetta

Nicotiana sylvestris

Nymphaea 'Blue Beauty'
   (Water lily)

Ornithogalum arabicum

Rosa The Pilgrim ('Auswalker')

Salvia officinalis (Common sage)

Salvia rosmarinus
   (Rosemary)

Wisteria sinensis 'Prolific'

SHRUBS FOR WALLS

Abelia x grandiflora
A semi-evergreen shrub with glossy, dark green leaves and an abundance of pink-flushed white flowers in summer. Best against a sunny wall in colder areas.
‡ 3m (10ft) ↔ 4m (12ft) ☼ ◊ ◊ ❀❀

Acacia dealbata
Mimosa is a fast-growing tree with silvery-green foliage and bright yellow, scented flowers that bring a bit of Australian sunshine into the garden in early spring.
‡↔ 15m (50ft) ☼ ◊ ❀❀

Buddleja crispa
The sweetly scented lilac summer flowers of this bushy shrub are highly attractive to bees and butterflies. It bears white woolly shoots and greyish-green leaves.
‡↔ 3m (10ft) ☼ ◊ ◊ ❀❀

Carpenteria californica
The tree anemone is an evergreen shrub with glossy, dark green leaves that bears large, fragrant white flowers with showy yellow stamens in summer.
‡↔ 2m (6ft) ☼ ◊ ❀❀

Ceanothus 'Concha'
A dense, evergreen, glossy-leaved shrub. Masses of purple buds appear in late spring that open up to dark blue flowers. A good choice for a sunny wall or fence.
‡↔ 3m (10ft) ☼ ◊ ◊ ❀❀

Chaenomeles speciosa 'Moerloosei'
Ornamental quinces can be trained against a shaded wall or fence. This variety bears clusters of white flowers, flushed pink, in early summer.
‡ 2.5m (8ft) ↔ 5m (15ft) ☼ ☼ ◊ ◊ ❀❀❀

Crinodendron hookerianum
The lantern tree is an upright, evergreen shrub, so called because of its large, scarlet to carmine-red flowers, which hang from upright shoots in late spring.
‡ 6m (20ft) ↔ 5m (15ft) ☼ ◊ ◊ ❀❀

Cytisus battandieri
The pineapple broom bears bright yellow, upright, pineapple-scented flowers from early to midsummer, above greyish-green leaves. It does best against a warm wall.
‡↔ 5m (15ft) ☼ ◊ ❀❀

Daphne odora 'Aureomarginata'
This evergreen shrub bears clusters of purple-pink and white fragrant flowers from midwinter to early spring, among yellow-edged green leaves.
‡↔ 1.5m (5ft) ☼ ◊ ◊ ❀❀

❀❀❀ FULLY HARDY   ❀❀ HARDY IN MILD REGIONS/SHELTERED SITES   ❀ PROTECT FROM FROST OVER WINTER   ❀ NO TOLERANCE TO FROST

☼ FULL SUN   ☼ PARTIAL SUN   ❋ FULL SHADE   ◊ WELL-DRAINED SOIL   ◐ MOIST SOIL   ● WET SOIL

Fremontodendron 'California Glory'
This vigorous shrub grows best against a warm, south-facing wall. It bears an abundance of bright yellow flowers between late spring and autumn.
↕ 6m (20ft) ↔ 4m (12ft) ☼ ◊ ◐ ❀❀

Garrya elliptica
The silk tassel bush bears waxy, dark green leaves and between midwinter and late spring, male plants bear dangling grey catkins up to 20cm (8in) in length.
↕↔ 4m (12ft) ☼ ☼ ◊ ◐ ❀❀

Jasminum humile
Yellow jasmine is a bushy, evergreen shrub that bears bright yellow flowers between early spring and late autumn. It flowers best against a warm wall.
↕ 2.5m (8ft) ↔ 3m (10ft) ☼ ☼ ◊ ◐ ❀❀❀

Myrtus communis subsp. tarentina
Ideal for hedging, evergreen myrtle has a long season of interest: its fragrant white flowers, borne between spring and summer, are followed by white berries.
↕↔ 1.5m (5ft) ☼ ◊ ◐ ❀❀

Pyracantha 'Golden Charmer'
The bright orange berries of this spiny shrub provide striking autumn interest and are a useful food source for birds. It also bears white flowers in summer.
↕↔ 3m (10ft) ☼ ☼ ◊ ◐ ❀❀❀

ALSO RECOMMENDED

Abutilon megapotamicum

Acca sellowiana
(Pineapple guava)

Acradenia frankliniae

Azara serrata

Ceanothus arboreus
'Trewithen Blue'

Cestrum elegans

Chaenomeles x *superba* 'Crimson and Gold' (Japanese quince)

Dendromecon rigida

Desfontainia spinosa

Drimys lanceolata
(Mountain pepper)

Eriobotrya japonica (Loquat)

Fabiana imbricata f. *violacea*

Forsythia suspensa
(Golden bells)

Grevillea 'Canberra Gem'

Hydrangea anomala subsp.
petiolaris

Itea ilicifolia

Piptanthus nepalensis
(Evergreen laburnum)

Prostanthera cuneata
(Alpine mint bush)

Prostanthera rotundifolia 'Rosea'

Pyracantha 'Mohave'

Ribes speciosum

Stachyurus chinensis 'Joy Forever'
In spring, this deciduous shrub bears dangling clusters of yellow flowers; the leaves which later develop are gold-variegated. It prefers an acid soil.
↕ 2m (6ft) ↔ 4m (12ft) ☼ ☼ ◊ ◐ ❀❀❀

Vestia foetida
From mid-spring to midsummer this upright, evergreen shrub bears hanging clusters of pale yellow flowers. Its glossy dark green leaves are also attractive.
↕ 2m (6ft) ↔ 1.5m (5ft) ☼ ◊ ❀❀

CLIMBERS FOR SHADE

Climbers suitable for cold or shady north- or east-facing walls are those that naturally grow in shade or semi-shade – many of these can become "stressed" and vulnerable to pests if they receive too much hot midday sun. It is important to select suitable plants as the flowers and foliage will suffer in the wrong conditions. Shade-tolerant plants prefer moist soils so when planting, dig in plenty of organic matter, such as leafmould, to improve the soil structure. Position young plants at least 45cm (18in) from the base of the wall to avoid the driest soil.

CLIMBING PLANTS

Aconitum hemsleyanum

Asteranthera ovata

Celastrus orbiculatus
  (Oriental bittersweet)

Celastrus scandens
  (American bittersweet)

Clematis 'Carnaby'

Clematis 'Helsingborg'

Clematis 'Henryi'

Clematis 'Minuet'

Clematis montana

Clematis 'Niobe'

Clematis 'Venosa Violacea'

Codonopsis clematidea

Codonopsis convolvulacea

Dactylicapnos scandens

Ercilla volubilis

Forsythia suspensa (Golden bells)

Hedera algeriensis
  'Gloire de Marengo'
  (Algerian ivy)

Hedera colchica 'Dentata'
  (Bullock's heart ivy)

Hedera colchica 'Sulphur Heart'
  (Sulphur heart ivy)

Hedera helix 'Goldheart'

Itea ilicifolia

Lapageria rosea
  (Chilean bellflower)

Lonicera japonica 'Aureoreticulata'

Lonicera japonica 'Halliana'
  (Japanese honeysuckle)

Muehlenbeckia complexa

Parthenocissus henryana
  (Chinese Virginia creeper)

Rosa 'Albéric Barbier'

Rosa 'Danse du Feu'

Rosa Händel

Rosa 'Mermaid'

Schisandra chinensis

Schizophragma hydrangeoides

Vitis amurensis (Amur grape)

***Akebia quinata* (Chocolate vine)**

Ampelopsis brevipedunculata

***Berberidopsis corallina* (Coral plant)**

Clematis montana* var. *rubens

Clematis **'Nelly Moser'**

Parthenocissus tricuspidata
(Boston ivy)

Hydrangea anomala subsp. *petiolaris*
(Climbing hydrangea)

Pileostegia viburnoides

Lonicera periclymenum **'Serotina'**
(Honeysuckle)

Schisandra rubriflora

Schizophragma integrifolium

Trachelospermum jasminoides
(Star jasmine)

Vitis coignetiae

CLIMBERS FOR SUN

Sun-loving climbers will thrive in the warm, sheltered conditions provided by south- and west-facing walls or fences. Many marginally hardy climbers will fruit or flower better if grown in these conditions, as the wall will absorb the sun's heat during the day and store it, acting like a radiator. However, walls that face the sun are often at risk of producing very dry conditions, so plant climbers at least 45cm (18in) from the base of the wall to avoid the driest soil, and dig in organic matter to encourage the soil to retain as much moisture as possible.

CLIMBING PLANTS

Akebia trifoliata

Clematis 'Bill MacKenzie'

Clematis cirrhosa var.
 purpurascens 'Freckles'

Clematis 'Étoile Violette'

Clematis 'Jackmanii'

Clematis 'Lasurstern'

Clematis rehderiana

Clematis 'The President'

Jasminum officinale
 'Argenteovariegatum'
 (Common jasmine)

Jasminum x stephanense

Hardenbergia violacea
 (Purple coral pea)

Lonicera x italica (Honeysuckle)

Lonicera x tellmanniana
 (Honeysuckle)

Parthenocissus tricuspidata
 'Veitchii' (Virginia creeper)

Passiflora caerulea
 'Constance Eliot' (Blue passion flower)

Rosa 'Compassion'

Rosa filipes 'Kiftsgate'

Rosa 'Gloire de Dijon'

Rosa 'Golden Showers'

Rosa 'Madame Alfred Carrière'

Rosa 'Maigold'

Solanum laxum (Potato vine)

Tecoma capensis
 (Cape honeysuckle)

Thunbergia alata
 (Black-eyed Susan)

Trachelospermum asiaticum

Vitis 'Brant'

Vitis davidii

Vitis vinifera 'Purpurea'

Wisteria floribunda 'Alba'
 (Japanese wisteria)

Wisteria sinensis 'Prolific'
 (Chinese wisteria)

Actinidia kolomikta

Eccremocarpus scaber
(Chilean glory flower)

Campsis x tagliabuana
'Madame Galen'

Clematis armandii

Humulus lupulus 'Aureus'
(Golden hop)

Ipomoea purpurea (Common morning glory)

Parthenocissus quinquefolia
(Virginia creeper)

Rosa banksiae 'Lutea'

Passiflora caerulea
(Blue passion flower)

Solanum crispum 'Glasnevin'
(Potato tree)

Rhodochiton atrosanguineus

Tropaeolum speciosum (Flame creeper)

Wisteria brachybotrys 'Shiro-kapitan'

SCREENING AND HEDGING PLANTS

Hedges and plant screens can be used to define the garden or areas within it, and also to provide wind protection or shelter. The plants you choose for screening or hedging need to fit your garden's design and be resilient enough to withstand the forces of wind and weather – check that they will grow tall enough to do the job required. Fast-growing types are useful for quick results, but will result in a hedge that needs frequent clipping. Bamboos and grasses are worth considering as an attractive alternative to a traditional hedge.

TREES

Arbutus unedo (Strawberry tree)

Chamaecyparis lawsoniana (Lawson's cypress)

Juniperus communis (Common juniper)

Nothofagus dombeyi

Olea europaeua (Olive)

Populus x canadensis 'Robusta' (Canadian poplar)

Prunus lusitanica (Laurel)

Umbellularia californica (Californian laurel)

SHRUBS

Berberis thunbergii f. atropurpurea 'Rose Glow'

Buxus sempervirens 'Suffruticosa' (Dwarf box)

Cotoneaster salicifolius

Elaeagnus umbellata

Escallonia 'Donard Beauty'

Euonymus japonicus 'Macrophyllus' (Japanese spindle)

Forsythia x intermedia

Griselinia littoralis (Broadleaf)

Hibiscus rosa-sinensis (Chinese hibiscus)

Leptospermum scoparium (Manuka)

Ligustrum ovalifolium

Pyracantha 'Watereri'

Rhododendron 'Loderi King George'

Rhododendron 'Furnivall's Daughter'

Rosa gallica 'Versicolor'

Tamarix ramosissima

Viburnum tinus 'Eve Price'

GRASSES AND BAMBOOS

Arundo donax (Giant reed)

Chimonobambusa tumidissinoda

Cortaderia selloana 'Sunningdale Silver' (Pampas grass)

Fargesia nitida (Fountain bamboo)

Miscanthus sinensis

Phyllostachys flexuosa

Pseudosasa japonica

Semiarundinaria fastuosa (Narihira bamboo)

SHRUB: *Aucuba japonica* **'Gold Dust'** **(Spotted laurel)**

SHRUB: *Berberis darwinii*

TREE: *Carpinus betulus* **(Common hornbeam)**

SHRUB: *Cotoneaster lacteus*

TREE: *Crataegus laevigata* **'Paul's Scarlet' (Hawthorn)**

SHRUB: *Hydrangea paniculata*
'Floribunda'

SHRUB: *Ilex aquifolium* 'Madame Briot'
(Holly)

SHRUB: *Ligustrum obtusifolium*
(Privet)

SHRUB: *Lonicera nitida*
'Baggesen's Gold' (Honeysuckle)

TREE: *Laurus nobilis* (Bay laurel)

SHRUB: *Photinia* x *fraseri*
'Red Robin'

SHRUB: *Pittosporum tenuifolium*
'Abbotsbury Gold' (Kohuhu)

SHRUB: *Rhododendron* 'Hydon Dawn'

TREE: *Taxus baccata* (Yew)

ROCK PLANTS

Campanula cochlearifolia
Masses of pale blue or white bell-shaped flowers adorn this dwarf campanula in midsummer – the toothed, bright green leaves form rosettes beneath them.
‡ 8cm (3in) ↔ indefinite ☼ ◑ ◊ ❆❆❆

Convolvulus sabatius
This trailing plant produces its trumpet-shaped, bright lavender-blue flowers from summer to autumn, set against small, mid-green oval leaves.
‡ 20cm (8in) ↔ 30cm (12in) ☼ ◊ ❆❆

***Dianthus* 'Pike's Pink'**
Fragrant, pink, double flowers are produced in summer; the evergreen foliage is grey-green and spiky, forming compact cushions.
‡↔ 10cm (4in) ☼ ◊ ❆❆❆

***Diascia* 'Salmon Supreme'**
This trailing herbaceous perennial bears spikes of salmon-pink tubular flowers rising from heart-shaped green foliage in summer and through to autumn.
‡ 15cm (6in) ↔ 50cm (20in) ☼ ◊ ❆❆

Erigeron karvinskianus
A carpeting perennial with grey-green foliage and daisy-like summer flowers in white or pink, ageing to purple, this plant spreads freely once it is established.
‡ 10–15cm (4–6in) ↔ indefinite ☼ ◊ ❆❆❆

Erinus alpinus
In late spring and summer, small purple or pink flowers are profusely borne on this semi-evergreen perennial. It is short-lived but self-seeds freely.
‡↔ 5–8cm (2–3in) ☼ ◊ ❆❆❆

***Erysimum* 'Bredon'**
Clusters of bright yellow flowers, highly attractive to beneficial insects, are produced from spring to summer on a bushy, semi-evergreen perennial plant.
‡↔ 45cm (18in) ☼ ◊ ❆❆❆

Gentiana verna
This evergreen perennial produces small rosettes of dark green leaves. In early spring, bright blue flowers with white centres are borne on short stems.
‡↔ 5cm (2in) ☼ ◊ ❆❆❆

***Hebe pinguifolia* 'Pagei'**
Evergreen oval blue-green leaves are carried on purple stems, against which the abundant clusters of white flowers stand out in summer.
‡ 30cm (12in) ↔ 90cm (36in) ☼ ◑ ◊ ◊ ❆❆❆

Helianthemum apenninum
Saucer-shaped white flowers with bright yellow stamens are borne on this shrub in midsummer. The stems and evergreen leaves are covered with white down.
↕↔ 45cm (18in) ☼ ◊ ❀❀❀

Phlox bifida
Masses of slender-petalled, star-shaped, lilac or white flowers appear in summer, smothering the mound-forming stems and evergreen leaves.
↕ 10–15cm (4–6in) ↔ 15cm (6in) ☼ ◊ ❀❀❀

Saponaria ocymoides
Tumbling Ted forms a sprawling carpet of soft, hairy leaves, above which masses of tiny pale pink flowers appear in summer. Excellent for a dry bank.
↕ to 8cm (3in) ↔ 40cm (16in) ☼ ◊ ❀❀❀

Saxifraga 'Hindhead Seedling'
This low-growing evergreen perennial has slender, spiky, blue-green foliage; in spring it bears open cup-shaped pale yellow flowers with bright yellow stamens.
↕ 2.5cm (1in) ↔ 8cm (3in) ❀ ◊ ❀❀❀

Scabiosa lucida
A clump-forming dwarf perennial with finely cut, grey-green leaves, this pretty scabious bears lavender-blue pincushion flowers from late spring to summer.
↕ 20cm (8in) ↔ 15cm (6in) ☼ ◊ ❀❀❀

Sempervivum tectorum
Rosettes of broad, pointed leaves are tipped with purple, sometimes turning purple-red in summer. The star-shaped reddish-purple flowers bloom in summer.
↕ 10–15cm (4–6in) ↔ 20cm (8in) ☼ ◊ ❀❀❀

Thymus 'Bressingham'
A compact, carpeting, scented thyme, 'Bressingham' has small, hairy, grey-green leaves and bears clear pink flowers from early to midsummer.
↕ 3cm (1¼in) ↔ 12cm (5in) ☼ ◊ ❀❀❀

ALSO RECOMMENDED

Anchusa caespitosa

Androsace sempervivoides

Aquilegia alpina (Alpine columbine)

Armeria maritima 'Vindictive' (Sea thrift)

Aster alpinus

Aubrieta 'Purple Charm'

Calceolaria arachnoidea

Crambe maritima (Sea kale)

Daphne jasminea

Daphne petraea 'Grandiflora'

Dianthus alpinus (Alpine pink)

Draba mollissima

Draba rigida

Gentiana acaulis (Stemless gentian)

Geranium orientalitibeticum

Lewisia 'George Henley'

Lithodora oleifolia

Osteospermum jucundum

Penstemon newberryi f. humilior

Potentilla 'Gibson's Scarlet'

Saxifraga 'Jenkinsiae'

Saxifraga scardica

Sisyrinchium 'E.K. Balls'

Vitaliana primuliflora

SPRING-FLOWERING SHRUBS

Abeliophyllum distichum
The white forsythia bears clusters of white, fragrant flowers in early spring; it blooms more freely grown against a sunny wall. Its dark green leaves turn purple in autumn.
↕↔ 1.5m (4ft) ☼ ◊ ❀❀❀

Berberis julianae
Ideal as a screen, this evergreen shrub has glossy, deep green leaves. From spring to summer, clusters of scented yellow flowers appear, followed by blue-black fruits.
↕↔ 3m (10ft) ☼ ☀ ◊ ❀❀❀

Camellia x williamsii 'Donation'
This evergreen, shade-loving shrub bears semi-double, rich pink blooms through mid- and late spring. It requires acid soil and is suitable for growing in a large pot.
↕ 5m (15ft) ↔ 2.5m (8ft) ☀ ◊ ◑ ❀❀❀

Ceanothus thyrsiflorus 'Skylark'
This bushy shrub with glossy green leaves bears a profusion of deep blue flowers in late spring. In cold areas it benefits from the protection of a warm wall.
↕ 2m (6ft) ↔ 1.5m (5ft) ☼ ◊ ❀❀

Chaenomeles x superba 'Pink Lady'
In early spring, clusters of deep, rose-pink flowers appear on the bare branches of this showy Japanese quince, followed in autumn by apple-shaped, yellow fruits.
↕ 1.5m (5ft) ↔ 2m (6ft) ☼ ☀ ◊ ❀❀❀

Corylopsis sinensis var. sinensis 'Spring Purple'
This shrub bears hanging clusters of yellow flowers that will brighten up the garden in spring. It produces purple foliage that develops to green with age.
↕↔ 4m (12ft) ☀ ◑ ❀❀❀

Cytisus x praecox 'Allgold'
This ornamental broom is smothered by a mass of pea-like, golden-yellow flowers from mid- to late spring. Its tiny, silky, grey-green leaves are borne on arching stems.
↕ 1.2m (4ft) ↔ 1.5m (5ft) ☼ ◊ ❀❀❀

Daphne cneorum
A low-growing, trailing shrub with clusters of scented, rose-pink flowers in late spring; position to make the most of its fragrance. The leaves are leathery and dark green.
↕ 23cm (9in) ↔ 2m (6ft) ☼ ◊ ❀❀❀

Erica arborea var. alpina
This tree heath is an upright shrub, densely clothed with honey-scented, white flowers from late winter to late spring. The dark green, needle-like leaves are evergreen.
↕ 2m (6ft) ↔ 85cm (34in) ☼ ◊ ❀❀❀

❀❀❀ FULLY HARDY   ❀❀ HARDY IN MILD REGIONS/SHELTERED SITES   ❀ PROTECT FROM FROST OVER WINTER   ❀ NO TOLERANCE TO FROST

☼ FULL SUN   ☼ PARTIAL SUN   ☀ FULL SHADE   ◊ WELL-DRAINED SOIL   ◖ MOIST SOIL   ● WET SOIL

Exochorda x macrantha 'The Bride'
Pure white, showy, saucer-shaped flowers on arching branches cover this spreading evergreen shrub in late spring. It is ideal for growing as a specimen plant.
‡ 2m (6ft) ↔ 3m (10ft) ☼ ☼ ◊ ◖ ❀❀❀

Forsythia x intermedia 'Lynwood'
A vigorous, deciduous shrub with upright stems that arch slightly at the tips. An abundance of bright golden-yellow flowers appear on bare branches in early spring.
‡↔ 3m (10ft) ☼ ☼ ◊ ❀❀❀

Fothergilla major
Bearing spikes of bottlebrush-like, fragrant white flowers in late spring, this slow-growing shrub is also valued for its blaze of orange, yellow, and red autumn leaves.
‡↔ 6m (20ft) ☼ ◖ ❀❀❀

Kolkwitzia amabilis 'Pink Cloud'
The beauty bush is a deciduous shrub with an arching habit. Bell-shaped pink flowers with yellow flushed throats are borne in profusion from late spring to early summer.
‡ 3m (10ft) ↔ 4m (12ft) ☼ ◊ ❀❀❀

Magnolia stellata
The star magnolia bears pure white, or pink-flushed, star-shaped flowers in early spring, before the leaves emerge. Spring frosts may damage early blooms.
‡ 3m (10ft) ↔ 4m (12ft) ☼ ☼ ◊ ◖ ❀❀❀

Osmanthus x burkwoodii
This evergreen shrub is grown for its glossy leaves and clusters of tiny, creamy-white, trumpet-shaped flowers, which are sweetly scented and appear in mid-spring.
‡↔ 3m (10ft) ☼ ☼ ◊ ❀❀

Paeonia delavayi var. ludlowii
In late spring, the nodding, glossy, bright yellow flowers of this vigorous tree peony open among its deeply cut, bright green leaves. The flowers are attractive to bees.
‡ 2m (6ft) ↔ 3m (9ft) ☼ ☼ ◊ ◖ ❀❀❀

Philadelphus 'Belle Etoile'
This mock orange is an arching, deciduous shrub with tapering leaves. Its fragrant, single white flowers have a maroon centre, and are freely borne in late spring. ‡ 1.2m (4ft) ↔ 2.5m (8ft) ☼ ☼ ◊ ❀❀❀

Prunus laurocerasus 'Zabeliana'
The evergreen cherry laurel looks its best in spring when long spikes of fragrant white flowers appear. 'Zabeliana' has a low, spreading habit, ideal for ground cover.
‡ 1m (3ft) ↔ 2.5m (8ft) ☼ ☼ ◊ ◖ ❀❀❀

SPRING-FLOWERING SHRUBS *CONTINUED*

Prunus x cistena
A slow-growing, ornamental cherry with glossy oval leaves that are red when young, maturing to purple. Delicate white flowers appear in late spring.
↕↔ 1.5m (5ft) ☼ ◊ ❀❀❀

Rhododendron 'Hotspur'
Azaleas are unsurpassed for vivid spring colour, and 'Hotspur' is no exception, with its clusters of flame-red flowers. It also has brightly coloured autumn foliage.
↕↔ 2m (6ft) ☼ ☀ ◊ ❀❀❀

Ribes sanguineum 'Pulborough Scarlet'
This flowering currant has aromatic leaves and bears clusters of dark red, white-centred tubular flowers in spring, followed by blue-black berries.
↕ 2m (6ft) ↔ 2.5m (8ft) ☼ ◊ ❀❀❀

Spiraea 'Arguta'
At its peak in late spring, bridal wreath presents a marvellous display, with masses of white flowers carried all along the upper sides of its arching stems.
↕ 2m (6ft) ↔ 1.5m (5ft) ☼ ◊ ◑ ❀❀❀

Syringa meyeri 'Palibin'
This dwarf lilac has a neat, rounded shape and small, dark green oval leaves. It bears abundant clusters of fragrant, lavender-pink flowers in late spring.
↕↔ 1.5m (5ft) ☼ ◊ ❀❀❀

Viburnum plicatum f. tomentosum 'Mariesii' With its horizontal branches, this shrub creates a striking architectural effect. The flowers are white, and the dark green leaves turn red-purple in autumn.
↕ 3m (10ft) ↔ 4m (12ft) ☼ ◊ ❀❀❀

Weigela florida 'Foliis Purpureis'
Funnel-shaped flowers, deep pink on the outside and white inside, appear in spring and look striking against the bronze-green foliage of this dark-leaved cultivar.
↕ 1m (3ft) ↔ 1.5m (5ft) ☼ ◊ ❀❀❀

ALSO RECOMMENDED

Berberis darwinii
  (Darwin's barberry)

Berberis valdiviana

Chaenomeles speciosa 'Snow'

Corylopsis glabrescens

Deutzia x rosea

Dipelta floribunda

Edgeworthia chrysantha

Enkianthus cernuus f. *rubens*

Genista tinctoria
  (Dyer's greenweed)

Hamamelis x intermedia
  'Barmstedt Gold' (Witch hazel)

Hamamelis x intermedia 'Jelena'
  (Witch hazel)

Leptospermum scoparium
  'Red Damask' (Manuka)

Lindera benzoin (Benjamin)

Malus toringo

Pieris japonica

Rhododendron 'Percy Wiseman'

Ribes sanguineum 'King Edward VII'
  (Flowering currant)

Staphylea pinnata (Bladdernut)

Telopea truncata
  (Tasmanian waratah)

Viburnum bitchiuense

SUMMER-FLOWERING SHRUBS

Buddleja globosa
This eye-catching shrub bears bright, orange-yellow balls of honey-scented flowers above its handsome, dark green leaves in early summer.
↕↔ 5m (15ft) ☼ ◊ ❋❋

Caryopteris x clandonensis 'Worcester Gold' The small but vivid lavender-blue flowers of this pretty shrub appear in late summer, and stand out against the warm yellow, deciduous foliage.
↕ 1m (3ft) ↔ 1.5m (5ft) ☼ ◊ ❋❋❋

Ceanothus x delilenus 'Gloire de Versailles' A fast-growing, evergreen bushy shrub with glossy foliage and large, pale blue flowers in mid- to late summer. A good choice for a sunny wall.
↕↔ 1.5m (5ft) ☼ ◊ ❋❋

Ceratostigma willmottianum
The hardy plumbago bears pale to mid-blue flowers in late summer, and its dark green, purple-margined leaves turn shades of red in autumn.
↕ 1m (3ft) ↔ 1.5m (5ft) ☼ ◊ ◕ ❋❋❋

Choisya x dewitteana 'Aztec Pearl'
An elegant Mexican orange blossom with slim dark green leaves. Fragrant clusters of white, star-shaped flowers emerge from pink buds in late spring or early summer.
↕↔ 2.5m (8ft) ☼ ◊ ❋❋❋

Convolvulus cneorum
With its silky, silvery leaves, this shrub is an asset even when not in bloom. The delicate, funnel-shaped white flowers appear from late spring to summer.
↕ 60cm (2ft) ↔ 1m (3ft) ☼ ◊ ❋❋

Deutzia x elegantissima 'Rosealind'
Stunning when grown in the border or as a specimen plant, this sun-loving shrub bears thousands of star-shaped, pale pink flowers in early summer.
↕ 1.2m (4ft) ↔ 1.5m (5ft) ☼ ◊ ❋❋❋

Hebe 'Midsummer Beauty'
This adaptable, evergreen shrub, with purplish-brown stems and bright green leaves, bears tapering plumes of lilac flowers from midsummer to autumn.
↕ 2m (6ft) ↔ 1.5m (5ft) ☼ ◐ ◊ ◕ ❋❋❋

Helianthemum 'Wisley Primrose'
A sun-loving rock rose that forms low mounds of evergreen, grey-green foliage, and bears plenty of saucer-shaped, pale yellow flowers throughout summer.
↕ 23cm (9in) ↔ 30cm (12in) ☼ ◊ ❋❋❋

SUMMER-FLOWERING SHRUBS CONTINUED

Hibiscus syriacus 'Woodbridge'
Exotic flowers are the main allure of hibiscus cultivars. In late summer 'Woodbridge' produces a succession of large, pink flowers with deep red centres.
↕↔ 3m (10ft) ☼ ◊ ❄❄❄

Hydrangea macrophylla 'Mariesii Lilacina'
A handsome, free-standing hydrangea grown for its showy, mauve-pink to blue lacecap flowers, which appear in midsummer.
↕ 2m (6ft) ↔ 2.5m (8ft) ☼ ◐ ◊ ◑ ❄❄❄

Hydrangea paniculata 'Unique'
In midsummer this beautiful cultivar bears large, creamy-white flowerheads that develop pink tints as they age, and its leaves turn yellow before falling.
↕ 7m (22ft) ↔ 2.5m (8ft) ☼ ◐ ◊ ◑ ❄❄❄

Hypericum 'Hidcote'
The arching branches of 'Hidcote' are covered with lance-shaped leaves, and throughout summer clusters of golden yellow flowers are borne in profusion.
↕ 1.2m (4ft) ↔ 1.5m (5ft) ☼ ◊ ❄❄❄

Lavandula stoechas
In early summer, French lavender bears dense spikes of fragrant, dark purple flowers, topped by rose-purple bracts, on long stalks above silvery-grey leaves.
↕↔ 60cm (24in) ☼ ◊ ❄❄

Magnolia liliiflora 'Nigra'
One of the most reliable magnolias, this beautiful cultivar produces large, dark purple-red upright flowers in early summer and intermittently into autumn.
↕ 3m (10ft) ↔ 2.5m (8ft) ☼ ◐ ◊ ◑ ❄❄❄

Myrtus communis 'Flore Pleno'
Myrtle is a sun-loving, evergreen Mediterranean shrub with aromatic foliage. Masses of pretty, fragrant white pompon flowers appear in late summer.
↕↔ 3m (10ft) ☼ ◊ ◑ ❄❄

Nandina domestica
The leaves of this evergreen shrub have red tints in spring and autumn, and small, star-shaped white flowers emerge in midsummer, followed by red berries.
↕ 2m (6ft) ↔ 1.5m (5ft) ☼ ◊ ◑ ❄❄❄

Paeonia delavayi
In early summer, this magnificent tree peony produces single, dark crimson flowers on long, lax stems. The dark green leaves are tinged burgundy in spring.
↕↔ 2m (6ft) ☼ ◊ ❄❄❄

❀❀❀ FULLY HARDY   ❀❀ HARDY IN MILD REGIONS/SHELTERED SITES   ❀ PROTECT FROM FROST OVER WINTER   ❀ NO TOLERANCE TO FROST

☼ FULL SUN   ☀ PARTIAL SUN   ❂ FULL SHADE   ◊ WELL-DRAINED SOIL   ◐ MOIST SOIL   ◆ WET SOIL

Phygelius x *rectus* 'African Queen'
This evergreen shrub has graceful upward-curving branches. The long, tubular flowers, produced in midsummer, are soft red with yellow inside.
‡ 1m (3ft) ↔ 1.2m (4ft) ☼ ◊ ◆ ❀❀

Potentilla fruticosa 'Red Ace'
This shrub-like cinquefoil bears orange-red, single flowers, which contrast well with the small, divided leaves. It blooms from late spring to early autumn.
‡ 1m (3ft) ↔ 1.5m (5ft) ☀ ◊ ❀❀❀

Rosa 'Geranium'
A spectacular shrub rose with arching branches and dark green leaves. Masses of scarlet flowers appear in early summer, followed by orange-red hips in autumn.
‡ 2.5m (8ft) ↔ 1.5m (5ft) ☼ ◊ ◆ ❀❀❀

Rosa glauca
This delicate shrub has striking, deep purple stems and elegant grey-purple foliage. Clusters of clear pink flowers in early summer are followed by red hips.
‡ 2m (6ft) ↔ 1.5m (5ft) ☼ ◊ ❀❀❀

Rosa 'Roseraie de l'Hay'
A hardy rugosa shrub rose with attractive light green foliage that produces richly scented, velvety, purple-red flowers throughout summer.
‡ 2.2m (7ft) ↔ 2m (6ft) ☼ ◊ ❀❀❀

ALSO RECOMMENDED

Abutilon vitifolium
  'Veronica Tennant'

Cistus x *cyprius*

Clethra delavayi

Crinodendron patagua

Cuphea cyanea

Escallonia 'Apple Blossom'

Fuchsia magellanica
  'Thompsonii'

Genista cinerea

Hebe 'Bowles' Variety'

Hypericum x *inodorum* 'Elstead'

Hyssopus officinalis (Hyssop)

Indigofera dielsiana

Kalmia latifolia (Calico bush)

Lavatera x *clementii* 'Rosea'

Olearia ilicifolia
  (Mountain holly)

Penstemon isophyllus

Philadelphus 'Beauclerk'
  (Mock orange)

Potentilla fruticosa 'Abbotswood'

Spartium junceum
  (Spanish broom)

Spiraea japonica 'Goldflame'

Syringa vulgaris
  'Katherine Havemeyer'

Tamarix ramosissima

Sambucus nigra f. *porphyrophylla* 'Eva'
This graceful elder's dark purple, lacy foliage provides colour contrast in a mixed border. Showy, pale pink, flattened flowerheads appear in early summer.
‡ 3m (10ft) ↔ 2m (6ft) ☼ ☀ ◊ ◆ ❀❀❀

Spiraea nipponica 'Snowmound'
At its peak in early summer, this spiraea presents a marvellous display, with clusters of white flowers carried all along the upper sides of the arching stems.
‡↔ 2.5m (8ft) ☼ ◊ ◆ ❀❀❀

SHRUBS FOR AUTUMN INTEREST

Acer palmatum 'Atropurpureum'
The leaves of this small, elegant tree open crimson in spring, mature to purple-red, and then turn a fiery red that blazes in the autumn garden.
‡ 8m (25ft) ↔ 10m (30ft) ☼ ◐ ❋❋❋

Berberis x *ottawensis* f. *purpurea* 'Superba'
With graceful arching branches, this large shrub has an attractive habit and also offers red berries and purplish leaves that turn bright crimson in autumn.
‡↔ 2.5m (8ft) ☼ ☀ ◊ ❋❋❋

Callicarpa bodinieri var. *giraldii* 'Profusion'
An upright shrub providing interest from bronze-green leaves in spring, pink flowers in summer, and long-lasting violet berries in autumn.
‡ 3m (10ft) ↔ 2.5m (8ft) ☼ ☀ ◊ ◐ ❋❋

Calluna vulgaris 'Robert Chapman'
A heather with a spreading habit, bearing mauve-pink flowers. It has dense, golden-yellow foliage that turns orange in autumn then red in winter and spring.
‡ 25cm (10in) ↔ 65m (26in) ☼ ◊ ❋❋❋

Clerodendrum trichotomum
From late summer to mid-autumn, this tree-like, large-leaved shrub produces fragrant white flowers, followed by attractive blue berries.
‡↔ 5–6m (15–20ft) ☼ ◊ ◐ ❋❋❋

Cotinus 'Grace'
The purple foliage of *C.* 'Grace' turns a brilliant translucent red in autumn. A fast-growing shrub or small tree, it bears tiny pink-purple flowers in summer.
‡ 6m (20ft) ↔ 5m (15ft) ☼ ☀ ◊ ◐ ❋❋❋

Cotoneaster salicifolius 'Gnom'
The profusion of berries this dwarf shrub bears mature to red in autumn and last into winter, when the slender, glossy, dark green leaves take on a bronze tinge.
‡ 30cm (1ft) ↔ 2m (6ft) ☼ ◊ ❋❋❋

Disanthus cercidifolius
This rounded deciduous shrub produces dark red flowers in autumn, when the heart-shaped leaves turn shades of yellow, orange, purple and red.
‡↔ 3m (10ft) ☀ ◊ ❋❋

Euonymus alatus
A dense, bushy, deciduous shrub, *E. alatus* puts on a spectacular autumn display of purple and red fruits as the dark green leaves turn to scarlet.
‡ 2m (6ft) ↔ 3m (10ft) ☼ ☀ ◊ ❋❋❋

❈❈❈ FULLY HARDY   ❈❈ HARDY IN MILD REGIONS/SHELTERED SITES   ❈ PROTECT FROM FROST OVER WINTER   ❀ NO TOLERANCE TO FROST

☼ FULL SUN   ☼ PARTIAL SUN   ✳ FULL SHADE   ◊ WELL-DRAINED SOIL   ◖ MOIST SOIL   ● WET SOIL

Fothergilla major
In spring, this upright, slow-growing shrub produces bottlebrush-like white flowerheads; autumn turns the dark green leaves orange, yellow, and red.
↕ 2.5m (8ft) ↔ 2m (6ft) ☼ ◖ ❈❈❈

Hydrangea quercifolia Snow Queen
The large, oakleaf-shaped foliage of this shrub turns from green to striking shades of coral and red in autumn while the white flowers fade through pink to brown.
↕ 2m (6ft) ↔ 2.5m (8ft) ☼ ☼ ◊ ◖ ❈❈❈

Itea ilicifolia
Tiny, greenish-white flowers open in long, catkin-like plumes from summer through to autumn, standing out against the glossy dark green leaves.
↕ 3–5m (10–15ft) ↔ 3m (10ft) ☼ ◊ ❈❈❈

Rhus glabra
From the reddish-purple stems of this bushy shrub grow slender, deep blue-green leaves that turn red in autumn. Female plants bear red fruits.
↕ 2.5m (8ft) ↔ 2m (6ft) ☼ ◊ ❈❈❈

Sambucus racemosa 'Plumosa Aurea'
Deeply cut leaves, bronzed when young, mature to golden yellow and take on a red tinge in autumn. The creamy flowers are followed by red berries in summer.
↕↔ 3m (10ft) ☼ ☼ ◊ ◖ ❈❈❈

ALSO RECOMMENDED

Acer palmatum var. *heptalobum* (Japanese maple)

Berberis x *carminea* 'Barbarossa'

Berberis thunbergii f. *atropurpurea* 'Rose Glow'

Callicarpa bodinieri var. *giraldii* (Beautyberry)

Cornus alba 'Sibirica Variegata'

Cotinus 'Flame' (Smoke bush)

Decaisnea fargesii

Euonymus hamiltonianus 'Red Elf'

Euonymus oxyphyllus

Fothergilla gardenii (Witch alder)

Gaultheria tasmanica

Hamamelis virginiana (Witch hazel)

Hippophae rhamnoides (Sea buckthorn)

Leonotis leonurus (Lion's tail)

Rhus typhina 'Dissecta' (Stag's horn sumach)

Rosa 'Geranium'

Ruscus aculeatus (Butcher's broom)

Vaccinium angustifolium var. *laevifolium* (Low-bush blueberry)

Vaccinium parvifolium (Red bilberry)

Sorbus reducta
This deciduous shrub forms a low thicket of dense, upright branches, carrying finely divided grey-green leaves that turn to shades of red and purple in autumn.
↕↔ 30cm (12in) ☼ ◊ ❈❈❈

Viburnum opulus
The guelder rose bears flattened heads of white flowers in spring and summer, followed by bright red fruits and reddening leaves in autumn.
↕ 5m (15ft) ↔ 4m (12ft) ☼ ☼ ◊ ◖ ❈❈❈

SHRUBS FOR WINTER INTEREST

Azara microphylla
This upright, shrubby evergreen tree has attractively glossy dark green oval leaves; from late winter to spring it produces clusters of vanilla-scented yellow flowers.
↕ 10m (30ft) ↔ 4m (12ft) ☼ ◊ ❀❀

Chimonanthus praecox **'Grandiflorus'**
An upright, deciduous shrub with lance-shaped green leaves, this plant is prized for the very fragrant, deep yellow flowers borne on bare winter stems.
↕ 4m (12ft) ↔ 3m (10ft) ☼ ◊ ❀❀❀

Cornus alba **'Sibirica'**
The main attraction here is the bright coral-red stems that are exposed in winter; cutting back hard in spring produces the best results.
↕↔ 3m (10ft) ☼ ◊ ❀❀❀

Cornus mas
A vigorous shrub or small tree, *C. mas* offers red autumn foliage and fruits but is most notable in winter, when its bare branches are adorned with yellow flowers.
↕↔ 5m (15ft) ☼ ☀ ◊ ❀❀❀

Corylus avellana **'Contorta'**
Its twisted shoots give the corkscrew hazel its name, and in winter, when they are bare of leaf, long, pale yellow catkins dangle from them to striking effect.
↕↔ 6m (20ft) ☼ ◊ ❀❀❀

Cotoneaster lacteus
This evergreen shrub has handsome dark green leaves; white flowers in summer are succeeded by large clusters of bright red berries that last into winter.
↕↔ 4m (12ft) ☼ ◊ ❀❀❀

Daphne bholua **'Jacqueline Postill'**
The midwinter flowers of this evergreen *Daphne* are pink to purple with white or pale pink centres; their intense fragrance is a delight in colder months.
↕ 2m (6ft) ↔ 1.5m (5ft) ☼ ◊ ❀❀❀

Elaeagnus x *ebbingei* **'Gilt Edge'**
Broad, rich golden margins on the evergreen leaves make 'Gilt Edge' a cheerful sight in winter; the autumn flowers are small but very fragrant.
↕↔ 4m (12ft) ☼ ◊ ❀❀❀

Hamamelis x *intermedia* **'Pallida'**
Autumn leaf shades of yellow, orange, and red are followed by strongly scented sulphur-yellow flowers on bare branches, growing in graceful arched tiers.
↕↔ 4m (12ft) ☼ ☀ ◊ ◊ ❀❀❀

❋❋❋ FULLY HARDY   ❋❋ HARDY IN MILD REGIONS/SHELTERED SITES   ❋ PROTECT FROM FROST OVER WINTER   ❋ NO TOLERANCE TO FROST

☼ FULL SUN   ☀ PARTIAL SUN   ✻ FULL SHADE   ◊ WELL-DRAINED SOIL   ◐ MOIST SOIL   ● WET SOIL

Jasminum nudiflorum
Winter jasmine has arching green stems, clothed with dark green leaves in the growing season; they are replaced by bright yellow flowers in midwinter.
↕↔ 3m (10ft) ☼ ☀ ◊ ❋❋❋

Mahonia japonica
The dark green, spiny leaves of this upright shrub are complemented by long sprays of fragrant yellow flowers from late autumn to early spring.
↕ 2m (6ft) ↔ 3m (10ft) ☀ ◊ ◐ ❋❋❋

Salix hastata 'Wehrhahnii'
In winter, the bare purple-brown stems of this small, slow-growing, upright willow contrast beautifully with soft silvery-grey catkins.
↕↔ 1m (3ft) ☼ ◐ ❋❋❋

Sarcococca hookeriana var. digyna
A dense, spreading shrub with slender evergreen leaves, this plant produces tiny, fragrant, white flowers with prominent pink anthers in winter.
↕ 10m (30ft) ↔ 4m (12ft) ☀ ✻ ◊ ◐ ❋❋❋

Skimmia japonica 'Nymans'
Fragrant white flowers are borne in spring, and if a male variety is planted nearby they will be followed by long-lasting bright red berries in autumn.
↕ 1m (3ft) ↔ 2m (6ft) ☀ ✻ ◊ ◐ ❋❋❋

Viburnum x bodnantense
Fragrant flowers are borne on the bare stems of this deciduous shrub. Cultivars with flowers ranging from almost white through pale to dark pink are available.
↕ 3m (10ft) ↔ 2m (6ft) ☼ ☀ ◊ ● ❋❋❋

Viburnum tinus 'Eve Price'
From winter to spring, flat clusters of small, star-shaped white flowers develop from pink buds amid dark green leaves; they are followed by blue berries.
↕↔ 3m (10ft) ☼ ☀ ◊ ● ❋❋❋

ALSO RECOMMENDED

Correa pulchella

Cotoneaster serotinus

Daphne mezereum (Mezereon)

Daphne odora 'Aureomarginata'

Erica carnea 'Challenger' (Alpine heath)

Erica x *darleyensis* 'Furzey' (Darley Dale heath)

Hamamelis x *intermedia* 'Aphrodite' (Witch hazel)

Hamamelis japonica 'Sulphurea' (Witch hazel)

Lonicera x *purpusii* (Honeysuckle)

Mahonia x *media* 'Charity'

Nandina domestica 'Fire Power' (Heavenly bamboo)

Pyracantha atalantioides 'Aurea'

Pyracantha 'Golden Dome'

Rubus biflorus

Rubus thibetanus

Sarcococca confusa

Sarcococca humilis (Christmas box)

Stachyurus praecox

Symphoricarpos x *doorenbosii* 'White Hedge'

Viburnum farreri

GROUND-COVER PLANTS FOR SUN

Ground-cover plants make a useful addition to the garden as their dense, light-excluding canopies can help to suppress weeds, often requiring little maintenance, but with colourful and striking effects. Not all of the plants classed as "ground cover" are low-growing, so it can be easy to create a varied and visually stimulating design. Consider using the plant suggestions on these pages to fill sunny "problem areas", such as a steep, sloping bank, where access for planting, turfing, or mowing may be difficult.

SHRUBS
Ceanothus thyrsiflorus var. *repens* (Blue blossom)

Cotoneaster cashmiriensis

Erica x *darleyensis* 'Jenny Porter' (Darley Dale heath)

Genista hispanica (Spanish gorse)

Hypericum calycinum (Rose of Sharon)

Salvia rosmarinus 'Severn Sea' (Rosemary)

Thymus pulegioides 'Bertram Anderson' (Thyme)

PERENNIALS
Artemisia stelleriana 'Boughton Silver'

Campanula glomerata 'Superba' (Clustered bellflower)

Cerastium tomentosum (Snow-in-summer)

Dicentra 'Stuart Boothman'

Geranium x *oxonianum* 'Wargrave Pink'

Gypsophila repens 'Dorothy Teacher'

Hosta fortunei var. *aureomarginata*

Juniperus squamata 'Blue Carpet' (Flaky juniper)

Lamium maculatum 'White Nancy'

Mentha suaveolens 'Variegata' (Pineapple mint)

Persicaria vacciniifolia

Phalaris arundinacea var. *picta* (Gardener's garters)

Phlomis russeliana

Potentilla megalantha

Saponaria ocymoides (Tumbling Ted)

Scutellaria orientalis

Silene schafta

Veronica gentianoides

Viola 'Nellie Britton'

ROCK PLANTS
Phlox subulata 'McDaniel's Cushion' (Moss phlox)

Sempervivum ciliosum

PERENNIAL: *Alchemilla mollis* **(Lady's mantle)**

PERENNIAL: *Aubrieta* '**Joy**'

SHRUB: *Erica carnea* f. *alba* '**Springwood White**' **(Alpine heath)**

SHRUB: *Euonymus fortunei* '**Emerald 'n' Gold**'

PERENNIAL: *Euphorbia polychroma*

PERENNIAL: *Geranium* 'Johnson's Blue'

ROCK PLANT: *Hebe pinguifolia* 'Pagei'

PERENNIAL: *Osteospermum jucundum*

PERENNIAL: *Lysimachia nummularia* 'Aurea' (Golden creeping Jenny)

PERENNIAL: *Origanum vulgare* 'Aureum' (Golden wild marjoram)

PERENNIAL: *Persicaria bistorta* (Bistort)

SHRUB: *Santolina pinnata* subsp. *neapolitana* 'Sulphurea'

PERENNIAL: *Stachys byzantina* (Lamb's ears)

PERENNIAL: *Veronica prostrata* (Prostrate speedwell)

SHRUB: *Vinca minor* 'La Grave' (Lesser periwinkle)

GROUND-COVER PLANTS FOR SHADE

Many of the plants suggested on these pages are woodland natives and depend on the absence of bleaching sunlight to produce their lush foliage. They provide ground cover in shady "problem areas" that do not receive a lot of light, such as the base of walls or fences, or beneath trees or shrubs, To encourage strong, healthy growth, remove any weeds before planting, as these will compete with your plants for moisture and nutrients. Improve the soil structure by digging in plenty of well-rotted manure, compost, or leafmould before planting.

SHRUBS
Cotoneaster dammeri
Euonymus fortunei 'Emerald Gaiety'
Gaultheria procumbens
Leucothoe Scarletta (Switch ivy)
Mahonia repens 'Rotundifolia'
Vinca difformis

PERENNIALS
Aegopodium podagraria 'Variegatum'
   (Variegated ground elder)
Anemone x lipsiensis
Bergenia 'Silberlicht'
Cardamine trifolia
   (Trifoliate bittercress)
Chelidonium majus 'Flore Pleno'
   (Greater celandine)
Cornus canadensis
   (Creeping dogwood)
Cyclamen hederifolium
Epimedium x perralchicum
Euphorbia amygdaloides var. robbiae
   (Mrs Robb's bonnet)
Galax urceolata
Galium odoratum
   (Sweet woodruff)
Geranium sylvaticum 'Album'
   (Wood cranesbill)
Heuchera 'Red Spangles'
Hosta 'Frances Williams'
Polypodium vulgare
   (Common polypody)
Sanguinaria canadensis f. multiplex 'Plena'
   (Canadian puccoon)
Saxifraga x urbium (London pride)
Symphytum 'Goldsmith'
Tolmiea menziesii 'Taff's Gold'
   (Thousand mothers)
Tradescantia (Andersoniana Group)
   'Osprey'
Vinca minor 'Argenteovariegata'
   (Lesser periwinkle)

CLIMBERS
Hedera helix 'Glacier' (Common ivy)
Hedera hibernica (Irish ivy)

PERENNIAL: *Ajuga reptans*

PERENNIAL: *Asarum europaeum*
(Asarabacca)

PERENNIAL: *Brunnera macrophylla*

PERENNIAL: *Convallaria majalis*
(Lily of the valley)

PERENNIAL: *Epimedium x rubrum*

PERENNIAL: *Geranium macrorrhizum*

PERENNIAL: *Hosta* 'Francee'

PERENNIAL: *Lamium maculatum* 'White Nancy'

PERENNIAL: *Luzula sylvatica* 'Aurea' (Greater wood-rush)

PERENNIAL: *Omphalodes cappadocica*

PERENNIAL: *Pachysandra terminalis*

PERENNIAL: *Tiarella cordifolia* (Foam flower)

PERENNIAL: *Pulmonaria rubra* 'Redstart'

PERENNIAL: *Tellima grandiflora* Rubra Group

SHRUB: *Vinca major* 'Variegata' (Greater periwinkle)

GRASSES, SEDGES, AND BAMBOOS

Anemanthele lessoniana
Fine-leaved pheasant's tail grass has an arching habit. In summer it produces purplish flower spikes; in winter the evergreen leaves turn orange-brown.
↕ 1m (3ft) ↔ 1.2m (4ft) ☼ ☀ ◊ ◑ ❋❋

Briza maxima
One of the most attractive of the annual grasses, quaking grass has nodding flower-heads that rattle in the slightest breeze. Stems dry well for flower arranging.
↕ 30cm (1ft) ↔ 23cm (9in) ☼ ◊ ◑ ❋❋❋

Calamagrostis x acutiflora 'Overdam'
The striped feather reed makes a strong vertical accent in the border. As the leaves emerge in spring, there is a pink tinge to the green and white variegation.
↕ 1m (3ft) ↔ 1.2m (4ft) ☼ ◊ ❋❋❋

Carex buchananii
This striking evergreen sedge has slender, coppery-brown leaves with a hint of a curl. It is upright when young, becoming more arching with age.
↕↔ 60cm (2ft) ☼ ☀ ◊ ◑ ❋❋

Carex elata 'Aurea'
Bowles' golden sedge produces a broad spray of vibrant yellow leaves, edged in green. In summer there is the added bonus of feathery brown flower spikes.
↕ 75cm (30in) ↔ 1m (3ft) ☼ ☀ ◑ ◊ ❋❋❋

Cortaderia selloana 'Pumila'
Ideal for smaller gardens, this dwarf pampas is half the size of the parent species. Golden-brown plumes are produced in summer on stout stems.
↕↔ 2m (6ft) ☼ ◊ ◑ ❋❋❋

Elymus magellanicus
Blue wheatgrass is a wonderful blue steel colour that looks stunning against a gravel mulch. It bears herringbone flowerheads that look like ears of wheat.
↕↔ 45cm (18in) ☼ ◊ ◑ ❋❋❋

Fargesia murielae
A tough plant for tough situations, this evergreen bamboo copes well with dry soils and exposed sites, and makes an effective windbreak or screen.
↕↔ 4m (12ft) ☼ ☀ ◊ ◑ ❋❋❋

Festuca glauca 'Elijah Blue'
One of those useful plants that look good all year round. The silvery-blue, needle-like leaves of this little fescue form neat, round mounds.
↕ 30cm (12in) ↔ 60cm (24in) ☼ ☀ ◊ ◑ ❋❋❋

❋❋❋ FULLY HARDY   ❋❋ HARDY IN MILD REGIONS/SHELTERED SITES   ❋ PROTECT FROM FROST OVER WINTER   ❋ NO TOLERANCE TO FROST

☼ FULL SUN   ☀ PARTIAL SUN   ❋ FULL SHADE   ◊ WELL-DRAINED SOIL   ◊ MOIST SOIL   ◆ WET SOIL

Imperata cylindrica 'Rubra'
Japanese blood grass is one of the finest
foliage plants – fluffy white flowerspikes
are a bonus in summer. Its crimson-tipped,
upright leaves glow in the sun.
‡ 45cm (18in) ↔ 1.8m (6ft) ☼ ☀ ◊ ◆ ❋❋

Lagurus ovatus
Hare's tail grass is a popular annual that can
be grown easily from seed. The soft, hairy
spikelets are pale green at first, maturing
to pale cream.
‡ 50cm (20in) ↔ 30cm (12in) ☼ ◊ ❋❋❋

Miscanthus sinensis 'Kleine Silberspinne'
An attractive ornamental grass that
produces silky white and red flower
spikes in late summer. These turn silver
as they age and last all winter.
‡↔ 1.2m (4ft) ☼ ◊ ◆ ❋❋❋

Pennisetum alopecuroides 'Hameln'
This compact fountain grass has narrow
leaves that tumble from the centre of the
plant, joined in summer and autumn by
flowing, bristly, decorative flowerheads.
‡ to 1.5m (5ft) ↔ to 1.2m (4ft) ☼ ◊ ❋❋❋

Phyllostachys nigra
Black bamboo is a popular plant for
contemporary gardens, grown for its
distinctive tall stems, which are initially
green and then turn a glossy black.
‡ to 5m (15ft) ↔ 3m (10ft) ☼ ☀ ◊ ◆ ❋❋❋

ALSO RECOMMENDED

Calamagrostis brachytricha

Carex flagellifera

Chimonobambusa tumidissinoda

Chionochloa rubra

Chusquea culeou
   (Chilean bamboo)

Cortaderia richardii (Toe toe)

Cortaderia selloana 'Sunningdale Silver'
   (Pampas grass)

Elegia capensis

Eragrostis curvula
   'Totnes Burgundy'

Juncus effusus f. *spiralis*
   (Corkscrew rush)

Luzula nivea (Snowy wood-rush)

Miscanthus sinensis var.
   condensatus 'Cosmopolitan'

Miscanthus sinensis 'Zebrinus'
   (Zebra grass)

Molinia caerulea subsp. *caerulea*
   'Heidebraut' (Purple moor grass)

Panicum virgatum 'Northwind'
   (Switch grass)

Pleioblastus variegatus
   (Dwarf white-striped bamboo)

Sasa veitchii

Thamnocalamus crassinodus
   'Kew Beauty'

Phyllostachys vivax f. aureocaulis
This slow-growing bamboo has striking,
bright lemon yellow canes flecked with green,
and slim arching foliage. Control its spread
with a root guard.
‡ to 6m (20ft) ↔ 4m (12ft) ☼ ☀ ◊ ◆ ❋❋❋

Stipa gigantea
Giant feather grass is a fabulous plant
for a sunny border. Tall, fluttering plumes
of flowers emerge above the narrow
evergreen foliage in summer.
‡ 2.5m (8ft) ↔ 1m (3ft) ☼ ◊ ◆ ❋❋❋

CONIFERS FOR SMALL GARDENS

***Abies cephalonica* 'Meyer's Dwarf'**
Broad, nearly horizontal growth makes
'Meyer's Dwarf' a good conifer for a
rockery. The short branches bear dark
green, sturdy needles.
‡ 50cm (20in) ↔ 1.5m (5ft) ☼ ☀ ◊ ◑ ✳✳✳

***Cedrus deodara* 'Aurea'**
This evergreen conifer has a drooping habit
at first, developing a broad crown with age.
The foliage is golden yellow, becoming
greenish in late summer.
‡↔ 5m (15ft) ☼ ◑ ◊ ✳✳✳

***Chamaecyparis obtusa* 'Nana Gracilis'**
The glossy, bright green foliage of this bushy
Hinoki cypress makes it an asset to any
garden; it is ideal grown in a rock garden
or in a large container.
‡ 2m (6ft) ↔ 1.5–2m (5–6ft) ☼ ◊ ✳✳✳

***Cupressus macrocarpa* 'Goldcrest'**
A narrow, columnar tree, 'Goldcrest' has
aromatic golden yellow foliage held in
graceful sprays. It makes a good hedge,
needing only minor trimming in summer.
‡ 10m (30ft) ↔ 5m (15ft) ☼ ◊ ✳✳

***Juniperus communis* 'Compressa'**
A dwarf juniper forming a slim column,
'Compressa' has dense, aromatic, dark
green foliage. It produces small fruits that
ripen over three years.
‡ 75cm (30in) ↔ 15cm (6in) ☼ ◊ ✳✳✳

***Juniperus* x *pfitzeriana* 'Pfitzeriana
Aurea'** This low-growing, spreading
plant bears graceful tiers of golden foliage,
drooping slightly at the tips. In winter the
foliage takes on a greener hue.
‡↔ 1.5m (5ft) ☼ ◊ ✳✳✳

***Juniperus squamata* 'Blue Carpet'**
Light steel-blue, prickly foliage and a low,
spreading habit distinguish this juniper. It
is fast-growing and makes excellent ground
cover, forming a dense mat.
‡ 30cm (1ft) ↔ 2–3m (6–10ft) ☼ ◊ ✳✳✳

***Picea abies* 'Reflexa'**
While this Norway spruce variety is a
sprawling ground-cover plant, it is also
possible to train it up a stake to provide
an attractive mound of weeping foliage.
‡ 30cm (1ft) ↔ 5m (15ft) ☼ ◑ ◊ ✳✳✳

***Pinus heldreichii* 'Smidtii'**
This slow-growing dwarf plant makes a
neat, dense mound of upward-thrusting
long bright green needles, making it an
excellent choice for a rock garden.
‡ 50cm (1½ft) ↔ 1m (3ft) ☼ ◑ ✳✳✳

✿✿✿ FULLY HARDY   ✿✿ HARDY IN MILD REGIONS/SHELTERED SITES   ✿ PROTECT FROM FROST OVER WINTER   ✿ NO TOLERANCE TO FROST

☼ FULL SUN   ◐ PARTIAL SUN   ✹ FULL SHADE   ◊ WELL-DRAINED SOIL   ◗ MOIST SOIL   ◖ WET SOIL

Pinus mugo 'Mops'
This slow-growing dwarf plant forms an almost spherical shape of thick upright branches, which are clothed with long, bright to dark green needles.
‡ 1m (3ft) ↔ 2m (6ft) ☼ ◊ ✿✿✿

Pinus sylvestris Aurea Group
This is a slow-growing group of Scots pines, suitable for smaller gardens. The long needles are blue-green, turning golden-yellow in winter.
‡ 10m (30ft) ↔ 5m (15ft) ◐ ◗ ✿✿✿

Platycladus orientalis 'Aurea Nana'
The shape of this conifer varies from nearly spherical to columnar, with dense foliage held in flat sprays. It is golden yellow, sometimes bronzing in winter.
‡↔ 60cm (24in) ☼ ◊ ✿✿✿

Taxus baccata 'Dovastonii Aurea'
A spreading, slow-growing yew with horizontally tiered branches weeping at the tips, this has yellow-margined or wholly golden-yellow foliage.
‡ 10m (30ft) ↔ 5m (15ft) ✹ ◊ ✿✿✿

Taxus cuspidata
This bushy, spreading dwarf yew is clothed with flattened needle-like foliage that is deep golden yellow in the first year and then matures to dark green.
‡↔ 5m (15ft) ✹ ◊ ✿✿✿

Thuja plicata 'Stoneham Gold'
With bright golden aromatic foliage held in irregular sprays that form an overall conical shape, this slow-growing dwarf conifer is ideal for a rock garden.
‡ 1–2m (3–6ft) ↔ 1m (3ft) ☼ ◊ ◗ ✿✿✿

Tsuga canadensis 'Jeddeloh'
The arching branches of this plant form a spreading mound of dark green foliage, developing from the crown and leaving a hollow like a bird's nest at the centre.
‡ 60cm (2ft) ↔ 1.2m (4ft) ✹ ◗ ✿✿✿

ALSO RECOMMENDED

Abies balsamea Hudsonia Group
    (Balsam fir)

Abies concolor 'Compacta'
    (White fir)

Abies koreana (Korean fir)

Chamaecyparis lawsoniana
    'Columnaris' (Lawson cypress)

Chamaecyparis pisifera
    'Filifera Aurea' (Sawara cypress)

Cryptomeria japonica 'Cristata'
    (Japanese cedar)

Juniperus chinensis 'Obelisk'
    (Chinese juniper)

Juniperus x pfitzeriana 'Old Gold'

Juniperus squamata 'Holger'
    (Flaky juniper)

Microbiota decussata

Picea abies 'Ohlendorffii'
    (Norway spruce)

Picea glauca var. *albertiana*
    'Conica' (White spruce)

Picea pungens 'Globosa'

Pinus cembroides
    (Mexican stone pine)

Pinus sylvestris 'Beuvronensis'
    (Scots pine)

Taxus baccata 'Repens Aurea'

Thuja occidentalis 'Holmstrup'

STRUCTURAL PLANTS

Aralia elata 'Variegata'
Sparse, stout, prickly stems are carried in tiers, bearing dark green leaflets with broad yellow margins. Clusters of small white flowers appear in late summer.
‡↔ 5m (15ft) ☀ ◊ ◖ ❀❀❀

Buxus sempervirens 'Suffruticosa'
Very dense and slow-growing, with small, glossy, bright green leaves, this evergreen box is ideal for use as low hedging around beds or for topiary.
‡ 1m (3ft) ↔ 1.5m (5ft) ☀ ◊ ◖ ❀❀❀

Chamaerops humilis
A slow-growing evergreen palm bearing dramatic fan-like leaves with sharply pointed, slender leaflets, C. humilis will need winter cover in colder areas.
‡↔ 1.5m (5ft) ☀ ◊ ❀

Cordyline 'Red Star'
This dramatic foliage plant has long, sword-like, stiffly arching leaves coloured a deep bronze-red. When mature, it bears scented white flowers.
‡ 3–10m (10–30ft) ↔ 1–4m (3–12ft) ☀ ◐ ◊ ❀❀

Cornus sericea 'Flaviramea'
Bright yellow, slender stems lift the mood of any winter garden; in summer, small white flowers appear, followed by white fruit and attractive autumn leaf colour.
‡ 2m (6ft) ↔ 4m (12ft) ☀ ◐ ◊ ❀❀❀

Dicksonia antarctica
This tree fern is ideal for adding height to a fern planting, producing its arching, spreading fronds at the top of a sturdy trunk covered with brown fibres.
‡ 6m (20ft) ↔ 4m (12ft) ☀ ◐ ◊ ◖ ❀❀

Dryopteris wallichiana
With upright fronds forming a shuttlecock shape, this fern makes a dramatic statement. The fronds are yellow-green in spring and mature to dark green.
‡ 90cm (36in) ↔ 75cm (30in) ☀ ◖ ❀❀❀

Echinops bannaticus
The globe thistle has woolly grey stems and impressive spiny, hairy, grey-green leaves up to 25cm (10in) long. Spherical, blue, thistle flowers appear in summer.
‡ 0.5–1.2m (1½–4ft) ↔ 75cm (30in) ☀ ◊ ❀❀❀

Ensete ventricosum
The sword-shaped, glossy, dark green leaves of this perennial can reach up to 6m (20ft) long. Overlapping leaf sheaths form the "stem". Min. temp. 7°C (45°F).
‡ 6m (20ft) ↔ 5m (15ft) ☀ ◐ ◖ ❀

❋❋❋ FULLY HARDY   ❋❋ HARDY IN MILD REGIONS/SHELTERED SITES   ❋ PROTECT FROM FROST OVER WINTER   ❋ NO TOLERANCE TO FROST

☼ FULL SUN   ◑ PARTIAL SUN   ❂ FULL SHADE   ◊ WELL-DRAINED SOIL   ◖ MOIST SOIL   ⬤ WET SOIL

Eriobotrya japonica
The large, glossy, deep green leaves of this bushy shrub or tree have a whitish furry underside. Clusters of white flowers in autumn are followed by yellow fruits.
↕↔ 8m (25ft) ☼ ◊ ❋❋

Euphorbia characias
Upright stems bearing evergreen, narrow, grey-green leaves are joined in spring by domes of cup-shaped acid-green flowers with maroon eyes.
↕↔ 1.2m (4ft) ☼ ◊ ❋❋

Fatsia japonica
Huge, palm-shaped, glossy green leaves make a stunning display, which is complemented in summer by large heads of creamy-white flowers.
↕↔ 1.5–4m (5–12ft) ☼ ◑ ◊ ◖ ❋❋

Melianthus major
This sprawling evergreen shrub has leaves up to 45cm (18in) long, with feathery, jagged-edged, blue-grey leaflets. It bears brown-red flowers in summer.
↕ 2–3m (6–10ft) ↔ 1–3m (3–10ft) ☼ ◊ ◖ ❋

Musa basjoo
The Japanese banana has spectacular arching leaves up to 1m (3ft) long. Drooping pale yellow flowers are borne in summer, followed by green fruits.
↕ 5m (15ft) ↔ 4m (12ft) ☼ ◖ ❋❋

Woodwardia radicans
This strong-growing fern has large, broad, lance-shaped, arching fronds, mid-green in colour; it spreads by producing new little ferns at their tips.
↕ 2m (6ft) ↔ 3m (10ft) ◑ ◖ ❋❋

Yucca filamentosa 'Bright Edge'
The stiff, lance-shaped leaves of this yucca are dark green with striking broad yellow margins. In summer, tall spikes of white flowers tower above them.
↕ 75cm (30in) ↔ 1.5m (5ft) ☼ ◊ ❋❋❋

ALSO RECOMMENDED

Trees
Ailanthus altissima
  (Tree of heaven)
Araucaria heterophylla
  (Norfolk island pine)
Betula pendula 'Youngii'
  (Young's weeping birch)
Fagus sylvatica 'Pendula'
Prunus 'Kiku-shidare-zakura'

Shrubs
Aesculus parviflora
  (Bottlebrush buckeye)
Corylus avellana 'Contorta'
Paeonia delavayi
Viburnum plicatum f.
  tomentosum 'Pink Beauty'

Perennials
Acanthus spinosus
Kniphofia caulescens
  (Red hot poker)
Gunnera manicata
Phormium tenax Purpureum Group
  (New Zealand flax)
Phyllostachys nigra
  (Black bamboo)

TREES FOR SMALL GARDENS

Acacia baileyana 'Purpurea'
This small tree or shrub has finely divided
purple-flushed leaves which are deep
red-purple when young. Yellow flowers
are borne from winter to spring.
↕ 8m (25ft) ↔ 6m (20ft) ☼ ◊ ❁

Acer japonicum 'Vitifolium'
A vigorous deciduous tree or large shrub,
this maple has large, rounded, mid-green
leaves that turn vivid colours of red, orange,
and purple in autumn.
↕↔ 10m (30ft) ☼ ☀ ◊ ◐ ❁❁❁

Amelanchier lamarckii
In spring, bronze young leaves are
accompanied by abundant star-shaped white
flowers. The leaves mature to dark green,
turning red and orange in autumn.
↕ 10m (30ft) ↔ 12m (40ft) ☼ ☀ ◊ ◐ ❁❁❁

Cercis canadensis 'Forest Pansy'
This tree or multi-stemmed shrub has
heart-shaped red-purple leaves held on
spreading stems. In autumn, they turn briefly
yellow and orange before falling.
↕↔ 10m (30ft) ☼ ☀ ◊ ◐ ❁❁❁

Cornus controversa 'Variegata'
The spreading branches of this deciduous
tree are layered to lovely effect, bearing
bright green leaves margined creamy white.
White flowers appear in summer.
↕↔ 8m (25ft) ☼ ◊ ❁❁❁

Crataegus persimilis 'Prunifolia'
This variety of hawthorn makes a small,
rounded tree with green, oval leaves
that turn vivid red or orange in autumn,
accompanied by dark red fruits.
↕ 8m (25ft) ↔ 10m (30ft) ☼ ☀ ◊ ◐ ❁❁❁

Ficus carica 'Brown Turkey'
The large, lobed, bright green leaves are the
main attraction of this fig tree, though fruits
may ripen in long, hot summers, especially
if it is trained on a sunny wall.
↕ 3m (10ft) ↔ 4m (12ft) ☼ ◊ ◐ ❁❁

Laburnum x watereri 'Vossii'
Long clusters of yellow pea flowers hang
from the branches of this tree in spring and
early summer; they look particularly effective
when trained over an arch.
↕↔ 8m (25ft) ☼ ◊ ◐ ❁❁❁

Malus 'Evereste'
This crab apple puts on a magnificent display
of blossom in spring, with white flowers
opening from pink buds. The small apples
that follow last into winter.
↕ 7m (22ft) ↔ 6m (20ft) ☼ ☀ ◊ ◐ ❁❁❁

✱✱✱ FULLY HARDY   ✱✱ HARDY IN MILD REGIONS/SHELTERED SITES   ✱ PROTECT FROM FROST OVER WINTER   ❄ NO TOLERANCE TO FROST

☼ FULL SUN   ◗ PARTIAL SUN   ● FULL SHADE   ◊ WELL-DRAINED SOIL   ◖ MOIST SOIL   ◗ WET SOIL

Olea europaea
A slow-growing evergreen tree, the
European olive has attractive silvery
grey-green leaves. Small white flowers
are followed by fruits that ripen to black.
↨ 10m (30ft) ☼ ◊ ✱✱

Prunus **'Kiku-shidare-zakura'**
Large, clear pink, double flowers are borne
in dense clusters on weeping branches in
mid- to late spring; the young leaves are
flushed bronze.
↨ 3m (10ft) ☼ ◊ ◗ ✱✱✱

Pyrus salicifolia **'Pendula'**
Silvery-grey oval leaves clothe the weeping
branches of this attractive ornamental pear.
In spring, it produces dense clusters of
white flowers.
↕ 5m (15ft) ↔ 4m (12ft) ☼ ◊ ✱✱✱

Robinia x slavinii **'Hillieri'**
In early summer, trusses of lilac-pink flowers
similar to wisteria are profusely borne on
this rounded tree. The foliage is mid-green,
formed of feathery leaflets.
↨ 5m (15ft) ☼ ◊ ✱✱✱

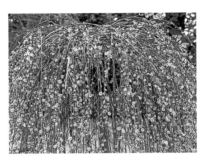

Salix caprea **'Kilmarnock'**
This beautiful weeping willow is densely
branched, with dark green foliage,
grey-green beneath. In spring it bears
grey catkins that later turn yellow.
↨ 2m (6ft) ☼ ◊ ◗ ✱✱✱

ALSO RECOMMENDED

Acer davidii 'Ernest Wilson'
  (Snake-bark maple)

Acer palmatum 'Atropurpureum'
  (Japanese maple)

Amelanchier x *grandiflora*
  'Ballerina'

Betula utilis var. *jacquemontii*
  (Himalayan birch)

Cercis siliquastrum (Judas tree)

Cornus kousa

Crataegus laevigata
  'Paul's Scarlet'

Cydonia oblonga 'Vranja'
  (Common quince)

Gleditsia triacanthos 'Rubylace'
  (Honey locust)

Hoheria angustifolia

Magnolia x *loebneri*
  'Leonard Messel'

Malus tschonoskii

Prunus incisa (Fuji cherry)

Prunus persica
  'Prince Charming'

Pyrus calleryana
  'Chanticleer'

Salix 'Erythroflexuosa'

Sorbus 'Joseph Rock'

Styrax japonicus

Sorbus aria **'Lutescens'**
The foliage of this whitebeam opens silvery,
maturing to grey-green. It bears white
flowers in spring and early summer;
orange-red fruits follow in autumn.
↕ 10m (30ft) ↔ 8m (25ft) ☼ ◗ ◊ ◖ ✱✱✱

Tsuga canadensis **'Aurea'**
This conifer has a broad, conical shape. The
grey shoots are spirally held, with flattened
needle-like leaves that are golden when
young and mature to green.
↕ 8m (25ft) ↔ 4m (12ft) ◗ ● ◊ ◖ ✱✱✱

MULTI-INTEREST TREES

Acer griseum
Peeling orange-brown bark is a major
attraction of the paper-bark maple; it also
has yellow flowers in spring, then brown
winged fruit and blazing autumn colour.
↕↔ 10m (30ft) ☼ ☀ ◊ ◑ ❋❋❋

Acer palmatum **'Sango-kaku'**
The lobed leaves of the coral-bark maple
open pink-green, maturing to dark green and
then yellow and orange in autumn. In winter,
the bark is bright coral red.
↕ 6m (20ft) ↔ 5m (15ft) ☼ ☀ ◊ ◑ ❋❋❋

Acer pensylvanicum **'Erythrocladum'**
The moosewood's bright green leaves turn
yellow in autumn; in winter, the young shoots
turn orange-red, developing white stripes as
they mature.
↕ 12m (40ft) ↔ 10m (30ft) ☼ ☀ ◊ ◑ ❋❋❋

Arbutus unedo
The bark of the spreading strawberry tree
is attractively red-brown and rough. White
flowers open in autumn as fruits from the
previous season ripen to red.
↕↔ 8m (25ft) ☼ ◊ ◑ ❋❋❋

Betula utilis **var.** *jacquemontii*
In winter, this tree's smooth, peeling white
bark is seen at its best; spring brings catkins,
while in autumn the dark green foliage turns
buttery yellow.
↕ 18m (60ft) ↔ 10m (30ft) ☼ ◊ ◑ ❋❋❋

Cornus kousa **var.** *chinensis* **'China Girl'**
Flowerheads with large white bracts are
profusely borne in late spring and early
summer; autumn brings deep red-purple
leaf colour and raspberry-like fruits.
↕ 7m (22ft) ↔ 5m (15ft) ☼ ☀ ◊ ◑ ❋❋❋

Eucalyptus pauciflora **subsp.** *niphophila*
The evergreen snow gum tree has open,
spreading branches clothed in peeling grey
and white bark, complemented by deep
blue-green lance-shaped leaves.
↕↔ 6m (20ft) ☼ ◊ ◑ ❋❋❋

Ilex aquifolium **'Handsworth New Silver'**
This dense, column-shaped holly is a female
variety bearing dark green leaves with cream
margins. It produces a generous crop of
bright red berries.
↕ 8m (25ft) ↔ 5m (15ft) ☼ ☀ ◊ ◑ ❋❋❋

Malus x purpurea **'Lemoinei'**
The leaves of this tree are reddish-purple
when young, bronzing when mature. In
spring, dark red flowers appear; red-
purple crab apples are borne in autumn.
↕↔ 10m (30ft) ☼ ◊ ◑ ❋❋❋

❋❋❋ FULLY HARDY   ❋❋ HARDY IN MILD REGIONS/SHELTERED SITES   ❋ PROTECT FROM FROST OVER WINTER   ❀ NO TOLERANCE TO FROST

☼ FULL SUN   ☀ PARTIAL SUN   ✹ FULL SHADE   ◊ WELL-DRAINED SOIL   ◖ MOIST SOIL   ◗ WET SOIL

Malus tschonoskii
Pink-tinged, single white flowers are borne in spring, followed by red-flushed crab apples. In autumn the green foliage turns to brilliant oranges and reds.
‡ 12m (40ft) ↔ 7m (22ft) ☼ ☀ ◊ ◖ ❋❋❋

Parrotia persica
This tree has flaking grey and fawn bark, and is still bare of foliage in spring when the small red flowers appear. In autumn, the leaves turn orange, red, and purple.
‡ 8m (25ft) ↔ 10m (30ft) ☼ ☀ ◊ ◖ ❋❋❋

Prunus serrula
Coppery-coloured peeling bark is the prettiest feature here; backlit by winter sun, the trailing bark is golden. Single white flowers appear in spring.
‡↔ 10m (30ft) ☼ ◊ ◖ ❋❋❋

Rhus typhina
The velvety shoots of this spreading tree are clad in dark green, leafleted foliage that turns brilliant red in autumn; female plants bear deep red fruits too.
‡ 5m (15ft) ↔ 6m (20ft) ☼ ◊ ◖ ❋❋❋

Sorbus commixta 'Embley'
A vigorous, spreading tree, 'Embley' has glossy dark green leaves with slender leaflets, which turn orange and red in autumn, with bright red fruit among them.
‡ 10m (30ft) ↔ 7m (22ft) ☼ ☀ ◊ ◖ ❋❋❋

ALSO RECOMMENDED

Acer campestre (Field maple)

Acer palmatum 'Osakazuki' (Japanese maple)

Acer rubrum 'October Glory' (Red maple)

Betula nigra (Black birch)

Cercidiphyllum japonicum (Katsura tree)

Crataegus persimilis 'Prunifolia' (Hawthorn)

Fraxinus excelsior 'Pendula' (Weeping ash)

Gleditsia triacanthos 'Sunburst' (Honey locust)

Malus 'Royalty' (Crab apple)

Nyssa sinensis (Chinese tupelo)

Prunus padus 'Watereri' (Bird cherry)

Prunus 'Shirotae' (Ornamental cherry)

Prunus 'Spire' (Ornamental cherry)

Prunus x *subhirtella* 'Autumnalis Rosea' (Rosebud cherry)

Robinia pseudoacacia 'Frisia' (False acacia)

Sorbus sargentiana (Sargent's rowan)

Stewartia sinensis
Dark green leaves provide contrast with the peeling reddish-brown bark before turning to blazing autumn colours. In summer, fragrant white flowers appear.
‡ 6m (20ft) ↔ 3m (10ft) ☼ ☀ ◊ ◖ ❋❋❋

Styrax hemsleyanus
In early summer this tree bears long plumes of bell-shaped, white flowers on graceful branches. The large, pointed leaves turn a buttery yellow in autumn.
‡ 5m (15ft) ↔ 4m (12ft) ☼ ☀ ◊ ❋❋❋

PLANTS FOR ACID SOIL

Although many plants will tolerate a slight variation in soil pH, some plants, such as rhododendrons, camellias, and most heathers, which are native to woodland or moorland, specifically require an acidic pH to thrive. Dig in lime-free compost before planting and mulch plants regularly. If conditions become too acidic, dig in some organic matter. If your soil is not acidic but you want to grow any of the plants suggested on these pages, consider planting them in a container, where they can be grown in special ericaceous soil or compost.

TREES

Acer davidii (Snake-bark maple)
Acer pensylvanicum 'Erythrocladum' (Moosewood)
Amelanchier lamarkii (Juneberry)
Arbutus unedo (Strawberry tree)
Cercis canadensis 'Forest Pansy' (Eastern redbud)
Halesia carolina (Snowdrop tree)
Stewartia monadelpha

SHRUBS

Acer palmatum var. *dissectum* (Japanese maple)
Andromeda polifolia 'Compacta' (Bog rosemary)
Camellia species
Cassiope 'Edinburgh'
Chamaedaphne calyculata
Disanthus cercidifolius
Embothrium coccineum (Chilean firebush)
Erica cinerea and cultivars (Heather)
Fothergilla major

Hamamelis **species** (Witch hazel)
Kalmia angustifolia (Sheep laurel)
Myrica gale (Bog myrtle)
Physocarpus opulifolius 'Dart's Gold'
Pieris 'Forest Flame'
Rhododendron species

CLIMBERS

Berberidopsis corallina
Crinodendron hookerianum
Desfontainia spinosa

PERENNIALS

Cirsium rivulare
Gentiana sino-ornata (Gentian)
Smilacina racemosa
Trillium erectum (Stinking Benjamin)
Uvularia grandiflora (Merrybells)

WATER AND BOG PLANTS

Osmunda regalis (Royal fern)
Sarracenia flava

SHRUB: *Calluna vulgaris* **'County Wicklow'** (Heather)

SHRUB: *Camellia* **'Leonard Messel'**

SHRUB: *Daboecia cantabrica* **'Bicolor'** (Cantabrian heath)

SHRUB: *Enkianthus campanulatus*

SHRUB: *Fothergilla gardenii* (Witch alder)

PERENNIAL: *Gillenia trifoliata* (Bowman's root)

SHRUB: *Kalmia latifolia* (Calico bush)

TREE: *Liquidambar styraciflua* (Sweet gum)

SHRUB: *Pieris japonica* 'Blush'

SHRUB: *Lithodora diffusa* 'Heavenly Blue'

SHRUB: *Rhododendron* Blue Tit Group

TREE: *Sorbus vilmorinii*

TREE: *Styrax japonicus* (Japanese snowbell)

SHRUB: *Vaccinium parvifolium* (Red bilberry)

PLANTS FOR CHALKY AND LIME-RICH SOILS

There is a vast number of plants to choose from if you can provide chalky or lime-rich soil conditions – the list given on these pages only contains a relatively small number. Chalky soils are often quite light and free-draining, so you may need to dig in well-rotted manure or compost to improve the soil structure and encourage water retention. Consider the fertility of your soil when selecting your plants: some will need a rich, fertile soil in order to flower well, while others, such as wildflowers, often do best on poorer soils. Feed plants accordingly.

TREES
Acer negundo 'Variegatum' (Ash-leaved maple)
Catalpa bignonioides 'Aurea' (Indian bean tree)
Cercis siliquastrum (Judas tree)
Fraxinus ornus (Manna ash)
Ilex species (Holly)
Laurus nobilis (Bay laurel)
Malus species (Crab apple)
Morus nigra (Black mulberry)
Prunus 'Pink Perfection' (Ornamental cherry)

SHRUBS
Abutilon 'Kentish Belle'
Berberis darwinii (Barberry)
Chaenomeles speciosa 'Nivalis' (Japanese quince)
Ceanothus impressus
Cistus species (Rock rose)
Cornus mas (Cornelian cherry)
Cotoneaster conspicuus 'Decorus'
Escallonia 'Donard Beauty'
Euonymus hamiltonianus
Fuchsia 'Prosperity'
Genista tenera 'Golden Shower' (Broom)
Helianthemum 'Jubilee' (Sun rose)
Magnolia salicifolia (Willow-leaved magnolia)
Potentilla fruticosa (Cinquefoil)

CLIMBERS
Campsis radicans (Trumpet vine)
Clematis 'Miss Bateman'
Fremontodendron 'California Glory'
Parthenocissus henryana (Chinese Virginia creeper)

PERENNIALS
Doronicum 'Miss Mason' (Leopard's bane)
Helenium 'Butterpat' (Helen's flower)
Knautia macedonica
Pulsatilla vulgaris (Pasque flower)
Verbascum 'Cotswold Beauty'

SHRUB: *Buddleja* **'Lochinch'**

PERENNIAL: *Campanula punctata*

TREE: *Cotinus coggygria*
Purpureus Group (Smoke bush)

SHRUB: *Hibiscus syriacus*
'Oiseau Bleu'

SHRUB: *Indigofera heterantha*

PERENNIAL: *Knautia macedonia*

PERENNIAL: *Malva moschata*
(Musk mallow)

SHRUB: *Osmanthus delavayi*

SHRUB: *Prunus tenella*
(Dwarf Russian almond)

SHRUB: *Philadelphus* 'Boule d'Argent'

PERENNIAL: *Rudbeckia laciniata*
'Herbstsonne'

SHRUB: *Rubus* 'Benenden'

SHRUB: *Syringa x persica*
(Persian lilac)

PLANTS FOR HEAVY CLAY

Clay soils can provide a hostile growing environment for plants: they are slow to warm in spring, sticky when wet, slow to drain, and quick to become solid when dry. However, given the right care and attention, clay soils can provide a rich, fertile growing medium, as their structure makes them excellent at retaining nutrients and therefore ideal for any of the plants listed here. Where possible, improve soils by digging them over in autumn and then again in spring, incorporating organic matter, coarse grit, or lime to improve the structure.

TREES
Acer palmatum 'Bloodgood' (Japanese maple)
Alnus glutinosa (Common alder)
Cornus kousa var. chinensis (Flowering dogwood)
Magnolia virginiana (Sweet bay)
Populus tremula 'Pendula' (Aspen)
Prunus maackii (Manchurian cherry)
Sorbus cashmiriana (Kashmir rowan)

SHRUBS
Aronia arbutifolia (Red chokeberry)
Berberis thunbergii f. purpurea 'Rose Glow' (Barberry)
Cotoneaster x watereri 'John Waterer'
Euonymus europaeus 'Red Cascade'
Ribes sanguineum 'King Edward VII' (Flowering currant)
Sambucus racemosa 'Plumosa Aurea' (Elder)
Viburnum opulus (Guelder rose)

CLIMBERS
Garrya elliptica 'James Roof' (Silk tassel bush)
Humulus lupulus 'Aureus' (Golden hop)
Rosa filipes 'Kiftsgate'
Vitis coignetiae (Vine)

PERENNIALS
Anemone x hybrida (Japanese anemone)
Bergenia species (Elephant's ears)
Campanula latiloba 'Hidcote Amethyst' (Bellflower)
Geranium Rozanne ('Gerwat')
Geum 'Bell Bank'
Heliopsis helianthoides var. scabra 'Sommersonne' (Ox-eye)
Hyacinthoides non-scripta (Bluebell)
Monarda 'Mahogany' (Bergamot)
Polygonatum hirtum (Solomon's seal)
Pulmonaria 'Sissinghurst White'
Symphotrichum novi-belgii 'Jenny' (Michaelmas daisy)

PERENNIAL: *Astrantia major* **'Claret'**

SHRUB: *Ceanothus* **'Joyce Coulter'**

SHRUB: *Chaenomeles* x *superba* **'Crimson and Gold'**

PERENNIAL: *Filipendula purpurea*

SHRUB: *Hydrangea arborescens* 'Grandiflora'

SHRUB: *Philadelphus* 'Manteau d'Hermine'

SHRUB: *Potentilla fruticosa* 'Abbotswood'

SHRUB: *Pyracantha* 'Mohave'

SHRUB: *Sinocalycanthus chinensis*

SHRUB: *Skimmia japonica* 'Rubella'

SHRUB: *Spiraea japonica* 'Anthony Waterer'

SHRUB: *Syringa vulgaris* 'Katherine Havemeyer' (Common lilac)

SHRUB: *Viburnum davidii*

PLANTS FOR HOT, DRY SITES

Plants that are native to very hot, dry climates have evolved a range of methods for coping. Many grey-, silver-, or blue-leaved plants are covered in fine hair or have a waxy surface, which deflects the sun's rays. Scented plants characteristically emit a haze of aromatic oils that create a barrier against the sun, while succulent plants store water in their fleshy leaves to prevent dehydration. Many heat-loving plants will suffer if grown in soil that is too fertile, so dig in leafmould to improve the soil structure, as it does not add as many nutrients as other organic matter.

TREES
Arbutus unedo (Strawberry tree)
Eucalyptus dalrympleana
Ficus carica (Common fig)
Gleditsia triacanthos 'Rubylace'
   (Honey locust)
Maackia amurensis
Pinus aristata (Bristlecone pine)
Rhus typhina (Stag's horn sumach)

SHRUBS
Abutilon vitifolium 'Veronica Tennant'
Ceanothus 'Cascade'
Convolvulus cneorum
Cytisus battandieri
Erysimum 'Bowles's Mauve'
x Halimiocistus wintonensis
Halimium lasianthum
Hebe macrantha
Lavandula pedunculata subsp. pedunculata
Parahebe perfoliata
Perovskia 'Blue Spire'

PERENNIALS
Agapanthus 'Loch Hope'
Agave victoriae-reginae
Amsonia orientalis Artemisia
   'Powis Castle'
Dianthus 'Haytor White'
Dictamnus albus var. purpureus
Dierama pulcherrimum
Eryngium bourgatii
Euphorbia characias subsp.
   wulfenii 'John Tomlinson'
Festuca glauca 'Blaufuchs' (Blue fescue)
Gaura lindheimeri
Geranium maderense
Verbascum 'Gainsborough'

BULBS
Allium hollandicum
Amaryllis belladonna
Cyclamen coum Pewter Group
Triteleia laxa
Tulipa tarda

SHRUB: *Ballota acetabulosa*

SHRUB: *Callistemon pallidus*
(Lemon bottlebrush)

SHRUB: *Cistus x dansereaui*
'Decumbens'

SHRUB: *Coronilla valentina* **subsp.**
glauca

SHRUB: *Genista hispanica*
(Spanish gorse)

SHRUB: *Helichrysum italicum* subsp.
serotinum (Curry plant)

SHRUB: *Hibiscus syriacus* 'Diana'

SHRUB: *Kerria japonica*
'Golden Guinea'

SHRUB: *Lavandula angustifolia*
'Munstead' (Lavender)

SHRUB: *Lavatera* x *clementii*
'Barnsley'

SHRUB: *Leptospermum scoparium*
'Kiwi' (Manuka)

SHRUB: *Phlomis fruticosa*
(Jerusalem sage)

SHRUB: *Romneya coulteri*
(Tree poppy)

SHRUB: *Salvia rosmarinus*
'Sissinghurst Blue' (Rosemary)

PLANTS FOR EXPOSED SITES

The biggest problem facing plants in exposed sites is likely to be high winds, which can loosen roots, break stems and branches, and scorch foliage by removing water from the leaves faster than the plant can replenish it. Choosing resilient plants, or those that will bend with the wind rather than resist it, will ensure that your garden can withstand the toughest conditions. Bear in mind that even in exposed sites, sheltered areas can be created for more delicate plants by arranging sturdy shrubs or trees to act as protective screens or windbreaks.

TREES

Acer platanoides (Norway maple)

Betula utilis var. *jacquemontii* (Himalayan birch)

Chamaecyparis pisifera 'Filifera Aurea' (Sawara cypress)

Crataegus laevigata 'Paul's Scarlet'
Fagus sylvatica (Common beech)

Fraxinus excelsior 'Jaspidea' (Ash)

Juniperus communis 'Hibernica' (Irish juniper)

Laburnum x watereri 'Vossii'

Picea breweriana (Brewer's spruce)

Taxus baccata (Yew)

Tsuga canadensis (Eastern hemlock)

SHRUBS

Berberis thunbergii f. *atropurpurea* 'Golden Ring'

Calluna vulgaris 'Kinlochruel' (Scots heather)

Corylus maxima 'Purpurea' (Filbert)

Cotinus coggygria Golden Spirit (Smoke bush)

Cotoneaster salicifolius

Elaeagnus umbellata

Erica carnea 'Vivellii' (Alpine heath)

Hypericum olympicum

Lonicera pileata (Honeysuckle)

Philadelphus 'Virginal'

Potentilla fruticosa 'Abbotswood'

Pyracantha 'Watereri'

Sambucus nigra f. *porphyrophylla* 'Guincho Purple' (Black elder)

Spiraea nipponica 'Snowmound'

Tamarix tetranda

Viburnum opulus 'Roseum' (Snowball tree)

PERENNIALS

Aster alpinus

Brunnera macrophylla (Siberian bugloss)

Dianthus gratianopolitanus (Cheddar pink)

Euphorbia cyparissias (Cypress spurge)

TREE: *Cupressus macrocarpa* **'Goldcrest' (Monterey cypress)**

SHRUB: *Deutzia gracilis*

SHRUB: *Dryas octopetala* (Mountain avens)

SHRUB: *Escallonia* 'Apple Blossom'

SHRUB: *Euonymus fortunei* 'Emerald Gaiety'

SHRUB: *Euphorbia mellifera* (Canary spurge)

SHRUB: *Fuchsia magellanica*

PERENNIAL: *Helianthemum* 'Fire Dragon'

SHRUB: *Olearia macrodonta* (New Zealand holly)

SHRUB: *Hippophae rhamnoides* (Sea buckthorn)

SHRUB: *Lupinus arboreus* (Tree lupin)

SHRUB: *Tamarix ramossisima* 'Pink Cascade'

SHRUB: *Salix reticulata*

SHRUB: *Spartium junceum*

INDEX

Page numbers that appear in italic in this index indicate an illustration.

PICTURE CREDITS

The publisher would like to thank the following for their kind permission to reproduce their photographs.
(Key: a-above; b-below/bottom; c-centre; f-far; l-left; r-right; t-top)

Every effort has been made to trace the copyright holders. Dorling Kindersley apologises for any unintentional omissions and would be pleased, in such cases, to add an acknowledgment in future editions.

8-9 Photolibrary: Pernilla Bergdahl. 10-11 The Garden Collection: Jonathan Buckley (t); Derek Harris (b). 10 Marianne Majerus Garden Images: Gilbert Folschette (cl). 11 Marianne Majerus Garden Images: Mount Ephraim Gardens, Kent (r). 13 Dorling Kindersley: Lucy Claxton (cr, bl). 14 Garden World Images: Rita Coates (cr); MAP / Nicole et Patrick Mioulane (tl); Andrea Jones (cl); Flowerphotos / Leonard Vucinic (bl); Louise A vHeusinkveld (br). 16 GAP Photos: Clive Nichols (bl). The Garden Collection: Andrew Lawson (tl). 17 The Garden Collection: Andrew Lawson (tl); John Glover (tr); Jonathan Buckley (bl); Nicola Stocken Tomkins (br). 24 Dorling Kindersley: Alan Buckingham (tl). 28 Marianne Majerus Garden Images: Claire Mee Designs (t); Lowder Mill (b). 29 Photolibrary: Mark Bolton (r). 30-31 Marianne Majerus Garden Images: The Fire Pit Garden, RHS Hampton Court Flower Show 2010, Arthur Northcott, John Gutteridge (bc). Photolibrary: Lee Anne White (tc). 32 Alamy Images: (bl). Marianne Majerus Garden Images: Nicola Gammon www.shootgardening. co.uk (br). 32-33 Marianne Majerus Garden Images: Joe Swift (t). 33 Marianne Majerus Garden Images: Claire Mee Designs (br). 34 Photolibrary: Ron Evans (c). 34-35 Marianne Majerus Garden Images: Stuart Craine (tc). 36-37 Garden World Images: MAP / Arnaud Descat (t). 36 GAP Photos: Elke Borkowski (bl). 38 The Garden Collection: Andrew Lawson (br). Marianne Majerus Garden Images: Kasteel Hex, Belgium (cl). 39 Garden World Images: Steffen Hauser (tr). 40-41 Marianne Majerus Garden Images: Ian Kitson (t). 40 The Garden Collection: Derek St Romaine (crb). 42-43 Alamy Images: Francisco Martinez (bc). Marianne Majerus Garden Images: Claire Mee Designs (tc). 44 Garden World Images: Liz Cole (clb). 44-45 GAP Photos: Elke Borkowski (t). 45 Garden World Images: Jayne Lloyd (bc). Marianne Majerus Garden Images: Stuart Craine (br). 46 GAP Photos: Fiona Lea (b). The Garden Collection: Nicola Stocken Tomkins (cl). 47 The Garden Collection: Jonathan Buckley

(tr). 48-49 Marianne Majerus Garden Images: Bennet Smith (t). 50 Photolibrary: Mark Bolton (c). 50-51 Marianne Majerus Garden Images: It's Only Natural, RHS Hampton Court Palace Flower Show 2010, Marianne Krogh Ali (t). Photolibrary: Paul Hart (b). 54 Marianne Majerus Garden Images: The Old Vicarage, East Ruston, Norfolk (bc). 54-55 Marianne Majerus Garden Images: Lynne Marcus and John Hall (tc); Sussex Prairie / Paul and Pauline McBride (bc). 55 Garden World Images: Country Life / IPC Media Ltd (tr). 57 Garden World Images: MAP / Nathalie Pasquel (br). 58 The Garden Collection: Andrew Lawson (bl). Marianne Majerus Garden Images: Susanne Blair (l); Julie Toll (c). 58-59 Garden World Images: Jonathan Need (t). 59 The Garden Collection: Michael O'Hara, Designer: Chameleon Gardens (t). 61 Alamy Images: Joe Fox (bl). 62 The Garden Collection: Andrew Lawson, Designer: Lesley Rosser (bc); Nicola Stocken Tomkins (c); Derek Harris (cr); Jonathan Buckley, Design: Helen Yemm, Ketley's (br). 64 Alamy Images: Sheila Halsall (t). Garden World Images: Dave Bevann (bc); Jacqui Dracup (br). 65 Alamy Images: CountrySideCollection - Homer Sykes (tl); vario images GmbH & Co.KG (br). 67 Garden World Images: Nicholas Appleby (bl). Marianne Majerus Garden Images: Charney Well, Cumbria, Christopher Holliday (br). 68 The Garden Collection: Andrew Lawson, Designer: Catherine Crouch (bl). 71 Marianne Majerus Garden Images: Bedfield Hall, Suffolk (t). 72 Garden World Images: Rowan Isaac (b). 75 GAP Photos: Jerry Harpur (clb). Marianne Majerus Garden Images: Anita Schweig-Bourg (t). Photolibrary: Clive Nichols (b). 76 Alamy Images: Stephen Mulcahey (br). Marianne Majerus Garden Images: Mathew Vincent (t). 77 Alamy Images: John Glover (b); Greg Ryan (c); Steffen Hauser / botanikfoto (cr). Clive Nichols: Design : Charlotte Rowe (br). Photolibrary: Steven Wooster (t). 78 The Garden Collection: Jonathan Buckley, Design : Diarmuid Gavin (t). 79 The Garden Collection: Jonathan Buckley, Design: Kim Wilde and Richard Lucas - Chelsea 2005 (bl).

Marianne Majerus Garden Images: Design: Lynne Marcus (tr); Palazzo Cappello, Malipiero, Barnabo, Venice (tl); Design: Laara Copley-Smith (tc). 82 The Garden Collection: Nicola Stocken Tomkins (t, b). 87 GAP Photos: Jerry Harpur (br). 89 GAP Photos: Elke Borkowski (cl). 91 Dorling Kindersley: Design: Martin Thornhill, RHS Tatton Park 2008 (tr). 99 GAP Photos: FhF Greenmedia (br). 100-101 GAP Photos: J S Sira (b). 102 GAP Photos: Jonathan Buckley (bc); Fiona Lea (br). 103 GAP Photos: Jerry Harpur (cl); Martin Schroder (r). 104 GAP Photos: Marion Brenner (tr, fbl, bl, bc, br). 105 GAP Photos: Jo Whitworth / Design: Piet Oudolf (cb). 110 Marshalls Seeds: (b). 111 GAP Photos: Richard Bloom (clb). Dorling Kindersley: Mark Winwood / RHS Wisley (tr). 112 GAP Photos: Jonathan Buckley / Design: John Massey, Ashwood Nurseries (tr); Heather Edwards (bl). 113 GAP Photos: Lee Avison / 39 Osborne Street / Geoff and Heather Hoyle (tr); Rachel Warne / Location: Saling Hall, Essex (bl). 115 GAP Photos: Flora Press (cr). 118-119 GAP Photos: Hanneke Reijbroek / Ada Hofman Gardens, Loozen, Holland (b). 119 GAP Photos: Elke Borkowski (cb). 120 GAP Photos: Marcus Harpur (tr). 121 GAP Photos: Paul Debois (c). 122 123RF.com: Nikolay Korzhov (tr).123 GAP Photos: Elke Borkowski (bl, br). 124-125 GAP Photos: Friedrich Strauss. 124 GAP Photos: Martin Hughes-Jones (c). 125 GAP Photos: Friedrich Strauss (br). 126 GAP Photos: Jo Whitworth (cl). Photolibrary: JS Sira / Garden Picture Library (tc). 126-127 Marianne Majerus Garden Images: Marianne Majerus (t); Marianne Majerus / Kew Gardens (b). Dorling Kindersley: Brian North / Waterperry Gardens (r). 129 GAP Photos: Richard Bloom / Location: Merriments Garden, East Sussex (cl). 130 GAP Photos: Geoff Kidd (tr). 134-135 Marianne Majerus Garden Images: Marianne Majerus / Scampston Hall, Yorks / Piet Oudolf (b). 139 GAP Photos: Neil Holmes / Design: Piet Oudolf (br, bl). Marianne Majerus Garden Images: Bennet Smith / Yvonne Inne and Olivia Harrison / From Life to Life: A garden for George, Chelsea

Flower Show 2008 (tl, cra). 140 Fotolia: Elena Blokhina (bl). 141 Marianne Majerus Garden Images: Marianne Majerus / 'Eco Cjoc', Helios, RHS Chelsea Flower Show 2009 / Kate Gould (t). 142-143 GAP Photos: Elke Borkowski / Location: Patricia van Roosmalen Garden (b). Harpur Garden Library: Jerry Harpur / Design: Marcus Barnett, London (t). 143 GAP Photos: Clive Nichols / Location: Vale End, Surrey (c). Marianne Majerus Garden Images: Marianne Majerus (tr). 144 Corbis: Nigel Cattlin / Visuals Unlimited (crb). 145 GAP Photos: Howard Rice (clb). 147 GAP Photos: Jerry Harpur (bl, br). Photolibrary: Friedrich Strauss (tl, tr). 148-149 Clive Nichols: Vale End, Surrey. 150-151 The Garden Collection: Nicola Stocken Tomkins (t). 151 GAP Photos: Lynn Keddie (cb); Friedrich Strauss (cra). 152 Jungle Giants Bamboo Specialists, www.junglegiants.co.uk: (tr, br). 155 RHS: Tim Sandall (t); Adrian Bloom (bl, br). 156 GAP Photos: Marg Cousens (bl). 156-157 GAP Photos: Gerald Majumdar (t). 158 GAP Photos: Hanneke Reijbroek / Design: Jacqueline van der Kloet / Location: Mien Ruys gardens (clb). Marianne Majerus Garden Images: Andrew Lawson (cra). 158-159 The Garden Collection: Nicola Stocken Tomkins (b). Harpur Garden Library: Jerry Harpur / Design: Nancy Heckler, USA (t). 159 Marianne Majerus Garden Images: Marianne Majerus (cr). 160 GAP Photos: Geoff Kidd (clb). 161 Dorling Kindersley: Lucy Claxton (bl). 163 GAP Photos: Friedrich Strauss (bc, br). Marianne Majerus Garden Images: Marianne Majerus / Hadspen Garden / Nori & Sandra Pope (tl, cr). 164-165 GAP Photos: Friedrich Strauss. 166-167 GAP Photos: BBC Magazines Ltd (b). Marianne Majerus Garden Images: Bennet Smith / RHS Hampton Court Flower Show 2009 (t). 167 GAP Photos: Carole Drake (t). 168 Dorling Kindersley: Bethany Dawn (bl). 170 GAP Photos: Jenny Lilly (tc). 172 GAP Photos: John Glover (cr). Getty Images: Marion Brenner (fbl). iStockphoto.com: Olaf Simon (tl). Suttons Seeds: (br, bl). 173 GAP Photos: Elke Borkowski (bl). 174-175 Photolibrary: Michael Paul / Garden Picture Library (t). 175 Marianne

Majerus Garden Images: Marianne Majerus (tr). **176 GAP Photos:** Michael King / Design: Marianne Krogh Ali (tr). **179 Harpur Garden Library:** Jerry Harpur / Design: Ian and Morag Hughes, Essex (tr, cla). **180-181 GAP Photos:** Lynn Keddie / Design: Michael Littlewood - Ecodesignscape (t). **180 Marianne Majerus:** Marianne Majerus / Sir Seewoosagur Ramgoolam Botanical Gardens, Pamplemousses, Mauritius (bl). **Photolibrary:** John Glover / Garden Picture Library (tr); Dan Kloeg / Garden Picture Library (br). **181 GAP Photos:** Lynn Keddie (clb); Jenny Lilly (br). **182-183 GAP Photos:** Elke Borkowski. **185 GAP Photos:** Geoff Kidd (bl). **Photolibrary:** JS Sira / Garden Picture Library (r). **186 GAP Photos:** Elke Borkowski (l); Juliette Wade (r). **187 GAP Photos:** Elke Borkowski (tr, bl). **188 GAP Photos:** Friedrich Strauss (tr); Graham Strong (bl). **189 GAP Photos:** Elke Borkowski (bl, r); Jonathan Buckley (tl). **192 Alamy Images:** Julian Marshall (tr). **GAP Photos:** Maxine Adcock (bl). **Photolibrary:** Mark Winwood (br). **194 Dorling Kindersley:** Alan Buckingham (br). **195 GAP Photos:** FhF Greenmedia (tl). **196 Photolibrary:** Gary k Smith / Garden Picture Library. **197 GAP Photos:** Michael Howes (l). **198 GAP Photos:** Hanneke Reijbroek (l). **207 GAP Photos:** Elke Borkowski (cb). **208 Dorling Kindersley:** Alan Buckingham (tr). **209 Photolibrary:** Cora Niele / Garden Picture Library (crb). **213 GAP**

Photos: Graham Strong (tr). **214 GAP Photos:** Juliette Wade (bl). **215 GAP Photos:** Maxine Adcock (crb); Juliette Wade (tc). **221 Alamy Images:** Steffan Hauser / botanikfoto (br). **Photolibrary:** FoodCollection (bl). **223 Dorling Kindersley:** Alan Buckingham (tr, bl, br). **224 Alamy Images:** Clive Sawyer (bc). **Photolibrary:** Alexandre Petzold / Bios (br). **230 GAP Photos:** Fiona Lea (bc); Mark Winwood (br). **231 GAP Photos:** BIOS / Gilles Le Scanff & Joelle-Caroline Mayer (crb). **233 Dorling Kindersley:** Alan Buckingham (tl). **234 GAP Photos:** Dave Bevan (bc); Sharon Pearson (bl); Tommy Tonsberg (br). **236 Dorling Kindersley:** Alan Buckingham (bl). **238 Dorling Kindersley:** Alan Buckingham (tr). **241 GAP Photos:** Geoff Kidd (tr); S & O (crb). **242 Dorling Kindersley:** Alan Buckingham (br). **243 Dorling Kindersley:** Alan Buckingham (bl). **244 GAP Photos:** Maxine Adcock (tr); Martin Hughes-Jones (bl); Michael Howes (br). **249 GAP Photos:** Mark Winwood (bl). **250 GAP Photos:** Rob Whitworth / Design: Claudia de Yong (tr). **252 GAP Photos:** Elke Borkowski (t); Lynn Keddie (br). **252-253 Photolibrary:** Jonathan Buckley / Practical Pictures (t). **253 GAP Photos:** Janet Johnson (tr). **Photolibrary:** Christopher Gallagher / Garden Picture Library (br). **254 Dorling Kindersley:** Alan Buckingham (tr). **256 GAP Photos:** Pernilla Bergdahl. **257 The Garden Collection:** Derek St Romaine (r). **262 Blackmoor Nurseries:** (b). **271 GAP**

Photos: Mark Winwood (tr). **276 GAP Photos:** John Glover (br). **281 Photolibrary:** Claire Higgins (cra). **286-287 GAP Photos:** Maayke de Ridder / Design: James Towillis. **290 FLPA:** Gary K. Smith (clb). **Garden World Images:** Sarah Lee (br). **291 The Garden Collection:** Liz Eddison (clb). **293 Photolibrary:** Leroy Alfonse (r). **299 Alamy Images:** Brian Hoffman (cr); Holmes Garden Photos (c). **GAP Photos:** BBC Magazines Ltd (cl). **300 Alamy Images:** Mark Boulton (bl). **301 GAP Photos:** (bc). **308 GAP Photos:** Lynn Keddie (tl). **309 Alamy Images:** Pete Thomas (clb). **327 Garden World Images:** Liz Cole (bc). **329 Garden World Images:** John Swithinbank (br). **336 Alamy Images:** Steven May (bl). **343 Alamy Images:** gardeningpix (br). **345 Photolibrary:** JS Sira (br). **346 GAP Photos:** Fiona Lea (bl). **347 Alamy Images:** Steve Welsh (tc). **GAP Photos:** Anne Green-Armytage (cr). **348-349 Photolibrary:** Stephen Hamilton. **351 GAP Photos:** Zara Napier (tl). **352 GAP Photos:** Martin Hughes-Jones (tl). **353 Photolibrary:** Bob Gibbons (tr); John Miller (tl). **Dorling Kindersley:** Neil Fletcher (cr). **354 GAP Photos:** Adrian Bloom (bl); Geoff Kidd (cr). **Photolibrary:** Carole Drake (br). **355 Dorling Kindersley:** Alan Buckingham (tr, bl). **FLPA:** Nigel Cattlin (tl). **GAP Photos:** J S Sira (br). **356 GAP Photos:** Christina Bollen (tl). **357 Dorling Kindersley:** Josef Hlasek (br); Kim Taylor (cr). **GAP Photos:**

Fiona Lea (cl). **NatureSpot:** Graham Calow (bc). **358 FLPA:** Nigel Cattlin (br). **GAP Photos:** Dave Bevan (t). **359 Alamy Images:** Grant Heilman Photography (t). **GAP Photos:** Simon Colmer (cb). **360 Dorling Kindersley:** Alan Buckingham (cb). **362 Dorling Kindersley:** Alan Buckingham (bl). **363 Dorling Kindersley:** Alan Buckingham (cb, br). **364 Dorling Kindersley:** Alan Buckingham (br). **GAP Photos:** Dave Bevan (bl). **366 Dorling Kindersley:** Alan Buckingham (br). **GAP Photos:** Dave Bevan (bl). **369 Alamy Images:** Nigel Cattlin (bc). **Dorling Kindersley:** Alan Buckingham (br). **372 Dorling Kindersley:** Courtesy of Unwins (tr). **373 Dorling Kindersley:** Mark Winwood / Ball Colegrave (br). **374 Dorling Kindersley:** Courtesy of the Lechlade Garden and Fuchsia Centre, Gloucestershire (bl). **377 Clive Nichols:** (c). **380 Photolibrary:** Jacqui Hurst (br). **381 Dorling Kindersley:** Emma Firth (tr). **Science Photo Library:** (bc). **390 Garden World Images:** MAP / Arnaud Descat (bc). **418 GAP Photos:** Adrian Bloom (br). **419 GAP Photos:** Adrian Bloom (cl). **423 GAP Photos:** Martin Staffler (tc). **427 Photos Horticultural:** Michael Warren (cb). **433 Photos Horticultural:** Michael Warren / Photoshot (br).

All other images © Dorling Kindersley. For further information see: www.dkimages.com

ACKNOWLEDGMENTS

Author acknowledgments:
Zia Allaway would like to thank the teams at the RHS and Dorling Kindersley, in particular Sarah Ruddick who steered the project so well, and Alison Donovan and Becky Tennant for their unfailing design expertise.

Helena Caldon would like to thank the team at DK for staying calm and friendly, and Nick, Tomas and Millie for bearing with her through the process.

Jenny Hendy would like to thank the book's editorial and design team at DK for their endless good humour, professionalism and attention to detail.

Martyn Cox would like to thank his mum and dad.

Publisher acknowledgments:
Dorling Kindersley would like to thank Sarah Ruddick, Chauney Dunford, Caroline Reed, Becky Shackleton, Diana Vowles, Helena Caldon, Vicky Read, Alison Shackleton, Rebecca Tennant, Joanne Doran, Elaine Hewson, Mark Cavanagh, Joanna Byrne, Lucy Claxton, Sarah Hopper, Esther Ripley, Alison Donovan, Liz Wheeler, Jonathan Metcalf, and Peter Luff for their work on the first edition, along with Fiona Wild and Ingrid Lock. Thanks also to Simon Maughan, Rae Spencer-Jones, Guy Barter, and Andrew Halstead at the RHS for their invaluable help and expertise.

For their work on this edition, Dorling Kindersley would like to thank Zia Allaway, Simon Akeroyd, and Martyn Cox for supplying updates, Myriam Megharbi for picture research, Andrew Salisbury and Leigh Hunt for reviewing pest and disease guidance, and Simon Maughan and Guy Barter for all their help.

Illustrations Vanessa Hamilton except p.78 by Peter Thomas; and pp.84, 86, 88, 90, 94, 96, and 98 by Richard Lee.

Additional photography Peter Anderson.

Authors Simon Akeroyd, Zia Allaway,
Helena Caldon, Martyn Cox, Jenny Hendy

DK UK
Project Editor Amy Slack
Senior Designer Glenda Fisher
Editor Jane Simmonds
Designer Jessica Tapolcai
Editorial Assistant Lucy Philpott
Senior Jacket Designer Nicola Powling
Jackets Co-ordinator Lucy Philpott
Pre-production Producer David Almond
Senior Producer Samantha Cross
Managing Editor Ruth O'Rourke
Managing Art Editor Christine Keilty
Art Director Maxine Pedliham
Publishing Director Mary-Clare Jerram

DK DELHI
Senior Editor Janashree Singha
Assistant Editor Ankita Gupta
Managing Editor Soma B. Chowdhury
Senior DTP Designer Pushpak Tyagi
DTP Designers Manish Upreti, Anurag Trivedi,
Satish Gaur
Pre-production Manager Sunil Sharma

ROYAL HORTICULTURAL SOCIETY
Consultant Guy Barter
Editor Simon Maughan
Publisher Rae Spencer-Jones
Head of Editorial Chris Young

This edition published in 2020
First published in Great Britain in 2011 by
Dorling Kindersley Limited
DK, One Embassy Gardens, 8 Viaduct Gardens,
London, SW11 7BW

The authorised representative in the EEA is
Dorling Kindersley Verlag GmbH. Arnulfstr. 124,
80636 Munich, Germany

A CIP catalogue record for this book
is available from the British Library.
ISBN: 978-0-2414-3243-3

Printed and bound in China

www.dk.com